Single Season Sitcoms, 1948–1979

Single Season Sitcoms, 1948–1979

A Complete Guide

Bob Leszczak

McFarland & Company, Inc., Publishers
Jefferson, North Carolina, and London

LIBRARY OF CONGRESS CATALOGUING-IN-PUBLICATION DATA

Leszczak, Bob, 1959–
Single season sitcoms, 1948–1979 : a complete
guide / Bob Leszczak.
p. cm.
Includes index.

ISBN 978-0-7864-6812-6
softcover : acid free paper ♾

1. Situation comedies (Television programs)—United States.
2. Television serials—United States. I. Title.
PN1992.8.C66L47 2012 791.45'617—dc23 2012038434

BRITISH LIBRARY CATALOGUING DATA ARE AVAILABLE

Manufactured in the United States of America

McFarland & Company, Inc., Publishers
Box 611, Jefferson, North Carolina 28640
www.mcfarlandpub.com

To my mom and dad—
my real life Ward and June Cleaver,
who never discouraged my TV viewing

Acknowledgments

This author would like to give warm, heartfelt thanks to the following people who made this first foray into publication a smooth and most enjoyable venture. This reads like a "Who's Who" of classic television—a cross section of actors, writers, producers, executive producers, directors, creators, and musicians: Sherry Alberoni, Oliver Andes, Candice Azzara, Olivia Barash, Bruce Bilson, Jimmy Brogan, Joyce Bulifant, Carol Burnett, Mel Carter, Ron Dante, Mickey Deems, Leo DeLyon, Elinor Donahue, Stephanie Edwards, John Eimen, Alix Elias, David Fox, Dawn Nickerson Fox, Kathy Garver, Dick Gautier, Danny Goldman, Monty Hall, James Hampton, Ron Harper, Darryl Hickman, Tab Hunter, Renne Jarrett, Jackie Joseph, Marvin Kaplan, Caren Kaye, Mimi Kennedy, Ruta Lee, Murray MacLeod, Rose Marie, Ron Masak, Lee Meriwether, Denny Miller, Karen Morrow, Julie Newmar, Harrison Page, Dennis Palumbo, Stuart Pankin, Van Dyke Parks, Cynthia Pepper, Roger Perry, David Pollock, Carl Reiner, Robert Rietty, Robbie Rist, Marcia Rodd, Beverly Sanders, Ralph Senensky, Bernard Slade, Marilyn Tokuda, Mike Wagner, Janet Waldo, Beverly Washburn, Dennis Wilson, Renn Woods, and Joel Zwick. Others who aren't quoted, but were nonetheless helpful in this journey are: Sidney Bloomberg, Brian J. Bohnett, Harlan Boll, Jean Cummings, Michael Dante, Rob Falcone, Rina Fox, Brian Garris, Allan Glaser, Martin Gostanian, John Kimock, Tom Kleinschmidt, Jack Kratoville, James Robert Parish, Mark Quigley, Richard Reicheg, Andy Taylor, Steve Vericker, Josie Walters-Johnston, and Fred Wostbrock. And, finally, there are two people whom I can never fully repay. My sincerest thanks for assistance, mentorship, kindness, and most of all encouragement goes to fellow authors, TV historians, and friends David Schwartz and Vincent Terrace—truly two of the most generous and patient people I know.

Table of Contents

Preface

Whenever one hears the term "must-see TV," said term is usually paired with the title of and information about a long-running mega-hit show such as *I Love Lucy, M*A*S*H, Seinfeld,* or *The Mary Tyler Moore Show.* However, to be fair, television history is also rife with programs which didn't quite achieve that same stature, longevity, or level of success. And yet, said shows were still "must-see TV" for a few million viewers each week, and are fondly remembered by them to this day.

My purpose in this book is to shed new light upon those short-lived shows which have been shrouded in darkness for way too long. I focus on sitcoms of a very finite nature—those which lasted a single season. Many of these shows have never been made available for syndication, most haven't been seen since their initial run, and only a select few have been singled out for release on DVD. If a show was invited back for a second season, no matter how briefly, it will not be included in this volume (examples being *Operation: Petticoat; Hey, Jeannie; Doc; The Bill Dana Show; Joe and Valerie; Colonel Humphrey Flack; The Practice; Szysznyk; The Good Guys; Detective School; Happy; Jamie; That's My Boy; A Date with the Angels; The Corner Bar; Temperature's Rising; The Governor and J. J.;* and *Busting Loose*). Also missing are the animated sitcoms (even though they all had laugh tracks) such as *Where's Huddles?, Calvin and the Colonel, The Jetsons, Top Cat* and *Wait 'Til Your Father Gets Home,* as well as the British sitcoms *Father, Dear Father, Fawlty Towers,* and *No, Honestly,* which I feel should be the subject of their own books.

Are the single season sitcoms as historically significant as *The Dick Van Dyke Show, The Donna Reed Show, Leave It to Beaver,* or *The Beverly Hillbillies*? Certainly not. And yet, as an impressionable youth of the 1960s and 1970s, I find that many are permanently and pleasantly ensconced in my own memory banks. Some were my very own brand of "must-see TV," albeit briefly. My interest in these shows has never waned. Through the years I've come to the realization that I am not alone in my eccentric fascination with shows which had a short shelf life on network television. Considering their age, the fact that there are still so many extant episodes of shows many would consider to be "flops" is nothing short of amazing. Oh, the long-running sitcoms will indeed be referenced in this book, but only where historically significant. The focus is on their second cousins quickly-removed, the single season sitcoms.

These shows came and went very quickly, and yet a choice few served as "stepping stones to stardom" for people like Barbara Billingsley (*Professional Father, The Brothers*), Natalie Wood (*Pride of the Family, Mayor of the Town*), Jack Lemmon (*Heaven for Betsy, That Wonderful Guy*), Marion Ross (*Mrs. G. Goes to College*), Carol Burnett (*Stanley*), Judy Carne (*Fair Exchange, The Baileys of Balboa, Love on a Rooftop*), Jack Klugman (*Harris against the World*) and Goldie Hawn (*Good Morning, World*).

While very useful and very well-done, books such as *The Complete Directory to Prime Time Network TV Shows*, by Tim Brooks and Earle Marsh, *Total Television*, by Alex McNeil, *The Great TV Sitcom Book*, by Rick Mitz, and *The Encyclopedia of Television Programs 1925–2010*, by Vincent Terrace are limited to very brief entries because of the sheer number of shows covered. *Lost Laughs of '50s and '60s Television*, by David C. Tucker, while very informative, limits

its scope to thirty sitcoms. My book takes on the unenviable task of covering every single season sitcom from television's infancy (1948) through the 1970s (alphabetically). I chose 1948 as the starting point as that was the first year the networks had a full slate of prime time programming.

A goodly amount of the information in this book has been culled from my large collection of episodes of these hard-to-find shows. Many gaps were filled at the UCLA TV Archives viewing rooms, as well as both of the Paley Centers for Media (New York and Los Angeles). The forum at www.sitcomsonline.com, and Desmond Martin's "Classic TV Archive" website (www.ctva.biz/) were also useful. Still more valuable and unique information was garnered from interviews with cast members, writers, directors, producers, musicians, guest stars, and others associated with these series.

For each of the shows contained in this book there is an overview of what it was all about, where it took place, the characters involved, time slot and network affiliation. In most cases, I was also able to supply the name of the production company, a list of important guest stars, directors and writers, sponsors, essential episodic information, and the number of episodes aired vs. number filmed or videotaped. Where available, cast pictures are included. Here, for the first time, is previously unpublished information such as *Doc Corkle*'s first name; Buddy's real first name on *Bringing up Buddy;* "Spider's" real first name on *Karen*; Celia's last name on *Stanley*; the professional name actress Beverly Garland used on her first show called *Mama Rosa*; Babbo's real first name on *Bonino*; the role Roger Perry gave up for a starring role in *Harrigan and Son*; the sponsor of the short-lived *Honestly, Celeste*; the legendary theme song that was first heard on the 1957 sitcom called *Sally*; the story of how Carl Reiner got the lead role in *Good Heavens*; the surname of Cadet Monk on *McKeever and the Colonel*; the only known photograph from the short-lived DuMont series *It's a Business?* and dozens upon dozens of more examples. At the end of the alphabetical descriptions of the programs is a litany of interesting lists, breaking the shows down into informative subsets.

So whether you're skimming through the book seeking out your own favorite short-lived sitcoms, or reading it from cover to cover, thank you for a shared interest in television history, and those single season sitcoms.

Single Season Sitcoms, 1948–1979

Accidental Family A Sheldon Leonard Production. NBC. Friday nights at 9:30. September 15, 1967-January 5, 1968. 16 color episodes were produced with a laugh track. Sponsors included Playtex, Carnation Instant Breakfast, and Hai Karate cologne.

This show opened with an animated slot machine and a jazzed-up version of "Old MacDonald Had a Farm" playing during the credits. The original working title was *Everywhere a Chick Chick*, but it became *Accidental Family* at the last minute. Jerry Webster, played by Jerry Van Dyke, was a recently widowed Las Vegas performer who got custody of his 8-year-old son, Sandy (Teddy Quinn), with a proviso that he was to secure a "non-show business environment" for the boy. Since Jerry was on the road performing so much, his farm in California's San Fernando Valley sounded ideal. But on that farm he had a tenant—an attractive divorcee named Sue Kramer (Lois Nettleton) who wouldn't leave. So a deal was struck that when Jerry was away, she became his son's ward (and wouldn't have to pay rent). Her very competitive daughter Tracy lived there, too, and was played by Susan Benjamin. The farm hand was a retired vaudevillian named Ben McGrath (Ben Blue); Jerry's agent, Marty, was played by Larry D. Mann; and his friend Dewey Davis, an impressionist, was portrayed by John Byner in one of his first recurring roles.

Notable guest stars included Jim Backus as Uncle Henry in an episode called "What Is This, Thanksgiving or Nightmare?" John Aniston (father of Jennifer) and Ellen Corby appeared together in an episode called "A Funny Thing Happened on the Way to the Playground"; Joyce Van Patten and Herb Edelman (later paired on *The Good Guys*) were teamed in an episode titled "If You Knew Martha"; and a very young Danny Bonaduce made his TV debut with a minor role in an episode called "Halloween's on Us." Even with a small role, he got billing in the credits above other guest stars, but that was understandable—his dad, Joseph Bonaduce, wrote the episode. Actor David Fox, who had a big role in that same episode (Brian, the bossy head of the "junior gargoyles" kid's club), told me, "I was amazed that Lois Nettleton would rehearse without make-up, and with her hair up in a kerchief. On the day of the filming, she was beautiful in full make-up, and her hair was done—we almost didn't recognize her as the same woman." Even as an 11-year-old boy, he said he realized that "the show wasn't going to be a hit—it just wasn't going anywhere." David also told me that "whenever Sheldon Leonard was around, the entire cast was on its best behavior." Sheldon made an uncredited cameo appearance in an episode called "The Making of a Vegetarian." Jackie Joseph guest-starred in the episode titled "Sandy Gets Tough," and it must have felt like she was surrounded by family because she told me that "Jerry Van Dyke's manager, Richard Linke, was also my former husband Ken Berry's manager. There were lots of parties back then—nice times. Dave Ketchum also guest-starred in that episode—he and his wife Louise were our closest friends in the mid sixties."

Directors included Bob Sweeney, William Wiard, and Earl Bellamy; writers included Sydney Zelinka, Treva Silverman, Jim Brooks, Mary Loos, Richard Sale, and Melville Shavelson. Sy Gomberg, who had previously worked on *The Law and Mr. Jones*, served as producer. Music was provided by Earle Hagen. Several episodes can be viewed in the UCLA TV Archives.

Actor's Hotel Productions for Television, Inc. ABC. Tuesday nights 10:30. September 25, 1951-May 13, 1952. Broadcast live. Sponsored by Ronzoni Macaroni.

William Edwards portrayed likable Carlo

Corelli who, along with his Uncle Antonio (Alan Dale), managed a small boarding house in a rural area. Episodes of this live show involved their dealings with a wide variety of colorful, unpredictable folks (mostly out-of-work actors) who dwelt there. The premise for this show is similar to that of another single season sitcom, *Mama Rosa*.

The program was produced by Carlo DeAngelo; the director was Ted Nathanson; and writers included Flora Frank and John Fleming. To my knowledge, no episodes exist.

Adam's Rib MGM Studios. ABC. Friday nights 9:30. September 14, 1973-December 28, 1973. 13 color episodes were filmed without a laugh track. Sponsors included Bristol Myers, Procter and Gamble, and The Gillette Company.

With very few exceptions, successful movies didn't translate well to the small screen—but that didn't stop TV executives from attempt after attempt. The original 1949 movie version of *Adam's Rib*, which starred Spencer Tracy and Katherine Hepburn, was a whopping success. The television version only lasted 13 weeks. Ken Howard and Blythe Danner (Gwyneth Paltrow's mom) took on the lead roles (as Adam and Amanda Bonner, respectively). He was a young, staid assistant district attorney. She was a maverick junior law partner. They would often meet in the courtroom on opposite sides of a case (and yet they would frequently meet discreetly under a table for a quick kiss or a smile during a trial). They had pet names for one another—sometimes he would call her "Pinkie" and she would call him "Cookie," and then other times it was the exact opposite. Others in the cast included Dena Dietrich as Amanda's secretary Grace Peterson; Edward Winter played her law partner Kip Kipple of the Kipple, Kipple and Smith law firm; Norman Bartold played district attorney Anthony Donahue; and Ron Rifkin was assistant district attorney Roy Mendelsohn.

The program had a very large female staff behind-the-scenes, and they were represented in a lot of the episodes (with very noticeable women's lib undertones). In the episode titled "Illegal Aid," Amanda was upset about defending a prostitute in the courtroom. Amanda felt that the man involved was just as much to blame in this situation, but it was the woman who was arrested. While doing research on hookers in a seedy bar, Amanda herself was mistakenly arrested for soliciting, and husband Adam had to come to her rescue. In a very special hour-long episode titled "The Unwritten Law," Adam and Amanda Bonner had their hands full with a case about a cheating husband and the irate wife who shot him.

The show's creator was Peter H. Hunt; the producer was William Froug; directors included Gary Nelson and Hunt; and writers included Peter Stone, Nora Ephron, and George Kirgo. The theme song, "Two People," was written by Perry Botkin, Jr. and Gil Garfield. A few episodes can be viewed in the UCLA TV Archives.

The Adventures of Hiram Holliday California National Productions. NBC. Wednesday nights 8:00. October 3, 1956-February 27, 1957. 27 black-and-white episodes were filmed with a laugh track, but only 20 aired. Sponsors included Jello, and Sanka Brand Coffee.

After a nice run on the live sitcom *Mr. Peepers*, Wally Cox starred in this filmed sitcom about a polite, mild-mannered little nebbish named Hiram Holliday (based on stories by Paul Gallico) who could do practically anything. The opening credits showed Holliday in a suit of armor, and despite his meek persona, he was a master at fencing, he could also diffuse a bomb, fly a plane, speak almost any language, scuba dive, and dance flamenco. He was an expert on birds, animals, plant life, gems, rocks and art, and only the surface has been scratched. All of these and other amazing talents came into play and were very useful on his free trip around the world. Holliday was awarded this trip and a cash bonus by the newspaper for which he was employed, the *New York Chronicle*, because as a proofreader for the paper, he caught a misplaced comma in a story which, had it been printed as is, would have brought about a libel suit and cost the company millions. To accompany Holliday on his adventures was Joel Smith (Ainslie Pryor)—a reporter for the newspaper who was to write about each stop. Unfortunately, Joel either just missed each escapade, or had to promise those involved not to print their story. The lack of good stories angered the publisher of the newspaper, Harrison Prentice (Thurston Hall). There was one consistent thread through all of the episodes—Holliday somehow unwittingly became involved in international intrigue, the syndicate, and spy rings. He was also amidst jewel thieves and murderers, but always emerged unscathed (usually with the help of his trusty umbrella). The handle of that same umbrella tapped the inside of our TV sets, attached to a note saying things like, "A moment please—you'll like what's next," just before commercial breaks.

Among the episodes available is "Lapidary Wheel," in which Holliday, on a train bound for Scotland, discovered the body of a passenger from India who had been stabbed alongside a venomous, hissing cobra. Upon alerting the authorities, both the body and cobra mysteriously disappeared. Initially, it was thought that Holliday was losing his marbles, but we would later find out the disappearances were related to a valuable missing diamond. In "Sea Cucumber," Hiram went looking for a rare plant in Hong Kong called the "sea cucumber," but a spy ring suspected him of sinister intentions (blowing up an ocean liner). Sebastian Cabot appeared in that episode as the nefarious Monsieur Cerveaux (a recurring role).

The program was produced by Philip Rapp; writers included Rapp, Joel Malcolm Rapp, Siegfried Herzig, Richard Powell, Bernard Drew, John Kohn and Doris Gilbert; and directors included Rapp, William J. Hole and George Cahan. A few episodes are available on DVD from the Cascadia Company.

The Adventures of Tugboat Annie Normandie Productions, Inc., Canadian Subsidiary of TPA, Television Programs of America/An Anthony Veiller Production. Filmed in Ontario, Canada. Syndicated. 1958. 39 black-and-white episodes were filmed with a laugh track. Sponsors included Lever Brothers.

The story of Tugboat Annie has a long history. Her adventures were regular features in *The Saturday Evening Post* written by Norman Reilly Raine. Raine would also go on to write the screenplay for the 1933 Warner Brothers *Tugboat Annie* movie which starred Marie Dressler and Wallace Beery. There were a few movie sequels, and in 1958, Annie even got her own TV sitcom which opened every week with this dialogue: "Hi, Bullwinkle, you old baboon" (said by Annie), followed by, "Annie Brennan, I'll get even with you if it takes the rest of my natural life" (said by Bullwinkle). The title of the show was written in letters made to resemble a ship's rope. Annie was the skipper of a tugboat in the Pacific Northwest named the *Narcissus*. Bullwinkle's tugboat was called the *Salamander*. They were fierce competitors, they fought a lot, and yet down deep they really did like one another. Annie was played by Minerva Urecal, and Captain Horatio Bullwinkle was played by Walter Sande. Each skipper had his or her own crew. Annie's crew consisted of Don Orlando as Pinto (the cook) and Eric Clavering as Shiftless. Bullwinkle's helper was Jake, played by James Barron.

Episodes include "The Romance of Horatio Bullwinkle," in which Bullwinkle's new love interest named Lydia (Charmion King) turned out to be a con artist who, along with her real boyfriend, tried to trick Bullwinkle into transporting their stolen goods. In "Operation: Hotcake," Annie suggested that timid Pinto ask the big boss Murdock Severn (Stan Francis) for a raise. When the suggestion backfired, Pinto decided to go into business for himself by opening his own diner (formerly Fogerty's Beanery). In "The Sixth Santa," Annie went all out to convince a fatherless young boy named Georgie Moore (Stephen Barrington) that there really was a Santa Claus, even though his friends tried to convince him otherwise.

The program was produced by Leon Fromkess; writers included Milton Pascal, Earl Baldwin, Maurice Richlin, Fred Fox, Joel Rapp, Bill Freedman, and Larry Rhine; and directors included Leo Goodwins and Sam Newfield. The theme song was the old traditional maritime classic "Sailor's Hornpipe." Several episodes are available for viewing at the Paley Center for Media.

AES Hudson Street The Triseme Corporation/Four D Productions. ABC. Thursday nights 9:30. March 23, 1978-April 20, 1978. Seven episodes were videotaped before a live audience, only five aired.

After successful supporting roles in *Sanford and Son* and *Barney Miller*, Gregory Sierra was tapped for his own sitcom. From Four D Productions, who gave us *Barney Miller*, came *AES Hudson Street* (AES meant Ambulance Emergency Service). Sierra portrayed frenzied Dr. Tony Menzies—the chief resident at a cash-strapped emergency ward in a rundown area of Hudson Street in New York City. J. Powell Karbo (Stefan Gierasch) was the difficult hospital administrator; Dr. Glick (Allan Miller) was the hospital's shrink; Rosa Santiago (Rosana DeSoto) was a nurse; Newton (Ray Stewart) was a male nurse; Foshko and Stanke (Susan Peretz and Ralph Manza, respectively) were ambulance workers; and Dr. Jerry Mackler (Bill Cort) was a surgeon.

Episodes include one in which a schizophrenic man attempted to blend in with the staff, posing as a doctor. In another untitled episode, a blackout came at the most inopportune time—a woman was about to give birth, and a South

African man had a badly infected leg. In still another untitled episode, Tony found out that he was being considered for an administrative hospital job in beautiful Honolulu.

The program was produced by Roland Kibbee; the executive producer and creator was Danny Arnold; writers included Arnold, Chris Hayward and Tony Sheehan; and directors included Noam Pitlik. Music was provided by Jack Elliott and Allyn Ferguson.

All's Fair T. A. T. Communications. CBS. Monday nights 9:30. September 20, 1976-August 15, 1977. 24 episodes were videotaped before a live audience at KTTV Studios.

Sitcom veteran Richard Crenna returned to prime time in this very topical, very political show set in Washington, D. C., which revolved around the problems of a May/December romance. Crenna portrayed political columnist Richard C. Barrington—age 49; and Bernadette Peters made her series debut as the "May" part of that romance—23-year-old Charlotte "Charley" Drake, a freelance photographer. He was very conservative, she was extremely liberal, and yet the romance worked. There were, however, numerous flare-ups between them over politics, age, and marriage. Allen Brooks (J. A. Preston) was Richard's equally conservative African American assistant; Lucy Daniels (Lee Chamberlain) was Allen's girlfriend and also a CBS News reporter; Ginger Livingston (Judy Kahan) was Charley's roommate, who was romantically involved with a married congressman; and Senator Wayne Joplin (Jack Dodson) was a liberal friend of Richard's who often sided with Charley. The show took a new direction midstream, as Richard became a special assistant to President Carter, and Ginger became his secretary. At that point, a new character, Lanny Wolf (Michael Keaton), was added as President Carter's aide and joke writer.

Episodes include "Strange Bedfellows," in which Charley attempted to chronicle an average day in Richard's life, but it turned out to be anything but average; in "Presidential Request," Charley was outraged and dubbed Richard a sellout when he edited one of his articles to please President Carter; and in "Jealousy," Richard was the jealous one when Charley allowed an old beau to briefly stay in her apartment. Turnabout was fair play when Charley was jealous of Richard's reunion with a French girl named Desiree (Andra Akers) in an episode titled "Remembrance."

The program was produced by Norman Lear; the creators included Rod Parker, Bob Schiller and Bob Weiskopf; writers included Parker, Albert E. Lewin, Howard Ostroff, Sybil Adelman, Michael Elias, Michael Loman, Tom Whedon, Bud Wiser, Don Hinkley, Ron Friedman, Peter Gallay, Dixie Brown Grossman and Robert Van Scoyk; and directors included Bob Claver and Hal Cooper. Richard Crenna later starred in yet another single season sitcom—*It Takes Two*, on which he was paired with Patty Duke.

Angel Burlingame Productions/Desilu Studios. CBS. Thursday nights 9:00 (October 6, 1960-December 1960), and Thursday nights 8:00 (January 1961-April 1961), and Wednesday nights 9:00 (April 1961-September 30, 1961). 33 black-and-white episodes were filmed before a live audience. Sponsors included Post Cereals and Johnson's Wax.

Not to be confused with the later David Boreanaz show of same name, this was the sitcom called *Angel*. *Angel* was short for Angelique. Angelique was a young French girl (Annie Farge, who had understudied in the Broadway play *The World of Susie Wong*) who had recently married a successful American architect named John Smith (whom she called Johnny), played by Marshall Thompson (later of *Daktari*). He called her "Angel" most of the time (sometimes "Annie"), but it was always "Angelique" when he was angry. And he often had good reasons to be quite angry—Angel was very stubborn, and she had a fiery French temper (and a thick French accent). Most episodes revolved around her trouble with the English language and American customs. The Smiths set up house in Los Angeles, next door to future good friends George and Susie Carpenter (Don Keefer and Doris Singleton, respectively). Hanley Stafford played Johnny's boss, Mr. Corwin, and Bella Bruck had a very funny recurring role as neighbor and friend, Mrs. Spiegelman.

When the series began, the couple was already married. However, in a flashback episode called "The Wedding," we saw Angelique coming over on the boat to meet Johnny on their scheduled wedding day. After vouching for and sponsoring a couple of shady Hungarian men so the men could leave the ship, Angelique was then unable to find her own passport and had to remain on board until it was found. All was well much later when she recalled that the passport was sewn into her coat so that she wouldn't lose it. This delay, however, caused her to miss the wedding. Meanwhile, something even worse had occurred—Johnny had been drowning his sorrows with the two Hungarian men, and was in no condition to be married. Somehow, Annie and the Hungarians propped Johnny up long enough for him to say his "I do" in front of a justice of the peace. Only moments later, he collapsed on the floor and spent his wedding night there.

Guest stars included James Garner as himself in "The French Lesson." Former Three Stooges member Joe Besser appeared in an episode called "The Museum." Child actor Johnny Eimen was also in that episode and he told me, "Joe Besser was even funnier off camera than he was on camera." However, Eimen also let me know that he himself was "scared to death of the live audience. Every sitcom I'd done up to that point had used a laugh track." Joseph Kearns guest starred in "Voting Can Be Fun," in which voting booths were set up in the Smith household; Alan Reed (Fred Flintstone) guested in "The Goat Dog" as zoning commissioner Stanley Pritchard who was attempting to get rid of Angel's pet goat, which she was trying to pass off as a dog; Gale Gordon was Mr. Johnson in "Unpopular Mechanics," in which Angel and Susie tried to repair an expensive and rare automobile, only to take the whole thing apart; and Mel Blanc made a cameo appearance in "Annie's Temper." Angelique always believed people were inherently good and trustworthy, but she got burned for her naïveté in "The Honest Man," in which she posted a not-vague-enough ad in the newspaper about money she found in the grocery store parking lot. The ad led to numerous opportunists cashing in at the Smith's front door.

Most of the 33 episodes were directed by Ezra Stone, Lamont Johnson, or Jess Oppenheimer. Oppenheimer created the show and also wrote many episodes. Being a Desilu show, much of the transitional music between scenes is very similar to that used in other Desilu shows, including *I Love Lucy*, *December Bride*, and *Those Whiting Girls*.

Anna and the King 20th Century–Fox. CBS. Sunday nights 7:30. September 17, 1972-December 31, 1972. 13 color episodes were filmed with a laugh track.

The 1952 Broadway musical *The King and I* won a Tony; the 1956 movie musical version garnered Yul Brynner an Academy Award. Even with all of that history and success, somehow the TV sitcom version fell flat. The title for the pilot was *Anna and the King of Siam*, much like the original Margaret Landon novel on which all versions were based. However, once it became a series, the title was shortened to *Anna and the King*. Yul Brynner reprised his role as stubborn King Mongkut. In the Anna Owens role was Samantha Eggar, hired as personal educator to the King's many children. Anna had a child of her own—a 12-year-old son named Louis (Eric Shea) who came with his mother to live in Siam. Louis was able to handle himself very well in a fight, and even gave a black eye to Crown Prince Chulalongkorn (Brian Tochi), which was a crime punishable by death—but luckily the charge didn't stick. Anna proved to be as headstrong as the King, and wasn't afraid to stand up to him and give her opinions, while others around her merely cowered or ran away. While the two lead characters did indeed have many conflicts, there arose a mutual respect and friendship (the King liked "skinny women"). The Anna Owens character was based upon the real-life experiences of Anna Leonowens.

In the debut episode, Anna had signed an agreement to become the children's teacher (replacing the King's right-hand man, Kralahome, played by Keye Luke). There was an immediate breach of contract, however (the King demanded that Anna and her son live inside the palace, even though they were promised a house of their own). Just as Anna and Louis were ready to leave because of the breach, the King softened, agreed to the house, and the Owens family stayed.

The program was produced by Bill Idelson; Gene Reynolds served as executive producer; writers included Bill Idelson, Harvey Miller, Lester and Tina Pine, Austin and Irma Kalish, Jim Fritzell, Jerry Mayer, Gene Thompson and Maurice Richlin; and directors included E.W. Swackhamer, Jeff Corey, Lee Philips, Michael Gordon, James Sheldon, Hy Averback, Terry Becker, Jack Donohue, and William Wiard. The theme music was by Jerry Goldsmith and Richard Shores.

Another Day The Komack Company. CBS. Saturday nights 9:00. April 8, 1978-April 29, 1978. 13 episodes were videotaped before a live audience, only four aired.

When Rhoda and Joe's divorce became final, David Groh was free to pursue other interests. CBS gave him a starring role in this extremely short-lived sitcom from James Komack. *Another Day* was an attempt to showcase a new trend toward two-income families. Groh was cast as Don Gardner—a Los Angeles ad executive; Joan Hackett was his wife, Ginny, who worked for an insurance company; and Hope Summers played Don's overbearing, meddling mother, Olive, who minded the kids while the couple was at work. Al Eisenmann portrayed painfully shy 11-year-old son Mark, and Lisa Lindgren played outgoing 16-year-old daughter, Kelly.

The program was produced by Paul Mason and George Kirgo; the executive producer and creator was James Komack; writers included Charlie Hauck, Dinah Kirgo, Julie Kirgo, Carl Kleinschmidt, Bill Taub, and Lynn Phillips; and directors included Hal Cooper, Nick Havinga, Gary Shimokawa, Burt Brinckerhoff, and James Komack. Paul Williams performed and composed the theme song. David Groh died at the age of 69 early in 2008.

Apartment 3-C A Harvey Marlowe Production. First-run syndication. 1949. Monday, Wednesday and Friday nights 7:15. A 15-minute live show.

This live early sitcom originated from WOR–TV in New York. This was the story of a couple of newlyweds—John and Barbara Gay (as themselves), who resided at 46 Perry Street in New York City in apartment 3-C. This was one of those seminal shows which helped set the standard for husband and wife sitcoms for decades. John Gay wrote every episode and, after a few months, his ideas began to dry up, and the ratings began to suffer. This was good practice for John, who later wrote episodes of *Lux Video Theater*, *Playhouse 90*, *Kraft Television Theater*, and *The Travels of Jaimie McPheeters*. For the silver screen, he was a contract writer for *Run Silent, Run Deep* and *The Courtship of Eddie's Father*.

In the October 22, 1949, edition of *Billboard Magazine*, the program was reviewed this way: "It's a standard domestic situation comedy, well produced, with Barbara and John Gay. Direction, though, was bad. Both Gays spoke so loudly and so quickly that neither could be understood. Both walked on one another's lines." To my knowledge, no episodes exist.

Apple Pie T. A. T. Communications. ABC. Saturday nights 8:30. September 23, 1978-September 30, 1978. Seven episodes were videotaped at Metromedia Studios before a live audience, only two aired.

The premise of this show sounded very promising and intriguing. Contrary to the old adage, "you can't pick your family," Ginger-Nell Hollyhock (Rue McClanahan) did just that. In the heart of the depression year of 1933, on Morning Glory Road in Kansas City, Ginger-Nell placed an ad in the classifieds to "assemble a family." What she got was a houseful of zanies. Her husband "Fast Eddie" Barnes (Dabney Coleman) was a con man; her daughter was a tap dancer named Anna Marie (Caitlin O'Heaney); her son, Junior (Derrel Maury), wanted nothing more than to be a bird; and Grandpa (Jack Gilford) was blind and very cranky.

Qualifying as one of Norman Lear's biggest flops, seven episodes were videotaped but only two ever aired. Those two were the pilot and "Fast Eddie Slows Down." Episode titles for those left in the can are "Ginger-Nell Goes Hollywood," "Rich Man, Poor Girl," "Ginger-Nell Loses Her Touch," "A Man from Ginger-Nell's Past," and "They Walk Among Us."

The program was produced by Charlie Hauck; the creator was Norman Lear; writers included Sy Rosen, Arthur Julian, Bill Davenport, Charlie Hauck, Lawrence J. Cohen, and Fred Freeman; and the director of all episodes was Peter Bonerz. *Apple Pie* was loosely based upon a book called *Nourish the Beast* by Steve Tesich, who would later go on to win an Academy Award for Best Screenplay for *Breaking Away*.

The Associates John Charles Walters Productions/Paramount Studios. ABC. Sundays 8:30 (September 23, 1979-October 28, 1979), and Thursday nights 9:30 (March 27, 1980-April 17, 1980). 13 episodes were filmed before a live audience, only nine aired.

This highly-touted sitcom came from the same folks who had given us *Taxi*. Critics loved it, but it was a colossal flop with viewers. This was the story of three young law graduates who had just become part of the big Wall Street law firm of Bass and Marshall. Big-hearted Leslie Dunn (Alley Mills) was of working class stock and had a huge soft spot for the oppressed; Tucker Kerwin (Martin Short) was a bit nerdy and naïve, and yet quite charming; Sara James (Shelley Smith) was from Boston and was tall, blonde, sexy, bright and very confident. She was usually the target of the overtly testosterone-laden mailroom boy named Johnny Danko (Tim

Thomerson). The firm's obnoxious kiss-up of a junior partner was Elliott Streeter (Joe Regalbuto), and the daft and forgetful Senior Partner was Emerson Marshall (British character actor Wilfrid Hyde-White).

Episodes include "Elliott's Deadly Serve," in which the law firm was about to change its name to Bass, Marshall and Milestone—Mr. Milestone (William Prince) was to become a partner in the firm. The ever-opportunistic Elliott had done vast amounts of research on the man, and knew that he had a penchant for the game of squash. Elliott then challenged Milestone to a no-holds-barred game with a $135 bet, only to see the elderly gentleman die of a heart attack on the court. This particular episode was the fifth episode of the series. Immediately after it aired, ABC put the show on hiatus until late March when another four new episodes debuted (now on Thursday nights). The show once again failed to catch on, and the remaining four episodes were kept in the can (guest stars included Georgia Engel and Danny DeVito).

The program was developed by Michael Leeson; the executive producers were James L. Brooks, Stan Daniels, Charlie Hauck and Ed Weinberger; writers included John Steven Owen; and directors included Tony Mordente. The show's theme song, "Wall Street Blues," was written by A. Brooks, and performed by blues legend B.B. King. *The Associates* was loosely based upon the book of same name by John Jay Osborn, Jr. Reruns, as well as previously unaired episodes, were briefly syndicated on the long-defunct cable channel, Entertainment.

Baby, I'm Back Charles Fries Productions/ Lila Garrett Productions/Dewil Productions, Inc. CBS. Monday nights 8:30. January 30, 1978-August 12, 1978. 12 episodes were recorded before a live audience.

After leaving *Sanford and Son* in a salary dispute (after six seasons), Demond Wilson came back in *Baby, I'm Back*. His return to television was short-lived. The story took place in a tough neighborhood on Richmond Drive in Washington, D.C. Demond portrayed Ray Ellis, a man who had abandoned his family seven years earlier and headed to sunny California. In the opening credits, his character, Ray Ellis, said his reason for leaving was that he "was supporting one wife, two kids, and three bookies—then one day my luck ran out, and like any right-thinking horse player, I ran with it." Yes, Ray had a gambling problem and owed a lot of people a lot of money. While away, his lovely wife Olivia (Denise Nicholas) had him declared legally dead, raised their two children Jordan (Tony Holmes) and Angie (Kim Fields), and hooked up with a new beau named Colonel Wallace Dickey (Ed Hall). Upon hearing of Olivia's upcoming nuptials to Colonel Dickey, Ray suddenly returned to try to erase the past, halt the marriage, and prove he was the better father. In fact, he moved directly upstairs from Olivia (she was in apartment 1A, and he was in 2A). His biggest obstacle in picking up where he had left off was his acerbic mother-in-law Luzelle Carter (Helen Martin). In the opening credits, Ray stated, "Luzelle is French for killer. The day she moved in with us, the rats moved next door."

Episodes of note included "Pay or Die," in which Ray was threatened by loan sharks who demanded payment or else. We found out later in the episode that the thugs were hired by Luzelle to give him a good scare, and hopefully put an end to his gambling problem. In "Olivia's Job Offer," the newly reunited family was on the verge of being separated once again as Olivia debated accepting a job offer on Guam. In "Survival of the Fittest," the relationship between Ray and Luzelle turned even frostier as they found themselves stranded together in a blizzard.

The program was created by Lila Garrett and Mort Lachman; producers included Sandy Krinski and Chet Dowling; writers included David Garber, Lila Garrett, Dowling, George Geiger, Kevin Hartigan, April Kelly, Lachman, Marion Freeman, Krinski, Bill Persky, April Kelly, and Mark Evanier; and directors included Dick Harwood, Mark Warren, and Nick Havinga. Music was provided by Jeff Berry. Reruns were shown on the BET Network.

The Baileys of Balboa Antelo Productions, Inc./Grandandy Productions, Inc./Richelieu Productions, Inc. CBS. Thursday nights 9:30. September 24, 1964-April 1, 1965. 26 black-and-white episodes were filmed at CBS Studio City with a laugh track. Sponsors included Reynolds Metals, American Home Products, and Philip Morris Cigarettes.

Keefe Brasselle was the executive producer (Richelieu Productions) for three single season shows which were greenlighted without pilot episodes—*The Cara Williams Show*, *The Reporter*, and this one, *The Baileys of Balboa*. It featured Paul Ford as widower Sam Bailey who owned the

Island Princess (with CF 2122 AW on its side), a decrepit charter fishing boat at Bailey's Landing in Balboa Beach, California. Director Bruce Bilson told me, "They were looking for ocean front property for the series, and found it next to the Balboa Yacht Club, where they got permission to build a pier for location shoots." The Balboa Yacht Club, headed by Commander Cecil Wyntoon (John Dehner), considered the *Island Princess* an eyesore. Wyntoon did everything in his power to get the Baileys to leave. Yes, there were more Baileys—Sam's beachcomber son, Jim (Les Brown, Jr.), and an occasional visitor such as genius cousin Chester Bailey (Michael J. Pollard). Sam's best friend of 15 years was the inept and forgetful shipmate Buck Singleton (Sterling Holloway). Buck, however, was a very good cook, known for his pancakes. Neighbor kid, Stanley, was played by Clint Howard. To break up the all-male cast, Judy Carne was given a recurring role as Commander Wyntoon's daughter Barbara—a love interest for young Jim Bailey (but she wasn't in every episode). It was this romance which rendered the rift between Sam Bailey and Cecil Wyntoon a bit more civil. Also appearing frequently was John Banner as Hans, who worked for Wyntoon at the Yacht Club.

Episodes include "Sam and the Invisible Man," with guest star Raquel Welch as Beverly Johnson, a Yacht Club beauty pageant contestant who got engaged to cousin Chester. Cecil Wyntoon was dead set against the engagement and tried to get Chester sent back to his home in Muncie, Indiana. Chester then had them believing that he had created a potion in his lab which made him invisible so that they couldn't send him home. This episode was directed by Bruce Bilson, who told me, "This was a very important show—it started my directorial career. Producer Bob Sweeney was my mentor." Dick Gautier guest starred as Tani in the episode titled, "To Sam, He's a Swimmer." Dick recalled, "I was never really much of a swimmer. I got to use my friend Peter Marshall's pool to rehearse in. I got diving down pretty well, but I had some trouble treading water. Somehow, with camera trickery, we managed to pull it off pretty well."

The program was produced by Bob Sweeney. Bruce Bilson remembered, "Antelo Productions was named for the street on which Sweeney lived." Writers included Sid Morse and Arthur Julian; directors included Gary Nelson, Charles Barton, and Bruce Bilson. Bruce told me, "Because of this series, I'm still into boating to this very day." *The Baileys of Balboa* was pummeled in the ratings by *Peyton Place* on ABC and *Hazel* on NBC.

Ball Four CBS. Wednesday nights 8:30. September 22, 1976–October 27, 1976. Seven episodes were videotaped before a live audience in New York City, only five aired.

Based upon the very successful Jim Bouton book of the same name, CBS brought the sitcom version of *Ball Four* to its Wednesday night lineup in the fall of 1976, albeit briefly. The program had the ideal time slot, tucked between *Good Times* and *All in the Family*. However, it only lasted five weeks. This was the story of relief pitcher Jim Barton (Jim Bouton) who wore number 56 on his jersey and played for the Washington Americans baseball team (likely a play on the hapless and defunct Washington Senators). Also in the cast were number 41 Coach Pinky Pinkney (Bill McCutcheon); number 37 (the manager) Cap Capograsso (Jack Somack); the massive and short-tempered Rhino Rhinelander (Ben Davidson)—the bullpen catcher who had a very soft spot for his mother; Lenny "Birdman" Siegel (who was always in the tub), played by Lenny Schultz (Gary Sandy in the unaired pilot); number 18 Rayford Plunkett who loved country music (Marco St. John); the oft-injured utility infielder Orlando Lopez (Jaime Tirelli); David James Carroll as rookie pitcher Bill Westlake; and outfielder C. B. "Cool Breeze" Travis (Sam Wright). Most of the action took place in the locker room. Because of its time slot (within the family hour), the sensors were very strict about what the guys could and couldn't say, and realism suffered in the G-rated locker room dialogue.

In the unaired pilot episode, Jim Barton was upset by cutbacks—the guys could only take three-minute showers, they assumed responsibility for lost baseballs and broken bats, and injured players were being denied coverage. The team held an election for a player representative and it went down to the wire between Plunkett and Barton, with Rhino casting the winning ballot for Barton.

The program was produced by Don Segall; creators and writers included Jim Bouton, Marvin Kitman and Vic Ziegel; and directors included Noam Pitlik, Jay Sandrich, Peter Lewis, and Nick Havinga. Joe Raposo composed the theme, which was performed by Harry Chapin. *Ball Four* was one of only a handful of sitcoms produced in New York in the 1970s. The unaired pilot episode can be viewed at the Paley Center for Media.

Barefoot in the Park Paramount Studios. ABC. Thursday nights 9:00. September 24, 1970-January 14, 1971. 12 color episodes were filmed with a laugh track. Sponsors included American Brands, General Foods, Lever Brothers, and Warner Lambert.

On September 24, 1970, two hit Neil Simon plays which became hit Neil Simon movies debuted in sitcom form. The one at 9:30 (*The Odd Couple*) quickly settled in for a five-season run. The one which preceded it on Thursday nights on ABC only ran for 12 weeks—it was the TV adaptation of *Barefoot in the Park*, which starred Jane Fonda and Robert Redford on the silver screen. The 1969 TV pilot episode had a white cast and had been an episode of *Love, American Style* titled "Love and the Good Deal" (Skye Aubrey as Corey and Philip Clark as Paul). The series, however, was done with an African American cast, and Tracy Reed and Scoey Mitchlll (yes, he spelled it with three "Ls") were the stars (as Corie and Paul Bratter, respectively). The Bratters were newlyweds, married only three weeks, and living in a run-down one room walk-up on the top floor of an old brownstone in lower Manhattan on West 10th Street. Paul Bratter had just landed a job (after six years of law school) at the prestigious firm of Kendricks, Keene and Klein (leading to several KKK jokes). Paul's immediate boss, Arthur Kendricks, was played by Harry Holcombe; Vito Scotti portrayed the building's klutzy superintendent, Mr. Velasquez; and Nipsey Russell played a friend of the Bratter's named Honey Robinson, who was the proprietor of Honey Robinson's Pool and Billiard Emporium. Honey had a crush on Corie's sassy widowed mom, Mabel Bates (Thelma Carpenter), who was a maid for a wealthy Park Avenue family.

In the debut, Paul reluctantly agreed to help out Corie and her mom at a posh dinner party. He later regretted this decision when Arthur Kendricks from his law firm showed up as a guest, and saw Paul serving food and drinks. Familiar sitcom faces Agnes Moorehead and Herbert Rudley guest starred in that debut. Other guest stars included Penny Marshall in "In Sickness and in Health;" Cindy Williams in "The Marriage Proposal;" boxing legend Sugar Ray Robinson in "Down with the Landlord;" and Huntz Hall and Jackie Coogan in "Disorder in the Court."

The program was produced by William P. D'Angelo, and devised for TV by Bill Idelson and Harvey Miller; writers included Idelson, Miller, Jerry Belson, Garry Marshall, Susan Harris, William S. Bickley, Charles Shyer, Alan Mandel, Stanley Ross, Richard DeRoy, Jack Winter, David Ketchum, and Bruce Shelly; and directors included Bruce Bilson, Jerry Paris, and Charles R. Rondeau. Music was provided by Neil Hefti. The theme song was performed by Rock and Roll Hall of Fame Inductee, Darlene Love. Ten of the 12 episodes were rerun as part of *Love, American Style's* 1971-1972 season. Cecil Smith of the *Los Angeles Times* called *Barefoot in the Park* "funny, young, bright, and quite delicious." One episode aired on TV Land.

The Betty Hutton Show (a.k.a. *Goldie*) Desilu Studios/A Hutton Production. CBS. Thursday nights 8:00. October 1, 1959-June 30, 1960. 30 black-and-white episodes were filmed with a laugh track. Sponsors included Post Cereal and General Foods.

The actress most famous for *The Greatest Show on Earth* and *Annie Get Your Gun* took a stab at TV stardom in this eponymous series, sometimes called *Goldie*. Goldie Appleby was a former showgirl-turned-manicurist-turned-legal guardian. She was mentioned in the will of one of her customers, a Mr. Strickland, who passed away suddenly. In fact, she got everything in the will—the estate (a Park Avenue duplex), and also Mr. Strickland's three children: Roy, the youngest, who attended the Ezra Taft Preparatory Day School for Boys (Dennis Joel); Pat, the artist (Gigi Perrault); and Nicky, who loved sports cars (Richard Miles). Goldie also inherited the family's lawyer Howard Seaton (Tom Conway, the actor who made another Tom Conway become Tim Conway). Goldie's attempts to adjust to her newfound wealth, status, and three children were at times overwhelming. Whenever things were going well, however, Goldie would utter the word "cu-cu." Goldie's former roommates (appearing occasionally) were Lorna (Joan Shawlee) and Rosemary (Jean Carson).

Episodes include "Art for Goldie's Sake," in which Goldie urged Pat to take up a hobby. Pat took Goldie's suggestion a bit too seriously, and moved into a Greenwich Village apartment to study art amidst an amusing array of beatniks. Goldie kept tabs on Pat, however, by donning a long black wig and mixing in with the younger generation and their bohemian ways. In "Gullible

Goldie," the sob story of a crooked elderly couple posing as down-and-out managers of a children's home, got Goldie in gear to raise money for them. Even the kids from the home were in on the ruse.

Guest stars included a very young Don Grady as Joey Simpson who started a school fight with Roy in the episode titled "Roy Runs Away;" Dennis Hopper portrayed Mike in the aptly titled "Goldie Meets Mike;" Phil Harris was Colonel Barker (an Elvis Presley send-off) in the episode called "Rock and Roll;" and Cesar Romero played himself in the episode called "Goldie Without Men."

The program was produced by William Harmon; the creator was Stanley Roberts; directors included Jodie Copeland, Richard Kinon, Jerry Hopper, and Robert Sidney; and writers included Laurence Marks, Ed Jurist, Marvin Marx, Terry Ryan, Edward Ludwig, Jack Wilson, Bob Kaufman, Ralph Goodman, Philip Lloyd, and Kip King. The theme song (during which, the letters in the name "Goldie" descended a large spiral staircase) was written by Jerry Fielding. Several episodes can be viewed in the UCLA TV Archives.

The Betty White Show MTM Productions. CBS. Monday nights 9:00 (September 12, 1977-November 14, 1977), and 9:30 (December 12, 1977-January 9, 1978). 14 episodes were videotaped before a live audience at CBS Studio Center.

This was the third time *The Betty White Show* was used as a program title—first in 1954 on her daytime show, then on her 1958 prime time comedy/variety show, and once more in 1977 following a successful run on *The Mary Tyler Moore Show*. This new show was also an MTM production, and another MTM alumnus, Georgia Engel, came along for the short ride. Georgia played Mitzi Maloney, Joyce Whitman's (Betty's) best friend and roommate. Joyce first met Mitzi at the unemployment office (Mitzi worked there, but was now, ironically, laid off). Here Betty portrayed a divorced, out-of-work actress with limited ability who got a break by being cast in a pilot episode for a possible series to be called *Undercover Woman* (somewhat of a parody of Angie Dickinson's *Police Woman*). Just as things were looking up for Joyce, she got word that her ex-husband, the emotionless John Elliott (John Hillerman), would be directing the series.

The Betty White Show—John Hillerman and Betty White (CBS).

Even with their unceasing animosity for one another (she called him "pickle-puss" and made sport of his mustache), they agreed to work together amicably. It's interesting to note that Joyce was making the pilot episode of *Undercover Woman* for CBS. While filming the pilot for this "show-within-the-show," Joyce began to have feelings for John once again. When those feelings weren't reciprocated it led to a funny scene in which Joyce, in a fit of rage, destroyed all of the props on the set (most were irreplaceable). Others in the cast included Barney Phillips as Fletcher Huff, the nervous, insecure actor who portrayed the police chief on Joyce's show. Caren Kaye was Joyce's sexy and dimwitted co-star, Tracy Garrett—but that character's name was Lisa Vincent (played by Carla Borelli) in the debut episode. Caren Kaye didn't recall why that change was made, but told me, "I was working mostly for Paramount and Garry Marshall at that time, so perhaps great timing came into play." Also in the cast were Charles Cyphers as Joyce's "male stunt double" Hugo Muncy (he donned a dress and wig); and Alex Henteloff as Doug Porterfield, a CBS Network liaison assigned to the series (his official title was Vice President in charge of prime time dramatic development, although prior to this he had been working in the mailroom). He was weak, ineffective, and never taken seriously. *Undercover Woman* became a series, and the love/hate relationship between Joyce and John was fodder for the remaining episodes of *The Betty White Show*.

The program was created by Ed Weinberger and Stan Daniels (who also served as executive producers); the producer was Bob Ellison; writers included David Lloyd; and directors included Bill Persky, Doug Rogers, Harvey Medlinsky, Burt Brinckerhoff, James Burrows, Jay Sandrich, and Noam Pitlik. Music was provided by Dick DeBenedictis. Betty White would later have a long run in *The Golden Girls*, she'd host an episode of *Saturday Night Live*, and star in a new sitcom for TV Land called *Hot in Cleveland*. Caren Kaye's memories of her co-stars are: "Love Betty White, and learned so much from this show, as well as John Hillerman. Georgia Engel is really that kind and sweet—a pure soul." The program was rerun on Nick at Nite.

The Bickersons First-run syndication. 1951-1952.

The Bickersons originated on radio and starred Frances Langford as the long-suffering Blanche Bickerson and Don Ameche as her harried husband of too many unpleasant years, John Bickerson. This couple truly lived up to their surname—they bickered constantly. Unlike *The Honeymooners* who did indeed fight a lot (and yet displayed great love and admiration for one another), the Bickersons' love was rarely obvious. When *The Bickersons* came to TV, they were originally seen as a semi-regular live feature on the DuMont Network's *Star Time* series. Frances Langford reprised her role as Blanche, but now in the role of John was comic Lew Parker (later Lew Marie on *That Girl*). These episodes are grainy kinescopes, most take place in the couple's drab and barren bedroom (twin beds, or course), and most are about 17 minutes in length.

The Bickersons did become a weekly single season syndicated filmed series in 1951, and again starred Lew Parker as John, but now Virginia Grey was Blanche (a prettier Blanche with less of an edge). These episodes are sometimes called *It's The Bickersons*, and the opening credits featured two birds on a perch squawking at one another. The couple resided in apartment number 22, and had a cat named Nature Boy. Also in the cast were Blanche's judgmental sister next door on Englewood Drive, Clara Gollup (Lois Austin), and her brother-in-law Barney Gollup (Sam Lee), who could never quite satisfy his appetite for food or gambling. These episodes were written and directed by Phil Rapp and produced by Jack Denove. Unlike the live episodes from *Star Time*, in these episodes the couple occasionally left the bedroom. They still threw barbs at one another on a consistent basis, but there was a palpable softening of the two main characters. This syndicated version of *The Bickersons* only lasted one season, but the story doesn't end there. These unhappily marrieds surfaced as a semi-regular erratically-timed feature on variety shows through 1953—still with Lew Parker as John, but now with Betty Kean as Blanche. Sadly, it seems none of the Betty Kean episodes have survived. The *Star Time* kinescopes of *The Bickersons*, and the filmed syndicated single season sitcom series as *It's The Bickersons*, are available in very inexpensive DVD box sets, which are available through the website *www.bickersons.com*.

Common threads through all of the many incarnations of *The Bickersons* include his snoring, her mother, his drinking, her cooking, his cheapness, and her spending.

Big Eddie Persky/Denoff Productions. CBS. Saturday nights 8:30 (August 23, 1975-September 6, 1975), and Friday nights 8:00 (September 19, 1975-November 7, 1975). Ten color episodes were videotaped before a live audience at KTLA Stage Five.

How ironic that Sheldon Leonard, who produced so many hit TV shows, was himself the star of such a colossal flop. It seemed like the ideal vehicle for him, as he had a real knack for portraying New Yorkers, tough guys, and gangsters. As "Big Eddie" Smith, he was the owner and promoter of the Big E Sports Arena. A reformed gambler who had gone legit, he was seeking culture, intellect and better manners. He played a tough guy on the show, but it was often very evident that he had a soft side, too. His new wife, Honey Smith (Sheree North), had a colorful past; she was an ex-stripper. Together they resided on East 56th Street in Manhattan. Quinn Cummings played their perky granddaughter, Ginger; Billy Sands played Monte "Bang Bang" Valentine, the Smith's cook; Alan Oppenheimer, who had previously played an accountant on *He and She*, played Big Eddie's accountant and brother, Jessie Smith; and Ralph Wilcox was an African American employee of Eddie's named Raymond McKay. The program got a jump on the fall TV season with an early start on Saturday nights beginning in late August of 1975, but when the program was placed into its regular Friday night slot against *Sanford and Son*, it spelled doom.

Episodes include "One Nation Invisible," in which Eddie and his granddaughter filed suit against a store who sold them a defective toy; in "Too Many Grandmothers," Big Eddie's first wife (Eva Gabor) made a surprise visit and instantly locked horns with Honey; in "One of Our Red Shoes Is Missing," the Smith family almost incited an international incident when they gave safe harbor to a defecting Soviet dancer.

The program was created by Bill Persky and Sam Denoff; it was produced and directed by Hy Averback.

Big John, Little John Redwood Productions and D'Angelo-Bullock-Allen Productions/NBC. Saturday mornings. September 11, 1976-September 3, 1977. 13 episodes were filmed with a laugh track.

Once again, the great Sherwood Schwartz made the unbelievable very fun and funny. This was the story of a 45-year-old junior high school science teacher (Herb Edelman as "Big" John Martin) who, while on a vacation in Florida at Ponce DeLeon Park, drank a small handful of water from the same "fountain of youth" for which Ponce DeLeon had been searching. The tiny amount of water he consumed caused him to frequently change back into a youthful 12-year-old John Martin ("Little" John, portrayed by Robbie Rist). The change, however, occurred at the most inopportune times. The only other people who knew about this were John's wife, Marjorie (Joyce Bulifant), and his 14-year-old

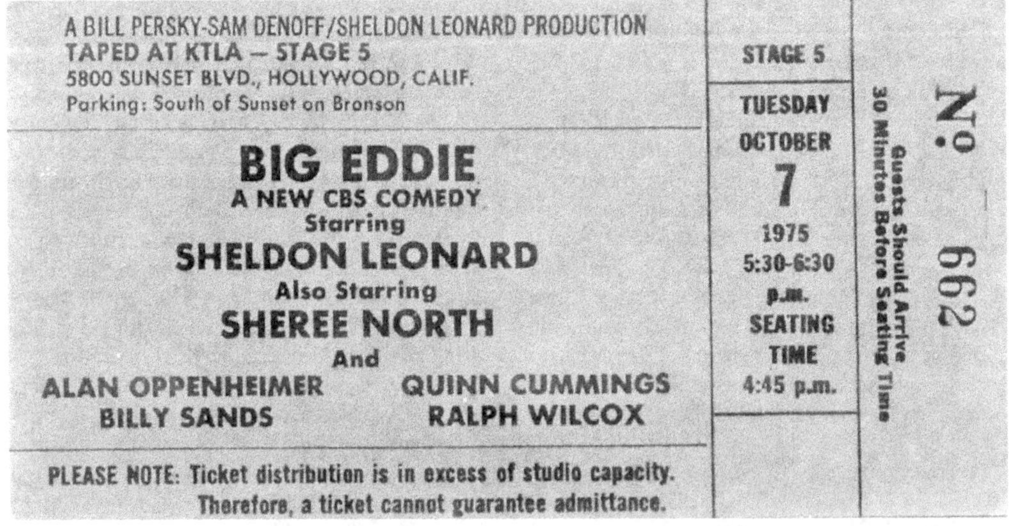
A BILL PERSKY-SAM DENOFF/SHELDON LEONARD PRODUCTION
TAPED AT KTLA — STAGE 5
5800 SUNSET BLVD., HOLLYWOOD, CALIF.
Parking: South of Sunset on Bronson

BIG EDDIE
A NEW CBS COMEDY
Starring
SHELDON LEONARD
Also Starring
SHEREE NORTH
And
ALAN OPPENHEIMER QUINN CUMMINGS
BILLY SANDS RALPH WILCOX

PLEASE NOTE: Ticket distribution is in excess of studio capacity.
Therefore, a ticket cannot guarantee admittance.

STAGE 5
TUESDAY
OCTOBER
7
1975
5:30-6:30
p.m.
SEATING
TIME
4:45 p.m.

Guests Should Arrive
30 Minutes Before Seating Time

No. 662

Big Eddie—Unredeemed ticket to a taping.

son, Ricky Martin (not to be confused with any other Ricky Martin), played by Mike Darnell. Olive Dunbar portrayed fellow teacher Miss Bertha Bottomly, who hadn't taken a vacation in 22 years. She was not "in on" John's secret, and she never did pick up on the running jokes that both Johns continually forgot her name (Miss Bottomly), and that they were never in the same room at the same time. The unpredictable change from "Big" to "Little" John, and vice-versa, created many a confused bystander, teacher, and student. The music always clued the audience into the fact that the "change" was coming. I asked Robbie Rist if wearing the oversized clothing whenever "Big John" became "Little John" ever caused him to trip and fall, and he said no: "In fact, the big clothes made my job easier. Every movement in those clothes was very funny. I didn't have to do a lot to get laughs." Robbie also recalled, "My natural eye color is green, and Herb Edelman's were brown, so I had to wear very uncomfortable contact lenses to make my eyes appear brown. I'm usually seen wearing glasses, but since I had the contact lenses on, I didn't wear glasses on this show."

Joyce Bulifant had an incredible memory about working with Sherwood Schwartz: "Up until the last possible moment, I was to be Carol Brady on *The Brady Bunch.* One of the powers-that-be at ABC wanted Florence Henderson in the role, and even though Sherwood Schwartz and others rallied for me, Florence got the role. I did get to do another show with Sherwood Schwartz, however, and this was it."

The debut, which explains the "growing" pains of the two Johns, was titled "A Sizeable Problem." Other episodes include "Peter Panic," in which both Johns were cast in a school production of "Peter Pan;" in "Big Shot, Little Shot," it was a two-shot vaccination day at school for John Martin—both "Big" and "Little" John got one; in "Time for Change," Big John thought he had finally figured out the schedule for his "changes" through a chemical equation, which proved grossly inaccurate.

The program was created by Sherwood Schwartz and Lloyd Schwartz; the executive producer was Sherwood Schwartz; producers included William P. D'Angelo, R. S. Allen, Harvey Bullock, and Lloyd Schwartz; writers included Ron Friedman, William Freedman, Sherwood and Lloyd Schwartz, Albert A. Schwartz, Mark Fink, Sam Locke, Paul Roberts, Ben Gershman, Harry Winkler, Bruce Howard, David P. Harmon, Jerome Zucker, Davis Samuel Zucker, James S. Abrahams, Bruce Kalish, Ron Sellz, Herbert Finn, and Alan Dinehart; and directors included Gordon Wiles and Ross Bowman. The theme song was written by John Thomas Fox and Sherwood Schwartz, and performed by Jerry Whitman. Joyce Bulifant remembered, "Harvey Bullock and Ron Friedman became great friends of mine for many, many years." All 13 original episodes are available in a DVD set from Fabulous Films, Limited, in the UK.

Robbie Rist revealed, "The guy who played my older brother Ricky, Mike Darnell, is the same Mike Darnell who is now the President of Alternative Entertainment for the Fox Network. Mike is really the father of reality TV. He very much wanted to be a producer, and through his own persistence, began with *When Animals Attack*, and parlayed it into *American Idol*, *Temptation Island*, *Joe Millionaire*, *X-Factor*, *Alien Autopsy*, and *So You Think You Can Dance?* Quite an amazing success story."

Billy John Rich Productions/20th Century-Fox. CBS. Monday nights 8:30 (February 26, 1979-March 12, 1979), and Saturday nights 8:30 (March 24, 1979-April 28, 1979). Seven color episodes were filmed with a laugh track.

This show, hastily selected to replace the abysmal lone episode of *Co-Ed Fever* on CBS, didn't fare any better than its predecessor. The premise worked well in the movies with James Thurber's *The Secret World of Walter Mitty*, and in cartoon form years later in *Bobby's World.* In sitcom form, however, it didn't jell. A young Steve Guttenberg portrayed Billy Fisher, a 19-year-old who hated the job arranged for him by his dad at the Shadrack and Shadrack Funeral Home in Pittsburgh, Pennsylvania. As an escape, Billy liked to daydream, and envisioned great things in his future. The program was actually based upon a British play called "Billy Liar," by Thomas Courteney, and "Billy Liar" was the name of one of the show's episodes (in which Billy saw himself as a superstar guest on *The Merv Griffin Show*). In the debut titled "The Letter," Billy got an interview for a job with the local radio station (WBK), and so he imagined becoming a famous disk jockey and media mogul who hired Don Adams to star in a sitcom which tried to put "fun" in funerals. In another episode, "Brief Encounter," Billy imagined himself as a famous athlete (NFL star Larry Czonka guest starred in this episode). In "The Prize," Billy envisioned himself taking Suzanne Somers to the annual Mortician's Ball.

The rest of the cast consisted of James Gallery as Billy's disappointed father George Fisher; Peggy Pope played Billy's mom Alice Fisher, and she was much more supportive of her son's "exaggerations." Also in the Fisher household was Gran, Billy's frail, forgetful grandmother, played by Paula Trueman. At the funeral parlor was Billy's co-worker and friend Arthur Milliken (Bruce Talkington) who was always trying to protect Billy from getting fired—not an easy task. Billy's boss was uptight funeral director Norville Shadrack (Michael Alaimo) who spoke slowly, always with perfect diction. Most of that perfect diction involved condescending remarks aimed at Billy for dereliction of duties. In the debut, Shadrack was angry with Billy because he used the company hearse to take a girl to a drive-in movie, and came back with a big scratch on the rear bumper.

The program was produced and directed by John Rich; writers included Dick Clement and Ian La Frenais (formerly of *On the Rocks*). *Billy* debuted on the same night as another short-lived CBS sitcom, *Flatbush*. This *Billy* is not to be confused with the short-lived 1992 sitcom of the same name which starred comedian Billy Connolly.

The Billy Bean Show ABC. Tuesday nights 9:00. 1951. Broadcast live.

Extremely little is known about this live sitcom, except that it starred Arnold Stang as Billy Bean—a soda jerk; Phil Tead was his boss; and Billie Lou Watt was the boss' daughter (on whom Billy had a schoolboy crush). Others in the cast included Harry Bellaver and Mort Stephens. The program was produced by Jeffrey Hayden, and directed by Sean Dillon. To my knowledge, no episodes exist.

The Bing Crosby Show Bing Crosby Productions/Desilu Studios. ABC. Monday nights 9:30. September 14, 1964-June 14, 1965. 28 black-and-white episodes were filmed with a laugh track. Sponsors included Mennen, Wisk, Lucky Whip, Pepto Bismol, Gillette, Imperial Margarine, Lever Brothers, and Ford-Lincoln-Mercury.

Recording and movie star Bing Crosby also had his own TV production company—BCP (Bing Crosby Productions), which gave us *Ben Casey* and *Hogan's Heroes*. BCP also brought us Bing's own eponymous short-lived sitcom. Bing was one of those stars who just couldn't make the successful transition to the small screen. The ABC Monday night lineup looked good on paper, though—George Burns in *Wendy and Me*, followed by *The Bing Crosby Show*—but neither show went on to a second season. Bing portrayed Bing Collins, a once-successful crooner who left show business for a less hectic life as an electronics engineer (he had designed the recording studio for local Culver University) and family man. He also loved baseball and was often pictured in front of the TV set sporting a Pittsburgh Pirates hat (Bing was part owner of the Pirates in real life), even though the TV series was set on Valley Tree Lane in Los Angeles. Bing was often heard humming the seasonal favorite "Greensleeves" on the show year round. Beverly Garland played his wife Ellie. At least once an episode, Bing and sometimes even Ellie broke into song. The Collinses also had two daughters—a blonde boy-crazy 15-year-old named Janice (Carol Faylen) and a 10-year-old walking encyclopedia named Joyce (Diane Sherry). They also had the luxury of a live-in handyman named Willie Walters (Frank McHugh).

Episodes include the debut "A Fine Romance," in which Bing and Ellie's marriage was called dull and predictable by their children, so the couple tried to get out of their rut by trying new things, only to discover it was the rut they liked best; in "Exactly Like Who?," Bing's real-life son, Gary, portrayed a wannabe singer/songwriter named Don, only to discover that the marketing of talent was really his bailiwick; in "The Test," while teaching Janice how to drive, Bing found out the hard way that his own driver's license had expired, necessitating his taking the driving test again; in "The Christmas Show," of course, Bing got to sing his legendary "White Christmas." Actress Kathy Garver recalled an episode on which she guest starred called "The Keefers Come Calling": "I played a party guest having a great time with dreamy guest star Frankie Avalon. Singer Vikki Carr played his wife, and accompanied him to this party at Bing's house. Together, they comprised the Keefers. I was going to UCLA at the time, and a chance to work not only with Bing Crosby, but also with my heartthrob, Frankie, was too good a role to turn down! The scenes went quickly—Bing was the ultimate pro."

The program was produced by Steven Gethers; writers included Dan Beaumont, Tom and Helen August, Jerome Ross, Irving Gaynor Neiman, and Jack Sher; and the director was James Sheldon. Music was provided by John Scott Trotter, and the theme songs "That's Life" and "It All Adds Up to Love" (performed by Bing) were written by Sammy Cahn and Jimmy Van Heusen. Numerous episodes can be viewed in the UCLA TV Archives.

Blansky's Beauties Henderson Production Company, Inc./Miller-Milkis Productions, Inc./ Paramount Studios. ABC. Saturday nights 8:00. February 12, 1977-May 21, 1977. 13 color episodes were filmed before a live audience.

Earlier in the TV season, Nancy Walker had her own eponymous sitcom from Norman Lear, which failed. This one didn't fare much better. The original working title was *Mrs. Blansky's Beauties*, but that was shortened. Walker portrayed Nancy Blansky, who was in charge of staging a crew of Las Vegas showgirls at the Oasis Hotel's Major Putnam Spectacular every night. To cut expenses, Nancy and a few of the girls as well as some family members (this show had a huge cast) lived together in an apartment (number 7). Nancy's roommates included bubbly Ethel "Sunshine" Akalino (Lynda Goodfriend) and daft blonde Bambi Benton (a take-off on Barbi Benton), played by Caren Kaye. Caren Kaye told me, "I was modeled to become the Fonz in this venue—a female Fonz." Also in the cast were nephew Joey DeLuca (Eddie Mekka), the choreographer, and his younger brother, the girl-crazy 12-year-old Anthony DeLuca (Scott Baio). Singer Johnny Desmond played Emilio, the maître d (Nancy's boyfriend) and George Pentecost played Horace "Stubbs" Wilmington, Nancy's persnickety boss and costume designer. After the quick demise of his own sitcom, *Mr. T. and Tina*, Pat Morita joined the cast of *Blansky's Beauties* midstream. He was back to playing Arnold and owned a Las Vegas coffee shop near the Oasis. Like *Happy Days* with its "Sit on it," and *Welcome Back, Kotter* with its "Up your nose with a rubber hose," this show, too had its own catch phrase: "Put a sock in it."

Even though this show was canceled after only 13 episodes, its story doesn't end there. Apparently, Miller-Milkis Productions really thought they had something here keeping the show set in Las Vegas and a few of the cast members—Caren Kaye, Lynda Goodfriend, and Scott Baio. With a bit of re-tooling, they made a new pilot called *Legs*, which aired on ABC almost exactly a year after the demise of *Blansky's Beauties*. In this show, Kaye and Goodfriend were once again Las Vegas showgirls with different character names. The pilot did well, and that led to a series with an additional element—the girls now had to look after younger siblings. This series ended up on NBC with a new title, *Who's Watching the Kids?* All of the tweaking and retooling didn't help very much, and it, too, only lasted 13 weeks.

Blansky's Beauties was created by Garry Marshall, Bob Brunner, and Arthur Silver; writers included Warren S. Murray, Joe Glauberg, Marc Sotkin, Judy Ervin, Roger Garrett, Chris Thompson, Robert Keats, Arnold Kane, Steve Zacharias, Toni DiMarco, and David Ketchum; and directors included Marshall, Alan Rafkin, and Jerry Paris. There were lots of guest stars from other Paramount sitcoms—Penny Marshall, Doris Roberts, Roz Kelly, and Phil Foster. Even the theme song, "I Want It All," was performed by Cyndi Grecco, who also performed the *Laverne and Shirley* theme. Nancy Walker never again attempted sitcom success, but she did go on to direct a couple of episodes of *13 Queens Boulevard*. Caren Kaye remembered Nancy Walker: "She was a pro but didn't enjoy working with showgirls, children or dogs. She was very kind to me when my back went out from wearing those uncomfortable costumes and shoes." Several episodes can be viewed in the UCLA TV Archives. One episode aired on TV Land.

Blondie Hal Roach Studios/King Features. NBC. Friday nights 8:00. January 4, 1957-September 27, 1957. 26 black-and-white episodes were filmed with a laugh track. Sponsors included Toni Hair Care Products.

This was TV's first version of *Blondie*. It was only marginally more successful than the second version in that it lasted for 26 episodes (the 1968 color version only lasted 13 weeks). It had the same identical theme song as the TV version of *The Great Gildersleeve*, which starred Willard Waterman, and was also filmed at Hal Roach Studios. Here again was that familiar story of Dagwood Bumstead (Arthur Lake, who had played Dagwood in the movies), and his lovely tow-headed wife Blondie (Pamela Britton), who lived at 4224 Shady Lane Avenue with their two children Alexander and Cookie (Stuffy Singer and Ann Barnes, respectively). In this version, their dog Daisy had a large litter of puppies (and all of the dogs were trained by Rennie Renfro).

Dagwood's boss at the Dithers Construction Company was cranky old Julius Caesar Dithers (Florenz Ames). Cora Dithers, his shrew of a wife, was played by two different women—Leal Bliss in the very early episodes, and Elvia Allman in the rest of the episodes. One of the biggest differences between this version of *Blondie*, and its color cousin a decade later, was the Woodleys—the Bumstead's next-door neighbors. True to the comic strip, Herbert and Tootsie Woodley were a big part of this first version of *Blondie*. Herbert was played by Harold Peary and wife Harriet "Tootsie" Woodley was played by Lois Collier in the very early episodes, and by Hollis Erving in the rest.

Episodes include the debut, "Dagwood's Ego for the Third Time," in which Blondie wanted Dagwood to get a promotion (an office with many windows was her gauge for success), so she cooked up a scheme to make him think he was a wealthy heir so that he'd think he had nothing to lose and would muster the courage to stand up to Mr. Dithers and demand the vice-presidency; in "I Spy," Dagwood unwittingly got involved with the syndicate, who had placed sensitive microfilm in his hat as a hiding place. The hard part for these crooks was getting the hat back. In "The Quiz Show," Dagwood got to show off his skilled number-crunching brain on a game show on which he became a "human adding machine" to win cash and prizes.

The program was produced by William Harmon; the executive producer was Hal Roach, Jr.; directors included Hal Yates, Paul Landres, and Gerald Freedman; and writers included John L. Greene, Frank Gill, Jr., and George Carlton Brown.

Blondie Paramount Studios/King Features. CBS. Thursday nights 7:30. September 26, 1968-January 9, 1969. 14 color episodes were filmed with a laugh track, only 13 aired.

This was the second unsuccessful attempt to bring Chic Young's *Blondie* comic strip to the small screen. This version was much more colorful than its predecessor. Actual color *Blondie* comic strips were shown during the opening and closing credits. This was the story of the always hurried, always harried Dagwood Bumstead (Will Hutchins)—an architect at Dithers Construction Company; his lovely, understanding, spendthrift wife Blondie was played by Patricia Harty. Blondie and Dagwood had two young children—Alexander and Cookie (Peter Robbins and Pamelyn Ferdin respectively). Both lent their voices to Charlie Brown and Lucy in animated TV specials. The Bumsteads also had a dog—Daisy, played by Daisy. Dagwood's boss, referred to as "Dithers, that screamer" in the opening credits, was portrayed by Jim Backus. Backus's real-life wife, Henny, played his wife Cora.

The debut, "Sayonara, Dagwood," involved a misunderstanding. Dagwood's plans were to be presented to the client, H.H. Hilton (Edward Andrews) at a Japanese restaurant called Chez Sukiyaki. Blondie got a glimpse of Dagwood entering the restaurant with Mr. Hilton's wife, Honey (Melinda Fee) and thought he was cheating on her. Dressed as a Japanese waitress, Blondie managed to create quite a scene. However, Dagwood got his raise, and Blondie apologized for what she had been thinking. A young Pat Morita had a minor role in this episode as Manny, the host at the restaurant.

The program was produced by Joe Connelly; writers included George Tibbles, Gary Belkin, and Danny Simon; and directors included Norman Abbott, Peter Baldwin, Gene Nelson, and Bruce Bilson. Music was provided by Bernard Green. Replacing this show was the equally short-lived *The Queen and I*, starring Larry Storch.

Bob & Carol & Ted & Alice Frankovich Enterprises, Inc./Screen Gems. ABC. Wednesday nights 8:00. September 26, 1973-November 7, 1973. 12 episodes were filmed before a live audience, but only seven aired. Sponsors included J. C. Penney.

The 1969 movie version by Paul Mazursky and Larry Tucker was nominated for four Academy Awards. Every one of the four main characters in the movie version was played by a very well-known entity—Robert Culp was Bob, Natalie Wood was Carol, Elliott Gould was Ted, and Dyan Cannon was Alice. There were no slouches in the TV sitcom version either—filmmaker Bob Sanders was played by Robert Urich, Carol Sanders was played by Anne Archer, Ted Henderson was played by David Spielberg, and Alice Henderson was played by Anita Gillette. The TV version, however, was not a hit. Bob and Carol Sanders were in their twenties, progressive, and "with it," while Ted and Alice Henderson were in their thirties, conservative, and "square." Bob and Carol had a young son named Sean, played by Brad Savage, and Ted and Alice had a pre-teen daughter named Elizabeth played by

Jodie Foster. They were all neighbors in Los Angeles, and they were friends, but their vastly different moral values, and some generation gap issues were the fodder for most of the comedy.

Episodes include "Nobody Wants to Talk About It," in which Carol wanted her husband to join her in becoming an organ donor. She then went a step farther and wanted the Hendersons to designate the Sanders family as guardians for Elizabeth, should anything happen to them (and vice versa). In the pilot episode, free spirits Bob and Carol asked Ted and Alice to "go naked swimming with them."

The program was produced by Jim Henerson (Larry Rosen produced the pilot episode); writers included Henerson, David G. Lloyd, Bernie Kahn, Larry Tucker, Rick Mittleman, Gene Thompson, Karyl Geld, Ron Friedman, George Atkins, James Ritz and Michael Weinberg; and directors included Rick Edelstein and Leo Penn. Reruns were briefly shown on Comedy Central.

The Bob Crane Show MTM Productions. NBC. Thursday nights 8:30. March 6, 1975-June 19, 1975. 14 color episodes were filmed before a live audience.

After a successful radio career came a brief stint on *The Donna Reed Show*, and then the long-running *Hogan's Heroes*, there were great expectations for this next venture in the career of Bob Crane—his own eponymous sitcom. And with the track record of success for MTM Productions, this seemed like "a sure thing." In his new show, Bob portrayed Bob Wilcox, who had been a highly successful and well paid big-wig in the insurance industry. That is, until the day he realized he just wasn't happy in his work. The opening credits explained it pretty well—Bob was on several phone lines at the same time and then mouthed the word "Stop!" In the next scene, he threw his briefcase into the lake. Even though he was now well into his forties, and much older than all of the other students, Bob decided to go to medical school to become a doctor. His wife Ellie Wilcox, played by Trisha Hart (formerly Patricia Harty), became the breadwinner (she was in real estate), and they, along with their seldom-seen daughter Pam (Erica Petal) moved from a glamorous home into a factory-turned-apartment in the old Star Trucking Company building in a less-than-desirable neighborhood. Apparently, Bob had also sold his car because he traveled everywhere by bicycle. Their landlord was a widower named Mr. Ernest Busso (Ronny Graham), who also owned the Busso and Petrie Toy And Novelty Company next door. Busso was always inventing new gag items, like toothpaste which turned your teeth black and itching bath salts.

That was Bob's home life. At City School of Medicine in Los Angeles, the assistant dean was the fastidious Dr. Lyle Ingersoll (Jack Fletcher). Bob's fellow students included Marvin Susman (Todd Susman), Lester Schmidt (Will Seltzer), and Jerry Mallory (James Sutorious). Harold Gould had a recurring role as Dr. Strauss. Situations were derived from the family's adjustments to the huge change in income status, and Bob's attempts to fit in with students half his age.

Episodes include the debut "Mid-Term Blues" in which Bob had the sinking feeling that he failed his mid-term exam and considered returning to the insurance industry when he saw the impact his new life was having upon his family; in "But I Love My Wife," Bob's new study partner, Janet Whitehall (Trisha Noble), was a beautiful 23-year-old who had designs on Bob. It's interesting to note that one year later, she'd reprise that role in another MTM show, *The Mary Tyler Moore Show* (as Whitney Lewis) in an episode titled "Ted's Temptation," and yet again she played a temptress (Carol Tyson) in an episode of *Husbands, Wives and Lovers*. The show's 13th and final episode, "Son of Campus Capers" was significant mostly for its guest star—an up-and-coming John Ritter in rare form as Hornbeck, who had been sabotaging the other students' lab experiments and book reports so that he could keep academic pace with them.

The program was created by Norman S. Powell, Jim Allen, and Martin Cohan. Powell and Cohan also produced the show. Writers included Cohan, Martin Donovan, Lloyd Garver, and Ken Hecht; directors included Jay Sandrich, Buddy Tyne, and Jack Shea. In June of 1978, Bob Crane's off-camera life caught up with him and he was found brutally murdered in a hotel room. David Pollock, who wrote for many of the MTM sitcoms told me, "Sadly, no one had any idea that Bob was leading this sordid double life."

The Bob Cummings Show (see *The New Bob Cummings Show*)

Bonino A Fred Coe Production. NBC. Saturday nights 8:00. September 12, 1953-December 26, 1953. 16 live episodes were broadcast with a live audience. Sponsors included Philip Morris

Cigarettes (Dunhill Cigarettes) and Lady Esther Cosmetics.

Fortunato Bonino (Ezio Pinza) was, as in real-life, an opera singer who loved to perform, and he toured the world. Called "Babbo" by his kids, he was a widower with eight children, and was away from his large family for long periods of time. When he forgot his son Carlo's birthday (Oliver Andes in the series, Jonathon Marlow in the pilot episode) because of a photo-op, he cut back performances in order to spend more time with his family. This decision greatly pleased Babbo's daughter, Doris (played in the pilot episode by future star, Eva Marie Saint, but later by Lenka Peterson), who was about to be married. His eldest son, Edward (Conrad Janis) was attending college, and his ten-year-old son, Andrew, who felt he now had a real father, was portrayed by actor/musician Van Dyke Parks. Parks told me, "I was originally selected to be in four episodes ... getting $450 a week, plus $100 in expenses. However, I became a close friend of Ezio Pinza's, and those four episodes expanded into the entire run of 16 episodes. Mr. Pinza took me out for my first Italian meal—spaghetti. I also became friends with his real-life son, Peter Pinza. I used to stay at the Pinza house often. I loved that their doorbell played "Some Enchanted Evening." Mr. Pinza drove a beautiful Kaiser and had a very beautiful wife, Doris, who had performed with the Ballet Russes." Oliver Andes, who played Carlo agrees, "Mr. Pinza was a very warm and generous man. Although he was a famous opera and stage star, he didn't act like one during rehearsals or the show. He gave the entire cast Christmas gifts at the end of the show, and mine was a gold Bulova Watch." Also in the cast were Chet Allen as son Terry Bonino; Gaye Huston as daughter Francesca Bonino; Paul Jonali as son Michael; Lucille Graygor as daughter Angela; the ubiquitous Mary Wickes as Martha the maid; Mike Kellin as Rusty (Babbo's valet and confidant); and David Opatoshu as Babbo's manager, Walter Rogers (Murray Matheson in the pilot episode). Oliver Andes recalled, "Mary Wickes left the show during the run to fulfill a movie contract which left a big void. Her character was very important to the whole series. She returned for one or two shows at the very end." Unlike *Life with Luigi*, this show about an Italian-American family did not raise the ire of the Italian-American community, although its life in prime time was just as short.

Ezio sang in each episode of the show, and Van Dyke Parks remembers, "I performed at least one duet with him on the show. In fact, our agent, Lucy Kroll, made sure to get kids who could act and sing for the *Bonino* show." Oliver Andes recalled, "Anthony Eisley was brought in to play Doris' boyfriend, John, and when they became engaged, it was the opportunity for Mr. Pinza to sing the 'My Little Girl' half of the soliloquy from *Carousel*." Doing a live sitcom with eight children and several pets was really risky. Andes remembered an episode with a live parrot: "There was an actor off-stage who spoke for it, but at a dress rehearsal, the real parrot started to speak lines that were not in the script, so a stuffed parrot was quickly substituted. And we all held our breaths when a pony was brought on in the first episode. We didn't want it to have an 'accident' during the show."

The program was produced by Fred Coe. *Bonino* was performed live from the Hudson Theater on West 44th Street in New York City, where *The Kate Smith Show* was also done. Van Dyke Parks told me, "I was never intimidated by the live broadcast or the live audience. I was able to emote, learn my lines, cry on cue. I was a very obedient kid and was very aware of all the talent surrounding me on the show." Oliver Andes concurred, saying, "You were only aware of the audience when they laughed or applauded." Among the guest stars on the show were Reta Shaw and Brett Somers.

The program was created by Thomas Phipps and Robert Alan Aurthur (who was also the writer); the director was Gordon Duff. A kinescope of the pilot is available for viewing in the New York City branch of the Paley Center for Media. This pilot episode is titled "I, Bonino," a play on *I, Pagliacci*.

In a *New York Times* review of *Bonino*, dated September 16, 1953, Jack Gould wrote, "*Bonino* is a program that obviously needs lots of work, and Saturday's show perhaps should have been tried out first on WNHC-TV in New Haven. A few more weeks may tell quite a different story." Sadly, after those few more weeks, *Bonino* was gone from the NBC schedule.

Boss Lady Wrather Television Productions, Inc. NBC. Tuesday nights 9:00. July 1, 1952-September 23, 1952. 13 episodes were filmed without a laugh track. Sponsors included Proctor and Gamble—Ivory, Lilt, and Duz.

By the time this summer replacement series began, its star, Lynn Bari, had already spent two decades in show business—mostly in "B" movies for 20th Century–Fox. A beautiful, statuesque brunette, she was also frequently seen in pin-up girl poses. She also danced and sang, but usually played "the other woman." Her move to the new medium of television did not prove to be an immensely successful one. In the summer of 1950, she co-starred with Donald Curtis in a CBS show similar to *The Thin Man* called *Detective's Wife*. Two years later, she starred in yet another summer replacement series (for *Fireside Theater*) called *Boss Lady*, but this one was way ahead of its time. At a time when *I Love Lucy* couldn't use the word "pregnant," and most TV women were housewives, Bari portrayed Gwen F. Allen, the successful CEO of a California construction company known as Hillandale Homes. Not only was she in management, but she was in management in a very male-dominated business, at the most successful builder in the United States. Gwen's inept father (Nicholas Joy) was the chairman of the board, and continually overstepped his bounds and interfered in his daughter's work. The staff was always trying to figure out ways to get the old man to step down or take another job, but to no avail. Gwen had a female secretary named Aggie, played by Lee Patrick, a male assistant named Roger (Richard Gaines), and a boyfriend named Jeff Standish (Glenn Langan).

Episodes include "Boss Vacations," in which the vastly overworked Gwen was forced into taking a vacation by her co-workers, but had to come back early to salvage a deal which was almost ruined by her meddling dad's silly invention called "the screenless window." In an untitled episode, Gwen was interviewed for the cover of *Executive* magazine at a most inopportune time. She was just about to hire a new general manager, but behind-the-scenes at the office, her reputation for hiring men who fell in love with her was leading to something resembling a mutiny. In another untitled episode, Gwen became a blonde in an attempt to get a construction contract with a Nicaraguan businessman who had an affinity for towheads.

The program was produced by Jack Wrather and Robert Mann; writers included Mann; and directors included William D. Russell. Several episodes can be viewed at both The Paley Center for Media and the UCLA TV Archives.

Bridget Loves Bernie Screen Gems/Douglas S. Cramer Company. CBS. Saturday nights 8:30. September 16, 1972-September 8, 1973. 24 color episodes were filmed with a laugh track.

This program had a lot in common with *Life with Luigi*, which aired two decades earlier. In *Luigi*'s case, the show was doing well in the ratings, but because of pressure from the Italian-American community (who were up-in-arms over their portrayal on the show), it was canceled. *Bridget Loves Bernie* suffered a similar fate. It was a sandwich hit, tucked in between *All in the Family* and *The Mary Tyler Moore Show* on Saturday nights on CBS. However, the subject matter raised such an uproar that, despite its very decent ratings, CBS bowed to the pressure and *Bridget Loves Bernie* became a single season sitcom. The uproar arose, mostly from the Jewish community, because of the "condoned" marriage between Bridget Theresa Mary Coleen Fitzgerald (an Irish-Catholic fourth grade school teacher), played by Meredith Baxter, and Bernie Steinberg (a poor cabbie who drove yellow cab number 12, was an aspiring actor and writer, and was the son of Jewish delicatessen owners), played by David Birney. The young couple, who met and fell in love in Bernie's cab, lived in the apartment above Steinberg's Delicatessen, run by Sam and Sophie Steinberg (Harold J. Stone and Bibi Osterwald, respectively). Because of their proximity to the newlywed couple, they meddled a lot. Bridget's parents meddled as well, and often dropped in unexpectedly (David Doyle played wealthy executive Walter "Walt" Fitzgerald, and Audra Lindley was his somewhat stuffy wife, Amy). The Fitzgeralds lived in a luxurious apartment at Central Park West. Not unlike Broadway's runaway hit, *Abie's Irish Rose*, the situations in this sitcom emerged from the star-crossed lovers and their families. How they adapted and adjusted along the way provided a seemingly endless array of script possibilities.

Episodes include "A Funny Thing Happened on the Way to the Vatican," in which the Steinbergs bought raffle tickets from the Fitzgeralds and won a trip to Rome (which included a private audience with the Pope). This was a prize the Fitzgeralds really wanted to win, so the Fitzgeralds bought round-trip tickets to Tel Aviv with the intention of trading. To avoid any hurt feelings, clever Uncle Moe Plotnick (Ned Glass) acted as a go-between, and made the switch, and all was well. In "Tis the Season," the newlywed couple couldn't decide which holiday to celebrate, Christmas or Hanukkah, for fear of offending one set of in-laws.

The show was created by Screen Gems staple Bernard Slade; the producers were Arthur Alsberg and Don Nelson; writers included Alsberg and Nelson, as well as John McGreevey, Elias Davis, Marty Roth, Bill Dana, Don Sherman, Howard Merrill, Slade, Jack Hanrahan, Jerry Mayer, Gordon Farr, Rick Mittleman, Warren S. Murray, Lloyd Turner, Gordon Mitchell, Joanna Lee, and Arnold Kane; and directors included Richard Kinon, Lee Philips, James Sheldon, Hal Cooper, Ezra Stone, Alan Rafkin, Coby Ruskin, Bill Bixby, and Ozzie Nelson. Ozzie also made a cameo appearance in the episode titled "With This Ring." The theme song, "Love Is Crazy," was written by Jerry Fielding with lyrics by Diane Hilderbrand. Those lyrics are performed at the beginning of the debut episode. This show was briefly rerun on a short-lived cable channel called HA! in the early 1990s. After the show's demise, David Birney and Meredith Baxter got married in 1973 in real-life. They divorced in 1989.

Bringing Up Buddy Kayro Productions, Inc./ Revue Studios in Hollywood. CBS Monday nights 8:30. October 10, 1960-September 25, 1961. 39 black-and-white episodes were filmed with a laugh track. Sponsored by Scott Paper Company.

This sitcom starred Frank Aletter as investment counselor Richard David "Buddy" Flower who lived in the town of Bradley Falls. The original working title for the show was *The Flower Girls*, but that title would have proven confusing to viewers. Bachelor Buddy lived with his two spinster aunts—Iris Flower (Doro Merande of *Our Town*) and Violet "Vi" Flower (Enid Markey, who had been Tarzan's first Jane in vintage films). Violet called everyone "Love." It wasn't a secret that Enid and Doro didn't get along very well (this sitcom didn't have the happiest set). Even though the aunts were never themselves wed, they were always playing matchmaker to get Buddy married off. Buddy was taken in by the aunts after his biological parents died in a car crash. Yvonne Lime portrayed Buddy's secretary and frequent love interest, Penny.

Episodes of note include "Cesare Comes Calling," in which a visiting, down-on-his-luck opera singer took advantage of the good-natured aunts by borrowing money from them, much to Buddy's dismay. In "Poppa's Eagle," Buddy tried not to look a gift eagle in the beak when a stuffed eagle heirloom was given to him by his aunts to spruce up his newly redecorated office. This placed Buddy on the horns of a dilemma—the bird was an eyesore, and he was allergic to feathers. In "The Aunts Have a Baby," an infant was abandoned in the backseat of the aunts' convertible while they were shopping. A note affixed to the baby's blanket let the aunts know that the foundling's name was Robert. With only that piece of information to go on, the aunts took care of the little guy until the mother could be tracked down. The hardest part was keeping it from Buddy.

Guest stars included Aletter's wife in real life, Lee Meriwether (playing a nurse named Gloria Arnold), in an episode titled "Buddy and the Amazon" (including a cameo by their new baby girl Kyle). Lee told me, "I was worried about keeping Kyle happy and quiet there on the set. Frank and I had to get her a Social Security card to appear on the show. That card still bears her teeth marks." Lee also recalled, "Enid was just amazing, adorable, as sweet as can be. Behind-the-scenes, she reassured me that, being a new mother I shouldn't worry—everything would be fine. Doro was much more reserved, but she eventually warmed up to me. I remember her having a minor incident in her dressing room, something about someone having moved her bobby pins." Other guest stars included Edgar Buchanan appearing in the episode called "Big Game Hunter" as Captain Cunningham, who was chosen to speak at a local women's league function. The problem was that all of his big adventures were tall tales. Sherry Jackson had a crush on Buddy in the episode called "Buddy and Janie;" Arte Johnson appeared in "Auntie's Cake," in which the aunts endorsed a line of frozen desserts; Irene Ryan and George Chandler appeared together in the episode titled "Cynthia's Boyfriend;" and Ryan reprised her role as Cynthia in an episode called "The Singer," in which Buddy and a nightclub performer were trapped together in an elevator.

The program was produced by Joe Connelly and Bob Mosher; the creator was George Tibbles; writers included the teams of Si Rose and Seaman Jacobs, Joe Connelly and Mosher, and Alan Lipscott, Bob Fisher and George Tibbles; and directors included David Butler, Sidney Lanfield, and Andrew McCullough.

The transitional music in this show is identical to that used in *Leave It to Beaver*. That's very understandable—both were filmed at Revue Studios for Kayro Productions. The entire run of this

Bringing up Buddy—**Left to right, Enid Markey, Frank Aletter, and Doro Merande (CBS).**

series is housed in the UCLA TV Archives. A program with a similar premise, *Young Mr. Bobbin*, aired several years earlier and also became a "single season sitcom."

Broadside Universal City Studios. ABC. Sunday nights 8:30. September 20, 1964-September 5, 1965. 32 black-and-white episodes were filmed with a laugh track. Sponsors included Plymouth.

In an experiment to release more men for combat in World War II, women were called upon as replacements for the motor pool in 1944. The action took place on Ranakai in the South Pacific in this female spinoff of *McHale's Navy*—thus the clever title of *Broadside.* Kathy Nolan, who for five seasons had been Kate on *The Real McCoys*, was the star of the show as Lt. Anne Morgan. She was one of five "women" newly stationed on Ranakai. The word "women" is in quotations for a reason to be explained later in this paragraph. Along with Anne Morgan were Waves Selma Kowalski (Sheila James); former exotic dancer Roberta Love (Joan Staley); the morale-deficient Molly McGuire (Lois Roberts); and here's that promised explanation—the fifth Wave was a guy named Marion Botnik (Jimmy Boyd of *I Saw Mommy Kissing Santa Claus* fame). He was a Wave because of a clerical error, and because of his ambiguous first name. Before all of the new arrivals, Cdr. Rogers Adrian (Edward Andrews) had it made. There was very little action on Ranakai, and he had the "Life of Riley." He was served lobster or steak for dinner each night and had a rather impressive vintage wine collection behind a curtain in his office. We'd also find out in the episode "Adrian's Phantom Staff Car" that he had a rare and valuable 12-cylinder Flotsam Town Car, which met an untimely end when it was borrowed by Wave Selma Kowalski, and ended up in a tree. Having these women on Ranakai was a huge disruption to Adrian's routine, and every episode centered around his attempts to get rid of the female motor pool. His disdain for the women might be related to his disdain for his wife, who is pictured on a dartboard in his office. Also in the cast were Dick Sargent as Lt. Maxwell Trotter; George Furth as Ensign Beasley; and Arnold Stang (the voice of *Top Cat*) as the ship's cook, First Class Stanley Stubbs.

Many episodes of the show had clever titles such as "Don't Make Waves," "The Non-Permanent Wave," and "The Stowawaves." Like *McHale's Navy*, this show was produced by Edward J. Montagne; writers included Robert C. Dennis, Earl Barret, Barry Blitzer, Elroy Schwartz, Ray Brenner, and *McHale's Navy* regulars Frank Gill, Jr., G. Carleton Brown, and Si Rose; and directors included Jean Yarbrough and Montagne. Music was provided by Jerry Fielding.

The Brothers Dallad Productions/Desilu Studios. CBS. Tuesday nights 8:30. October 2, 1956-March 26, 1957. 26 black-and-white episodes were filmed before a live audience. Sponsors were Proctor and Gamble (Joy Dishwashing Liquid), The American Tobacco Company, Lever Brothers, and Shaeffer Fountain Pens.

This situation comedy called *The Brothers* has no relation to the sitcoms of same name which ran years later on Showtime and Fox. This show's opening credits appeared in a diagonal film strip, and that has a direct correlation to the main characters, Harvey and Gilmore Box, who owned a photography studio in San Francisco. The family had been in the "city by the bay" for decades, and had developed a reputation as "the San Francisco Boxes." The elder brother, Harvey Box, was played by Gale Gordon—a role not unlike the blustery Osgood Conklin he portrayed previously on *Our Miss Brooks.* The younger, much more timid and naïve brother, Gilmore Box, was played by Bob Sweeney. Each of the Box brothers had a girlfriend with a personality much like their own. The aggressive Margaret Kleeb (Ann Morriss) was teamed with Harvey, and the quiet Marilee Dorf (Nancy Hadley) was paired with Gilmore. Barbara Billingsley appeared as Barbara, another Gale Gordon girlfriend, in five episodes.

In an episode called "Renting the Attic," the Box brothers realized that they needed to divest of their old 1937 La Salle. They decided upon a used 1951 convertible, but as usual, money was their problem. Gilmore got the bright idea to take in a boarder to live in the attic. Harvey was against the idea, but acquiesced with the understanding that he must first approve of the tenant. Their first prospect was a hobo, but their second got the nod. He was H. Barrington Steele, Jr. (Robin Hughes). He seemed like the ideal boarder—that is, until he held an extremely loud celebration on his very first night in the attic. This boarder resurfaced in the episode called "The Quadrangle," in which Steele stole the Box brother's girlfriends.

A running theme in episodes of this show was competition between the Box brothers. In "Gilly's Birthday," Harvey blew off his brother's birthday party for a championship bowling meet; in "Little Theater Group," Harvey was expecting a role in an upcoming local Shakespearean production, but it was Gilmore who got the role of Romeo (Harvey was merely put in charge of painting the scenery); in "Gilly's Investment," Gilmore tried to show the Box family that he had

The Brothers—**Left to right, Gale Gordon, Nancy Hadley, and Bob Sweeney (CBS).**

as good a head for business as his brother, Harvey. However, Gilmore invested in, of all things, a dead whale.

The program's producer was Edward Feldman; directors included Hy Averback; and writers included Bill Davenport, Burt Styler, Jim Fritzell and Al Lewin. Music was provided by Wilbur Hatch.

Six rerun episodes were broadcast in prime time during the summer of 1958 on alternating weeks with *Bachelor Father* on CBS. One episode is available for viewing it the UCLA TV Archives.

Brothers and Sisters Paramount Studios. NBC. Sunday night 8:00 (January 21, 1979); Friday nights 8:30 (January 26, 1979-February 1979); and Friday nights 9:00 (February 1979-April 6, 1979). 13 episodes were filmed with a laugh track, only 12 aired.

Immediately following the meteoric success of *National Lampoon's Animal House*, all three networks vigorously assembled sitcoms about college life. ABC got the ball rolling with *Delta House*, CBS was last with the one-shot *Co-Ed Fever*, and in between NBC tried *Brothers and Sisters* (not to be confused with the Sally Field drama of the same name). *Brothers and Sisters* took place at Larry Krandall College (run by its namesake and founder, played by William Windom). In the Pi Nu Fraternity were Miles "Checko" Sabolcic (Chris Lemmon, son of Jack) who was dedicated to his studies; Ronald Holmes III (Randy Brooks), the only African American member of the fraternity; Stanley Zipper (Jon Cutler), the most slovenly frat member; Seymour (Roy Teicher, who also wrote a couple of episodes) who had an insatiable appetite; and Pi Nu President, Harlan Ramsey (Larry Anderson) who was filthy rich and overbearing. In the Gamma Delta Iota Sorority was Harlan's equally obnoxious girlfriend, social climber Mary Lee (Amy Johnston), and Zipper's unobtainable dream girl, Suzi Cooper (Mary Crosby, Bing's daughter). Marilyn Tokuda played a character named Yoko of the Gamma Delta Iota Sorority. She remembered, "I was in awe of Chris Lemmon, the son of one of my favorite actors, Jack Lemmon. Certain moments while watching him work, his mannerisms, even speech patterns would remind me of him. I wondered what a challenge it must have been forever being compared to such an iconic figure as his father. I was also a big fan of William Windom. I grew up watching him on *The Farmer's Daughter*. He was so nice."

Episodes include "Truth or Consequences," in which it was thought that either Ronald or Harlan cheated on their math test (as each had identical answers)—but which one? In "The Main Event," when Ronald said some hurtful things to Mary Lee, Harlan stepped in and challenged Ronald to a boxing match. In "Save the Monkey," Zipper was so upset that a monkey was to be used in a lab experiment, he set the animal free.

The program was produced by Hy Averback, Nick Abdo, and Jerry Mayer; the executive producers were Bob Brunner and Arthur Silver; writers included Roy Teicher, Jeff Franklin, Ron Leavitt, Allen Goldstein, Brian Levant, Bernie Kahn, Jerry Mayer, Paul Diamond, David Lerner, and Levi Taylor; and directors included Lowell Ganz, Buddy Tyne, Dennis Steinmetz, Abdo, Dick Martin, Will Mackenzie, John Bowab, and Tony Mordente. Music was provided by Mark Snow. The first episode aired immediately after Super Bowl XIII in which the Pittsburgh Steelers defeated the Dallas Cowboys 35–31, before moving to its regular Friday night timeslot.

The Buster Keaton Show *(Life with Buster Keaton)* Consolidated Television Productions/ Crown Pictures International. Syndicated. Black-and-white filmed episodes, some have laugh tracks. 1951.

Legendary silent film star Buster Keaton (*The General*) attempted to bring his comedy to television in the early 1950s, first in a live and local variety series in Los Angeles, and then in this nationally syndicated filmed sitcom. Neither show was very successful, but both used the same cast. Peter Leeds played Mr. Sharkey, Buster's boss, and Donna Gibson played the boss' daughter, Mabel. The filmed sitcom episodes took place in the Hollywood Sporting Goods store. This venue allowed Buster a lot of "alone time" on camera to "do his thing." Buster was, of course, the bumbling employee, almost getting fired from his job each and every week. He was not only clumsy, but also lazy. He'd often be caught goofing off in the back room, listening to the radio, reading, napping, daydreaming, or playing with the sporting goods.

The episode titled "Private Eye" had Buster in a Walter Mitty daydream state, envisioning himself as famous private eye Sam Keaton who was hired to deliver a mysterious yellow canary. Many episodes had a sporting goods theme, such as "Gone Fishing," "Buster in the Jungle," and "Tag Team Buster." Some classic and inspired slapstick moments were caught on film in an untitled episode in which Buster made taffy—creating some great belly laughs, as well as a huge mess.

The program was produced by Clyde Bruckman; writers included Jay Sommers and Carl K. Hittleman. Hittleman also served as executive producer. Directors included Arthur Hilton and Eddie Cline. The pressures of coming up with funny visual material each and every week became very taxing for Keaton, and he bowed out of the show before its run was completed. It is not known how many episodes were produced, nor are many of the episode titles

Calucci's Department—Left to right back row, Jose Perez, Bill Lazarus, Bernard Wexler, Jack Fletcher. Left to right front row, Candy Azzara, James Coco and Peggy Pope (photograph courtesy of Candy Azzara).

known. Guest stars were rarely credited, so the identities of many of the other actors on the show remain a mystery.

Calucci's Department A Sullivan Production. CBS. Friday nights 8:00. September 14, 1973–December 28, 1973. 13 color episodes were videotaped in New York before a live audience.

The Sullivan in Sullivan Productions was indeed Ed Sullivan. The premise for this show still sounds great on paper. One would think that a sitcom taking place in a New York City unemployment office would have unlimited possibilities. However, something went awry and this promising idea fell flat. Joe Calucci (James Coco) was the unemployment office supervisor, but in his heart of hearts he wanted to be a sportswriter. The opening credits pretty well summed up the caliber of employees he supervised: they all entered the building still looking half-asleep and extremely lethargic. This collection of miscreants consisted of Ramon Gonzalez (Jose Perez), the office narcissist, and Shirley Balukis (Candy Azzara), Joe's hunt-and-peck secretary and girlfriend (she was able to see the inner beauty beneath his girth). She called him "Joey." Azzara said, "I am not a singer, but my character would always break into a song that related to her situation." After a lot of flirting in the early episodes, the couple finally shared a kiss in the episode titled "The Bloom Is Off the Rose." In "Calucci and the Chicken or the Egg," Joe finally brought Shirley home to meet his mom. Joe lived with his mother, Mrs. Calucci (Vera Lockwood), a culinary savvy widow. Her cooking led to Joe's weight problems, as evidenced in the episode titled "Calucci Goes on a Diet," in which Joe's doctor issued a mandate to drastically change his diet. Others in the office included the high-strung Oscar Cosgrove (Jack Fletcher), who was the office claims adjuster; Peggy Pope was Elaine Fusco (who was a whiz in the stock market); Bill Lazarus was Jack Woods; Bernard Wexler was Walter Frohler; and Rosetta Lenoir was Mitzi Gordon. This incompetent staff, plus surly claimants, and government red tape kept Calucci constantly at wit's end. Azzara told me, "The unaired pilot was almost with the same cast, except William Hickey was in it, but his character didn't make it into the series. Also Claudia McNeil was in the pilot but was replaced in the series by Rosetta Lenoir. In that pilot, I had short hair and dressed like Marilyn Monroe—they made me a white dress like the one Marilyn was famous for wearing."

The program was produced by Howard Gottfried and Nick Arnold; writers included Arnold, Phil Mishkin, Renee Taylor and Joseph Bologna. Taylor and Bologna were also the show's creators. Azzara recalled, "It was easy for me working with Renee and Joseph—I knew their comedy—I was in their first Broadway play, *Lovers and Other Strangers*." Directors included Bruce Bilson, Burt Brinckerhoff, Arthur Storch, and Russ Petranto. This was one of just a small handful of shows from the 1970s videotaped in New York City (at CBS Broadcast Center). The theme song was written by Marvin Hamlisch. There was fierce ratings competition in this time slot, up against both *Sanford and Son* and *The Brady Bunch*. Candy told me, "After the show was canceled, one of the directors said they were sure I'd still be bringing snacks. I would always bring cheese crackers and candy for the company and crew while we were taping."

Camp Runamuck A Runamuck Production/Screen Gems. NBC. Friday nights 7:30. September 17, 1965–September 2, 1966. 26 color episodes were filmed with a laugh track.

There were two distinctly different summer camps on opposite sides of the lake. The girls' camp, Camp Divine, was just that—divine, impeccably run, and managed. Just across the water on the boys' side, however, the goings-on were certainly no picnic at the slipshod, mismanaged, aptly named *Camp Runamuck*. To begin with, Commander Wallace "Wally" Wivenhoe (Arch Johnson) was not a big fan of children and had an eyelash curler in his baseball mitt. Second in command was 32-year-old Senior Counselor George Spiffy, played by Dave Ketchum, who often got letters of disappointment from his mother (he constantly sought her approval to no avail). Under him was the eternally cheerful chronic snorer Counselor Stanley Pruett, played by Dave Madden, and Counselor Doc Joslyn (played by Frank DeVol in the debut episode, but rather by Leonard Stone for the rest of the series). Mike Wagner portrayed the camp cook, Counselor Malden. In charge on the girls' side of the lake was Alice Nunn as matronly Mahala May Gruenecker; Nina Wayne (Carol's sexy older sister) was Rhodes Scholar Caprice Yeudleman (who evoked in Pruett involuntary, violent shaking from head-to-toe); and Hermione Baddeley was the owner of the girls' camp, Eulalia Divine. The girls communicated by sending arrows across the lake with an attached message, but the arrows always landed in the worst possible locations. The girls sang a cloying "good morning song" every day, which drove the counselors on the boys' side of the lake to distraction.

Episodes include "Rabbits of the World Unite," in which Mahala May and Wivenhoe had a falling out. Wivenhoe later discovered that Mahala May's father worked for the very exclusive Apperson Meadows Golf Club which he wished to join, and besides just apologizing profusely, committed his crew to appear at the girls' pageant dressed in bunny costumes. In "Turtle?"

because of poor attendance in the boys' camp, the crew set up a plan to take pictures for new brochures to express the fun environment of Camp Runamuck. Their plan was ill-timed and few smiles could be found as all of the boys were grief-stricken at the death of their beloved pet turtle. Among the best episodes was "Tomboy," featuring a very young Maureen McCormick as Maureen, who was continually caught sneaking out of the girls' camp and infiltrating the boys' camp. She liked doing "boy" things much more than "girly" things, so the Runamuck counselors devised a plan to alter their own schedule to include cooking and sewing. The plan worked like a charm, and Maureen went running back to the girls' side of the lake.

A DAVID SWIFT ENTERPRISE

"We are gathered here today on this solemn occasion to lay to rest-----a TURTLE????"

(#4116)

Written by
Sid Mandel and
Bob Rodgers
FINAL DRAFT
June 16, 1965

A SCREEN GEMS · RUNAMUCK PRODUCTION

Camp Runamuck—**Script from the episode titled "Turtle?" which aired October 29, 1965.**

The program was created and produced by David Swift; writers included Swift, Bob Rodgers, Sid Mandel, Ann Marcus, William Freedman, and Ben Gershman; directors included Swift, Robert Rosenbaum, Hal March, Howard Duff, Charles Barton, David Butler, and Bruce Bilson. The music was provided by Hugo Montenegro, and the theme was written by Howard Greenfield and Jack Keller. Dell Comics released one *Camp Runamuck* comic book in April of 1966. It sold for twelve cents. This program was briefly rerun on Comedy Central.

Captain Nice Paramount Studios. NBC. Monday nights 8:30. January 9, 1967–August 28, 1967. 15 episodes were filmed in color with a laugh track. Sponsors included General Mills, Arrid Deodorant, Glad Sandwich Bags, and Sani-Flush.

Two very similar single season sitcoms debuted and ended on the very same night. Both were superhero parodies. On one show, a scrawny little nebbish took a special pill to give him superhuman strength, while in the other our meek little man drank a potion he had created in a laboratory, making him virile and invincible. One aired on Monday nights at 8:00 on CBS (*Mr. Terrific*), and the other aired on Monday nights at 8:30 on NBC. Here we're discussing the latter, called *Captain Nice.* The action took place in the city of Bigtown (population: 112,000), somewhere in the Midwestern part of America. This was the story of a shy chemist for the police department named Carter Nash (William Daniels), a momma's boy who still lived at home with his parents, Mrs. Esther Nash (Alice Ghostley) and Mr. Harvey Nash (Byron Foulger, who was always behind a newspaper). Carter got his job through his uncle, Fred Finney, the mayor of Bigtown (Liam Dunn), but they tried their best to keep that a secret. Also in the cast were William Zuckert as

Chief Segal, and Ann Prentiss as Sgt. Candy Kane, who found the sensitive and timid Carter Nash very attractive. One day in the lab, Carter had a major breakthrough and invented a potion which would make a weakling very strong (which he displayed to the mayor and the police chief using a cat and mouse in a cage). However, no one on the police force saw its potential and dismissed it as folly. Carter then ingested the potion himself, saved a damsel in distress, and returned an escaped felon to prison. When he drank his potion, he suddenly and temporarily was able to fly, and attained superhuman strength to subdue the bad guys. He used the initials on his Carter Nash belt buckle (C.N.) for the name of his alter-ego, *Captain Nice*. Upon admitting his heroism to his mother, she encouraged him to continue to help mankind. She even made his new red, white and blue *Captain Nice* costume, complete with cape. Unlike Superman, Carter's costume changes were slow and methodical—he even hung up his suit and put shoe-trees in his footwear.

There were only 15 episodes of *Captain Nice*, but they were jam-packed with famous guest stars like Vic Tayback, Barbara Stuart, Dick Wilson, Victor French, Pat Harrington, Jr., John Fiedler, Burt Mustin, Bob Newhart, Jo Anne Worley, Charles Grodin, John Dehner, and Joseph Campanella.

The program was produced by Jay Sandrich; the executive producer was Buck Henry; writers included Henry, Al Gordon, Hal Goldman, Treva Silverman, Peter Meyerson, Arne Sultan, Mike Marmer, Stan Burns, David Ketchum, and Bruce Shelly; and directors included Jud Taylor, Gary Nelson, Richard Kinon, Hollingsworth Morse and Charles Rondeau. Vic Mizzy provided the show's theme song, and one of the vocalists greatly resembles Don Adams. The program was briefly rerun on the HA! cable channel.

The Cara Williams Show Richelieu Productions. CBS. Wednesday nights 9:30 (September 23, 1964–April 21, 1965), and Friday nights 8:30 (April 30, 1965–September 10, 1965). 30 black-and-white episodes were filmed with laugh track. Sponsors included General Foods, and Procter and Gamble.

This show followed *The Dick Van Dyke Show* on Wednesday nights—it should have been a big hit. It was produced and developed by a known quantity in Keefe Brasselle. The star of the show was familiar—she had been in several successful movies (*The Helen Morgan Story*, *Never Steal Anything Small*, *The Defiant Ones*) and had spent two wacky seasons as Gladys Porter on *Pete and Gladys*. Here, in her own eponymous sitcom, Cara Williams portrayed Cara Wilton at work and Cara Bridges at home. She was the file clerk for Fenwick Diversified, Incorporated—a company which didn't allow employees to be married to one another—thus the two different surnames. Cara was married to the company's efficiency expert Frank Bridges, played by Frank Aletter. Comedic situations arose from the couple's attempts to keep their married status from their boss Damon Burkhardt (Paul Reed). The program altered its format somewhat midseason as Cara finally divulged her secret to the boss, while explaining that married couples were keeping Fenwick Diversified afloat. Both she and Frank got to keep their jobs. Also in the cast were Jeanne Arnold as Mr. Burkhardt's secretary Mary Hammilmeyer; Reta Shaw as Mrs. Burkhardt; and Jack Sheldon as musician, neighbor and friend Fletcher Kincaid.

Maybe the character of Cara was just too similar to her earlier role of Gladys. Cara got into the same kind of outrageous predicaments. In the episode titled "What Television Show Does Your Dog Watch," Cara got into an automobile accident with the star of the children's show, "Mighty Man of Mars" (John Lupton), and agreed to babysit the star's dog to pay for the damages. While babysitting, she tried on his "Mighty Man" costume and became airborne. We got to see another side of her in the episode titled "Will Cara's Success Spoil Frank Bridges?" Here Cara showed her vocal talents while filling in for Fletcher's regular vocalist. She sang "You Made Me Love You." Guest stars included Jerry Van Dyke as the owner of a glue factory in "Cara Fiddles While Her Hero Burns," and Paul Lynde was the head of a computer dating service in "Three on a Mismatch." After all of the first-run episodes had aired, the show moved to Friday nights for the summer rerun season. Cara returned to television, albeit briefly, in the 1970s, in *Rhoda*, as Mae.

Phil Sharp served as the show's producer; writers included Larry Tucker, Laurence Marks, Michael Morris, and Paul Mazursky; and directors included Howard Morris and Gene Reynolds. Cara's two different theme songs were from Kenyon Hopkins (one was an instrumental, and one was a vocal).

The Charlie Farrell Show Hal Roach Studios, Hollywood. CBS. Monday nights 9:00. July 2, 1956–September 24, 1956. 12 black-and-white episodes were filmed. Sponsors included Procter and Gamble, Sanka Coffee, Lilt Home Permanents, and General Foods.

Charlie Farrell had previously portrayed Vern Albright, Gale Storm's dad, on *My Little Margie*. On *The Charlie Farrell Show*, Charlie portrayed himself. The goings-on were semi-autobiographical (scripts were based upon real events). Both on the show and in real-life, Charlie owned and managed the Racquet Club on Racquet Club Drive in Palm Springs, California (which runs right into Farrell Drive, named for Charlie). It was also noted in several episodes that he was a retired film star. A couple of fictional members of his family were employed at the Racquet Club—Charles Winninger played Charlie's hard-working dad and young Jeff Silver played Charlie's nephew, Rodney, who was always attempting to get a raise. Others in the cast were Noreen Nash as Doris Mayfield, Charlie's girlfriend; Kathryn Card was housekeeper Mrs. Papernow; Richard Deacon was club director Sherman Hall; and Leon Askin was the very French head chef Pierre.

Episodes include "Secret Love," in which a young woman, who was in a doubles tennis tournament with Charlie, secretly developed a big crush on him. She then began sending anonymous love letters to Charlie, leading him to wonder from whence the letters came. In "Fashion Show," Charlie and his crew had to safeguard fashion designer Don Loper's new line of net dresses from rival designers' prying eyes, and thus they were hidden in plain view—as the new net for the tennis court. In "French Love," a visiting restaurant reviewer named Boulanger (Marcel Dallo) was wooed, wined and dined by the Racquet Club, because of the great business a good review would bring. However, his lovely daughter became the real center of attention, and a huge distraction for Chef Pierre.

The program was produced and created by Gordon Hughes; the executive producer was Hal Roach, Jr.; writers included John L. Greene, Hughes, Lee Karson, Phil Shuken, and Jack Harvey; and directors included Ralph Murphy and Rod Amateau. This show served as a summer replacement for *I Love Lucy* in 1956. For a series consisting of only 12 episodes, it had an impressive life in reruns—seen on NBC prime time during the summer of 1957, and again on CBS prime time during the summer of 1960.

The Chicago Teddy Bears Dean Jones Productions, Inc./Equinox Productions/Warner Brothers Television. CBS. Friday nights 8:00. September 17, 1971–December 17, 1971. 15 color episodes were filmed with a laugh track.

The pilot episode was titled "A Cellar Full of Frogs" (with guest stars Ann Sothern and George Raft) and it was hilarious. It's very easy to see why CBS greenlighted this period piece on its 1971 fall schedule. Unfortunately, none of the other episodes could quite live up. This was the story of a 1920s Chicago speakeasy (in the era of prohibition) called Linc and Latzi's. It even had a retractable bar which, in emergencies, would spin around to hide the adult beverages, instead revealing an old-fashioned church organ. The "Linc" in Linc and Latzi's was Linc McCray (Dean Jones). Dean had attempted TV success twice before in the sitcom *Ensign O'Toole* and in the variety series *What's It All About, World?* Sadly, *The Chicago Teddy Bears* was not the answer. The "Latzi" in Linc and Latzi's was John Banner, although he did not appear in the pilot. He was Uncle Latzi to Linc and also to gangster Big Nick Marr, (Art Metrano), Linc's cousin. Uncle Latzi seemed oblivious to Nick's activities, but Linc was quite adept at thwarting Nick's frequent attempts to push people around (mostly Marvin [Marvin Kaplan], Linc's accountant whose real ambition was to be a dentist) and take over the speakeasy. Big Nick also had three rather useless gray matter-challenged goons following him around for protection—Huntz Hall as Dutch, Jamie Farr as Lefty, and Mickey Shaughnessy as Duke. Nick would often hit all three in the jaw with one well-aimed punch.

Episodes include "The Alderman," in which the very crooked Big Nick attempted to run for alderman in his district of Chicago with a clean set of "cooked books." Linc, however, had copies of Nick's real financial statements in his safe, leading Nick to reconsider his bid for political office. In "Nick's Sister," Rosalie Marr (Sarah Fankboner) was stood up at the altar by a guy with cold feet named Herman (Elliot Street). Big brother Nick then quickly sought a replacement, and set his eyes on Marvin with an offer he simply couldn't refuse—or else. Marvin Kaplan told me about an episode called "Horse of Another Color": "I have a horse phobia. I'm terrified of horses and I had to get behind this horse to push it while John Banner pulled. Well, suddenly without warning the horse raised his tail, and my glasses fogged up—one of the hazards of working with animals came true. Meanwhile, John Banner thought the crew was laughing at what he was doing, totally unaware of what was happening behind the horse." In another incident with an animal, "We had a goat which wouldn't do anything it was supposed to do. We finally figured out that if we fed it peanut butter it would cooperate. That ploy only seemed to work in the rehearsals, however, and not while filming."

The program was produced by Jerry Thorpe, and created by R.S. Allen and Harvey Bullock. Allen and Bullock also wrote some episodes, along with Laurence Marks. Directors included Hy Averback, Leslie Martinson, and Murray Golden. The show's '20s-era retro music was courtesy of Jerry Fielding. Marvin Kaplan added, "It was a very funny show, but where it ran into its biggest challenge was using violence and attempting to make it funny. Also, showing gangsters with lollypops in their mouths instead of cigarettes was not very believable." A few episodes are available for viewing in the UCLA TV Archives.

The Cliffwood Avenue Kids Premore Productions, Inc. First-run syndication. 1976–1977. 13 episodes were broadcast.

This syndicated sitcom followed the lives of a group of pre-teens who were members of the Cliffwood Avenue Club and solved mysteries. Members included Poindexter Yothers as Poindexter; J. Brennan Smith as Samwich; Tara Taboy as Tara; Melora Hardin as Melora; Kris Maarquis as Sheldon; Andre Broudin as Andre; and Jeremy Lawrence as Jeremy. Most of the cast members and their characters shared the same first name.

Episode titles include "Gentlemen, Start Your Lawnmowers," "The Cat Burglar Caper," "The Kids Go Ape," "Spy Jinks," "The Great Trainer Robbery," and "The Search for the Lost Indian Mine."

The program was produced by Win Opie. Premore Productions was also responsible for *Jabberwocky*.

Co-Ed Fever Ransohoff Productions. CBS. Sunday night 10:30. February 4, 1979. One episode aired.

After the amazing success of the movie *National Lampoon's Animal House*, all three networks quickly pounced upon the idea of creating a show about college hijinks. ABC had *Delta House*, NBC had *Brothers and Sisters*, and CBS had *Co-Ed Fever*, which debuted in a special Sunday night preview before moving in to its regular Monday night timeslot. That special airing of the show was greeted by a huge yawn, and it was pulled from the lineup even before it could settle into its Monday night timeslot.

The program opened with a female student writing a letter home to her parents. It began, "Dear Mom and Dad, I'm fine." She then told her parents that she was giving her schoolwork (even trigonometry) the old college try, but she also told them about a guy who lived across the hall in the Brewster House Dorm at Baxter College—an Eastern women's college which had just started admitting men. She met him at the laundromat and liked him a lot. The opening credits closed with, "I'll bring him home at the end of the quarter, gotta go now, Your Loving Daughter." There was a huge jukebox at the foot of the dorm stairs.

Characters included the very romantic Tuck (David Keith); the compulsive eater Mousie (Alexa Kenin), who had designs on Tuck; the very wealthy Doug (Christopher S. Nelson); the madcap Gobo (Michael Pasternak); sexy Sandi (Heather Thomas); Elizabeth (Cathryn O'Neil); Hope (Tacey Phillips); Melba (Jillian Kesner); housemother Mrs. Selby (Jane Rose); and Mr. Peabody (Hamilton Camp).

The program was produced by Frank Shaw; the executive producer was Martin Ransohoff; the creators were Ransohoff, Michael Elias and Shaw; writers included Elias and Shaw; and the director was Marc Daniels. Music was provided by Henry Mancini; the theme song was written by Marilyn and Alan Bergman.

The Cop and the Kid Playboy Productions/ Paramount. NBC. Thursday nights 8:30 (December 4, 1975–December 18, 1975), and Thursday nights 8:00 (January 8, 1976–March 4, 1976). 13 episodes were recorded with a laugh track.

The premise for *The Cop and the Kid* was vastly more successful years later when employed on *Diff'rent Strokes*. Charles Durning portrayed Los Angeles police officer Frank Murphy. While running after a shoplifting suspect named Lucas Adams (Tierre Turner), Officer Murphy had an asthma attack. Because news of such an attack could have cost him his job, Murphy agreed to leniency in Lucas's court case in exchange for his silence about the asthma incident. Murphy was so convincing at trial that he was awarded custody of the boy—an orphaned, streetwise,

African American youth. Murphy and his mother, Brigid Murphy (Patsy Kelly), made continued efforts to reform the young man, and these efforts supplied the fodder for each episode. Mary Goodhew (Sharon Spelman) was Lucas's school principal; his best buddies were Mouse and Shortstuff (Eric Laneuville and Curtiz Willis, respectively). Lucas's dog was named "Killer," but he was anything but.

Episodes include "You'll Look Great in Basic Black," in which Murphy was involved in a sting operation. He dressed as a woman to help nab a purse snatcher. In "Not with My Teacher," Lucas encouraged Murphy to date his teacher (Arlene Golonka) for his own classroom benefit. In "Danger: Men Working," Murphy and Lucas became short order cooks to help raise money for a much needed automobile.

The program was produced by Ben Joelson and Art Baer; Jerry Davis was executive producer and creator; and directors included Alex March and Gary Nelson.

Dave and Charley NBC Daytime. January 7, 1952–March 28, 1952. Monday—Friday morning 11:30–11:45, broadcast live.

Dave was Dave Willock; he appeared as himself. He has a long list of TV credits—*Pantomime Quiz; Margie; The Beautiful Phyllis Diller Show; My Mother, the Car;* and *The Queen and I.* Charley was Cliff Arquette as Charley Weaver, complete with suspenders, ragged hat and glasses—always yearning for his "Mount Ida Mama." Charley's many TV credits include *The Dennis Day Show, The Jack Paar Show, Hobby Lobby, The Roy Rogers and Dale Evans Show* (1962), *The Hollywood Squares*, and *The Jonathan Winters Show.* Previously, the two had worked together on a local Los Angeles program in 1950 called *Willock and Arquette.* Arquette was the senior member of the duo. Together they also briefly starred in this national live daily daytime 15-minute NBC sitcom called *Dave and Charley.* Both characters did their level best each day to avoid physical labor and instead sat back and enjoyed life. This homespun show's set was Charley's living room, which was in the proximity of a railroad track. An ongoing joke was the shaking house and twirling pictures on the wall every time a train passed by. There were other characters on the show—Charley's wife, Berle; Mr. Bixby, the man who lived upstairs; Wedgewood, the newsboy; and Orlie Gibson who ran the railroad's signal tower—but they didn't actually appear on camera, but rather were spoken to on the telephone or through a window.

Episodes include one in which Charley washed the landlady's fine stemware to pay his rent, with calamitous results; in another, an attempt to trade in an old wood-burning stove went badly. In yet another episode, Charley got his hand stuck in a mailbox while trying to retrieve a kiss-off letter to Dave's girlfriend Valeria. A lot of the dialogue was ad-libbed. Three episodes are available for viewing in the UCLA TV Archives.

The director was John B. Lyman III; Willock and Weaver were the producers and writers. Willock and Weaver teamed up for yet another NBC show, this one in prime time, during the summer of 1955, titled *Do It Yourself* which featured a lot of comedy and clowning, but also quite a bit of instruction from handy Dave Willock.

Dear Phoebe Conne Stephens, Inc./American National Studios Hollywood. NBC. Friday nights 9:30. September 10, 1954–September 2, 1955. 32 episodes were filmed, some with a laugh track. Sponsors included Campbell's Soup and General Electric.

Peter Lawford, a member of the famous Rat Pack, starred in this single season sitcom prior to his success in *The Thin Man. Dear Phoebe* was the story of a college psychology professor named Bill Hastings who gave up teaching to become a writer. He got a job at the *Los Angeles Daily Blade* giving advice to the lovelorn. However, there was a catch—he answered all of the questions, and gave advice to all of those seeking it, under the alias of an elderly woman named Phoebe Goodheart. In an amusing little twist of fate, Bill (a.k.a. Phoebe) had a blossoming relationship with a coworker at the newspaper named Mickey Riley. Mickey was the name of the female sports reporter played by Marcia Henderson. Even though Bill and Mickey were sweethearts, they were also competitors for stories, and that conflict of interest fueled most of the episodes. There was another reason their romance was rocky—he was very demonstrative with his affection, but she constantly tried to keep it under wraps. Also on the staff of the newspaper were Joe Corey as Humphrey Humpsteader, the copyboy trying the make it big in the business, and the ubiquitous Charles Lane as the cranky old penny-pinching Mr. Fosdick (who really did have a kind heart under all that bluster).

Episodes include "Mickey's Engagement," in which Bill got really jealous of an erroneous rumor that Mickey was getting engaged to a wealthy socialite. In "A Face for Phoebe," Mr. Fosdick staged a publicity campaign for Phoebe Goodheart. The problem came when people wanted to see what she looked like. In "Mind Over Muscle," Bill's psychology training came in handy when picking the winner of a boxing match featuring copyboy Humphrey. That same episode featured an uncredited early appearance by Jamie Farr. In the very touching "Christmas Show," after many attempts Bill finally got to reunite a little boy with his mysterious absentee father (Jesse White), and in doing so rekindled the boy's belief in Santa Claus.

The program was created and produced by Alex Gottlieb; writers included Barbara Hammer and Gottlieb; and the director was Don Weis. Reruns of *Dear Phoebe* were shown in prime time during the summer of 1956 on NBC on Tuesday nights at 8:00.

The Debbie Reynolds Show MGM Studios/Raymax Productions/Filmways. NBC. Tuesday nights 8:00. September 16, 1969–September 1, 1970. 26 color episodes were filmed with a laugh track. Sponsors included The American Tobacco Company.

She was being touted as the next Lucy and signed a two-year deal. However, during the airing of the very first episode of *The Debbie Reynolds Show*, titled "That's Debbie" (also the original working title for the series), the star of the show was in quite a huff. Maybe it was more of a huff and a puff because Debbie was outraged that the first commercial in her new series was for Pall Mall Cigarettes. The network had promised her there would be no cigarette advertising in the show, but they broke that promise in the very first commercial break. Debbie was angry because she had been forced to learn to smoke for movie roles in *The Rat Race* and *Mary, Mary*. It then took her years to quit the habit, so she wanted to protect others from becoming addicted as well. Since Debbie had a two-year contract and owned fifty percent of the show, she couldn't be fired, so she quit—a decision which cost her millions. In retrospect, Debbie regrets the decision.

There was a lot of slapstick on the show, and not unlike Lucy Ricardo's attempts to get into her husband's nightclub act, Debbie Thompson wanted to become a feature writer for the *Los Angeles Sun*, like her husband Jim (Don Chastain). The Thompsons lived at 804 Devon Lane in Los Angeles. Also in the cast (resembling Fred and Ethel Mertz) were Debbie's sister Charlotte Landers played by Patricia Smith (most folks called her "Char") and Debbie's brother-in-law Bob Landers (Tom Bosley). The Thompsons were childless, but the Landers had an eleven-year-old son named Bruce (Bobby Riha) who frequently visited his Aunt Debbie. A lot of the plots were very *Lucy*-esque. In the debut, Debbie dressed up as a man to caddy for the governor to try to get a scoop for the newspaper; in "It's a Bird, It's a Plane, It's Debbie," our star took flying lessons with nearly disastrous results; and in "You Bet Your Wife," Debbie's husband Jim was a terrible game player, so she and brother-in-law Bob pretended to be married to get on a game show to win cash and prizes.

The program was created and produced by Jess Oppenheimer; directors included Ezra Stone and Jay Sandrich; writers included Gene Thompson, Stanley Ralph Ross, Oppenheimer, Phil Leslie, Peggy Chantler Dick, Ann Marcus, Joseph Bonaduce, Barbara Avedon, Lionel Burt, Jim McGinn, and Pat McCormick. Debbie stepped out of character at the end of each episode to address the audience. The show's theme song, "With a Little Love," was sung by Reynolds. However, near the end of the show's run, the theme song was abruptly changed to an instrumental. Music was provided by Jack Marshall. The program was briefly rerun on Galaxy, a British satellite channel.

Delta House Universal Studios. ABC. Thursday nights 8:30 (January 18, 1979), Saturday nights 8:00 (January 27, 1979–March 1979), and Saturday nights 8:30 (March 1979–April 28, 1979). Nine color episodes were filmed with a laugh track.

National Lampoon's Animal House was such a huge and surprise success story, all three networks instantly began scrambling to assemble a TV ensemble—and all three failed. CBS had *Co-Ed Fever*, NBC had *Brothers and Sisters*, and ABC had the best known of the three with *Delta House*. The latter was most like the original in that the executive producers again were Marty Simmons and Ivan Reitman, and four members of the movie's cast came over to do this TV adaptation (as *Delta House* instead of *Animal House*). John Vernon was back as Dean Vernon Wormer, who was constantly conspiring with the Omega

House to rid Pennsylvania's Faber College of those party animals known as the Deltas; Stephen Furst was back as the sad sack Kent "Flounder" Dorfman, bedecked in his multicolor beany; Bruce McGill reprised his role as the mustachioed motorcycle maniac Daniel Simpson Day (nicknamed "D-Day"); and James Widdoes returned as Delta President/prankster Robert Hoover. However, one key ingredient was missing—John Belushi was unavailable to reprise his role as Bluto, so Josh Mostel (Zero's son) joined the cast as Bluto's younger brother, Jim "Blotto" Blutarsky (who ate peanuts, shell and all), but realized he could never live up to his brother's infamy. Peter Fox portrayed womanizer Eric "Otter" Stratton. Other cast members of note included Peter Kastner (*The Ugliest Girl in Town*) as Professor Jennings. And maybe "the prettiest girl in town," a young and yet-unknown Michelle Pfeiffer, portrayed "The Bombshell."

Unfortunately, the TV version was broadcast in "the family hour," and so stringent rules were placed upon the program from the censors. One of the show's producers and writers, David Pollock, told me, "The show suffered greatly because so much of what made the movie a box office smash was not allowed in the series because of its time slot. We began throwing in multiple items we knew the sensors wouldn't allow, so that we could get some compromises on the things we really wanted to include. We'd say, okay, we'll remove that part if you let us keep this part." Episodes include "The Fall of Dean Wormer," in which the Deltas and Mrs. Wormer caught the dean in a compromising position with a co-ed named Gloria (Elaine Joyce). In "The Blotto Who Came to Dinner," Dean Wormer was hit with a lawsuit after injuring Blotto with his car. Blotto and the Deltas then moved in to the Dean's home until Blotto was well enough to leave. In "The Draft," Dean Wormer used his connections to get D-Day drafted. Much to the Dean's dismay, D-Day failed the physical because of a foot deformity.

The show was produced by Elias Davis and David Pollock; writers included Marty Simmons, Tod Carroll, Davis, Pollock, and Michael Stotter; and directors included Hollingsworth Morse and Joshua White. The show's time slot changed often, and the Deltas never graduated to a second season. *Delta House* was briefly shown in reruns on WWOR-TV.

The Dennis O'Keefe Show A Cypress Production/United Artists Television. CBS. Tuesday nights 8:00. September 22, 1959–June 7, 1960. 32 black-and-white episodes were filmed with a laugh track. Sponsors included Oldsmobile.

Dennis O'Keefe had been in dozens of movies dating back to the 1930s (*Topper Returns*, *The Lady Wants Mink*, *Woman on the Run*), but now in his fifties, with movie roles on the wane, he sought fame in the new medium of television. From that decision came *The Dennis O'Keefe Show*, which had a subtitle—*All Around Towne* (also the name of the fictional nationally syndicated column by Dennis's character, 42-year-old Henry "Hal" Towne). The column originated in a fictional newspaper called *The News Chronicle*. Hal had been raised on a Fort Andrews, Iowa, farm, but now resided in the Park View Apartments (apartment 12-A) in Manhattan (the address on the awning outside the apartment complex was 22). His alarm clock was set for 7:00 every weekday morning, but that didn't mean he got up at that time. (Hal had somewhat of a reputation for being tardy.) He also had a ten-year-old attention-starved son named Randy (Rickey Kelman) and a housekeeper who was referred to as a "pinch-hitting mother"—Miss Amelia Sargent (Hope Emerson), nicknamed "Sarge," who had performed as a child in community theater in Omaha. In his line of work, Hal Towne was frequently surrounded and wooed by some very attractive women, but his steady girl (also his publishing agent) was Karen Hadley (Eloise Hardt). At *The News Chronicle*, Hal's somewhat harried, impatient, bespectacled editor and "guy Friday" was named Elliot (Eddie Ryder).

Episodes include "Shake Hands with Hal," in which we discovered that Hal Towne had never signed a contract for anything (every deal he ever made was completed with a handshake). This revelation got him in Dutch with his new landlord, Mr. Howell (Howard McNear), who wanted to evict Hal, Randy and Sarge (who had no lease) so that his own recently married daughter (Connie Hines) and her new husband could move in. In "Go Home, Aunt Millie," Hal's Aunt Millie (Lee Patrick) came for a visit from England, and quickly disrupted the Townes' routine, and was responsible for getting young Randy into a fight at his school. In "Quints," Hal was torn between getting a byline for the biggest story of the year (a visiting United Nations delegate's wife gave birth to five baby boys in his apartment) and keeping a promise to the delegate (Mr. Marino, played by Franco Corsaro) not to tell a soul. Actor Marvin Kaplan guest starred in an unnamed episode, recalling, "It was on film and was shot in three days. Dennis O'Keefe was one of the underappreciated leading men, who had a great light touch. He was very pleasant and a lot of fun." Speaking of series co-star Hope Emerson, Kaplan remembered, "I had the pleasure of working with her again. I had first met her on the set of the movie version of *Adam's Rib*. She was a fun-loving woman and she was glad to be part of the series."

The program was created by John Fenton Murray; the producer was Les Hafner; writers included Murray, Benedict Freedman, Jack Michael, Joel Kane, Robert Gottlieb, Alan Lipscott, Bob Fisher, Seaman Jacobs, and Si Rose; and directors included James V. Kern, Jerry Hopper, Abby Berlin, and Don Weis. The program had a brief run in syndication in the early nineties on the now-defunct Nostalgia cable channel. A DVD set of four original episodes of *The Dennis O'Keefe Show* is available very inexpensively from Alpha Video.

Diana Talent Associates/Norton Simon Productions. NBC. Monday nights 8:30. September 10, 1973–January 7, 1974. 15 color episodes were filmed at CBS Studio Center before a live audience.

***Diana*—Diana Rigg as fashion designer Diana Smythe (NBC).**

After a successful run as Emma Peel on *The Avengers*, NBC had high hopes for this Diana Rigg sitcom. The title of the show in the unaired pilot was *The Diana Rigg Show*, but that was shortened to simply *Diana* for the series. Here she was Diana Smythe, an English divorcee in her mid-thirties who had moved to the United States with aspirations of making it big in New York's fashion district. She moved into her brother Roger's apartment (11 B) while he was out of the country on business. Roger, however, had given keys to the apartment to dozens of his friends, and they seemed to barge in at the most inopportune moments, leading to many funny, embarrassing and confrontational situations. Among those with keys were Diana's neighbor, Holly Green (Carol Androsky), a hand and foot model for TV commercials (she always seemed to fall in love with married men), and Jeff Harmon (Richard Mulligan), a mystery novelist. Diana got a job at Butley's Department Store as fashion coordinator (it was called Sue Ellen Frocks in the pilot). Her boss at the store was the serious, hard-working head of merchandising, Norman Brodnik (David Sheiner); his wife, Norma worked at the store, too (she was played by Nanette Fabray in the pilot, and Barbara Barrie in the series). Richard B. Shull played Howard Tolbrook, the copywriter who hated exercise and had a gambling problem, and Robert Moore (who also directed a few episodes) played flamboyant window dresser Marshall Tyler (a close friend of Tolbrook and his wife).

One of the most memorable episodes was titled "You Can't Go Back," in which Diana was reunited with her *Avengers* co-star Patrick Macnee as Bryan, who attempted to win her back with his wit and charm, but lost her again because of his self-centered ways. In "Long Shots and Fat Chances," Howard asked Diana to hold on to fifty dollars for him. The money was for a birthday gift for his wife and Howard was afraid he would just gamble it away. The plan backfired when the horse on which he planned to bet won and would have garnered him four hundred dollars. In "Kung Who," Dick Gautier guest starred as Benton Fowler, a karate instructor whom Diana accidentally knocked out in her apartment. Legendary sitcom director Ezra Stone (radio's Henry Aldrich) had a cameo in this episode as the doctor who revived Fowler. Dick Gautier remembered, "There's one scene where Diana flips me onto the floor. We did several takes so that I landed in the ideal spot for the director, Gene

Nelson. Well, we did one take too many—on that sixth flip, I broke a toe."

The program was created and produced by Leonard Stern; writers included Sam Bobrick, Ron Clark, Leonard Stern, Gordon Farr, Arnold Kane, Jerry Mayer, Sir Harry Swanson, Charlotte Brown, Stan Cutler, and Stanley Charles; and directors included Stern, Jay Sandrich, Robert Moore, and Gene Nelson. Music was provided by Jerry Fielding. Cecil Smith of *The Washington Post* wrote, "*Diana* is as cool, as sophisticated, and as elegant as its star. I admit prejudice—Diana Rigg is, to me, as good a reason as any to be alive in this haphazard century." Dick Gautier agrees, and told me, "She was marvelous, a delight, and so very gracious." A few episodes are available for viewing in the UCLA TV Archives.

Dick and the Duchess Sheldon Reynolds Productions/MGM British Studios and Elstree Studios, London. CBS. Saturday nights 8:30 (September 28, 1957–March 1958), and Friday nights 7:30 (March 1958–May 16, 1958). 26 black-and-white episodes were filmed with a laugh track. Sponsored by Mogen David and Key Wines (some commercials starring Hans Conried), and Helene Curtis.

Produced by Sheldon Reynolds, who had also produced the syndicated *Sherlock Holmes* TV series, *Dick and the Duchess* was the story of an American named Dick Starrett (Patrick O'Neal) who, while living in London, happened to meet a duchess named Jane (Hazel Court). They fell in love and were married, much to her elitist family's chagrin. They hated seeing her with a mere commoner, and Dick was indeed of common stock—he was an insurance claims investigator and adjuster. His duchess, Jane, somehow always managed to get involved in her husband's work, and would invariably wreak havoc upon his investigations, to the dismay of Dick's British boss Peter Jamison (Richard Wattis). Others in the cast included Beatrice Varley as Mathilda, the housekeeper; Michael Shepley as Inspector Stark of Scotland Yard; and Ronnie Stevens as Rodney, Dick's co-worker.

Several episodes are available for viewing at the Paley Center for Media's New York branch. Among those is "The Swedish Story," in which the duchess attempted to make Dick think he was unwell so that they might take a long overdue vacation. What they got was a working vacation, as Peter Jamison sent the Starretts to Naples to investigate a jewelry heist. That visit was short-lived, as it was then discovered that the perpetrators had hightailed it to Sweden. Dick and the Duchess followed them to the town of Salts Jobden, but to avoid suspicion, Jane posed as Dick's sister—a choice which led to even more problems as an endless parade of Swedish men flirted with "single Jane." In "An American," when Dick missed an important meeting with a man who had information about a looting racket, Peter Jamison stepped in, posing as Dick Starrett, an American (and failed miserably).

The executive producer was Nicole Milinair; writers included Harvey Bullock, Ray Allen, Sheldon Reynolds, Dennis Freeman, and Robert Shannon; and directors included Reynolds, Gerard Bryant, Henry Kaplan, Allan Davis, and McLean Rogers.

Doc Corkle Key Productions. NBC. Sunday nights 7:30. October 5, 1952–October 19, 1952. Three episodes were filmed at Eagle Lion Studios, Hollywood. Sponsored by Reynolds Aluminum.

This program was originally scheduled to be called *The Eddie Mayehoff Show*, but that was changed at the last minute. The program aired right before *The Colgate Comedy Hour* on Sunday nights, and the sponsor, Reynolds Aluminum, was so disappointed with this show that they abruptly pulled out and the show was instantly cancelled. Its quick demise couldn't be blamed on a lack of stars in its cast: Eddie Mayehoff (formerly of one of TV's earliest variety shows, *Hour Glass*) played friendly neighborhood dentist "Doc" Ambrose Corkle; Doc's dad, "Pop" Corkle, was played by Chester Conklin (one of the original Keystone Kops); Doc's zany, trouble-inciting stepsister Melinda was played by Billie Burke; Doc's sister Nellie was played by Hope Emerson; Nellie's son Winfield Dill (a.k.a. "Dilly") was portrayed by Arnold Stang; and Doc's daughter Laurie was played by Connie Marshall. Even though Doc had a relatively successful dental practice, he was always flat broke. Sister Nellie, however, had a bright future—she was a wealthy widow.

In the debut episode, Doc's daughter Laurie needed fifty dollars for a senior prom gown at the very same time the doctor needed the money for a new dental chair. In the second episode, Doc lost a tooth and reluctantly had to visit the town's newest dentist. In the third and final episode, Laurie was in need of $150 for college. Doc was able to raise that amount, but lost the money after falling victim to one of his dad's hairbrained inventions.

The program was produced by Lou Place; the directors were Richard Bare and Place; and writers included Robert Fisher, Alan Lipscott, and Devery Freeman. *Doc Corkle*'s timeslot was hurriedly filled by another Reynolds Aluminum show, *Mr. Peepers*, which had just completed a successful summer run on NBC and quickly went back into production. *Doc Corkle* initially had a 39-week contractual commitment. Upon its quick cancellation, Mayehoff negotiated a settlement of $50,000; Stang was awarded $10,000. Damages for others in the cast were not known, but all had been promised 39 weeks. Two episodes exist in the Library of Congress.

The Don Rickles Show A Warmth Production/Paramount Studios. CBS. Friday nights 10:30. January 14, 1972–May 26, 1972. 13 color episodes were filmed before a live audience.

This single season sitcom had a terrible time slot—after the Friday night movie on CBS at 10:30. Not to be confused with his earlier eponymous variety show (produced by Goodson and Todman), this *Don Rickles Show* featured the insult-spewing comedian as Don Florenz Robinson, a New York ad agency executive for Kingston, Cohen and VanDerPool, Inc. Yes, his middle name was Florenz (as revealed in the episode titled "Greetings from Uncle Sam"), and it was often mistaken as "Florence," and many jokes and laughs were mined from that. Don had a pretty wife named Barbara (Louise Sorel) and a pre-teen daughter named Janie (Erin Moran). At the office (the building's address was 600, but the street was never mentioned), Don had a friend in co-worker Tyler Benedict (Robert Hogan). Tyler's wife, Jean (Joyce Van Patten) was friends with Don's wife, Barbara. Also in the cast were former child actor Barry Gordon (famous for *Nuttin' For Christmas*) as aggressive and persnickety ad agency executive Conrad Musk. Judy Cassmore was Audrey, Don's assistant (who got promoted to the legal department in the final episode titled "Audrey, Come Home"). Don's family situations were compounded by his continual frustrations with all things technical.

CBS promoted this show heavily, but to no avail. Used in the promo was a scene from the episode titled "The Mercy of the Court," in which Don had a disagreement with his TV repairman whom he told to remove all of the tubes so that he could turn the broken TV set into a guest room. In "Greetings from Uncle Sam," Don mistakenly got a draft notice, and because of government red tape still had to report for his physical (much to the amusement of the army doctor played by comedian Milt Kamen). In "The Moo Cow Child," Don's daughter Janie was selected to be the star of a milk commercial filmed in the Robinson's own kitchen by the obnoxious Conrad Musk. In "Where There's a Will," Don's real-life buddy Bob Newhart played an attorney (and golf partner) named Jerry, who encouraged Don to create a will and designate a legal guardian for their daughter, Janie. This subject led to a spat between Don and Barbara over whose mother would be a more apt choice—her mother Eleanor or his mother Etta.

The program was produced by Sam Denoff and Hy Averback; the executive producer was Sheldon Leonard; directors included Leonard and Averback; and writers included Sam Denoff, Susan Silver, Rick Mittleman, Elias Davis and David Pollock. Writer Pollock, who co-wrote the episode "Split Ticket" (along with Davis), told me, "There was a tram which transported the studio audience to the soundstage. On that tram, the people were treated to a pre-recorded batch of insults from Don Rickles, himself. It was a ploy used as a pre-warm-up for the folks, and they loved it. It was very popular and very well-received." *The Don Rickles Show* was also unique in that it showed the studio audience in the closing credits. A few episodes can be viewed at the Paley Center for Media. Don would again attempt sitcom success in the ill-fated *CPO Sharkey* and *Daddy Dearest.*

Don't Call Me Charlie The McGuire Company/General Services Studio. NBC. Friday nights at 9:30. September 21, 1962–January 25, 1963. 26 black-and-white episodes were produced, but only 18 aired. Sponsors included Lipton Soup, Bayer Aspirin, Scott Paper Company, and Brown and Williamson Tobacco.

This short-lived sitcom was supposed to be titled *Vive Judson McKay*, and requires considerable explanation—especially the odd and confusing title eventually chosen. *Don't Call Me Charlie* was a phrase uttered often by gin rummy-loving Colonel Charles Barker (John Hubbard) to garner some respect, but those surrounding him still called him Charlie. However, I'm getting ahead of myself. Charlie was not the star of the show—that was newbie veterinarian Judson McKay (Josh Peine), who had just joined old Dr.

Martin's veterinary practice. Dr. Martin had been looking for someone to take over as he neared retirement age. However, that retirement was put on hold when McKay was drafted and had to immediately report to Paris. The differences between McKay's hometown of Muscatine, Iowa, and Paris, France, were staggering, and provided many of the show's laughs. McKay was a rather shy, hard-working, small town guy. In fact, anyone else visiting Paris might instantly wish to take in its nightlife. Not McKay. First and second on his itinerary were visiting Louis Pasteur's workplace and seeing Normandy Beach (where his older brother was buried).

His first meeting with Charlie (Colonel Charles Barker) at the Seine Army Command in Paris was short-lived. McKay explained in great detail that he was with the "Veterinarian's Corps, which concerns itself with the care and health of animals of the military establishment, and with the inspection and certification of all food supplies of animal origin for the troops." Charlie then came to the realization that there had been a clerical error—he wanted a bandmaster who played trombone—not a veterinarian. Charlie had a lot of free time as this post didn't see very much action. In fact, the colonel jokingly admitted that his "only combat experience came in his first marriage." It was to take about three weeks to return McKay stateside, so he set up temporary residence in an apartment which just happened to be next to a lovely woman (who was originally from Boston) named Pat Parry (Linda Lawson). McKay later found out that she was Charlie's girlfriend, but she had begun falling for McKay. This revelation led Charlie to expedite McKay's return to the United States. However, when McKay came to the aid of a sick parakeet belonging to a young relative of Charles DeGaulle, Charlie had a change of heart and asked McKay to stay on in Paris. Arte Johnson appeared on occasion as Corporal Lefkowitz, and was featured in the episode titled "Who Stole My Boots?" Alan Napier appeared frequently as General Steele.

The program was created, frequently written, and produced by Don McGuire. McGuire even did a guest shot as General Nuxhall in the episode titled "Play It, Sam." Directors included Joseph Depew. The animals used on the show (and there were many) were trained by Frank Inn. Music was supplied by Jack Marshall. The show's theme song was a jazzed-up version of the children's classic, "Where, Oh Where Has My Little Dog Gone."

Dorothy The Konigsberg Company/Davis-Carroll Productions, Inc/Warner Brothers. CBS. Wednesday nights 8:00. August 8, 1979–August 29, 1979. Four color episodes were videotaped before a live audience.

In the late seventies, Dorothy Loudon's career had a resurgence because of the Broadway musical *Annie*. Loudon won a Tony Award for her role as Miss Hannigan and then got a shot at a sitcom on CBS. Much like her first sitcom, *It's A Business?* on the old DuMont Network decades earlier, this new show, *Dorothy*, featured comedy and some music. This was Loudon's bailiwick—musical comedy. In *Dorothy*, Loudon portrayed Dorothy Banks, a former showgirl, whose husband had run off and left her years before. She was a live-in teacher at the exclusive Hannah Huntley School for Girls, somewhere in the eastern portion of the United States, and her subjects were music and drama (which allowed for at least one musical number in each show). She was a good teacher, but the very stern administration didn't always appreciate her unorthodox methods. Others on the faculty included the young bespectacled biology teacher, T. Jack Landis (Kenneth Gilman); dizzy and emotional French teacher Lorna Cathcart (Priscilla Morrill), who unnecessarily added a French phrase to almost every sentence of dialogue; the very prissy and demanding headmaster/grandson of the school's founder Burton Foley (Russell Nype); and his mom Mrs. Foley (Irene Tedrow). Among student body members was the hardscrabble, underachieving super tomboy Frankie Sumpter (Linda Manz), who was never expelled because of the large endowment contributed yearly by her family; the bookworm Meredith (Susan Brecht), who had a crush on Mr. Landis; the pretty and popular blonde Cissy (Elissa Leeds), and the brunette Margo (Michele Greene).

Episodes include one in which a rumor about the upcoming firing of one of the teachers put the entire faculty on edge—that is, until they found out the intended victim was Headmaster Foley. Upon hearing that news, fierce competition for Foley's old position arose. In another untitled episode, Frankie's mischief on a field trip led to the cancellation of all future field trips. The angry response from the other female students led to Frankie's attempt to run away. Getting her to change her mind was job one for Dorothy.

The program's creators and executive producers were Bob Carroll, Jr., Madelyn Davis, and

Frank Konisgberg; writers included Rick Hawkins, Liz Sage, Vic Rauseo, and Linda Morris. The lone director was John Rich. The theme song was provided by Billy Goldenberg and Bill Dyer.

The Double Life of Henry Phyfe Luther Davis Productions/Filmways. ABC. Thursday nights 8:30. January 13, 1966–September 1, 1966. 17 color episodes were filmed with a laugh track. Sponsors included Chiffon Margarine, Score Hair Tonic, Fact Toothpaste, Clairol Hair Products, Quaker Oats, and Bristol Myers.

This midseason entry replaced *O.K. Crackerby*, but didn't meet with much more success than its predecessor. In between *The Red Buttons Show* and *The Dean Martin Celebrity Roasts*, Academy Award-winner Red Buttons starred in this sitcom called *The Double Life of Henry Phyfe*, which attempted to mirror the success of *Get Smart*. Timid, mousey Henry Phyfe had the misfortune of being the exact double of U-31, a spy for the C.I.S. (a United States counterintelligence agency), who had been killed in a hit-and-run accident. If Phyfe could be convincing enough, all of U-31's unfinished business could be completed. There were complications, however. U-31 was fearless, a real ladies man, multi-lingual, a marksman, very athletic, and a black belt in karate. Phyfe was none of the above. Phyfe already had a job as an accountant, and Parley Baer played his boss, Mr. Hamble. Hamble had no idea of Phyfe's "double life," and neither did Phyfe's girlfriend (Judy, played by Zeme North), or his future mother-in-law (Florence, played by Marge Redmond). Judy and Florence were deemed superfluous after only a few episodes, and simply vanished from all future scripts without explanation. Phyfe's boss at C.I.S. was Gerald B. Hannahan (Fred Clark). Hannahan knew that Phyfe was extremely patriotic, and it was that patriotism which allowed him to cajole Phyfe into taking on each and every dangerous mission.

Missions included "Whatever Happened to Yesterday?" in which Phyfe had to take a crash course in the Japanese language, culture, and karate to obtain an important piece of microfilm. In "Phyfe Goes Skiing," Phyfe had to become an expert skier like U-31 in order to find out about a defecting foreign agent. In "Phyfe on a Ferry," Phyfe had to push an old woman off of a ferry boat to gain the trust of a spy nicknamed "the liquidator." A male contact who was supposed to be dressed as an old woman missed the ferry (which left the dock early) and Phyfe pushed a real elderly woman into the sea.

The program was created and produced by Luther Davis (although Nat Perrin produced the pilot); writers included Ben Starr, Leo Rifkin, Rich Eustis, Al Rogers, Charles Marion, Monroe Manning, Sloan Nibley, Bill Lutz, Harry Winkler, Hannibal Coons, and Ronald Axe; and directors included Leslie Martinson, Howard Morris, and Charles Rondeau. The theme song and its clever lyrics were written by the brilliant Vic Mizzy. Many episodes are available for viewing in the UCLA TV Archives.

Duffy's Tavern MPTV (Motion Pictures for TV)/Hal Roach Studios. First-run syndication. 1954–1955. 39 black-and-white episodes were filmed with a laugh track. Sponsors included the Arizona Brewing Company, Arnold Bakeries, and Roma Wines.

Duffy's Tavern was a seedy little bar and grill on Third Avenue in New York City. This place was no *Cheers*. The show opened every week with Archie (Ed Gardner) on the telephone saying, "Duffy's Tavern where the elite meet to eat, Archie the manager speaking, Duffy ain't here." In fact, Duffy was never there. Archie would speak with him on the phone on occasion, but we never did get to see him on screen. However, we did get to see his husband-hungry daughter Miss Duffy (she was always called Miss Duffy; we never found out her first name), played by Pattee Chapman. In the original radio version of the show, Shirley Booth portrayed Miss Duffy. Archie always had get-rich-quick schemes up his sleeve, but none of them ever seemed to pan out. Some of the funniest lines in this show revolved around Archie's butchering of the English language—weddings were "maritime relations," clothing purchased for a wedding was a "torso," the plural of spouse was "spices," a wealthy person was a "money maggot," when a lady was treated with respect that was called "chiselry," and after dinner one had to go for a walk to let one's "drastic juices" do their job. Also in the cast was Alan Reed as the dim-witted Charlie Finnegan. There was another Charley in the cast—Charley the cook (Jimmy Conlin), who always sported a bow tie. Archie had an on-again, off-again romance with gold-digger Peaches La Tour (Veda Ann Borg) who performed striptease down at the Bijou Burlesque.

Episodes include the debut titled "Grand Opening," in which a local illegal gambling joint had taken away all of Archie's potential customers, and he devised a plan to get them to come back to *Duffy's Tavern*. In "Archie Gets Engaged," Archie was jilted by Peaches, and to make her jealous, he proposed to the wealthy but unattractive Mrs. Van Clyde (Barbara Morrison) who had been trying to get Archie's attention and affection for many years. In "A Date for Miss Duffy," Archie fixed Miss Duffy up with a wealthy old friend nicknamed Egghead Anderson (Larry Dobkin), whom he hadn't seen in years. However, Egghead turned out to be a wanted con-man who thought Miss Duffy had money.

The program was produced by Hal Roach, Jr.; writers included Larry Rhine, Ben Starr, and Kenneth T. Earl; and directors included Harve Foster and Howard Bretherton. *Duffy's Tavern* had a 10-year-run on radio, but didn't translate as well to TV where it became a single season sitcom, although the original deal with Hal Roach called for three seasons and 117 episodes. A few episodes are available for viewing in the UCLA TV Archives.

The Duke NBC. Friday nights 8:00. July 2, 1954–September 3, 1954. 13 episodes were broadcast live, originating in Hollywood (from the El Capitan Theater). Sponsors included Toni Hair Products.

As a summer replacement for *The Dave Garroway Show*, *The Duke* had an interesting premise—a prizefighter who opted to go "classy," and leave the ring for more highbrow and intellectual pursuits. The Duke was Duke London (Paul Gilbert, whose birth name was Ed McMahon), a retired boxer who, thanks to a friend named Rudy Cromwell (Claude Stroud) who graduated from Harvard, now enjoyed more elitist diversions, such as reading, the opera, and fine art. The Duke was becoming quite an accomplished painter, and also (with Rudy as his business partner) decided to open a "classy" nightclub to be called "The Duke's." Meanwhile, this new version of Duke London was very upsetting to his former promoter, Sam Marco (Sheldon Leonard), and his former trainer, Johnny (Allen Jenkins), both of whom were gearing up for a Duke London comeback. They did eventually lure Duke back into the ring—but only to paint other fighters. The Duke also had a girlfriend named Gloria, who was played by Phyllis Coates.

Several episodes of this show are available for viewing at the UCLA TV Archives. Among those is the debut in which Duke and Rudy opened the nightclub. Once the Duke's nightclub was open, we really got to experience the many varied talents of actor Paul Gilbert. In this episode, he sang "I Can't Give You Anything But Love" and "Figaro," performed a dance routine, juggled, and played every instrument in the band (drums, piano, bass, and trumpet). In real life, Paul Gilbert came from a Vaudevillian family of performers, and began his career as an aerialist, but after a fall turned to music, comedy and dancing. In another episode, in an attempt to render his new nightclub classier still, Duke wanted to bring in a Shakespearean performance, but the show instead became a fundraiser for underprivileged children from the Third Avenue Settlement House—*A Midsummer Night's Dream* performed completely by child actors. Among those child actors was a very young Steven Wootton, later of *This Is Alice*.

The program was produced by Bill Harmon; writers included Charles Isaacs and Jack Elinson; and directors included Dick McDonough and Sid Smith. Music was provided by Lou Bring. Paul Gilbert later went on to co-star in the hit Jane Fonda film *Cat Ballou*.

The Dumplings NRW Productions/T. A. T. Communications. NBC. Wednesday nights 9:30.

***The Dumplings*—James Coco and Geraldine Brooks (NBC).**

January 28, 1976–March 24, 1976. Eleven episodes were recorded before a live audience, but only ten aired.

After having created numerous immensely popular shows such as *All in the Family*, *Maude*, *Good Times*, *Sanford and Son*, *One Day at a Time*, *Mary Hartman, Mary Hartman* and *The Jeffersons*, Norman Lear came up with this very friendly but short-lived show. Marcia Rodd, who co-starred on the show told me, "It was a nice change of pace. Everyone was yelling at one another and fighting on TV in the 1970's. This show, however, was about two chubby people who loved each other very much and got along extremely well." The title characters, Joe and Angela Dumpling (James Coco and Geraldine Brooks, respectively), even worked well together at a luncheonette on the ground floor of a New York skyscraper which housed the offices of the huge Bristol Oil Company. Their regular customers were conniving City Councilman Frederick Steele (George Furth); Bristol Oil Company bigwig Charles Sweetzer (George S. Irving); and Mr. Sweetzer's secretary, Bridget McKenna (Jane Connell). *The Dumplings* also had a helper in the luncheonette named Cully (Mort Marshall). Tony Award nominee Rodd (she was nominated for her role in *Shelter*) told me, "I portrayed Angela Dumpling's very 'hyper' sister, Stephanie." Marcia also said, "The show's creators loved my laugh very much and they tried to incorporate it into every episode."

In the pilot episode, the Dumplings were in a quandary—they had the opportunity to cater a big function and maybe even get to market their mushroom and barley soup and make lots of money. The function, however, coincided with their anniversary, and love won out. This episode can be viewed in the UCLA TV Archives.

Notable *Dumplings* directors include Hal Cooper (whom Marcia Rodd calls "the best of the best") and Dennis Steinmetz; producers included Bernie West, Michael Ross, and Don Nicholl. The theme song was written by Alan and Marilyn Bergman, and music was provided by Billy Goldenberg.

Dusty's Trail Redwood and Writer First Productions/Metromedia Producer's Corporation. First-run syndication. 1973–1974. 26 color episodes were filmed with a laugh track.

One might call this show "Go West, Young Gilligan" or even "Gilligan's Wagon." Set in the 1880s, *Dusty's Trail* (like *Gilligan's Island*) was also created by Sherwood Schwartz, and every single character was, unabashedly, the mirror image of the entire cast of the earlier show. For all intents and purposes, the bumbling scout named Dusty (Bob Denver) was Gilligan; the wagon master Mr. Callahan (Forrest Tucker) was the Skipper; stuffy Carter Brookhaven (Ivor Francis) was Thurston Howell III; pompous Daphne Brookhaven (Lynn Wood) was Lovie Howell; showgirl Lulu McQueen (Jeannine Riley) was Ginger Grant; school teacher Betsy (Lori Saunders) was Maryann (Lori and Jeannine were both *Petticoat Junction* alumni); and Andy (Bill Cort) was bright like the professor. Instead of "little buddy," Mr. Callahan called Dusty "little pal." Callahan's horse was named Blarney, and Dusty's horse was named Freckles. The program focused upon this group of seven misfits whose Conestoga wagon had been separated from the rest of the train on the way to California. As they fended for themselves, they were constantly attempting to avoid bears, Indians, and outlaws along their way.

Some of the 26 episodes of *Dusty's Trail* had very clever titles. There was "The Phony Express" in which a wounded soldier sought the assistance of Dusty to deliver a pouch to Fort Hale (without it winding up in the hands of outlaws). In "Here Come the Grooms," Dusty and Callahan were held captive by hillbillies and forced to wed their ugly sisters. In "The Wizard of Ooze," Dusty's amnesia kept him from warning the others about an active volcano beneath their wagons. In "The Treasure of C. Henry Matres," Dusty found a treasure map, and discovered just how greedy the other six passengers were.

The program was produced by Elroy Schwartz; the executive producer was Sherwood Schwartz; writers included Al Schwartz, Larry Rhine, David Harmon, Brad Radnitz, and Bruce Howard; and directors included Jack Arnold, Leslie Martinson, Bruce Bilson, and Oscar Rudolph. The theme song was written by Sherwood and Ross Schwartz, and performed by Mel Street. Four episodes of *Dusty's Trail* ("Tomahawk Territory," "Horse of Another Color," "There Is Nothing Like a Dame," and "The Not-So-Magnificent Seven") were edited to make a full-length feature in August of 1976 called *The Wackiest Wagon Train in the West*. Seventeen of the original 26 episodes are available in a DVD box set from Brentwood Home Video.

Easy Aces Ziv Television Productions/DuMont Network. Wednesday nights 7:45. December 14, 1949–June 14, 1950. Sponsors included the Phillips Soup Company and Hudson Automobiles. An unknown number of episodes were filmed.

Goodman Ace and Jane Sherwood Ace had a long and successful history in radio—his character was witty and her character was batty. Jane was malapropism prone, uttering classic lines such as, "Time wounds all heels," "I'm his awful wedded wife," and "You could've knocked me over with a fender." After each of those, Goodman (Mr. Ace, as he was called on the show) would inquire, "Isn't that awful?" Jane frequently uttered a very nasal-sounding, "All right," in answer to Goodman's questions. The Aces also did many commercials together for companies such as Lincoln Mercury. Jane had a friend named Dorothy on this TV version, played by Bette Garde. It's interesting to note that a lot of the show's dialogue was ad-libbed. After the demise of *Easy Aces*, for all intents and purposes, Jane went into retirement, but Goodman had success writing for Milton Berle, Danny Kaye, and Perry Como. He was also the writer and producer of a nightly five-minute program called *Ruthie on the Telephone* on CBS in 1949. Years later, Goodman became involved with a Canadian sitcom shown in America called *The Trouble with Tracy* (many episodes were old *Easy Aces* plots revamped).

The program was produced by Herbert Gordon; the director was Jeanne Harrison; and writers included Goodman Ace, George Foster, J. Raymond, and Mort Green. To my knowledge, no episodes exist.

The Ed Wynn Show Thalia-Keethwyn Productions/Screen Gems. NBC. Thursday nights 8:00. September 25, 1958–January 1, 1959. 16 episodes were filmed with a laugh track, only 15 aired. Sponsors included Bulova and L and M Cigarettes.

Elderly John Beamer (Ed Wynn), a retired businessman living in the Midwest, suddenly became the ward of his two granddaughters, young Midge (Sherry Alberoni) and teenager Laurie (Jacklyn O'Donnell), while their widowed father was stationed in Saudi Arabia. This was the new, legit Ed Wynn—the one who came to be because of *Requiem for a Heavyweight* and that immensely popular episode of *Westinghouse Desilu Playhouse* called "The Man in the Funny Suit," on which Ed co-starred with his real-life son Keenan. Left behind were the baggy pants and the outdated vaudevillian material. Two granddaughters joining him in that big old house was just not enough, so upon Laurie's urging, Beamer agreed to take in her college friends as boarders, including one chimpanzee.

In the debut, Beamer came to realize too late that a town zoning ordinance forbade turning one's home into a boarding house (he was even jailed over the ordeal). However, he refused to give in to the old saying, "You can't fight city hall," and eventually all ended well. In the second episode, "The Crossing Guard," Beamer did a good deed and filled in for the crossing guard (Guy Kennedy) who desperately needed the day off to attend his grandson's christening. However, the overzealous Beamer almost got the crossing guard job eliminated in favor of a traffic light after an altercation with a stubborn driver who turned out to be the town's new traffic manager.

Sherry Alberoni Van Meter (Midge) recalls that Ed Wynn would "make funny, rubbery faces at me to try to make me laugh. The crew laughed with him a lot—they knew what a classic old vaudevillian he was, and everyone was very respectful to him. He was always so sweet, funny and nice to me. I really loved him."

***The Ed Wynn Show*—Left to right, Sherry Alberoni, Ed Wynn and Jacklyn O'Donnell (photograph courtesy of Sherry Alberoni Van Meter).**

The ratings for the show were not encouraging, but there was another reason for the show's early demise. Sherry remembers, "Ed's health played a major role in not continuing. He was very frail. I could see that, even as a child, because he constantly shook."

Another Screen Gems show began in that same fall TV season of 1958, but met with far greater success. Sherry recalls being on the same lot with the cast of *The Donna Reed Show*: "Many days I would go to school with Paul (Petersen) and Shelley (Fabares). Also, in May of 1959, I appeared on their show in an episode titled 'Going Steady' as Jeff's girlfriend, Meredith Penner."

Writers of note included Devery Freeman, Arthur Julian, Clifford Goldsmith, Harry Kronman, Phil Sharp, Howard Leeds, Paul and Margaret Schneider, Si Rose, Seaman Jacobs, and Bill Davenport; directors included Arthur Lubin, William D. Russell, and Sherry's favorite, Jack Donohue, whom she says, "would sing and do the soft shoe between takes. He was just great with us kids." Other regulars on the show included Jesslyn Fax as cranky neighbor Mrs. Creavy and the ubiquitous Herb Vigran as Beamer's friend Ernest Henshaw, whom Sherry recalls as "really fun. Such a great character face." *The Ed Wynn Show* used a lot of the same transitional music as *Dennis the Menace* and *This Is Alice*. Several episodes can be viewed in the UCLA TV Archives.

The Egg and I CBS. Weekdays at noon. September 3, 1951–August 1, 1952. 237 fifteen-minute episodes were broadcast live five days a week without a laugh track. The sponsor on Monday, Wednesday and Friday was Colgate, and on Tuesday and Thursday was Procter and Gamble.

Based upon the book by Betty McDonald (and the 1947 movie starring Claudette Colbert and Fred MacMurray), *The Egg and I* was a fifteen-minute comedy serial which aired daily on CBS at noon. The original plans for the show had Claudette Colbert reprising her role, but the part of Betty Blake was instead given to Pat Kirkland and later to Betty Lynn (as of March 10, 1952). She was called "Betty" by most people, but her Gammy (Mary Perry) called her "Elizabeth." Betty's very tall husband, Jim Blake, was portrayed by John Craven. Together, they tried to make a profit out of a run-down old farm in Allegain County. Among their farmhands was Jed Simmons, played by Grady Sutton. Betty's neighbors (the famous Maw and Paw Kettle) were played by Doris Rich and Frank Tweddell, respectively. William A. Lee played Ed Peabody, the owner of the local general store.

Episodes in existence include "Paw Turns a Leaf," in which the first day of spring put a little spring in Paw's step, actually making him volunteer to work on the planting of begonias and daffodils. However, true to form, he later came to his senses and complained of an aching back and that ended that. In "The Purloined Jacket," Betty gave Ma Kettle's visiting son Joe Kettle (Richard Carlyle) a nice sport jacket from Jim's closet (but forgot to tell Jim) so that Joe could come home with his head held high. Joe tried to make it in the movies in New York City, but only got about as far as usher in a movie theater (although he had tall tales to tell about his involvement in the executive branch of the movie industry for anyone within earshot). Jim ran into Joe at Ed Peabody's store and recognized the jacket instantly, but politely didn't make a big scene.

The program was produced by Montgomery Ford; the directors were Jack Gage and Judson Whiting; and writers included Mel Goldberg, Robert Soderberg and Manya Starr. The announcer was Alan Edwards. The show did extremely well in the ratings upon its debut and owned its timeslot, but wasn't able to stay on top, and after 237 episodes, it was gone from the CBS daytime lineup.

Ensign O'Toole Four Star Lederer Productions. NBC. Sunday nights at 7:00. September 23, 1962–September 15, 1963. 32 black-and-white episodes were filmed with a laugh track. Sponsors included L & M Cigarettes and Ford.

It was peacetime in the South Pacific where the destroyer the *USS Appleby* sailed. On board was Ensign O'Toole, portrayed by Disney movie regular, Dean Jones. Screen Gems originally showed interest in creating the series, but Four Star Studios got the honor. It wasn't announced often, but O'Toole had a first name—Terrence (revealed in the episode "Operation: Arrividerci"). Normally, he was simply referred to as O'Toole, and he had many unique talents. He could answer almost any trivia question; he spoke several languages; and he had an uncanny knack of getting out of work, getting out of paying the check, and getting in good with the ladies. His best friend, bunkmate, and occasional patsy was Lieutenant Rex St. John, portrayed by Jack Mullaney. O'Toole always seemed to be butting heads with Chief Petty Officer Homer

Nelson (Jay C. Flippen), who was always in search of a poker game. Jack Albertson played Lieutenant Commander Virgil Stoner, who was usually addressed as Mr. Stoner by the crew. Appearing occasionally were Beau Bridges as Seaman Howard Spicer; Bob Sorrels as Seaman Claude White; Stuart Margolin as Lieutenant Miller; and Ken Berry as Lieutenant Melton. Mrs. Ken Berry, Jackie Joseph, appeared in the episode titled "Operation: Casanova" as Mary Lou. Harvey Lembeck played Seaman Gabby Di Julio, and the captain was never seen, only heard barking orders on the ship's "squawk box."

The title of every episode of the show began with the word "Operation." Guest stars included Soupy Sales in the episode called "Operation: Jinx" as Seaman Jerome J. Johnson, whose reputation for bad luck followed him aboard *The Appleby;* Dick Powell, one of the "stars" in Four Star Studios, appeared as Chief Richard Powell in the episode called "Operation: Benefit"; comedian Jack Carter played Steve Turner, a con artist who wanted to open a Geisha house in "Operation: Geisha"; Harry Morgan was Charlie the cook, whose food was practically inedible, in "Operation: Mess"; and John McGiver played Stoner's psychologist brother-in-law, Arthur Ainsley, in "Operation: Psychology."

Ensign O'Toole—Dean Jones.

Directors included Hy Averback, Don Taylor, Jackie Cooper, Lawrence Dobkin, James Komack, Robert Gordon, and Richard Kinon; writers included Howard Leeds, Jack Raymond, and the teams of Bill Davenport and Charles Tannen, Jim Fritzell and Everett Greenbaum, James Allardice and Tom Adair, and Sheldon Keller and Howard Merrill. The program was based upon the books of Bill Lederer (*All the Ships at Sea* and *Ensign O'Toole and Me*). Lederer was a consultant on the series. When the show was canceled in September of 1963 by NBC, *The Bill Dana Show* took its place on the Sunday night schedule. ABC showed reruns of *Ensign O'Toole* during the summer of 1964 in prime time. More recently, reruns were shown on the Performance Channel in the UK. Dell put out two *Ensign O'-Toole* comic books during the show's initial run. Each sold for twelve cents.

The Eve Arden Show

Westhaven Enterprises/Desilu Productions. CBS. Tuesday nights 8:30. September 17, 1957–March 25, 1958. 26 black-and-white episodes were filmed before a live audience. Sponsors included

Lever House (Dove Soap) and Shulton (Old Spice).

In between her successes in *Our Miss Brooks* and *The Mothers-in-Law*, Eve Arden starred in this eponymous sitcom for Desilu. An earlier sitcom called *Young and Gay* had been based upon a work by Emily Kimbrough, and this show was based upon her autobiography titled *It Gives Me Great Pleasure*. Here Eve portrayed a widow named Liza Hammond who had two children—fraternal twin 13-year-old daughters Mary and Jenny (Karen Green and Gail Stone, respectively). Liza was an author and reluctant lecturer whose latest work, called "Summer's End," was quite a success. Allyn Joslyn played George Howell, Liza's agent. He was responsible for foisting the timid Liza onto the lecture circuit (he was also the head of the Howell Lecture Bureau). Whenever Liza was away, her mother, Nora Martin (Frances Bavier), dealt with the trials and tribulations of raising the twins. Willard Waterman made frequent guest appearances as their very frugal landlord, Carl Foster.

Quite a few episodes had a recurring theme—Liza's insecurities and how she attempted to overcome them. In the debut episode, "It Gives Me Great Pleasure," Liza dealt with stage fright in her first stop on her lecture tour. Using the old chestnut of picturing everyone in the audience in their underwear got Liza through the ordeal quite successfully. However, her fears did not end there. In the episode titled "The New Liza Hammond," she was seeing a psychiatrist to lessen her inferiority complex. The therapy, however, worked much too well, and Liza became uncharacteristically aggressive. In one of the show's best episodes, "Cover Girl," Liza was flattered by all of the attention she was suddenly receiving from the opposite sex—that is, until she found out why. The picture on the cover of her latest book only utilized her head, which was atop the body of a sexy young model. In "White Elephant Sale," Liza had new feelings of insecurity because of all of the attention the new "it girl" in the building, Mrs. Kenyon (Margaret Chapman) was getting. To get her daughters back into her own corner, Liza donated one of her most prized possessions for their charity event: her autographed Ernest Hemingway book.

First Edmund Hartmann, and later Al Lewis, produced the show; writers included William Cowley, Sol Saks, Sherman Marks, and Peggy Chantler; and directors included William D. Russell and John Rich. Four episodes of the program are available on DVD from Alpha Video. The original concept for the show in 1955 envisioned actress Myrna Loy in the starring role.

Fair Exchange Cy Howard Productions, Inc./Desilu Studios. CBS. Friday nights 9:30 (September 21, 1962–December 28, 1962—60 minute episodes), and Thursday nights 7:30 (March 28, 1963–September 19, 1963—30 minute episodes). 15 hour-long episodes and 12 half-hour episodes were filmed with a laugh track. Sponsors included Shell Gasoline, Pillsbury, Chesterfield Cigarettes, Coty Cosmetics, and Vicks Vaporub.

This was one of the first unsuccessful attempts to produce an hour-long sitcom. This one, called *Fair Exchange*, had a huge obstacle—stiff competition from *77 Sunset Strip* on ABC. This was the story of two middle class families, one American and one British, who exchanged daughters (they were exchange students going to college in each other's native country). The families weren't complete strangers—the two male stars knew each other from World War II. Beginning with the American family (the Walkers), there was the patriarch Eddie (Eddie Foy, Jr.), who, besides being a veteran of World War II, was also a veteran song and dance man from Vaudeville and owned a New York ticket agency. His wife, Dorothy, was played by Audrey Christie. They had two children—Flip Mark played Larry and Lynn Loring played Patty, their exchange student daughter. Patty was studying at the Royal Academy of Dramatic Arts in London. Eddie's poker buddy, Jerry Dale, was played by Ned Glass. The British family, the Finches, was headed by Tommy Finch (Victor Maddern), who owned a sporting goods store. His wife, Sybil, was played by Diana Chesney. They, too, had two children—Neville (Dennis Waterman) and their exchange student daughter, Heather (Judy Carne), who wanted to become a model. Both of the young men on the show developed crushes on their female visitors (a point which was emphasized in the episode titled "A Young Man's Fancy"). Tommy's best friend was Willie Shorthouse, played by Maurice Dallimore. The hour-long experiment failed, and the program was canceled after its two-part Christmas episode ("'Twas The Fortnight Before Christmas" and "Innocents Abroad"), in which each family tried to surprise the other by flying to visit their respective daughters. Their planes, unwittingly, passed one another in flight. Realizing their mistake, each family spent the holiday in the other family's country.

After the cancellation, CBS was said to have received volumes of angry letters, and after a three-month hiatus, *Fair Exchange* returned with new shorter (half-hour) episodes, now on Thursday nights at 7:30 (moving *Mister Ed* to Sunday nights). However, the new day and time slot, and the more compact episodes, still didn't equal big ratings, and this time the show's cancellation was final.

The program was created by Cy Howard; the producer was Edward H. Feldman; and writers included William Raynor and Myles Wilder. This part is really interesting: the British segments were directed by Sherman Marks and were filmed in London, while the American segments were directed by Richard Kinon and were filmed in Hollywood. Music was provided by Cyril Mockridge. Jack Gould of *The New York Times* wrote, "*Fair Exchange* should be a winner. The two families are altogether reasonable and real human beings who bring a note of charm and warmth to the readjustment that attends the arrival of young visitors in their homes."

Family Genius DuMont Network. Friday nights 9:00. September 9, 1949–September 30, 1949. Episodes were broadcast live.

This was a very short-lived live sitcom. Information on this program is extremely scarce and to my knowledge, no episodes exist. Featured was Jack Diamond as Tommy Howard, the "family genius." The parents of this child prodigy were played by Phyllis Love and Arthur Edwards. Others in the cast included Edith Gresham, Alan MacAteer, Joan Tighe, and Elizabeth York. The program was produced by James L. Caddigan and Elwood Hoffman; the directors were Caddigan and Jack Weiser.

Far Out Space Nuts A Sid and Marty Krofft Production/CBS. September 6, 1975–September 4, 1976. 15 episodes were videotaped at Samuel Goldwyn Studios with a laugh track.

As one would expect, there was a lot of slapstick fun on this program with Bob Denver as Junior, Chuck McCann as Barney, and Patty Maloney as an alien creature called Honk (who never spoke, only honked). Barney and Junior were bumbling Cape Kennedy food concessionaires. While aboard the spaceship PXL-1236 loading the food supply, Junior misunderstood Barney's "lunch" command for the word "launch," and they were instantly hurled into orbit. During their adventure in space, the trio was captured by a different set of evil aliens each week, and along for the ride was that character named Honk. Extracting themselves from the aliens' clutches was always a bunch of silly fun. Luckily, Barney had received some training in flying the spaceship, while Junior had not (but that didn't stop him from occasionally giving it a whirl—always with disastrous results).

Episode titles include "The Three Spaceketeers," "Crystallitis," "Flight of the Fippets," "Barney's Begonia," and "Captain Torque, Space Pirate."

Far Out Space Nuts—**Left to right, Chuck McCann, Bob Denver, and Patty Maloney (photograph courtesy of Jean Cummings).**

The program was created by Sid and Marty Krofft, who also served as executive producers; the producer was Al Schwartz; writers included Earle Doud, Chuck McCann, John Mendelsohn, and Sid and Marty Krofft; and directors included Wes Kenney, Walter C. Miller, and Claudio Guzman. Music was provided by Michael Lloyd.

Father of the Bride Father Productions, Inc./MGM Studios. CBS. Friday nights 9:30. September 29, 1961–September 14, 1962. 34 black-and-white episodes were filmed with a laugh track. Sponsors included Campbell's Soup and General Mills.

It began as a book by Edward Streeter. Then came the MGM movie of the same name (which starred Spencer Tracy) and eventually the MGM TV series a decade later. The latter starred Leon Ames as Stanley Banks of Williston and Banks, attorneys-at-law (office number 416). Stanley was played by Jim Backus in the pilot. Stanley was married to Ellie (Ruth Warrick). Together, they were the parents of Tommy (Rickie Sorensen) and Kay (Myrna Fahey). Kay was in love with, then engaged to, and eventually married to Buckley Dunston (Burt Metcalfe)—much to "father's" chagrin. On the Dunston side of the family were Buckley's father, Herbert (Ransom Sherman), and mother, Doris (Lurene Tuttle, who had played Leon Ames's wife for two seasons on *Life with Father*). Also in the cast, were Irene Tedrow as Stanley's secretary Miss Bellamy; and Ruby Dandridge as the Banks's housekeeper, Delilah. Stanley Banks managed to wink at the audience at the end of almost every episode.

Early episodes of the show took us from the day the parents were told of the kids' intentions ("Bombshell at Breakfast") to the first meeting of the groom's side of the family ("Buckley's Parents"). Then there was "The Engagement Party," "The Guest List," "Maid of Honor," "The Shower," "The Rehearsal," and then finally "The Wedding," "The Honeymoon," and eventually the first argument in "Quibbling." The show's final episode, "The Visit," involved Kay's parents badly wanting to visit the newlyweds, but because of a book of etiquette by an author named Gelbert, they insisted upon waiting for an invitation.

The program was produced by Rudy E. Abel; directors included Fletcher Markle, Gene Reynolds, Tony Leader, and Richard Whorf; and writers included the teams of Theodore and Mathilde Ferro, Katherine and Dale Eunson, Mort Green and Ken Cooper, Jim Henerson, and Lou Hazam. The theme song was by David Raksin (also from *Life with Father*). Early episodes of the show featured animated opening credits with a cartoon cupid holding a magic wand, but later episodes had the entire cast gathered on the Banks' staircase. The final episode is available for viewing in the UCLA TV Archives.

Fay Danny Thomas Productions/Universal. NBC. Thursday nights 8:30 (September 4, 1975–October 23, 1975), and Wednesday nights 9:30 (May 12, 1976–June 2, 1976). Ten color episodes were filmed before a live audience.

This show, and its predecessor on Thursday nights, *The Montefuscos*, suffered very quick cancellations. Both took a direct hit from *The Waltons* on CBS and *Barney Miller*, followed by *On the Rocks*, on ABC. The star of the show, Lee Grant, exacerbated the situation by lambasting NBC for the abrupt cancellation of *Fay* during a guest appearance on *The Tonight Show* (October 30, 1975), and also by "flipping the bird" to the powers-that-be on that same telecast. To this day,

***Fay*—Joe Silver, Lee Grant (photograph courtesy of Jean Cummings).**

Lee insists that she found out about the show coming to an end from a stagehand. Initially, the program was being compared to *The Mary Tyler Moore Show*, because the star was a single woman trying to "make it on her own." *Fay* was Fay Stewart—a 43-year-old recent divorcee trying to readjust to single life. In the debut episode, she acquired an apartment on Langley Avenue, and a new job as a law secretary in San Francisco. Fay was still very good friends with her ex-husband, Jack Stewart (Joe Silver), who called her "his best friend" in the episode titled "Jack Remarries." It was nice that they still liked one another (even though he had cheated on her several times during the marriage), because they had a daughter together, 23-year-old Linda ([played by Margaret Willock] who was married to plastic surgeon Dr. Elliot Baines [played by Stewart Moss]). Fay also befriended a nosey neighbor named Lillian (Audra Lindley). In a very interesting bit of foreshadowing, Audra Lindley and Norman Fell played husband and wife in the episode titled "Lillian's Separation." Years later, Lindley and Fell would again be husband and wife on both *Three's Company* and *The Ropers*.

The show had a rather large cast. At the law office was Fay's boss, the very young and insecure Danny Messina, played by Bill Gerber (who developed a big crush on her in the episode titled "Danny Falls in Love"); Danny's elder law partner Al Cassidy (Norman Alden); and his African American secretary Letty Gilmore (Lillian Lehman).

The program was created by Susan Harris; the executive producer was Paul Junger Witt; writers included Harris, Max Pisk, Richard Clair, Jenna McMahon, and Jerry Mayer; and directors included Richard Kinon and Joan Darling. The theme song, "Coming into My Own," was performed by Jaye P. Morgan; the lyrics were written by Elayne Heilveil and Stuart Margolin, with music by George Aliceson Tipton. Danny Thomas warmed up the live audience before each of the show's tapings. The program got another chance to prove itself in prime time during the summer of 1976, but again failed to garner high ratings (even though it was now on Wednesday nights). Ironically, Lee Grant was nominated for an Emmy Award for her role in *Fay*, but lost to Mary Tyler Moore. Lee admitted years after the show's demise that working in front of those live studio audiences brought about incredible bouts of stage fright, from which she never fully recovered. Sander Vanocur reviewed the program in *The Washington Post* writing, "After you have watched Lee Grant and Joe Silver for half-an-hour, your head may be in the clouds. *Fay* looks like a winner."

Fibber McGee and Molly MGM, Hollywood. NBC. Tuesday nights 8:30. September 15, 1959–January 19, 1960. 12 black-and-white episodes were filmed with a laugh track. Sponsors included Singer Sewing Machines and Standard Brands (Chase and Sanborn Coffee and Fleischmann's Margarine).

In 1955, there was an attempt to bring a character named The Great Gildersleeve to television, but that only lasted a single season. Throckmorton P. Gildersleeve's character originated on one of radio's longest-running shows, *Fibber McGee and Molly* (it ran for 22 seasons), but when Fibber was brought to the small screen, it too failed (lasting only 12 weeks). This was the story of a childless couple who lived at 79 Wistful Vista. "Fibber" (Bob Sweeney) got his nickname because he was notorious for being a very proficient liar—yet most people simply called him "McGee" (that included his long-suffering wife, Molly, played by Cathy Lewis). Harold Peary,

***Fibber McGee and Molly*—Bob Sweeney and Cathy Lewis (photograph courtesy of Jean Cummings).**

who portrayed Gildersleeve in the radio version of *Fibber McGee and Molly*, appeared in this TV version as Mayor LaTrivia. The McGee's neighbors, the Norris family, were familiar faces—Elisabeth Fraser played Hazel Norris and Paul Smith played her husband, Roy Norris. In an episode titled "The Good Neighbor," the McGees and Norrises were about to celebrate their fifth anniversary as neighbors, when suddenly all went awry as the husbands got into a heated dispute over who owned the apple tree in the backyard. The situation mushroomed, necessitating the formerly friendly neighbors to settle things in a courtroom. In the debut titled "The Trailer," Fibber, a man devoid of sales resistance, went out to buy a simple $60 trailer for an upcoming vacation and brought back a $9,500 behemoth. Fibber then told Molly a whopper of a fib—that he had won the trailer at the local "Wistful Vista Trailer Show." Jack Kirkwood, who would again work with Elisabeth Fraser on *One Happy Family*, appeared occasionally as Fred Nitney, Fibber's old vaudeville partner. In the episode titled "The Fred Nitney Story," Fred stayed with the McGees while he finished writing a book about their act known as "Nitney and McGee."

The program was produced and directed by William Asher; writers included Bill Davenport, Hugh Wedlock, Howard Snyder, Larry Rhine, and Bill Freedman. In the opening credits, Fibber and Molly are seen as clay figures, and Molly chases her husband across the screen with the second "L" in Molly. Sadly, the show didn't translate well to television. Evidently, it was much funnier to envision Fibber opening his overstuffed closet (which invariably led to a huge crash on radio) than to actually see it on the screen. A few episodes were rerun on NBC in the spring of 1960 under the umbrella of *Comedy Playhouse*.

Flatbush Lorimar Productions. CBS. Monday nights 8:30. February 26, 1979–March 12, 1979. Six episodes were filmed at the MGM lot in Culver City, California, but only three aired.

Much in the same manner as *Life with Luigi* and *Bridget Loves Bernie*, *Flatbush* caused an uproar because of extreme ethnic stereotyping and an offensive portrayal of the borough of Brooklyn, New York. However, there was one big difference here—*Life with Luigi* and *Bridget Loves Bernie* were actually high-rated shows, but *Flatbush* was not. Writer Dennis Palumbo told me, "In hindsight it was stereotypical. Remember, this show was 'inspired' (stolen from) the film *The Lords of Flatbush*, which starred Sylvester Stallone and Henry Winkler. I think I was the only Italian-American writer on the show. All I remember at the time was trying to make the scripts funnier. What social/cultural concerns there might have been didn't really enter into the picture." Well, because of all the flak, CBS had no problem pulling it off of their Monday night schedule. The program's original working title was *The Flatbush Fungoes*, and it was the story of five recent high school graduates from the Italian-American section of Flatbush, Brooklyn. Each of the main characters had a nickname and each belonged to a rather tame, fun-seeking gang called the Flatbush Fungoes. Dennis Palumbo said, "Being from Pittsburgh rather than New York, I had to have the term fungo explained to me."

The main cast consisted of Presto Prestopopolous (Joseph Cali), who drove a cab; Socks Palermo (Adrian Zmed), who worked in a men's clothing store; Joey Dee, not to be confused with the singer of *The Peppermint Twist* (played by Randy Stumpf), who was an apprentice plumber who went to law school at night; Turtle Romero (Vincent Bufano), who worked in his family's restaurant; and Figgy Figueroa (Sandy Helberg), who was the nerdy guy in the group, worked in a supermarket, and delivered food on a bicycle. Also in the cast were Esposito (Antony Ponzini), who owned the pool hall where the Fungos hung out, and Mrs. Fortunato (Helen Verbit), the nosy neighborhood gossip.

Episodes include "Kar Kannibals," in which the treasured "Fungomobile" was stolen by car thieves, and the Fungoes vowed to seek revenge. Other episode titles included "Movin' Out," and "The Heist." Dennis Palumbo remembered that when writing several of these episodes, "I kept trying to imagine our guys as the Italian Marx Brothers. I was going for that manic, high-energy quality."

The program was produced by Philip Capice and Gary Adelson; the creator was David Epstein; writers included Epstein, Terry Hart, Mike Weinberger, and Dennis Palumbo; and directors included some big names—William Asher, Mel Ferber and Tony Mordente. Palumbo shared, "I recall the writers' general surprise that guys of that caliber were willing to direct this show." Music was provided by Mark Snow.

Flying High Mark Carliner Productions/CBS. Friday nights 10:00 (September 29, 1978–December 29, 1978), and Tuesday nights 10:00

(January 2, 1979–January 23, 1979). 18 episodes were filmed, only 13 aired.

One might call this program a mile-high version of *The Love Boat*. The similarity, in fact, was intentional. This was the story of three beautiful stewardesses from diverse backgrounds and totally different parts of the United States who all came together at the same time to work for Sun West Airlines. Marcy Bowers (Pat Klous) was 19 years old and a native of Sweetwater, Texas, where she worked on the family farm; Pam Bellagio (Kathryn Witt) was 22 years old, and was still living at home in Trenton, New Jersey, with her very large Italian-American family; and Lisa Benton (Connie Sellecca) was 21 years old and was tired of living off of her wealthy parents' money in Greenwich, Connecticut—she wanted to earn her own way in the world. Others in the cast included pilot Captain Doug March (Howard Platt); Mac Carabasi (Stephen Parr); and Raymond Strickman (Ken Olfson). In the two-hour pilot episode, guest stars included Timothy Hutton and Marcia Wallace.

Episodes include "Fear of Cheesecake," which was reminiscent of the movie *Airplane* in that the cockpit crew came down with food poisoning. In "High Rollers," the girls worked a flight to Las Vegas where a comedian attempted to woo Lisa, and Marcy won big at one of the casinos. In "Swan Song for an Ugly Duckling," Marcy's old school chum (Melinda Naud) wanted to change her ugly duckling ways in an attempt to keep her very wealthy husband (Terry Lester). "South by Southwest" was written by Dennis Palumbo, who recalled, "They brought me in to do a hurry-up script because another script was shelved. Given the speed with which the script was written and shot, I thought the episode came out reasonably well. The best part about it for me was that the guest actor was Ross Martin, one of my favorite TV stars. At the screening of my episode, watching the scenes where he said my dialogue was the high point of the experience. I chose the title of the episode, and was constantly checking maps to make sure the narrative was indeed taking our characters south by southwest across the country. This was all pre-internet, remember."

The program was created by Dawn Aldredge and Martin Cohan; the executive producer was Mark Carliner; the producer was Robert Van Scoyk; writers included Aldredge, Cohan, Robert Van Scoyk, Terry Ryan, Jerry Ross, Judie Neer, Katharyn Michaelian Powers, Joyce Amor, and Dennis Palumbo; and directors included Peter H. Hunt, Sigmund Neufeld, Jr., Nicolas Sgarro, Dennis Donnelly, and William K. Jurgensen. Music was provided by David Shire. This was yet another example of a failed attempt to create a successful hour-long sitcom.

Free Country Reiner/Mishkin Productions/ Columbia Pictures Television. ABC. Saturday nights 8:00. June 24, 1978–July 22, 1978.

VIDEO-TAPED AT KTLA — STAGE 1
5800 Sunset Blvd. at Van Ness
Entrance — Van Ness Avenue

REINER/MISHKIN in association with
COLUMBIA PICTURES TELEVISION
presents
FREE COUNTRY
starring
ROB REINER JUDY KAHAN

Children under 16 will not be admitted

FRIDAY
APRIL
14
1978

SHOW TIME
8:00 p.m.

GUESTS MUST
ARRIVE
7:00 p.m.

№ 293

Free Country—Unredeemed ticket to a taping.

Five episodes were videotaped at KTLA Stage One.

Rob Reiner was not happy with ABC's treatment of this show. He wanted 13 episodes, ABC gave him five and relegated it to be a summer replacement series. This was the story of a Lithuanian immigrant named Joseph Bresner (Rob Reiner) who came to New York in 1906. His bride-to-be, Anna (Judy Kahan), followed suit in 1909. Reiner got to play dual roles—he began each episode as the 89-year-old Joseph Bresner in the current day, and when he'd reminisce, we would see the same Joseph Bresner in his youth at the turn of the century. The Bresners had neighbors named Sidney and Ida Gewertzman (Fred McCarren and Renee Lippin, respectively); a friend named Louis Peschi (Joe Pantoliano); and a boarder named Leo Gold (Larry Gelman). Stories each week dealt with how the Bresners adapted to the sometimes odd customs of this "free country." Joseph was always afraid of being deported because he was somewhat of a revolutionary in the old country.

Episode titles pretty well spell out each chapter of this short-lived series—"Anna's Arrival," "Anna's Adjustment," "Citizenship," "When Already," and "Special Delivery." The last two episodes were concerned with Anna's pregnancy, and the eventual birth of their first child (which arrived before the doctor).

The program was produced by Gareth Davies; the creators were Rob Reiner and Phil Mishkin, who also served as executive producers; writers included Reiner, Earl Pomerantz, Mishkin, Arnold Kane, and Sy Rosen; and directors included Hal Cooper and James Burrows. Reiner was probably secretly relieved when the show only lasted for five weeks, as his makeup for the elder Joseph Bresner took several hours to apply.

Friends 20th Century–Fox/ABC. Sunday nights 7:00. March 25, 1979–April 22, 1979. Five hour-long episodes were filmed with a laugh track.

There wasn't a Ross or Rachel on this program called *Friends*. This one saw life through the eyes of three Southern California eleven-year-old kids from vastly different upbringings, and was recommended by the NEA (National Education Association). There was Pete Richards (Charles Aiken), and his parents Frank and Pamela (Andy Romano and Karen Morrow); Nancy Wilks (Jill Whelan), who was from a broken home, and her father (Dennis Redfield); and Randy Summerfield (Jarred Johnson), an African American lawyer's son, and his parents (Roger Robinson and Janet MacLachlan). Episodes focused upon the trials and tribulations of adolescence, and involved subjects such as dating, family, school, growing pains, and friendship. Also in the cast, Charles Lampkin as Randy's granddad, and Alicia Fleer as Pete's elder sister, Cynthia. The role of Cynthia was originally intended for someone else. Karen Morrow told me, "Helen Hunt was supposed to play my daughter, but when she saw that her part was greatly overshadowed by her younger brother on the show, she bowed out."

Episodes include "Going Out," which was about dating, and "Grandfather Arrives," about a visit from Randy's granddad. "Pressure" was an episode about Randy's falling grades. His schoolwork was suffering because of his many extracurricular activities and his attempts at cheating (copying a book report from an encyclopedia, and stealing answers for a geography test) only got him in bigger trouble (benched for an upcoming basketball game). In that same episode, Pete's older sister, Cynthia, fell in with the wrong crowd, changed her hair, and became a totally different person—until she realized the error of her ways. Karen Morrow remembered, "I was really disappointed when this show was canceled so quickly. I really enjoyed and felt really comfortable in this role. I guess the competition from *60 Minutes* and *Disney's Wonderful World* was just insurmountable."

The program was created by A. J. Carothers, with whom Karen Morrow became close friends. Producers included Bob Sand, Bo Kapprall and Cindy Dunne; the executive producers were Aaron Spelling and Douglas S. Cramer. Karen Morrow described Spelling as "very nice and very loyal," and Cramer as "a lovely man who was also a fan." Writers included Michael Russnow and Liz Coe; and directors included Roger Duchowny, Buddy Tyne, James Sheldon, Glenn Jordan and Arnold Laven. Music was provided by Fred Karlin. One episode is available for viewing at the UCLA TV Archives. Karen Morrow said, "When most people see *Friends* on my resume they think it's the Courtney Cox show. To avoid a lengthy explanation, I usually just play along and tell them that I was the lady who lived upstairs with the annoying kid, to which they usually respond, 'I remember that.'"

Friends and Lovers (see *Paul Sand in Friends and Lovers*)

From a Bird's Eye View ITC (Incorporated Television Company) Production. NBC. Monday nights 7:30. March 29, 1971–August 16, 1971. 16 color episodes were filmed.

Flying was certainly a lot more fun before 9/11. This show is proof. Filmed in the United Kingdom for ITC, it starred Millicent Martin as British stewardess Millie Grover, who had really good intentions, which invariably backfired. Her American roommate and co-worker was Maggie Ralston played by Patte Finley. It was always Maggie's responsibility to get Millie out of predicaments. Their boss at the London airline, the impatient Clive Beauchamp, was portrayed by Peter Jones.

Actor Robert Rietty appeared in three episodes of the show. Rietty had previously worked with director Ralph Levy in the pilot episode of *Harry's Girls*. He remembers, "Faithful as always, when Ralph Levy came to London to do this series with Millicent Martin, he engaged me to play in several episodes and left the dialogue for me to invent." In the episode titled "Hurricane Millie," Rietty played a casino manager who had a confrontation with a ne'er-do-well songwriter whose luck at the gaming tables changed negatively every single time Millie showed up to place a bet. This episode also had a cute song performed by Millie and Maggie called "Head in the Clouds," written by Frank Barber and Jack Fishman (who also wrote the program's theme song). In an episode titled "Wife Trouble," Millie's good nature again got her in Dutch when she helped an attractive male passenger secure a promotion by pretending to be his wife. In that episode, Rietty played the hotel clerk. In "All in a Day's Work," Millie was linked romantically to a movie star once the paparazzi had seen them together. Truth is, she was only helping him get onto the plane (he had way too much to drink). Rietty played the porter in that episode. He recalled, "Millicent was a delight to work with, and so was the rest of the cast." He added that executive producer Sheldon Leonard "never visited us on the set, at least not when I was working."

In the debut episode called "The Hate-In" (a play on the "love-ins" of the '60s), Millie was depressed because her boyfriend George Lemon (Richard Briers) hadn't yet made a move, even after several dates. She began to think George might have been gay—that is, until she realized that he had fallen head-over-heels for her roommate Maggie. Maggie had absolutely no interest in George, but that didn't stop the two best friends from having a huge fight.

A majority of the episodes were directed by Ralph Levy; writers included Sid Dorfman, Carl Kleinschmitt, Pat Dunlop, R. S. Allen, Harvey Bullock, Stan Cutler and Martin Donovan. The opening credits were animated. All 16 episodes of the show are available on DVD from Network Video in the United Kingdom.

Funny Face Paramount Studios. CBS. Saturday nights 8:30. September 18, 1971–December 11, 1971. 13 color episodes were filmed with a laugh track. Sponsors included Bristol Myers.

This was the story of young Sandy Stockton of Taylorville, Illinois. Taylorville was a small town with a population of 10,425. Make that 10,424, because Sandy Stockton left her home town to major in education at UCLA. To earn money while in college, Sandy did some work in TV commercials (when she could find work, that is) through the Prescott Advertising Agency, run by Maggie Prescott (Nita Talbot). Sandy's best friend was star-struck neighbor Alice McRaven (Valorie Armstrong). Sandy also befriended her landlord (Pat Harwell, played by Henry Beckman) and his wife (Kate Harwell, played by Kathleen Freeman). In the episode titled "Don't Worry, I'll Manage," Sandy took over for her landlords who hadn't had a vacation in eons. However, unhandy Sandy was immediately overwhelmed by a leaky pipe, a tenant who took in a dog (there was a no pet clause in the lease), and angry tenants who accused Sandy of favoritism. In "A Star Is Born on a Stretcher," Sandy was discovered by an agent named Manny Pitler (Avery Schreiber), who got her a bit part on *Mission: Impossible*. Appropriately, the episode's locale was the Paramount Studios lot. Sandy landed a non-speaking role on the show (in a scene with guest star Peter Graves) in which a booby-trapped music box exploded in her face. Comedy ensued when the scene had to be reshot numerous times.

The program was produced by Carl Kleinschmidt; the executive producer was Jerry Davis; directors included Hal Cooper and Peter Baldwin; and writers included Susan Silver and Ron Friedman. *Funny Face* was a sandwich hit, situated between *All in the Family* and *The New Dick Van Dyke Show* on Saturday nights in the fall of 1971. However, Sandy needed emergency eye surgery, and production was halted. It was one of the top ten most successful shows of the 1971–

1972 television season. The following season, Sandy was back in *The Sandy Duncan Show*, again as Sandy Stockton, but with an entirely new set of circumstances, writers, producers, co-stars, and a live audience. It's interesting to note that Tom Bosley had been a guest star on *Funny Face* as a used car salesman in the episode titled "The Used Car"—but on *The Sandy Duncan Show*, he played her boss, Bert Quinn. Both *Funny Face* and *The Sandy Duncan Show* used the same theme song called "The Kind of Girl She Is," written by Alan and Marilyn Bergman, and both shows used the same photo album pictures during the opening credits. Jack Jones sang the theme song for *Funny Face*, but not for *The Sandy Duncan Show*. It's unclear why the successful *Funny Face* was retooled in the first place. See the entry for *The Sandy Duncan Show* for more. Several episodes of *Funny Face* can be viewed in the UCLA TV Archives.

The George Burns Show B and A Productions/McCadden Productions. NBC. Tuesday nights 9:00. October 21, 1958–April 14, 1959. 18 black-and-white episodes were filmed with a laugh track, 7 others (the variety format) were done live with a live studio audience. The sponsors were Colgate-Palmolive and Carnation.

Numerous times in the debut episode titled "George and the Private Eye" (sometimes called "George Becomes a Producer"), the following question arose in the dialogue: "Can George Burns be successful on TV by himself?" Sadly, that question was answered rather quickly. Even with an array of guest stars such as Bob Cummings, Jack Benny, Tommy Sands, Tony Martin, and Eddie Fisher, George Burns just wasn't making it on his own. Most of the regulars were there: Harry Von Zell as himself, Ronnie Burns as himself, Larry Keating as Harry H. Morton (now George's accountant) and Bea Benederet as Blanche Morton (now George's secretary—she hired herself for the position so George wouldn't be tempted by all the pretty starlets who would be coming through the office). Well, there was one regular who wasn't there—Gracie Allen, and that made all of the difference in the world. Also, the show was now on NBC, not CBS, where *The George Burns and Gracie Allen Show* had thrived and reigned for eight seasons. This show limped through several formats for one abbreviated season.

The show's opening credits featured a burning cigar in an ashtray. In the debut, a very forlorn George was seated alone, looking out the window (obviously wishing Gracie was there). He was on the horns of a dilemma—Gracie had retired, but he wasn't ready to make that same commitment yet. The two Harrys urged him to take a stab at the producing end of the business, so he set up shop in an empty office in Harry Morton's office building. George was just very out of his element in this new venture, and after the sitcom's Christmas episode titled "A Wife for Christmas" (in which Harry Von Zell almost got married), the program abruptly changed direction. Suddenly, *The George Burns Show* was a live weekly half-hour variety show. All of the regulars were still there, but there was now a George Burns monologue, singing and dancing, and some sketch comedy, involving a celebrity guest (Carol Channing appeared in a few of these variety episodes). This second format lasted for all of seven weeks, when suddenly, on February 24, 1959, the program resurrected its sitcom format and picked up right where it had left off. None of these changes made a difference in the ratings, and on April 14, 1959, George Burns got his question answered—apparently, he couldn't be successful on TV by himself. This would be proven twice more, on *Wendy and Me* in the mid–1960s, and on *The George Burns Comedy Week* in the mid–1980s.

The program was produced by Rod Amateau; writers included Norman Paul, Keith Fowler, Harvey Helm, and William Burns (George's younger brother). The sitcom episodes were directed by Amateau; the variety show episodes by Bob Henry. Music was provided by Jeff Alexander. On the debut episode, Ronnie Burns auditioned both sides of his Verve Label (Verve 10125) 45rpm record "Double Date" backed with "Kinda Cute" (actor Joby Baker portrayed one of the background singers). Ricky Nelson had released his first two singles on Verve and enjoyed major chart success, but Burns was not able to duplicate that success. However, he would later get two seasons out of a sitcom set in Palm Springs, California titled *Happy*, about a baby who could share his thoughts with the audience (not unlike Cleo the basset hound in *The People's Choice*).

The Gertrude Berg Show (see *Mrs. G. Goes to College*)

Getting Together Thornhill Productions/Screen Gems. ABC. Saturday nights 8:00. September 18, 1971–January 8, 1972. 14 color episodes were filmed with a laugh track. Sponsors included General Foods and Warner Lambert.

This show was thoroughly crushed by the competition provided by *All in the Family* on CBS. It was also ill-timed, as Bobby Sherman's recording career was in a real lull—thus, he didn't attract the same number of viewers he had on his previous ABC series, *Here Come the Brides*. This series was originally to be titled *The Bobby Sherman Show* but was changed at the last minute. *Getting Together* was actually a spinoff of *The Partridge Family*—introduced in the episode titled "A Knight in Shining Armor." A struggling Los Angeles songwriter named Bobby Conway (Bobby Sherman) was introduced to a nerdy, tone-deaf lyricist named Lionel Poindexter (even his name was nerdy) played by Wes Stern. This episode, which aired on March 19, 1971, served as the pilot for *Getting Together*, which made its official debut in the fall of 1971. To eke out a living, Bobby worked as a recording studio engineer, and Lionel took any odd job that came along. The songwriters lived together in an antique shop along with Bobby's 12-year-old sister, Jennifer (freckle-faced Susan Neher). In fact, Bobby had a minor hit single record called "Jennifer," which was introduced on the show, and dedicated to his TV sister. Also in the cast was Pat Carroll as Rita Simon, the motherly landlady (owner of the antique shop), and her policeman boyfriend Rudy Colcheck (Jack Burns).

The title of every episode was also the title of a major hit "oldies" song—"Jenny, Jenny" (Little Richard), "Cathy's Clown" (Everly Brothers), "All Shook Up" (Elvis Presley), "Where Are You, Little Star?" (The Elegants), "Singing the Blues" (Guy Mitchell), "Why Do Fools Fall in Love" (Frankie Lymon and the Teenagers), "Beep Beep" (The Playmates), "I Want You, I Need You, I Love You" (Elvis Presley), "Those Oldies but Goodies Remind Me of You" (Little Caesar and the Romans), "The Great Pretender" (The Platters), "Breaking Up Is Hard to Do" (Neil Sedaka), "Broken-Hearted Melody" (Sarah Vaughan), "Blue Christmas" (Elvis Presley), and "Memories Are Made of This" (Dean Martin). In "Memories Are Made of This," cash-starved songwriters Bobby and Lionel signed up as guinea pigs for scientific experimentation to help pay the rent. In "Blue Christmas," Bobby wanted his sister, Jennifer to experience a real Christmas with snow and a real tree, so he booked a cabin in the mountains. What he didn't know was that it came complete with a hole in the roof and an outhouse. Actress Beverly Washburn, who appeared in the "Great Pretender" episode recalled, "I played an encyclopedia salesman in the episode, and Bobby Sherman made me feel so welcome. He was one of the most fan-friendly people in the business. Every week, there was a large crowd of teenage girls there seeking autographs, and he was kind and took time to acknowledge each and every one of them consistently. On the same lot, David Cassidy was doing *The Partridge Family*, and, unlike Bobby, he totally ignored or was rude to the fans lined up at his door."

The program was created by Bernard Slade; the executive producer was Bob Claver; the producer was Paul Junger Witt; writers included Charles Shyer, Alan Mandel, Jack Winter, Dennis Klein, Steve Zacharias, John D. F. Black, Richard Bensfield, William S. Bickley, Perry Grant, Richard Baer, and Lee Kalcheim; and directors included Richard Kinon, Ron Winston, Hal Cooper, Roger Duchowny, Jerry Bernstein, Lou Antonio, and Ralph Senensky. Senensky told me, "This was during a brief period when I was exclusively directing sitcoms. I recall very little about *Getting Together*." The *Getting Together* theme song was written by Helen Miller and Roger Atkins, and performed by Bobby Sherman. During the show's run, Bobby released a *Getting Together* album on the Metromedia record label (Metromedia 1045). Bernard Slade's Thornhill Productions later gave us another single season sitcom, *The Girl with Something Extra*, which starred Sally Field. Clarence Petersen of *The Chicago Tribune* called *Getting Together*, "A pleasant little story for the kiddies—harmless and entertaining, and neither preachy nor patronizing." The entire run of this series is available for viewing in the UCLA TV Archives.

Ghost Busters A Filmation Production. CBS. Saturday mornings. September 6, 1975–September 4, 1976. 15 episodes were videotaped with a laugh track.

This was a live action Saturday morning kid's sitcom which accomplished the reuniting of Larry Storch and Forrest Tucker of *F Troop*, and their respective roles on this show didn't differ all that much. Their character names were a play on actor Spencer Tracy's name—"Spenser, Tracy, and Kong—Ghost Busters" was emblazoned on the door to their business office. Storch was Spenser (spelled Spen*s*er on the door, but spelled Spen*c*er in the opening credits), Tracy was an ape who didn't speak (Bob Burns in a monkey suit), and, oddly enough, Tucker was Kong. This show preceded the blockbuster movie of the same name.

Not unlike Mr. Phelps in *Mission: Impossible*, Spenser and Tracy received their weekly instructions from a self-destructing tape recorder, hidden in a different item each week (moose head, typewriter, painting, etc.). There was a lot of slapstick and many sight gags, and without fail, the tape recorder self-destructed in Tracy's face. There was also a TV set at the office which, whenever a weather report was tuned in, would spray rain in the faces of those sitting in front of it.

Each episode featured different ghosts which necessitated busting, including Billy the Kid, The Red Baron, Count Dracula, and Frankenstein's monster. Episode titles included "The Maltese Monkey," "Which Witch Is Which," and "A Worthless Gauze."

The program was produced by Norman Abbott; the executive producers were Lou Scheiner, Norm Prescott, and Dick Rosenbloom; and the writer and creator was Marc Richards. The theme song was written by Diane Hildebrand and Jackie Mills. After the successful Columbia picture starring Bill Murray and Dan Aykroyd, new episodes of *Ghost Busters* were created—this time in cartoon form, again utilizing the voices of Forrest Tucker and Larry Storch.

Gidget Screen Gems. ABC. Wednesday nights 8:30 (September 15, 1965–June 1966), and Thursday nights 8:00 (June 1966–September 1, 1966). 32 color episodes were filmed with a laugh track. Sponsors included Armstrong, Campbell's Soup, and Contac.

Many will be amazed to discover that the TV version of *Gidget* was a single season sitcom, because it has certainly had a long and successful life in syndication (with only 32 original episodes). The story of Gidget, a contraction of the words "girl" and "midget" (although she was a rather normal five-feet-two-inches), began in 1959 with the movie starring Sandra Dee, James Darren, and Cliff Robertson. In 1965, a young Sally Field, plucked from total obscurity, became her on TV. Her full name was Frances Elizabeth Lawrence, but her dad only called her "Frances" on a couple of occasions when she had done something really wrong (usually it was "Gidget," and occasionally "Francee"). She was fifteen-and-a-half years old, lived near the beach in sunny southern California, and attended Westside High School. She had a boyfriend named Jeff "Moondoggie" Matthews (Stephen Mines), who attended Princeton University and only appeared occasionally on the show. While he was away, both he and Gidget agreed to see other people, but they knew in their heart of hearts that one day they would marry. Gidget's dad, widower Russ Lawrence (Don Porter), was an English professor at UCLA. Attempting to take the place of Gidget's mother was her older, very serious, worrywart sister Anne Cooper (Betty Conner) who lived in The Terrace Apartments in number 417. Anne (she had black hair in the pilot, but was a blonde and sometimes a strawberry blonde in the series) was married to a student of psychiatry named John Cooper, played by Peter Deuel (Peter E. Deuel in the pilot). Strangely, John didn't call his father-in-law "dad," but rather called him simply "Russ." Gidget's best friend was named Larue (Lynette Winter), she was allergic to the sun and was much less popular with the opposite sex than Gidget, even though she drove a beautiful red Mustang convertible (used mostly to transport surfboards to the beach). Every episode was 30 minutes chock full of fun, sun, surf, and the joys and woes of being a teenager. Gidget had her own unique lingo, including words and phrases such as "holy minestrone," "rest the bones" (meaning sit down) and, of course, "toodles" (meaning goodbye).

Bruce Bilson, who directed three episodes of the show ("In and Out with the In-Laws," "We Got Each Other," and "Independence: Gidget Style") told me, "The outdoor scenes weren't actually shot on a beach. They created a sandy walled-in area—a kind of berm in Burbank where all of those exterior scenes were shot." Bilson also recalled, "To save time filming the interior scenes, the set was ingeniously constructed so that scenery could merely be raised instead of broken down." In an episode titled "Don't Defrost the Alligator," guest star Marvin Kaplan recalled, "That really was a full-sized alligator on the set. The alligator was ushered in on a leash by a young actor playing a Western Union messenger. Not only weren't its jaws muzzled, but one also had to be careful of getting a good whack from its powerful tail. All of us, especially Sally Field and I, kept our distance."

Actress Beverly Washburn, who guest starred in two episodes of the show ("Slumber Party," and "Take a Lesson"), told me, "Sally Field's stepfather, Jock Mahoney, got me started in the business. He had seen me perform in a show at a Veteran's Hospital, and a short time later I ran into him again when I was auditioning for a part which I was unlikely to get. Well, Jock, out of the kindness of his heart, used his influence and swayed the producers into giving me a shot in a movie called *The Killer That Stalked New York*."

Guest stars included Paul Lynde, Daniel J. Travanti, Dick Gautier, Richard Dreyfuss, Martin Milner, Harvey Korman, Bonnie Franklin, and Judy Carne. Judy Carne and Peter Deuel would later meet up again in *Love on a Rooftop*.

The producer was William Sackheim; the executive producer was Harry Ackerman; writers included Ruth Brooks Flippen, Austin and Irma Kalish, Albert Mannheimer, Frederick Kohner, Barbara Avedon, Stephen Kandel, John McGreevey, Louella MacFarlane, A. J. Mady, Tony Wilson, Martin A. Ragaway, Pauline and Leo Townsend, Dorothy Cooper Foote, Joanna Lee, Lee Karson, Don Richman, Janet Carlson, and Gary Flaum; and directors included William Asher, Oscar Rudolph, Jerry Bernstein, E. W. Swackhamer, Gene Reynolds, Bruce Bilson, Hal Cooper, Christopher Cary, and Don Porter. The theme song was written by Howard Greenfield and Jack Keller, and was performed by The Four Freshmen in the pilot, but rather by Johnny Tillotson for the series (from the MGM album "Johnny Tillotson Sings"). The original pilot was merely a longer, unedited version of what became the debut episode, "Dear Diary." In 1986, an updated syndicated version called *The New Gidget*, starring Caryn Richman in the title role, ran for two seasons. Director Bruce Bilson told me, "I also directed the pilot for this sequel. We shot that in Hawaii, not Burbank." A DVD box set containing every original ABC episode is available from Sony Entertainment. Two Gidget comic books were released by Dell Comics, selling for twelve cents each.

The Girl with Something Extra Thornhill Productions/Screen Gems. NBC. Friday nights 8:30 (September 14, 1973–December 28, 1973), and Friday nights 9:00 (January 4, 1974–May 24, 1974). 22 color episodes were filmed with a laugh track.

It wasn't *When Harry Met Sally*, but rather "when John met Sally." On this show they used their real first names—John Davidson played John Burton, and Sally Field was the future Sally Burton. They met at an art exhibit. John knew instantly that there was something "special" about Sally, and she secretly knew that he was attracted to her. Even though John claimed that he didn't wish to be married for another 40 years, a very short time later they became husband and wife. It was on their wedding night (in the debut titled "Sally on My Mind") when Sally made that huge confession (much like Samantha did on *Bewitched*). Sally had a special power: she could read minds—some people none of the time, some people some of the time, and some people most of the time. John fell into the latter category and instantly a lot of things from their whirlwind courtship made sense to him. She could read his mind most of the time if he was with her (she couldn't read his mind when he was away). He was ill-at-ease with this; the uneven, unfair advantage she had in this relationship created most of the comedy. John's brother, Jerry the gambler (Jack Sheldon), was the only person John told about Sally's abilities. Jerry wanted Sally to use her powers to win big on a TV game show, at the horse track, and in a chess match with Bobby Fischer. Although most of the shows focused upon the couple's home life, John did have a job as an attorney at Metcalf, Kline and Associates. His boss was Owen Metcalf (Henry Jones), and his secretary was named Angela (Stephanie Edwards). Stephanie Edwards shared, "I don't think my character even had a last name—she was added midseason." Also in the cast was Sally's best friend, the very single Anne, played by Zohra Lampert.

Episodes include the "Everything You Wanted to Hide and Couldn't," in which John became embarrassed when he realized that Sally knew what he was thinking about other women (and also about his childhood crush on Annette Funicello). In "How Green Was Las Vegas," Sally threw her ethics aside to help Jerry win big at the tables in Sin City. In "All the Nudes That's Fit to Print," John was approached by a famous women's magazine to pose as their naked centerfold (he also later did this in real life). Edwards told me, "I made the mistake of mentioning that I played trombone in my high school band. Wouldn't you know it—they had me play that trombone in one of the episodes in front of Jack Sheldon, as well as Sally and John. I didn't know it at the time (and was surprised years later when I was a guest on *The Merv Griffin Show*) but Jack Sheldon (who played Jerry on our show) was a brilliant musician and bandleader. Had I know this then, I would've been too scared to play in front of him."

The program was created by Bernard Slade. Both *The Girl with Something Extra* and *Getting Together* were produced by Thornhill Productions, and Slade told me, "Thornhill was my production company." The program was produced by Larry Rosen (except for the debut episode which was produced by Mel Swope); writers included Slade, Warren S. Murray, Earl Barret, Stan Cutler, Dick Bensfield, Steve Zacharias, Perry Grant, William Davenport, Dale McRaven, Gordon "Whitey" Mitchell, Lou Derman, Everett Greenbaum, Jim Fritzell, and Lloyd Turner; and directors included Bob Claver, Charles Rondeau, Richard Kinon, Leo Penn, E. W. Swackhamer, William Wiard, Roger Duchowny, John Erman, and Alan Rafkin. Music was provided by Dave Grusin. Sally Field's transition to motion pictures proved to be magical—she went on to garner two Academy Awards for best actress (*Norma Rae* and *Places in the Heart*). Reruns were briefly shown on the USA Network. Stephanie Edwards told me, "We were really high on the idea of doing a second season. There was even talk of building up my character, but then we were abruptly and surprisingly cancelled. That's show biz."

The Girls (see *Young and Gay*)

Glynis Desilu Studios. An Esco Production. CBS. Wednesday nights 8:30. September 25, 1963–December 18, 1963. 13 black-and-white episodes were filmed with a laugh track. Sponsors included Lifebuoy Soap, R. J. Reynolds Tobacco, Ralston Purina, and Jello.

Most shows of this era were given a full season to prove themselves and find an audience. Such was not the case with *Glynis*, which was abruptly canceled after 13 weeks. Basically, this was *Murder, She Wrote*'s earlier comic cousin. The action took place in San Diego, California. British actress Glynis Johns played Glynis Granville, a neophyte mystery writer and amateur sleuth. Keith Andes was her attorney husband (and partner in crime-solving), Keith Granville. The childless couple always seemed to stumble upon the solution to a mystery, but certainly not without putting themselves in great peril.

The show began in a rather unconventional way—it was part of a summer run of pilots under the umbrella heading of *Vacation Playhouse*. The pilot episode was called "Hide and Seek," and it aired on August 5, 1963. The original working title for the series was to be *The Glynis Johns Show*, which was shortened to simply *Glynis* at the last minute. Only a few weeks after the pilot, the series made its official debut—with a couple of changes. In the pilot, Keith Andes's first name was John, but since Glynis used her real first name in the series, it made sense for Keith to do the same. Also, Michael Constantine, who was in the pilot, was replaced by George Mathews as Chick Rogers, a retired cop who acted as Glynis' crime consultant.

The best episodes had great guest stars. In "Three Men in a Tub," Harvey Korman portrayed Ken Bradford who was accused of foul play when his uncle disappeared. Ken was a prime suspect because he was the uncle's sole heir. In "A Little Knowledge Is Fatal," John Dehner played Willie the Fink, whose bookmaking operation was discovered by Glynis. Jack Albertson appeared in "The Pros and Cons" as Al, one of three convicts trying to go straight.

Directors included E. W. Swackhamer and Felix Feist; writers included Jerry Seelen, Elroy Schwartz, Leo Rifkin, Arthur Julian, and Jess Oppenheimer. Oppenheimer was also the producer.

This series was replaced by the short-lived *Tell It to the Camera* with Red Rowe. Eight of the original thirteen episodes of *Glynis* were rerun in prime time from July to September of 1965 in *The Lucy Show's* regular spot. In this time slot, *Glynis* ranked in the top ten. Glynis Johns attempted sitcom stardom again in 1988 in the short-lived *Coming of Age*.

Going My Way My Way Productions/Revue Studios-MCA. ABC. Wednesday nights 8:30. October 3, 1962–September 11, 1963. 30 hour-long episodes were filmed without a laugh track. Sponsors included The American Tobacco Company, Breck Shampoo, and Miles Laboratories.

This is the kind of show we would later dub a "dramedy." It is yet another example of an Academy Award-winning film which failed when adapted for television. Bing Crosby and Barry Fitzgerald starred in the motion picture, and some equally capable big names headed this version on the small screen which came to TV in a rather unorthodox way—no pilot episode was required. Gene Kelly played Father Chuck O'Malley, a young priest sent to the slums of New York's St. Dominic's Parish. Kelly borrowed from his own father's Irish speech patterns for the role. There was an instantaneous clash of progressive and conservative ideology as O'Malley attempted to be patient and understanding with the very staid and stubborn Father Fitzgibbon (Leo G. Carroll). Allegedly, Carroll was very fond of singing, and with very little provocation would burst into song between takes on the set (he also sings in the debut, "Back to Ballymora"). Nydia Westman played Mrs. Featherstone, the housekeeper at the rectory, and a young Dick York portrayed Tom Colwell—in charge of the wayward "Boys Club" at the parish's community center. Child actor John Eimen (who appeared in two episodes—"The Parish Car" and "A Tough Act to Follow") told me about working with Dick York: "He was very intense, focused on his role ... a very fine actor." Eimen also spoke about the rest of the cast: "I was thrilled to be working on a show with the great Gene Kelly and the wonderful Leo G. Carroll from one of my favorite shows, *Topper*." Also, appearing frequently was Regis Toomey as J. W. Dawson, director of the Boys Club.

Having Kelly in the cast certainly assisted in getting many big name guest stars, such as Harry Morgan, Eddie Bracken, George Kennedy, Anne Francis, Jack Warden, Dan Duryea, Keir Dullea, James Dunn, Cloris Leachman, Billy Mumy, Beverly Garland, James Whitmore, Michael J. Pollard, Jane Wyatt, Richard Denning, William Demarest, Pat O'Brien, Ray Walston, Anthony Eisley, and Richard Long.

The program was produced by Joe Connelly; writers included Emmet Lavery, Juanita Vaughn, Dale and Katherine Eunson, Carey Wilber, William Fay, Mark Weingart, Robert Hardy Andrews, Richard Baer, George Tibbles, Lewis Reed, Malcolm Stuart Boylan, James O'Hanlon, Mel Goldberg, Bob Mosher, and Joe Connelly; and directors included Joe Pevney (Joe's son, Jeff appeared as one of the community center boys), Fielder Cook, Alan Crosland, Jr., Robert Florey, James Sheldon, Allen Reisner, Herman Hoffman, Felix Feist, Paul Stewart, Alex March, Bernard Girard, and Paul Stanley. Music was provided by Cyril Mockridge. A *Going My Way* DVD box set is available from Timeless Media.

Goldie (see *The Betty Hutton Show*)

Good Heavens Columbia Pictures Television. ABC. Monday nights 8:30 (March 8. 1976–April 5, 1976), and Saturday nights 8:00 (May 22, 1976–June 26, 1976). 12 color episodes were filmed with a laugh track.

Good Heavens went through a few changes between the pilot and the actual series. The unaired pilot was titled "Everything Money Can't Buy," and it starred Jose Ferrer as Mr. Angel. Mr. Angel wore business attire and was sent back to Earth in the afterlife to reward good deeds. In the pilot, the recipient of the reward was a greasy spoon waitress named Doris (Brenda Vaccaro). On the way to work one morning, Doris gave up her seat on the bus to an elderly gentleman and immediately heard harp music. Shortly thereafter, she came face-to-face with Mr. Angel who acknowledged her good deed and told her to make a wish—but the wish had to be something that money couldn't buy. Her wish was to meet a handsome "Pseudo Sir Lancelot" to sweep her off her feet. She met her alleged "Mr. Right" (golf pro Chris Livingston, played by Bert Convy), only to realize at the altar that her real and true Mr. Right was her old boyfriend, the slovenly Ernie (Peter Bonerz). The moral of the story ("appreciate what you've got") carried through most of the episodes of the actual series. Once a series, however, the title became *Good Heavens*, and the star of the show was also its executive producer and sometimes director Carl Reiner. Reiner told me, "They asked me to play the angel in the series because they thought Jose Ferrer wasn't charming enough. I really didn't want to do it at first, but Jose said that I could do charming a lot better than he, and he talked me into it." Reiner's Mr. Angel was the only recurring character on the show; every episode had a totally new storyline and a totally new ensemble of actors—sort of a "comedy anthology." As in the pilot, Mr. Angel wore business attire and had no visible wings.

Episodes include "See Jane Run" (directed by Reiner), in which Florence Henderson had dual roles as twins Julia and Jane who were separated at birth. After an act of kindness at her job in Mr. D's Dress Shop, Julia was visited by Mr. Angel. Her wish was to finally meet her long-lost sister Jane—a decision she'd later rue when Jane's unsavory past was revealed. In "Coffee, Tea, or Gloria," a doctor named Brad (Dean Jones) did a good deed by returning a lost prescription for eyeglasses to its rightful owner and was then visited by Mr. Angel. Brad's wish was to know what it would have been like had he married his first love, Gloria (Sue Ane Landgon), instead of his wife, Joanne (Marcia Rodd). After the experience, he realized how lucky he was to have Joanne in his life. Carl Reiner's real-life son, Rob, and daughter-in-law (at that time) Penny Marshall appeared in the episode, "Take Me Out to the Ball Game," in which a sporting goods store clerk finally got to see what playing major league baseball was all about, and soon longed to get his old life back. Reiner fondly recalled the episode called "Good Neighbor Maxine," with guest stars Loretta Swit and Clu Gulager. Carl related, "Inspired by a real life event in which actress Eva Marie Saint was stung by a bee on her lip, Loretta Swit's Maxine character was also stung on the lip by a bee. Clu Gulager's character, Jim Pearson, treats it like a snake bite, sucks out the poison from her bottom lip, the two kiss and fall in love."

The program was produced by Austin and Irma Kalish; the creator was Bernard Slade. Because Reiner only appeared in the opening and closing scene each week, I asked Mr. Slade if the show was shot out of sequence and he said, "Yes, it was shot like a movie." Writers included Bob Fisher, Slade, Arthur Marx, Austin and Irma Kalish, Seaman Jacobs, and Fred Fox; directors included Reiner, Mel Swope, and Bud Molin. Music was provided by Pat Williams (which explains why it sounds so much like *The Mary Tyler Moore Show*). Reiner told me, "When the series ended, they let me keep the tan fedora I wore in the series. When I was given a star on the Hollywood Walk of Fame, the picture they used for a series of souvenir Hollywood trading cards is a picture of me wearing that hat on *Good Heavens*." Many episodes of the series are available for viewing in the UCLA TV Archives.

The Good Life Lee Rich Productions/Screen Gems. NBC. Saturday nights 8:30. September 18, 1971–January 8, 1972. 15 color episodes were filmed with a laugh track.

Not to be confused with the later John Caponera/Drew Carey sitcom called *The Good Life*, this one starred Larry Hagman in between his successes on *I Dream of Jeannie* and *Dallas*, and was based upon the book by Douglass Wallop. Hagman, along with Donna Mills, portrayed the middle-class Millers (Albert and Jane) who didn't like the direction their harried Wall Street lives had taken. In the words of Albert, "There's got to be a better way." That "better way" became obvious when their car broke down one day and they were taken, by a kindly butler, to the mansion where he was employed. From there they made a phone call to a tow company. However, while there, they saw the opulence of the butler's living quarters in the mansion and decided to become domestics as well. Even though they had no experience in the field, they were able to secure live-in employment at the Dutton Estate, owned by the often inebriated wealthy industrialist Charles Dutton (David Wayne). Mr. Dutton took an instant liking to the couple, as did his son with his third wife, Nick (Danny Goldman). This was very fortunate because Nick happened to hear the couple discussing their lack of experience on the intercom system, but he didn't snitch to his dad. Mr. Dutton's sister, Grace Dutton (played in the pilot by Kate Reed, but by Hermione Baddeley in the series), had little patience for the couple's mistakes and wanted nothing more than to get them fired. Danny Goldman told me, "Kate Reed was a wonderful serious actress, but they were looking for someone dizzier, and Hermione Baddeley was the ideal choice." Danny also had a couple of great stories about his audition for the show: "They liked my comic timing and decided to take it to the next level and gave me a live audition, working with Larry Hagman. Larry wanted to have his back to the audience so as to not upstage me, but I begged him not to do that. He was a bit taken aback as he thought he was doing me a favor, but I did get the part. I found out years later that I was up against Mark Hamill for the role. Mark, of course, would later go on to *Star Wars*." Danny also had another interesting observation: "The Millers weren't allowed to call the Duttons millionaires. It had something to do with standards and practices. Maybe they thought the show might offend millionaires, so we were gazillionaires."

Episodes include the debut "One of Our Rolls Is Missing," in which a dinner party for 15 proved to be overwhelming, so the Millers ordered out. However, the food was late in coming, and when they opted to instead pick up the order themselves, an automobile accident sent food everywhere except to the Dutton's table. In "Jane's Double Life," Jane became Nick's surrogate date for an elegant ball, but trouble began brewing when a handsome multi-millionaire named Rico (Alejandro Rey) tried to sweep her off her feet. In "Butterfield Ate," the Millers were asked to babysit for a neighbor's full-grown lion. Danny Goldman recalled, "While waiting around for rehearsals or filming to begin, one could always hear classical music blasting from Larry Hagman's trailer."

The program was created by Fred Freeman and Lawrence J. Cohen; the producer was Claudio Guzman; the executive producer was Lee Rich; writers included Gordon "Whitey"

Mitchell, Lloyd Turner, Cohen, Freeman, Albert Lewin, William Raynor, Myles Wilder, Susan Harris, William S. Bickley, Art Baer, Ben Joelson, and Ron Friedman; and directors included Hy Averback, Bruce Bilson, Charles Rondeau, Joseph Goodson, Hal Cooper, Ron Winston, Claudio Guzman, Larry Hagman, and Jay Sandrich. The theme song, "The Good Life," was performed by Tony Orlando and Dawn. Goldman remembered, "The exterior scenes of the Dutton Estate were actually shot at a large home in Pasadena, California."

Good Morning, World Discus Productions/ Paramount Studios. CBS. Tuesday nights 9:30. September 5, 1967–September 17, 1968. 26 color episodes were filmed before a live audience. Sponsors included Scope Mouthwash and Joy Dishwashing Liquid.

"Good morning, World" was a phrase uttered regularly by radio legend William B. Williams. It also became the title of a sitcom from the same people who brought us *The Dick Van Dyke Show*, though it was much less successful. This was the story of two morning disc jockeys named Lewis and Clark, who got their start at a small radio station in Hawaii. Dave Lewis was played by Joby Baker and Larry Clark was played by Ronnie Schell, on temporary "leave" from *Gomer Pyle, USMC.* While on vacation in Hawaii, a Los Angeles radio station manager named Roland B. Hutton, Jr. (Billy DeWolfe) heard *The Lewis and Clark Show*, and offered them two-and-a-half times what they were making, and a shot at success in the #2 radio market in the country. Before taking the job, Dave married the Hawaiian radio station's switchboard operator, Linda (Julie Parrish), at the Prince Kalahuli Tiki Lodge, and they all moved to Southern California. Larry remained single and moved into a swinging bachelor pad of his own. Meanwhile, Dave and Linda moved into a beautiful apartment (1B), where their new neighbor was cheerful and dizzy Sandy Kramer (Goldie Hawn). Sandy hooked up with Larry, and the two couples went on a lot of double dates. Carl Reiner recalled, "Goldie Hawn was quite a find. During the run of the show, George Schlatter 'borrowed' her for *Rowan and Martin's Laugh-in*, and never gave her back to us." However, most of the show's action was centered upon the radio station and the goings-on in Studio B, the very tenuous relationship between Larry and Mr. Hutton, and the difficulties in keeping egos in check on a two-man big city morning radio show. Joby Baker and Ronnie Schell got a feel for Los Angeles radio for real when they filled in for vacationing Lohman and Barkley on KFWB for one week early in *Good Morning, World's* run.

Episodes include "You vs. Me," in which both Larry Clark and David Lewis received nominations for a "Best Radio Personality" award. The problem was that they weren't nominated as a team, but rather, separately—one could win and one could lose. Luckily, neither of them won. In "Don't Call Us, We Won't Call You," Dave and Larry attempted to get out of doing a charity event—that is, until they found out that a lot of big names were scheduled to appear. Carl Reiner and Andy Griffith made cameo appearances in that episode. In "You Can't Say That about My Wife and Neither Can I," Dave's radio job and his life at home intermingled when his on-air "wife jokes" offended his wife Linda. Jackie Joseph had a big guest-starring role in an episode titled, "The Return of Bibian." She told me, "This was the best sitcom job ever. I had no idea it was such a big part until I went in for the table read. It was both thrilling and terrifying—the whole show was about Bibian." It just so happened, that week was not the happiest week for the cast. Jackie recalled, "During our rehearsal week, the show was canceled. Ronnie Schell nearly had a breakdown and kept wailing, 'No, no.'" Jackie tried to lighten the mood with a joke, and she told Ronnie, "Don't worry, Ronnie, Lassie will save you. Well, he cracked up so much at that line, he was able to carry on."

It was no secret that there were a few problems on the set—before the show went into production, Julie Parrish had a stroke and never again had the same energy she had in the pilot. Jackie Joseph recalled another "situation" in this situation comedy: "Joby Baker was a good friend and an incredibly talented performer, but something within him resisted learning lines. He just couldn't retain them."

The program was created by Bill Persky and Sam Denoff, who also served as producers; the executive producers were Carl Reiner and Sheldon Leonard; writers included Saul Turteltaub, Bernie Orenstein, Rick Mittleman, Jack Winter, Persky, Sam Denoff, Peggy Elliott, Ed Scharlach, Joseph Bonaduce, Carl Kleinschmidt, Dale McRaven, Bruce Howard, Sydney Zelinka, Jim Brooks, E. Duke Vincent, Bill Idelson, Sam Bobrick, Ronny Perlman, and Bruce Johnson; and directors included Gary Nelson, George Tyne,

Reiner, Danny Dayton, Robert Scheerer, and John Rich. Music was provided by Dave Grusin. The record playing in the opening and closing credits of the show was on the Columbia record label—appropriate because the program aired on CBS. Every episode is available in a DVD box set from S'More Entertainment.

Grady Bud Yorkin Productions, Inc./Tandem Productions. NBC. Thursday nights 8:00 (December 4, 1975–December 25, 1975), and Thursday nights 8:30 (January 1, 1976–March 4, 1976). 12 episodes were videotaped before a live audience, only ten aired.

Grady Wilson was one of Fred Sanford's best friends on *Sanford and Son*. Late in 1975, Grady (Whitman Mayo) got his own spinoff series (albeit briefly). It's interesting to note that Whitman Mayo didn't start out as an actor, but rather as an agent in New York City during a period in which there was a lot of interest in African American performers. He often submitted himself for choice roles instead of the actors he was representing. He snagged the choice role of Grady on *Sanford and Son* and never looked back. He was able to carry it off pretty well as a recurring character on *Sanford and Son*, but carrying his own show proved to be quite another story.

The opening credits for *Grady* showed him hopping on bus after bus to make the big move from Watts to a racially diverse middle class neighborhood at 636 Carlisle Street in Santa Monica to live with his daughter Ellie Wilson Marshall (Carole Cole); his schoolteacher son-in-law Hal Marshall (Joe Morton); and his grandchildren Laurie (Rosanne Katon) and Heywood Marshall (Heywood Nelson). Jack Fletcher played the prissy landlord Mr. Pratt (who lived only three houses down). There was an immediate problem with the Marshall family's new house—a deranged old man, Mr. Beardsley (Eric Christmas), who thought World War II was still going on, living in Grady's room and awaiting the arrival of the Japanese. When this old man was confronted by Grady, he had a heart attack and died. Fred Sanford (Redd Foxx) made a guest appearance on that debut episode of *Grady*, and upon seeing an ambulance leaving the Marshall's house he was told that an old man had died there. Comedy ensued as Fred, of course, thought that the old man who had passed on was Grady.

The Marshalls also had some kooky neighbors—Rose and George Kosinsky (Alix Elias and George Dzundza, respectively). George was an undercover policeman and Rose was a cheerful busybody who was always borrowing something. Dzundza left the show very early in its run, but his absence was never explained (Alix Elias continued in the role of Rose). Alix recalled, "I didn't know if I was a deserted wife or widow. There was a lot of confusion about who we were and what we were to play."

The show had a very brief run, but did manage to squeeze in a holiday episode titled "Merry Birthday, Happy Christmas." The widower Grady did get married on the show—well, at least in his daughter Ellie's dream (in the episode titled "Grady Takes a Wife") which occurred while she was awaiting his return from a vacation in Las Vegas. Her dream had him tying the knot with a circus performer.

The program was produced by Howard Leeds and Jerry Ross. The executive producers were Bud Yorkin, Saul Turteltaub and Bernie Orenstein, whose aim was to create a show during which, if one closed one's eyes, it would be difficult to figure out if the family was black or white. Writers included Ben Joelson and Art Baer; directors included Burt Brinckerhoff. Music was provided by John Addison. The debut titled "Be It Ever So Humble," was later placed into syndication as an episode of *Sanford and Son*. Grady would later return to *Sanford and Son*, and even stick around for the short-lived sequel called *The Sanford Arms*. Elias said about the show's demise, "We all saw the end coming. We tried to stave it off because of the money—everyone was trying to keep the gravy train going. We'd do anything, play anything they wanted just to keep the show afloat, but there was really not much we could do. I do remember that Jack Fletcher, Heywood Nelson, and Joe Morton all handled it with real gentility and dignity. I hope I behaved as well."

TV Land reran one episode of this show as part of a tribute to Norman Lear.

Grandpa Goes to Washington Paramount Studios. NBC. Tuesday nights 8:00. September 7, 1978–January 16, 1979. 11 hour-long episodes were filmed with a laugh track.

After the demise of *Chico and the Man*, NBC found another comedy vehicle for Jack Albertson: *Grandpa Goes to Washington*. This was an hour-long sitcom which, much like most other hour-long sitcoms, failed to catch on. Albertson portrayed a widower named Josephus "Joe" Kelley (of the Boston Kelleys), who formerly taught political science, but had to retire at the mandatory age of 66. The thing is, Joe wasn't ready to retire, so he sought political office and, as luck would have it, his two opponents were exposed as crooks, paving his way to the senate. Joe was certainly not your average senator—he drove a Volkswagen convertible, he played and occasionally taught the drums, he was proudest of his "friends in low places," and he was completely and totally honest. At least temporarily, Joe lived in a spare room above a garage where an airplane was housed. In the main part of that same house lived his son, Kevin, a milquetoast two-star Air Force General whom dad called "Fathead" (Larry Linville); Kevin's wife, Rosie, the health food nut (among her specialties were poached zucchini and rhubarb mousse), played by Sue Ane Langdon; and their children Kathleen (who supported very hip causes like the preservation of nude beaches), played by Michele Tobin, and Kevin, Jr. (who loved baseball), played by Sparky Marcus. At the office, Joe's overworked African American secretary Madge (she was always threatening to quit) was played by Madge Sinclair.

In the debut, Senator Kelley looked into the plans of a landowner named Mr. Green (Conrad Bain). The impatient Mr. Green claimed he was intending to build condominiums on the land currently occupied by Kelley's grandson Kevin Jr.'s baseball team (and he wouldn't even consider waiting two weeks before excavating so that the team could finish up their season unless he was paid $28,000). Senator Kelley then discovered that the plans for the condos were merely a ploy to jack up the price of the land for developers who wanted to put a mosque on that same lot.

The program was produced by Robert Stambler; the executive producers were Richard P. Rosetti and Leonora Thuna; writers included Barbara Avedon, Barbara Corday, Lane Slate, Noel Baldwin, Emily Levine, Harry Cauley, Leonora Thuna, Harry Spalding, John Dunkel, Bruce Taylor, and Paul West; and directors included Richard Crenna, Michael Caffey, Herbert Kenwith, Paul Stanley, George Tyne, Allen Baron, Joseph Pevney, and Larry Elikann. Music was provided by Artie Butler. This show shouldn't be confused with *Mr. Smith Goes to Washington*, which starred Fess Parker. One rerun episode aired on TV Land.

The Great Gildersleeve Hal Roach Studios. First-run syndication. 1955–1956. 39 black-and-white episodes were filmed with a laugh track.

In 1941, *The Great Gildersleeve* (on radio) became one of the first truly successful spin-offs in broadcast history. Gildersleeve had previously been a long-running character on the radio version of *Fibber McGee and Molly*. There were even four "Gildersleeve" motion pictures filmed in the early 1940s. In 1955, Gildersleeve was brought to television (albeit briefly). On radio, he'd been portrayed by both Harold Peary and later by Willard Waterman (who took the lead role in the television adaptation). It was purely coincidental that a man named "Waterman" would portray the Water Commissioner of Summerfield, Throckmorton P. Gildersleeve. He was called "Gildy" for short. The tall, rotund, mustachioed, cigar-chomping Gildersleeve had an orphaned niece and nephew in his ward—pretty teenager Marjorie Forrester (Stephanie Griffin) and her mischievous younger brother Leroy (Ronald Keith). Whenever Leroy misbehaved, Uncle Throckmorton would let out an elongated and quavering, "Leeeeeeeroyyyyyyyyyyy." Leroy called him "Unc." Gildy would also emit some interesting sounds when in the presence of beautiful women (mostly high-pitched sighs). Helping out around the Gildersleeve household at 217 Elm Street was Birdie Lee Coggins, his African American housekeeper played by Lillian Randolph. Others in the cast, seen less frequently, were Willis Bouchey as Mayor Terwilliger (Gildy's boss); Forrest Lewis as Mr. Peavey (Summerfield's pharmacist); Barbara Stuart as Bessie (Gildy's young secretary); and Doris Singleton as Lois (Gildy's regular girlfriend).

In the debut titled "Gildy Goes Broke," Uncle Throckmorton chastised young Leroy for spending all of his money on an opportunistic little girl named Brenda Knickerbocker (Mary Jane Saunders). When Gildy went to confront the girl's mother, the lovely Ellen Knickerbocker (Dorothy Green), he fell into the same trap and ended up spending a large amount of cash on the woman (the running theme being "like uncle, like nephew").

The program was produced by Matthew Rapf; writers included Andy White, John Elliotte, Jay Sommers, Don Nelson, Jerry Davis, Joseph Calvelli, and Richard Baer; and directors included Robert S. Finkel and Charles Barton. This program had the exact same theme song as another Hal Roach Studios show, the 1957 version of *Blondie*. Unfortunately, *Fibber McGee and Molly* and *The Great Gildersleeve* were unable to make the successful transition from radio to television. Reruns of *The Great Gildersleeve* ran in the early 1990s on the now-defunct "Nostalgia" cable network. Several episodes are available on DVD from Alpha Video.

Grindl A David Swift Production/Screen Gems. NBC. Sunday nights 8:30. September 15, 1963–September 13, 1964. 32 black-and-white episodes were filmed with a laugh track. Sponsors included Gleem Toothpaste, Lilt Home Permanents, and Thrill Dishwashing Liquid.

In between *Your Show of Shows* and *It's About Time*, Imogene Coca starred in this unusual sitcom with only two regular stars. James Millhollin played Anson Foster, the head of the Foster Temporary Employment Agency, and Imogene Coca played Grindl (although Mary Grace Canfield had the title role in the unaired pilot). CBS originally showed interest in the show, but it went to NBC. We never did find out Grindl's full name. Even in an episode in which she was being interrogated by the police, she told them her name was Grindl, and they seemed totally satisfied with that information. One can only assume that Grindl was her first name by a couple of episode titles, like "Lady Grindl" and "Aunt Grindl." Grindl was, for all intents and purposes, a "Jill-of-all-trades." Mr. Foster farmed her out to a new job, a new set of circumstances, and a new set of faces each week. Mostly, she did housekeeping work, but at times she was also a babysitter, receptionist, bookstore clerk, bank teller, gift-wrapper, nurse, telephone answerer, and vacuum cleaner salesperson. Almost every week, Grindl's latest job somehow involved great peril from counterfeiters, teenage thugs, bank robbers, mad bombers, kleptomaniacs, and even the infamous "Moon Killer."

Guest stars included Telly Savalas as Hartman in the debut titled "The Gruesome Basement"; Paul Lynde guest starred as Mr. Inchback in the holiday episode titled "'Twas the Week before Christmas"; Herschel Bernardi played a gambler named Joe Bostick in "The Lucky Piece"; and Frank Aletter, later Imogene Coca's co-star in *It's About Time*, played Mr. Sterling in the episode called "Active Retirement."

The program was a David Swift Production; the executive producer was Harry Ackerman; writers included James and George O'Hanlon, Swift, Joe Bigelow, Lee Loeb, Jay Sommers, Ray Singer, John McGreevey, Burt Styler, Albert Lewin, Bud Grossman, and William Davenport; directors included Paul Nickell, Sherman Marks, Stanley Prager, and Charles Barton.

The program employed two different openings—one in which Grindl was seen walking down the street holding her ever-ready umbrella; the other was animated with Grindl featured in a maid's uniform. It should be noted that the character of Grindl was not unlike the character Dorkus, which Imogene portrayed in the Jack Lemmon movie *Under the Yum Yum Tree.*

The Growing Paynes DuMont. Wednesday nights 8:30. October 20, 1948–August 3, 1949. Sponsors included John Wanamaker in association with Frank M. Whiting and Company. Broadcast live without a laugh track.

This *Growing Paynes* had absolutely no connection to the Alan Thicke and Kirk Cameron *Growing Pains* which came decades later. This was one of television's earliest sitcoms (they were actually called "domestic comedies" back then) for the short-lived DuMont Network. Every expense was spared in creating the sets for this series—some of the starkest sets in TV history, accompanied by obviously hand-drawn credits. The program starred Elaine Stritch as Ellie Payne, the sensible and long-suffering wife of the bumbling, dimwitted George Payne (Ed Holmes). John Harvey and Judy Parrish had originated the roles of the Paynes in a local version of *The Growing Paynes* before it became a national broadcast. George sold insurance and worked for the cantankerous, cigar-chomping Mr. Cartwright (Edward Cullen), but was continually falling for get-rich-quick schemes, only to be bailed out at the last possible nanosecond. Luring George into those get-rich-quick schemes was usually his friend Jim Garson (Donald Curtis). The Paynes also had a very inquisitive son named Johnny (David Anderson).

A couple of rough old kinescopes are available for viewing at the Paley Center for Media. In one untitled episode, George Payne and Jim Garson almost fell for an insurance scam in the South American countries of Peru, Paraguay and Bolivia. George and Jim were going to move there and corner the market on car insurance—that is, until Ellie, the voice of reason, delivered the factual bombshell that only a very small percentage of people in those countries have automobiles. In yet another untitled episode, Ellie was away for a few weeks, and in her stead George Payne hired an elderly, cranky, irascible woman (however, she was a great cook) named Abigail Sneed, played by Georgia Simmons as a temporary housekeeper. This intolerable woman became a heroine at the end of the episode when she recognized the man with whom George was about to do business as a wanted felon nicknamed "Confidence Al Orwell" (Blair Davies) and called the police.

The program employed George with a unique sense of humor—sarcasm delivered in a whisper. For example, when he presented a new client with a cigar, the client said that it must have cost a pretty penny, to which George whispered, "A pretty quarter." When George asked a potential client what he did for a living, the response was, "I market a lot of stuff," to which George whispered, "You've cornered the stuff market." The program was directed by Pat Fay; the writer and creator was A. S. Ginnes. Scoring for the show was provided by an uncredited organist (used to accentuate various scenes).

Guestward Ho A Desilu Production. ABC. Thursday nights 7:30. September 29, 1960–September 21, 1961. 38 black-and-white episodes were filmed. Sponsors were Ralston-Purina and Seven-up.

This charming sitcom went through a lot just to become a series. The first pilot didn't sell. In that first pilot, Vivian Vance played Babs Hooton and Leif Erickson played her husband, Bill. However, it was thought by the powers that be that the couple should be more youthful, so Vivian Vance was replaced by Joanne Dru (sister of game show host Peter Marshall). Dru had previously appeared in the unsold pilot called *Adventures of a Model* for Desilu. Her husband, Bill, was now to be played by Mark Miller.

Here's the plot: based upon the book by Patrick Dennis and Barbara Hooton titled *Guestward Ho*, Bill Hooton bought a dude ranch called Guestward Ho in Santa Fe, New Mexico, without first having consulted his wife. Wife Babs hated the idea of leaving the big city, but agreed to "give it a year" because she loved her husband very much, and she knew how much he wanted to return to the area in which he was born and raised. As expected, both she and their son Brook (Flip Mark) were like fish out of water in the desert of New Mexico. In the pilot, the Hootons had a dog named Gilbert, but no children.

Inspired by Sir Thomas Wolfe, the episode "You Can't Go Home Again" proved just that. Upon arrival, Bill realized that so much had changed since he lived there last—the people, the soda shop, even the rock upon which he carved his initials (it was about to be blasted to smithereens by a construction crew).

Long before Alan Alda was Hawkeye on *M*A*S*H*, brilliant character actor J. Carroll Naish was Hawkeye—an opportunistic Native American who had a trading post and set up a souvenir stand at Guestward Ho. His stand had a lot of "questionable" items for sale which he claimed to be authentic pieces of history. Jolene Brand played his assistant Pink Cloud. Long and lanky Earle Hodgins played the ranch foreman, simply known as "Lonesome."

Some of the best episodes include "The Thanksgiving Story," in which Bill refused to pay for a store bought turkey from Hawkeye and opted to shoot his own. Little did he realize how very scarce turkeys were in the New Mexico desert. In "Babs and the Lion," which borrowed the story from the original Vivian Vance pilot, Bill tried to hide the news of the sighting of a vicious mountain lion in the area for fear the news would drive Babs back to New York City for certain.

Guest stars included Natalie Schaefer as Mrs. Crawford, who visited her daughter in "Babs's Mother"; Richard Deacon played Mr. Andrews in "Too Many Cooks"; Adam West appeared in "Bill the Fireman"; ZaSu Pitts made Lonesome feel less lonesome in the episode titled "Lonesome's Gal"; and Louis Nye appeared as King Cool in one of the final episodes, "The Beatniks."

Directors included Claudio Guzman, Fred DeCordova, James Sheldon, and Desi Arnaz; writers included Arthur Julian and Ronald Alexander. The theme song and its clever lyrics were written by Arthur Hamilton.

The October 10, 1960, issue of *Time* magazine reviewed the show this way: "*Guestward Ho* (ABC), a series based on a book by Patrick Dennis and Barbara Hooton, follows a New York Family to New Mexico, where they open a dude ranch. The first episode was as dull as the wrinkled eyelid of a Gila monster. The family struggled to clean up their rundown property, meanwhile trying to avoid being cleaned out by a shrewd Indian called Hawkeye (inevitably J. Carroll Naish), who reads the *Wall Street Journal*." The entire run of the series is available for viewing in the UCLA TV Archives.

The Halls of Ivy TPA (Television Programs of America)/ITC (Incorporated Television Company, Ltd.) CBS. Tuesday nights 8:30. October 19, 1954–September 29, 1955. 38 black-and-white episodes were filmed—some with a laugh track. Sponsors included Nabisco, and International Harvester.

Based upon the Peabody Award-winning radio program of the same name, *The Halls of Ivy* (sponsored by Schlitz Beer on radio), had a much shorter and less successful run on television beginning in the fall of 1954. Featured were real-life husband and wife Ronald Colman and Benita Hume, reprising their roles as Dr. William Todhunter Hall (she called him Toddy) and Victoria Cromwell Hall (he called her Vicky), respectively. Colman had also garnered acclaim in his days as a leading man on the silver screen, in *Lost Horizon* and *The Prisoner of Zenda*, but they both exhibited a flair for comedy on the radio version of *The Jack Benny Show*, leading to their own radio show and eventually their own TV sitcom. Here they resided at Number One Faculty Row, in an unnamed Midwestern state in the town of Ivy at Ivy College. William was the college president. Members of the faculty included Ray Collins as Dr. Merriweather and Herb Butterfield was Clarence Wellman—the chairman of the board of trustees. The Hall's housekeeper, Alice, was portrayed by Mary Wickes.

In the only readily available episode titled "The Old Professor Forgot His Umbrella" (sometimes called simply "The Umbrella Man"), Professor Lucien Royce (Francis Pierlot), now an octogenarian and many years into his retirement, returned for a visit to Ivy. William hadn't seen the man since his own days as an undergrad and was very happy about the reunion. Chairman Wellman, however, wasn't as happy—he thought the old man's return might prove to be a liability and a distraction. William then came up with a wonderful compromise: hiring the elderly gentleman to be the college's historian. One other episode, "The Eleventh Commandment," is housed in the Peabody Awards Collection (The Walter J. Brown Media Archives) in Athens, Georgia, and revolves around a controversial plaque on a building constructed by a woman architect named Ann Garrick (Joanne Davis).

The program was created by Thendon "Don" Quinn; the executive producer was Leon Fromkess; the producer was William Frye; writers included Barbara Merlin, Decla Dunning, Nat Wolff and Don Quinn; and directors included William Cameron Menzies, Norman Z. McLeod, and William D. Russell. Allegedly, this show was very expensive to produce—over $50,000 an episode (a record for that time). *The Halls of Ivy* theme song (also used in the radio version) became quite popular and has been recorded numerous times by countless artists.

Hanging In T. A. T. Communications. CBS. Wednesday nights 8:30. August 8, 1979–August 29, 1979. Four episodes were videotaped before a live audience.

Getting this four-week show on the air was more trouble than it was worth. It began as a vehicle for Beatrice Arthur, who was to portray a congresswoman in Washington, D. C. When she decided not to do it, the show morphed into *Onward and Upward* with pretty much the same scripts and the same supporting cast, except that now the main character was an African American former pro football player who became a congressman. John Amos had first dibs on the role, but he turned it down. Lou Gossett, Jr., was the next candidate for the role, as the title became *Mr. Dooley*, but he also backed out. Next in line was Cleavon Little as the title of the show now became *Mr. Dugan*. This version almost got on the air, but when black politicians got a sneak preview of the show, their extremely negative reaction led to yet another change. CBS pulled its promos for the show at the last possible minute, plugged in a special episode of *Alice* in its stead, and once again, the show was retooled. It was now to be called *Hanging In* and it starred former *Maude* co-star, Bill Macy, as Louis Harper—a former football star who enjoyed helping the poor and underprivileged through special community projects. He was then offered the presidency at Braddock University, but brought along his humanitarian ways, which promised to get him into political red tape and hot water with the university board, staff, and fundraisers. Others in the cast included Maggie Gallagher (Barbara Rhodes), the high-pressure dean of faculty; Sam Dickey (Dennis Burkley), the slick director of admissions and public relations; diminutive Pinky Nolan (Nedra Volz), Harper's wise-cracking housekeeper; and Darian Mathias as Rita Zepperette.

Episodes include "Old Girlfriend," in which a visit from Sam Dickey's old flame caused him to become a nervous, compulsive eater. In "Sleep with the Fishes," Harper had cause for concern when threatening phone calls led him to believe the syndicate wanted him dead after he refused college admission to a mob man's son.

The program was produced by Sy Rosen; the executive producer was Norman Lear; writers included Arthur Julian, Rosen, William Davenport, Charlie Hauck, and Rod Parker; and directors included Alan Rafkin and Walter C. Miller. The show's theme was provided by Bill Byers. There are two schools of thought about what TAT Communications stood for—Tandem and Toy Communications or Tuchus Affen Tisch (Yiddish for putting one's butt on the line).

Hank Warner Brothers Studios. NBC. Friday nights 8:00. September 17, 1965–September 2, 1966. 26 episodes were produced with a laugh track. The pilot is black-and-white, the other 25 episodes are in color. Sponsors included Bell Telephone.

Not to be confused with the short-lived Kelsey Grammer show of same name, this *Hank* aired over 40 years earlier. This Hank was a guy to really admire. He was brilliant, kind, considerate, resourceful, clever, and very hard-working. Henry "Hank" Dearborn, played by up-and-coming Broadway star Dick Kallman, had lost both his parents in a traffic accident when he was only 15. Hank instantly had to quit high school and get a job to help support his nine-year-old sister Tina (Katie Sweet). Hank fully intended to finish high school and eventually go to college. However, that day seemed a long way off because of his current situation, so he devised a very complex plan. He became a "drop-in." He learned the schedules of a goodly amount of the students at Western State University and took their place when they were absent or cut class. He devised multiple disguises and used at least six different names, including Mr. Dunstetter and Waldo Smith. While on the campus, Hank took on many odd jobs, including driving an old ambulance-cum-lunch wagon. Besides food, there were also many items for sale on that wagon which students found useful, such as pens, pencils, bobby pins, nail files, and shoelaces. Hank also took in dry cleaning and laundry, fixed watches, repaired shoes and tennis rackets, and even set up a student dating service. All of this kept Hank really busy and yet he still had time for his girlfriend Doris Royal (played by Inelda DeMartin in the pilot and Linda Foster in the series). Doris was a student at Western State. To complicate Hank's life, she was also the daughter of the university's registrar Dr. Lewis Royal (Howard St. John). Doris tried her best to keep Hank's secret, as did the one person on campus who discovered the truth—Professor McKillup (Lloyd Corrigan). McKillup was so taken by Hank's ingenuity and hunger for knowledge, he pledged to go along with the charade (he also professed a love for "beating the system"). Hank was also a very proficient runner and hurdler and this got him out of jams when there was a chance of his secret being discovered by others. He could merely outrun and out-jump his pursuers.

Actor Marvin Kaplan, who guest starred on the episode titled "Campus Caper," remembered, "I didn't know this at first, but in the episode they needed me to ride a bicycle. There's one problem with that—I never learned how to ride a bicycle, so they rigged up an intricate bike propped up on a block of wood with pulleys and ropes, and made me look as though I were cycling by pulling the ropes." Mr. Kaplan also recalled, "I played a detective in that episode and there were bloodhounds. Well, bloodhounds just like lying around, and it was very hard to motivate them." Jackie Joseph appeared in an episode titled "Wedding, Anyone?" About that episode, she recalled, "I had to start out being really homely. I had pancake makeup to 'dull down' my face—every young actress's dream. Also guest-starring in that episode was Alan Reed, Jr., whom I knew while I was in college at LACC. He was a very nice young man. In fact, he even gave me a tip about a job his father was casting."

The program was created and produced by Hugh Benson; the director was John Rich; and writers included Everett Greenbaum and Jim Fritzell. The clever theme song was written by the great Johnny Mercer (lyrics) and Frank Perkins (music).

Some of the show's loose ends were tied up in the final episode called "Operation: Matriculation." In this episode, Hank's ruse was discovered when he was whisked off to the hospital after pretending to be a student who had been sent home with the measles. Dick Kallman also recorded an album and some singles for RCA Victor and Liberty Records.

The Hank McCune Show United Television Productions. NBC. Saturday nights 7:00. September 9, 1950–December 2, 1950. Sponsors included Peter Paul Candy and Lewis Foods.

The Hank McCune Show began locally in New York in 1949. The program went national on NBC, briefly, in the fall of 1950. This was a program on which the focus was slapstick comedy. Conveniently, Hank McCune played Hank McCune. Hank always had good intentions, but was easily confused and his curiosity continually got him into some outrageous predicaments. Hank shared a bungalow with a friend named Lester Mayberry (Hanley Stafford). In fact, Lester rued that day and kept track of the time (two months, seven days, three hours, 26 seconds) since Hank moved in. Lester worked at the West Trust and Savings Bank for 18 years. He was close to becoming first vice president of the bank, but his boss, Mr. Higgins (Thurston Hall), told him that the misadventures of McCune were actually holding him back from a promotion.

Episodes include one in which the always curious Hank McCune listened to a wire recording accidentally left on the receptionist's desk in the office of Dr. Willis (Charles Meredith). Hank thought the message was about his roommate, Lester, who had an appointment that same day. The message, which stated that the patient was very close to having a nervous breakdown, was actually about a different patient, but in the meantime Hank managed to completely soundproof the entire bungalow so Lester could get lots of peace and quiet. In another untitled episode, the hijinks of a would-be magician named Preston the Prestidigitator caused both Hank and Lester to believe that the other was a kleptomaniac.

The program was produced by Samuel Z. Arkoff, Dick Farrell, Hank McCune, and Ed Bernds; writers included Mort Lachman, Si Rose, Russ Bender, and Larry Clemmons. This show is significant for a couple of reasons. It was one of the first filmed sitcoms, and even more importantly, it is credited with being the very first show to employ a laugh track. In a review of the show, *Variety* didn't quite know what to make of the canned laughter. Little did they realize how often it would be used over the next few decades. A few episodes are available for viewing at the Paley Center for Media.

Harrigan and Son Desilu Productions. ABC. Friday nights 8:00. October 14, 1960–September 29, 1961. 34 black-and-white episodes were filmed without a laugh track. Sponsors included Reynolds Aluminum, and the announcer was Rex Marshall.

A young actor named Roger Perry had been cast in a new show for MGM called *Dr. Kildare*. However, at the time, he was under contract with Desilu, and said, "Desi Arnaz pulled me aside, and with his wonderful accent, told me that a much better part had just cropped up in a new Desilu series to be called *Harrigan and Son*, with Pat O'Brien. I opted out of the MGM deal and went with Desi." This sitcom was another Cy Howard creation, but not as broad a comedy as his other projects. *Harrigan and Son* was more of a "dramedy," and employed no laugh track. Perry told me, "That was one of the problems. We really didn't know the direction of the show—it wasn't a true sitcom, but it also wasn't a full-fledged drama. It was kind of on the fence." The show focused upon a crusty, curmudgeonly, widowed New York attorney named James Harrigan, Sr. (movie legend Pat O'Brien). His son, James Harrigan, Jr. (Roger Perry), had just graduated from Harvard Law School first in his class, and dad took him in as a law partner, changing the name

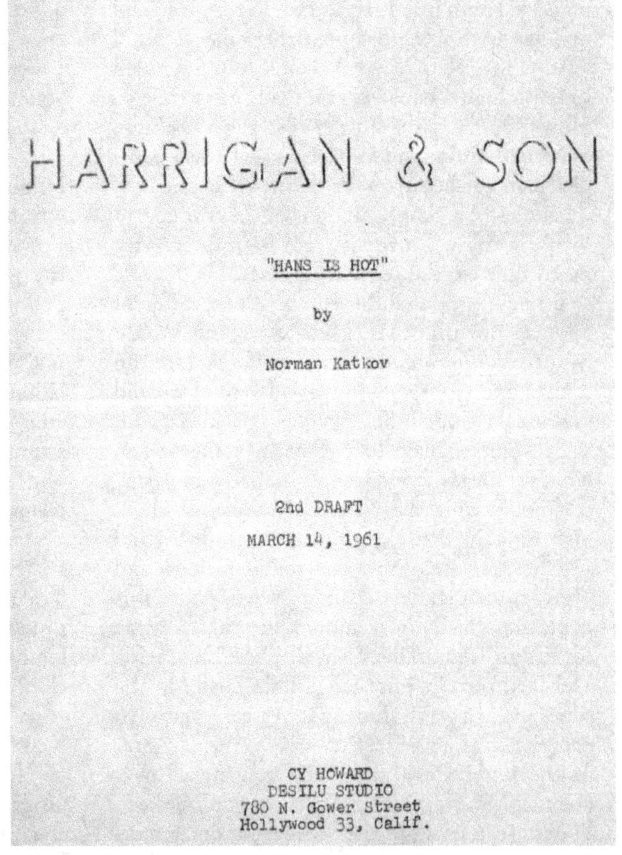
HARRIGAN & SON

"HANS IS HOT"

by

Norman Katkov

2nd DRAFT

MARCH 14, 1961

CY HOWARD
DESILU STUDIO
780 N. Gower Street
Hollywood 33, Calif.

Harrigan and Son—**The script for the episode titled "Hans Is Hot," which aired May 5, 1961.**

on the door to "Harrigan and Harrigan." The two Harrigans had very different approaches to the legal profession. The younger Harrigan practiced law "by the book," but the elder Harrigan took some chances along the way if he thought it could help that particular case—and that was the source for most of the stories and conflicts on *Harrigan and Son*. Even their choice in secretaries differed greatly. Dad chose the beautiful and bubbly Gypsy (Georgine Darcy) while Junior opted for the efficient "plain Jane," Miss Claridge (Helen Kleeb).

Episodes include "Hans Is Hot," in which Junior discovered that his efficient new German housekeeper had brought her young son to America against the father's wishes. In "The Comeback," Junior wanted to take an old professor of his into the practice in an advisory capacity for an upcoming copyright case. Dad was very supportive—that is, until he found out that this new addition to the practice, Walter Grant (David Lewis), had a penchant for the bottle. Perry recalled, "The show was filmed at Desilu in Culver City, California, but the show itself was set in New York. After we had been on a while, director Don Richardson took us all to New York for some atmosphere shots. We had to get up really early for those shots, and Pat O'Brien had so many friends in Manhattan, he got very little sleep, having gotten to his hotel room in the wee hours of the morning. What a great experience it was—Pat was such a wonderful guy and a wonderful, entertaining storyteller."

The program was directed by Claudio Guzman, Walter Grauman, Don Richardson, John H. Auer, and Sherman Marks; writers included Bob O'Brien and Henry Garson. The theme song, George M. Cohan's "Harrigan," originated in the 1907 musical titled *Fifty Miles from Boston*. Roger Perry is an accomplished musician and he played the piano and performed the theme song during the closing credits (in a duet with Pat O'Brien). Perry remembered, "We were up against *Rawhide* in our time slot, but we didn't do that badly. We really expected to be renewed for another season, but that's show business. And even though *Dr. Kildare* ran for several seasons, and *Harrigan and Son* only ran for one season, I wasn't bitter and I didn't really have any regrets." A couple of episodes can be viewed in the UCLA TV Archives.

Harris Against the World Kayro-Vue/Universal City Studios. NBC. Monday nights 8:00. October 5, 1964–January 4, 1965. 13 episodes were filmed with a laugh track.

Before he was Oscar Madison, and long before he was Dr. R. Quincy, Jack Klugman portrayed Alan Harris in *Harris Against the World*, sandwiched in between the two other shows (*Karen* and *Tom, Dick and Mary*) aired under the umbrella heading of *Ninety Bristol Court* (which conveniently was on NBC, the show's initials). Alan Harris worked at a big Hollywood movie studio, albeit as superintendent. He needed the job (and frequently some part-time jobs as well) to support his spendthrift wife, Kate (Patricia Barry), and their two children, a girl named Deedee (Claire Wilcox) and a boy named Billy (David Macklin). Alan was harassed by many problems in his daily life—money, family, his bosses, his job, and life in general. He certainly moaned and complained about his troubles a lot, but underneath it all beat a heart of pure gold. He did have a couple of good friends to help him cope—the Millers, Helen (Fay DeWitt) and Norm (Sheldon Allman). Just like the other shows in the *90 Bristol Court* triumvirate, Cliff Murdock (Guy Raymond) was the Harris's handyman.

Every one of the 13 episodes pitted Harris against someone—"His Secretary," "His Family," "The Old Rah-Rah," "His Dancing Teacher," "Kid Parties," "Sundays," "Aunt Cora," "The Simple Life," "The Studio," "The Stock Market," "His Housekeeper," "His Son, the Drop-out," and "Anniversary Gifts." However, it was Harris against *I've Got a Secret* on CBS and *Voyage to the Bottom of the Sea* on ABC which was his undoing. Only one of the *Ninety Bristol Court* shows, *Karen*, survived the entire season.

The program was produced by Joe Connelly and Devery Freeman; writers included Tom Adair, Danny Simon, Milt Rosen, Bill Idelson, Sam Bobrick, Marty Roth, Paul Mason, and James B. Allardice; and directors included Sidney Lanfield, Christian Nyby, Earl Bellamy, Wes Kenney, and Seymour Robbie.

Harry's Girls MGM Television/Michel Productions. NBC. Friday nights 9:30. September 13, 1963–January 3, 1964. 15 black-and-white episodes were filmed at Studios De La Victorine, France. Sponsors included Colgate.

This was Larry Blyden's second attempt at sitcom success. His first was *Joe and Mabel* in 1956. This one was for MGM Television. The original working title was *Me and My Gals*. Ralph

Harry's Girls—Rear—Larry Blyden. Front row, Dawn Nickerson, Diahn Williams, and Susan Silo (photograph courtesy of Dawn Nickerson-Fox).

Levy directed the pilot and he got actor Victor Rietty to portray restaurant owner Salvatore. Victor got to work with his son, Robert, in the pilot. Robert Rietty remembers, "I came along because my father had just come out of the hospital after a long stint, having broken his leg. Ralph Levy kindly suggested that I go with him in case he needed help, and he wrote in a character to justify a salary for me, too."

Very little from the pilot appeared up in the actual series. The three original girls, Kris Garner, Marsha Rivers, and Ellen McRae, were gone. McRae would do well for herself, however, years later as Ellen Burstyn. The show's star, Larry Blyden, appeared in 59 separate screen tests for the show to whittle down the 320 girls who applied for the roles down to the final three. Dawn Nickerson (nowadays known as Dawn Nickerson Fox), who played Lois Anderson, the naïve wide-eyed blond in the series, told me, "They knew those girls in the pilot weren't going to be in the actual cast for the series." Susan Silo played Rusty and Diahn Williams portrayed Terry. Since *Harry's Girls* was a trio of singers and dancers, the comely actresses got to show their musical talents in quite a few episodes. Dawn told me, "Diahn and Susan had more dancing experience than I, but I had been the stand-by for Carol Lawrence in the musical *Subways Are for Sleeping*, and that must've impressed the powers that be, as well as Larry Blyden, to get me the part of Lois in the series." Even Ralph Levy, the director of the pilot, was gone when the series began. Richard Kinon took his place. Dawn recalls that "Richard was a doll. He kept the peace and kept the pace. He was very easy to work with." The only carry-overs from the pilot were Blyden as Harry Burns (the star and manager of the touring song-and-dance act), and Victor Rietty again portrayed Salvatore in the series episode called "The Director" based upon the pilot. In this episode, the girls all tried to audition for an unconventional Italian director known simply as Gabrielli. Gabrielli liked to hire unknowns and liked to place them in very earthy circumstances. Well, he put the girls into a scene involving a mud fight. Dawn remembers, "the mud was very gritty and we all wound up with scratches. We really went at it. We went into it with a plan, and it was done in one take."

This series was unique in that it had no laugh track, but even more significantly, it was filmed overseas. Dawn Nickerson Fox remembers, "We were supposed to do the series in England, but British equity wanted us to guarantee a certain number of British actors would be used. They also wanted to okay each script. We said no, and so most of the episodes were done in France." Yes, they filmed in France even if that particular episode was set elsewhere in Europe. Dawn recalls, "The newspapers were just full of excitement over this series to be filmed in Europe. We got lots of publicity."

Dawn thinks that the series ultimately failed because "truthfully, if they had followed us around to see what was really going on as we were settling into our lives in Europe, they would've had some really wonderful ideas for some great scripts. However, most of the episodes were written far away from us behind closed doors." Dawn says that one of the funniest real-life events involved her and one of her co-stars, "Susan Silo and I hit it off as friends, and so we decided to share a villa in Nice, France. Well, the first night there we both woke up itching. There were bed bugs. Temporarily, we moved in with Larry Blyden who had a very small water heater in his place. We were always using all of his hot water."

Even though the show wasn't a huge success, Dawn believes that the show had a direct influence upon *Charlie's Angels*. Dawn said, "I always felt there was a little bit of copying going on there."

Larry Blyden went on to host numerous game shows (*Personality*, *You're Putting Me On*, *The Movie Game*, and *What's My Line?*) before his untimely death in a car accident in Morocco. The three girls are all still in touch. Dawn told me, "I left the business because of love; Diahn Williams went on to become a lawyer; and Susan Silo is a voiceover artist."

Writers included Bob O'Brien, and the teams of Joseph Stein and Sydney Zelinka, and Harry Goodman and Larry Klein. Ted Turner owns the MGM Television film archive, and thus owns the extant episodes of *Harry's Girls* which are alleged to be, according to Dawn Nickerson Fox, "in an underground vault somewhere in Kansas." After being canceled, this show was replaced by *That Was the Week That Was* in January of 1964. *Harry's Girls* was loosely based upon the MGM film, *Les Girls*.

The Hartmans NBC. February 27, 1949–May 22, 1949. Broadcast live. Sponsors included Textron, Inc.

The Hartmans had been a successful dance team in Vaudeville. Paul Hartman and his real-life wife, Grace, attempted to make the transition to TV in this seminal sitcom in 1949. In *The Hartmans* (sometimes referred to as *The Hartmans at Home*), they portrayed a newly married couple living in a suburb called Forest Heights, dealing with everyday life. Also in the cast was Paul's brother-in-law, played by Loring Smith, and a handyman played by Harold J. Stone (in one of his first TV appearances). Coincidentally, it was a role as a handyman for which Hartman is best remembered—Emmett Clark on both *The Andy Griffith Show* and *May-*

berry, R. F. D. The Hartmans failed to catch on and ran for less than three months on NBC. A short while after the show's demise Grace was diagnosed with cancer and Paul had to fend for himself in Hollywood. His next venture, a sitcom called *Pride of the Family*, also lasted only one season (see the entry for that show).

The program was produced and directed by Harry Herman; writers included Frank Wilson and Ted Luce. To my knowledge, no episodes exist.

The Harvey Korman Show Chrisma Productions. ABC. Tuesday nights 9:30. January 31, 1978–August 3, 1978. Six episodes were videotaped before a live audience.

Early in his career, Harvey Korman was the voice of The Great Gazoo on *The Flintstones*, and made many guest appearances on sitcoms such as *Glynis*, *The Hero*, *I'm Dickens*, *He's Fenster*, and *The Munsters*. He really garnered some deserved attention as a semi-regular on *The Danny Kaye Show*, which, of course led to a decade of inspired fun on *The Carol Burnett Show*. In 1977, he decided to strike out on his own and was replaced (at least temporarily) on that show by Dick Van Dyke. Coincidentally, Van Dyke's son Barry became a member of the cast of *The Harvey Korman Show*. Harvey's new show was doomed from the start, as it was scheduled extremely erratically on ABC. The pilot episode aired in 1977 and varied slightly from the actual series. In the pilot, Harvey played Francis Kavanaugh, who ran acting classes from his home. The first episode of the actual series didn't air until early in 1978. Harvey now portrayed hammy, out-of-work actor Harvey Kavanaugh, who lived in a big, old house with his daughter Maggie (Christine Lahti), who worked at the Friendly Community Bank. Her boyfriend and co-worker was Stuart Stafford (Barry Van Dyke). Harvey's hard-working agent, Jake Winkelman, was played by Milton Selzer.

The episode titles for *The Harvey Korman Show* resemble those for *Friends*, in that each one began with the words "the one where," followed by "Harvey Gets a Job as an Escort," "Stuart Moves In," "Harvey Won't Change," "There's a Hold-up," and "Harvey Goes On a Kid's Show."

The program was created by Hal Dresner, who also served as executive producer; the producer was Don Van Atta; writers included Mike Kagan, Harry Cauley, Carol Gray, Dresner, Jim Parker, Burt Prelutsky, and a yet-unknown Garry Shandling; and directors included Harvey Korman, Howard Morris, and Bill Persky. The theme song, "Living Life Today," was performed by Korman in a Broadway-esque manner.

The Hathaways Screen Gems. ABC. Friday nights 8:00. October 6, 1961–August 31, 1962. 26 black-and-white episodes were filmed with a laugh track. Sponsors included Ralston Purina and Mobil Gasoline.

The original working title for this show was *The Chimps*. Walter Hathaway (Jack Weston) was a successful real estate agent. His wife Elinor (game show maven, Peggy Cass) was a booking agent. They had a housekeeper named Amanda Allison (Mary Grace Canfield). Sounds like your normal American household in 1961—that is, until the "children" are brought into the equation; they were primates. They had three trained show business chimpanzees living with them, and they were always referred to as "the children" or "the kids." The two "boys" were named Charlie and Enoch and the little "girl" was named Candy. The "boys" were often dressed as cowboys and the "girl" was always in a dress. Elinor was their booking agent and Jerry Roper (Harvey Lembeck) was their real agent. Much like regular children, these kids got the Hathaways into a myriad of embarrassing situations on Magnolia Drive in Los Angeles.

In the debut, "Love Thy Neighbor," Walter was trying to sell the house next door. He finally found someone interested in it, but the potential buyer (Bert Brockwood, played by George Ives) was not fond of noise or pets. In fact, he and his family were moving to get away from the noisy and annoying dogs and pigeons of their current neighbors. To insure that the Brockwoods would buy the house, Walter and Elinor made every attempt to keep their "children" hidden for the first month. As fate would have it the Brockwoods discovered the truth, but decided to stay anyway because their own kids were so fond of the chimps. The four members of the Brockwood family had recurring roles on the show.

The program was produced by Ezra Stone; the executive producer was Robert Sparks; writers included Herbert Finn, John Elliotte, Leo Solomon, Ben Gershman, Hugh Wedlock, Howard Snyder, and Dick Wesson; and directors included Richard Kinon, Richard Donner, David Butler, and Don Taylor. Music was provided by Herbert W. Spencer. The opening credits were animated. The Marquis Chimps made numerous TV appearances, after the demise of *The Hath-*

aways, on *The Ed Sullivan Show*, *The Hollywood Palace*, and even an episode of *The Lucy Show* titled "Lucy, the Babysitter." A decade later, Ted Bessell and Anita Gillette starred in a similar sitcom called *Me and the Chimp*, which also lasted just one single season. Several episodes of *The Hathaways* are available for viewing in the UCLA TV Archives.

The Headmaster CBS. Friday nights 9:00. September 18, 1971–January 1, 1971. 14 color episodes were filmed without a laugh track. Sponsors included Bristol Myers and Lever Brothers.

At the end of the 1967–68 TV season, Andy Griffith left *The Andy Griffith Show*, the number one show on television. Finding another hit show would soon prove extremely elusive. His first attempt: a dramedy called *The Headmaster*. This time around, Andy was Andy Thompson, the headmaster at a small co-ed California prep school called The Concord; Andy's wife, Margaret (Claudette Nevins), was an English teacher at the school. Lee Meriwether told me, "I auditioned for that role, but they gave it to Claudette." Jerry Van Dyke played the coach and gym teacher Jerry Brownell. Parker Fennelly was the school's custodian, Mr. Purdy. Episodes dealt with teenage angst, the generation gap, fitting in, as well as sex, drugs and rock and roll. The edgy subject matter proved to be a turn-off to fans of the old Andy Griffith.

Episodes included "Will the Real Mother of Tony Landis, Please Stand Up," which marked the TV reunion of Andy and Ron Howard. In "One for the Gipper," Jerry's team was comprised of a bunch of lovable losers, and because of their lack of wins, he began to doubt himself, and resigned his position. He was talked into staying, however, after being told by many that he had made a big difference in the lives of so many students.

The program's producer was Aaron Ruben (who also created the program); the executive producer was Richard O. Linke; writers included Nate Monaster, Ruben, Rob Reiner, and Phil Mishkin; and directors included Lee Philips, Gary Nelson, and John Rich. The theme song, "Only a Man," was written by Dick Williams and performed by Linda Ronstadt. One episode is available for viewing at the Paley Center in Los Angeles. A few weeks after the cancellation of *The Headmaster*, Griffith was back with another short-lived series—*The New Andy Griffith Show*, which co-starred Lee Meriwether (see the entry for that show). After the quick demise of that program, reruns of *The Headmaster* returned for a brief time as a summer replacement.

He and She Talent Associates. CBS. Wednesday nights 9:30. September 6, 1967–September 18, 1968. 26 color episodes were filmed before a live audience. Sponsors included General Foods (Cool Whip, Maxwell House Coffee, and Gaines Burger Dog Food).

While this intelligent sitcom won an Emmy Award for comedy writing, and had a strong lead-in on Wednesday nights from *Green Acres*, it simply couldn't find an audience. This was the story of a childless "he"—Dick Hollister—and a "she"—Paula Hollister (real-life married couple Dick Benjamin and Paula Prentiss). She was a scatterbrained social worker (for the Tourist Aid Society) who was often bringing home foreigners to keep them from being deported. He was a cartoonist whose *Jetman* comic strip was so popular that it became a TV series. Jack Cassidy, in a role which greatly influenced Ted Baxter, played Oscar North, the arrogant, egocentric, smarmy, flamboyant, mama's boy actor who really thought he was Jetman and had constant disagreements with Dick about *Jetman*'s direction. Harold Gould appeared occasionally as Dick's boss Norman Nugent. Alan Oppenheimer had a recurring role as Dick's overly frugal accountant Murray Mouse (who had a wife named Minnie). At the apartment, the Hollisters lived next door to a firehouse (number 26), and Greek-fluent fireman Harry Zarakardos (Kenneth Mars) always entered the Hollisters's apartment via a wooden plank precariously placed between their windows. Diminutive Hamilton Camp played the Hollisters's inept handyman, New England-native Andrew Hummel, who was usually seen fixing either the front door or the bedroom door.

Episodes include the debut, the only one filmed at Desilu Studios (the others were filmed at CBS Studio Center), called "The Old Man and the She," in which Paula tried to keep an elderly Greek man named Orestes Ponopolis (Wolfe Barzell) from being deported. Dick decided to make him a silent companion for Jetman named Mr. Shush, and he became a recurring character on the show. In "Second Time Around," the Hollisters decided to have a big second wedding to celebrate their fifth anniversary, since their first one was so small and cheap, but a fire alarm during the ceremony took away the best man Harry.

He and She—Paula Prentiss left, behind door top to bottom—Jack Cassidy, Dick Benjamin, Julie Sommars from the episode "The Background Man" (photograph courtesy Jean Cummings).

He and She was often compared to *The Dick Van Dyke Show*, so, with tongue-in-cheek, there was an episode titled "Dick's Van Dyke," in which Dick sought a quiet little hideaway to finish his artwork, and came back after nine days with a van dyke (a beard), to which he quickly discovered wife Paula was allergic.

The program was produced by Arne Sultan; the creator and executive producer was Leonard Stern; writers included Stern, Sultan, Jim Parker, Arnold Margolin, Martin A. Ragaway, Irma and Austin Kalish, Allan Burns, Chris Hayward, and Joseph Bonaduce; and directors included Stern and Jay Sandrich. Music was provided by Jerry Fielding. Reruns of the program were shown on CBS during the summer of 1970, and all 26 episodes were briefly syndicated in the 1980s on the USA Network.

Heaven for Betsy A Jacyn Production. CBS. Tuesday and Thursday nights at 7:45. September 30, 1952–December 23, 1952. 26 black-and-white episodes of this 15-minute live show were broadcast without a laugh track. Sponsors included Pepsodent Toothpaste and Lever Brothers.

They had previously worked together as boyfriend and girlfriend on the short-lived TV series *That Wonderful Guy*. Here, as in real-life, they were husband and wife on a show inspired by a recurring skit about a newlywed couple on *The Frances Langford/Don Ameche Show*, and thought it might work as a regular series. Pete Bell, played by a young Jack Lemmon, was an impetuous assistant buyer for the toy department of the Wilmot Department Store in Manhattan. His wife, Betsy Bell, played by Cynthia Stone, was a former secretary-turned-homemaker who constantly had to get her impulsive husband out of jams. Most of the episodes revolved around this newlywed couple's attempts to adjust to married life on Oak Tree Lane. Being married in real life, the dialogue came very easily. Pete's no nonsense, cigar-smoking boss, Alonzo Wilmot, was played by Cliff Hall.

In maybe the only surviving episode, Pete, who hadn't gotten a raise at the department store in well over a year, tried to muster up the courage to ask the cantankerous Mr. Wilmot for more money. Betsy was very supportive and even helped her husband by jotting down a list of his attributes and demands, and orchestrating a "dry run" of his talk with Wilmot. At the actual meeting with Wilmot, however, the phone never stopped ringing and Pete never did get the opportunity to ask for that raise.

The program was produced by Marge Kerr; writers included Russell Beggs and Budd Grossman; directors included Dick Linkroum. Jacyn Productions was a combination of the names Jack and Cynthia. Jack and Cynthia had one son together (Chris) in 1954 and divorced in 1956. Chris would later star in his own short-lived sitcom, *Brothers and Sisters* on NBC.

Heavens to Betsy September 1948. NBC. Sunday night 9:00. Broadcast live.

Not to be confused with *Heaven for Betsy* with Jack Lemmon, this short-lived sitcom had similarities to *Two Girls Named Smith* in that it focused upon two young ladies trying to make it big on Broadway. They had considerable talent, but no name recognition and found many obstacles on their way to the "great white way." Producers just weren't willing to cast obscure actresses. Elizabeth "Betsy" Cote played Betsy; Mary Best played her friend Mary; Nick Dennis portrayed their landlord; and Russell Nype was their regular cabdriver. To my knowledge, no episodes exist.

Hee Haw Honeys Yongestreet Entertainment Corporation Productions in Association with Lexington Broadcast Company. First-run syndication. 1978–1979. 26 episodes were videotaped with a laugh track.

Hee Haw Honeys was basically a musical sitcom spin-off of *Hee Haw*. The pilot and the actual series differed somewhat. In the pilot, the *Hee Haw Honeys* were three female singers/entertainers who appeared in bit parts and performed in clubs, but were tired of merely being extras on the "Hee Haw Porch"—they wanted regular parts on *Hee Haw*, but were basically the "not yet ready for *Hee Haw* players." They attempted to pay their dues so that *Hee Haw* would want them, so they got their own *Hee Haw Honeys* bus and took to the road. The cast in this pilot consisted of Kathie Lee Johnson (later Kathie Lee Gifford) as Chrissy, who was big on women's liberation; Muffy Durham was Lee Ann, who longed to be back on the plantation (and whenever she flirted with any man, "Tara's Theme" from *Gone with the Wind* played); Catherine Hickland was near-sighted, husband-seeking Toby; Kenny Price played Kenny, who sang and drove their bus; Jackie Kahane played Gus, the drummer; John Toole played "Lettuce Leaf," who was a trucker for a vegetable company and was also the baby brother of Chrissy; and Bob McClure portrayed the sinister Silo Yutes, who was always trying to repossess the bus when payments were late. While in Plains, Georgia, the Honeys happened to meet President Carter's incorrigible brother, Billy, while making a pit stop.

In the series, things were different. It became the story of the Honey family. Lulu Honey (Lulu Roman) and Kenny Honey (Kenny Price) were proprietors of the Hee Haw Honeys Club in Nashville. Lulu and Kenny were the proud parents of Willie Billie Honey (Gailard Sartain); Misty Honey (Misty Rowe); and Kathie Honey (Kathie Lee Johnson, who had just wrapped up work on *Name That Tune*). There was a lot of typical corny *Hee Haw* humor, and many country music greats came by the club to perform (among them Loretta Lynn, Conway Twitty, Roy Clark, and The Oak Ridge Boys).

The program was produced by Sam Lovullo; the executive producers were Frank Peppialt and John Aylesworth; writers included Barry Adelman and Barry Silver; and directors included Ron Kantor. The theme song was by Ron Martin; music was provided by Charlie McCoy. The program was recorded at WTVF, Nashville. The pilot episode can be viewed at the Paley Center for Media.

Here We Go Again A Bobka Production/Metromedia Producers Corporation. ABC. Saturday nights 8:00. January 20, 1973–June 16, 1973. 13 color episodes were filmed with a laugh track.

Here We Go Again was a mid-season replacement for *Alias Smith and Jones*. Larry Hagman had just wrapped up another short-lived sitcom, *The Good Life*, and quickly entered this one in which the focus was divorce. This time he was architect Richard Evans and tried his hand at marriage a second time in the debut episode. He was marrying a divorcee and clothes horse named Susan Standish (soon with a hyphenated Evans tacked on), played by Diane Baker. Since it was their second marriage, they opted for a quickie wedding in Nevada. They each had children from their previous marriages—Susan had two little girls who lived with her, Cindy and Jan (Leslie Graves and Kim Richards, respectively). Richard had a teenage son, Jeff (Chris Beaumont), who lived with his mom. The conflict in this sitcom arose from the close proximity of the exes—Richard's ex-wife (and Chris's mom), the very handy and needy Judy Evans (Nita Talbot), who was an editor for *Screen World Magazine*, resided only a half-mile away; and Susan's ex, the womanizing, free-spirited, poker-loving, slovenly, former pro quarterback Jerry Standish (Dick Gau-

Here We Go Again—Left to right (back row)—Chris Beaumont, Nita Talbot, Dick Gautier. Left to right (middle row)—Larry Hagman, Leslie Graves. Left to right (front row)—Diane Baker, Kim Richards (photograph courtesy of Dick Gautier).

tier), lived a mere six blocks away, down the hill in the Encino Tower Apartments in 6A. Dick Gautier recalled, "There was one episode of the show on which I only had about three lines and, really nothing to do. To emphasize my lack of stuff to do, I recorded my three lines on a tape recorder, and when my turn came up, I just pressed 'play.' Anyway, they got the hint, and rewrote the script and gave me something more to do in that episode."

Episodes include "Sunday, Soggy Sunday," in which the newly wed Evanses tried to find some "alone time," away from the kids and the meddling exes, but met with little success. In "The Tax Man Cometh," the IRS audited Jerry for non-disclosure of his recent poker game winnings. In an episode which got its title from a sitcom from TV's infancy, "A Date with Judy," Richard's ex fell madly in love and was leaning towards marriage, and Richard envisioned finally being off the hook for any more alimony payments. The wedding, however, never came to fruition.

Dick Gautier told me, "It was a very happy, friendly set. I had worked with Larry Hagman in a movie in New York and he was great to work with. Diane Baker was just a wonderful lady, a beautiful person and a great actress. Nita Talbot had a bizarre, 'out there' side to her, but she was great."

The program was created and frequently written by Bob Kaufman (he was the Bobka in Bobka Productions); producers included Kaufman and Stan Schwimmer; directors included Jay Sandrich; and the executive producer was Charles Fries. *Here We Go Again* had two totally different problems which hampered its success—first and foremost, the show had stiff competition on Saturday nights, up against *All in the Family*; and second, few viewers found divorce to be a laughing matter. A few episodes can be viewed in the UCLA TV Archives.

The Hero Talent Associates. NBC. Thursday nights 9:30. September 8, 1966–January 5, 1967. 16 color episodes were filmed at Paramount Studios, Hollywood. Sponsors included Salem Cigarettes, Tempo Charcoal Filter Cigarettes, and Lifebuoy Soap.

Talent Associates was the production company of David Susskind and Leonard Stern. Together they were responsible for several hit shows, such as *Get Smart* and *McMillan and Wife*. However, a few of their shows had very short lives in prime time—a prime example being *The Hero*.

The Hero was the story of actor Sam Garret (Richard Mulligan). Sam had a hit TV Western show called *Jed Clayton, U.S. Marshall*. On-camera, Sam was cool, sure-footed, and confident. He was the fastest gun in the west. However, off-camera in real life, Sam was pure sugarfoot. He was klutzy, uncoordinated, insecure, and afraid of horses. Most of the stories and situations revolved around Sam's attempts to be as much of a hero at home and with his friends as he was on his TV show—but he always seemed to fall short. Sam was married to the lovely Ruth Garret (Mariette Hartley), and they had a son named Paul (Bobby Horan), who had a pet snake. Paul's best friend was Burton Gilman (Joey Baio, Scott's cousin), who was taking dancing lessons; and Burton's father was Fred (Victor French). Director Bruce Bilson told me, "Victor French and I became close friends. Victor had one problem on the set—he perspired a lot. Someone had to constantly mop his brow."

Episodes include "I Have a Friend," in which Sam tried to help a down on his luck nightclub owner (Bernie Kopell as Charlie Trendler) by arranging to have an actor break in his new act at the club. When that actor broke his leg, tone deaf Sam tried to work up an act of his own to fill the void. In "The Big Return of Little Eddie," Uncle Eddie (Paul B. Price) visited, and wanted to get back into show business after a long absence. Once again, our hero, Sam attempted to save the day by using Eddie in an episode of his TV show. Sam's good intentions backfired when everyone came to the realization that Eddie was a terrible actor, and this got on the nerves of Ralph Rayburn (Harvey Korman), the director. In the show's debut episode, "A Night to Remember to Forget," Chuck Connors of *The Rifleman* played himself.

Writers included Roswell Rogers, Budd Grossman, Martin A. Ragaway, Arne Sultan, and the teams of Leonard Stern and Don Hinkley, Joseph and Carol Cavella, Bill Idelson and Sam Bobrick, and Austin and Irma Kalish; directors included William Wiard, Bruce Bilson, Gene Nelson, and Robert Ellis Miller. The whistling theme song was written by Jack Marshall. A few episodes can be viewed in the UCLA TV Archives.

Hey, Landlord United Artists/Mirisch-Rich Productions (filmed at Desilu). NBC. Sunday nights 8:30. September 11, 1966–May 14, 1967. 31 color episodes were filmed before a live audience. Sponsors included Procter and Gamble.

The original working title for the show was *Woody*, named after Woodrow "Woody" Banner (Will Hutchins), who had aspirations of becoming a great writer, and inherited an old brownstone apartment building in Manhattan in the East 30s from his late uncle. He moved from his native Ohio and took up residence in one of the ten apartments there and became the landlord. Because the building was so old, it needed constant repairs, so Woody took in an old college friend (from Ohio State University), Elmer Charles "Chuck" Hookstratton (Sandy Baron), a wannabe comedian and native New Yorker, as his roommate and co-landlord (by the way, Sandy got this TV role as the result of a very successful stint sharing the bill with Steve Lawrence at the Copacabana). The boys' apartment was rather eclectic and came complete with a suit of armor, bunk beds, and stacks upon stacks of books blocking the staircase. Their tenants were every bit as unusual as Woody's apartment. Appearing most frequently was Jack Ellerhorn (Michael Constantine), a photographer with an ulcer who was constantly griping about the lack of heat in his apartment. On a less regular basis we would also get to see the fastidious Mrs. Henderson (Ann Morgan Guilbert) who had several very mischievous children, and was constantly requiring repairs to the things which the kids had broken. And on occasion we would also get to see the voluptuous, albeit scatterbrained Timothy Morgan played by Pamela Rodgers (Timothy was a girl) and her equally lovely roommate Kyoko Mitsui (Miko Mayama). In between starring roles as *Gidget* and *The Flying Nun*, Sally Field made occasional appearances as Woody's younger sister, Bonnie Banner.

Episodes include "Czech Your Wife, Sir," in which the wife (Leigh French) of an absent tenant (she didn't speak a word of English) was about to have a baby, turning Woody and Chuck into instant midwives. In "Divorce: Bachelor Style," Woody and Chuck had a falling out over Chuck's incessant borrowing, and divided the apartment into equal halves. In "Shapes of Wrath," quick-tempered Jack Ellerhorn, in a fit of rage, hired a hit man to "take care of" Chuck. Rose Marie told me about the episode, "Aunt Harriet Wants You," in which she guest-starred: "Garry Marshall liked my work a lot and brought me in to play Aunt Harriet. It was great fun."

The program was produced and created by Garry Marshall and Jerry Belson; writers included Marshall, Belson, Dale McRaven, Carl Kleinschmidt, James L. Brooks, Jack Winter, Peggy Elliott, and Ed Scharlach; and directors included Jerry Paris, John Rich, Belson, and Marshall, all of whom Rose Marie calls "the best of the best." Music was provided by the legendary Quincy Jones. This United Artists program was replaced by another in the same 8:30 Sunday night slot, *The Mothers-In-Law*. Lawrence Laurent of *The Washington Post* called *Hey, Landlord* "a gentle situation comedy."

Hey, Mulligan (The Mickey Rooney Show)

Volcano Pictures, Inc./Mickey Rooney Enterprises/Screencraft. NBC. Saturday nights 8:00. September 4, 1954–June 4, 1955. 36 black-and-white episodes were filmed with a sweetened laugh track. Sponsors included Green Giant Vegetables and Pillsbury.

Diminutive Mickey Rooney had an amazing string of successes on the silver screen, but just couldn't make the successful transition to television. *Hey, Mulligan*, also known as *The Mickey Rooney Show*, was his first of three attempts at sitcom success in three different decades. When this show debuted, Mickey was already in his mid-thirties, but he was playing a much younger character who still lived at home with his parents—Sgt. Joe Mulligan (a lifelong policeman), played by Regis Toomey, and Nell (a former burlesque dancer who met Joe when her dance hall was raided), played by Claire Carleton. Rooney was Mickey Mulligan, a page at a mythical TV network called IBC in Hollywood. There were pictures of NBC celebrities on every wall of the building (Groucho Marx, Martin and Lewis, Milton Berle, Jimmy Durante, and dozens more). Mickey may have been a lowly page, but he had tall hopes of becoming a star, and was enrolled at the Jonathan Swift Academy of Drama and Theatre Arts, which he attended at night. At the station, Mickey's boss was program director Charles Brown (John Hubbard) in office number 284, who, despite Mickey's constant screw-ups, was rather a patient man. Mr. Brown's receptionist, Pat, was also Mickey's girlfriend (played by Pat Walker in the pilot, and Carla Balenda in the series). Mickey's best friend, Freddie (Joey Forman), was also a page at IBC. Appearing in several episodes in small roles was a young Guy Williams.

Episodes include the most famous of the series, "The Lion Hunt," in which Mickey unwittingly freed a caged lion to be used in a jungle show at IBC, and the lion was later found hiding out in the Mulligan's home. In "Disk Jockey," a new vice president of programming (John Eldredge) gave Mickey a shot at TV stardom by giving him an overnight job announcing and playing records. Mickey's disk jockey TV show was a complete disaster, but it did lead to the capture of a wanted felon. In "The Grunion Hunt Mystery," Mickey and a blind date went grunion hunting on the beach after dark. It's interesting to note that an identical storyline involving grunion hunting was also used in an episode of Rooney's second sitcom called *Mickey* in the 1960s.

The program was based upon an idea by Richard Quine and a very young Blake Edwards; the producer was Joseph Santley; the executive producers were Mickey Rooney and Maurice Duke; writers included Quine, Edwards, John Fenton Murray, Benedict Freedman, Duke, Harry Clork, and Sumner Long; and directors included Quine and Leslie Martinson. Music was provided by Van Alexander. The series was briefly syndicated on the long-defunct CBN cable channel in the 1980s as *The Mickey Rooney Show*. Thirty episodes of the series are available in a box set from Timeless Video.

Highcliffe Manor T. A. T. Communications/ Metrotape West Studios. NBC. Tuesday nights 8:30. April 12, 1979–May 3, 1979. Six color episodes were videotaped before a live audience, only four aired.

1979 was a bad year for TV spoofs of horror films—*Struck by Lightning* and this program, *Highcliffe Manor*, both had very short TV lives. The latter requires some explanation and introduction to its rather large cast. Highcliffe Manor was a spooky old castle on an island off the coast of Massachusetts. The castle was the home of the Blacke Foundation where Berkeley Blacke performed scientific experiments and had an odd array of assistants. In the debut episode called "Blacke Death," Berkeley had been "blown to smithereens" in a laboratory explosion. His tearful widow, Helen Blacke (of Omaha, Nebraska), was played by Shelley Fabares. Bedecked in black, Mrs. Blacke arrived at the castle for the funeral services. Helen was a very attractive, naïve, positive and trusting soul. Even when she was informed by the evil scientist named Frances Kiskadden (Eugenie Ross Leming who also helped develop the show, and co-wrote many of the episodes) that the staff intended to harm her, she just sloughed it off. Frances, an MIT graduate, had previously created a handsome Frankenstein monster in her lab named Bram Shelley (Christian Marlowe). They were also lovers, but Bram was a work in progress—he temporarily had erector set parts for his left hand and right foot and he also had a very short-term memory. Cheng (Harold Sakata) was Frances's silent servant who brought her cadavers every night (for Bram's replacement parts); the Reverend Ian Glenville (Stephen McHattie) was a woman chasing clergyman who was carried to the castle by his African American valet Smythe, a graduate of Oxford University (Ernie Hudson) after having been involved in a canoeing accident. Glenville and Smythe were escapees from a South African prison. Glenville was instantly attracted to the widowed Helen (he finally kissed her in episode number four called "Love Blooms") and this raised the ire of pretty young Wendy Sparkes (Audrey Landers), who wanted Glenville for herself. Wendy's parents had been killed in a bizarre Grand Canyon accident. One could see a rivalry brewing as Dr. Felix Morger (Gerald Gordon) also found the widowed Mrs. Blacke extremely attractive (he loved massaging her feet and chewing on her hair). These were newfound feelings for Felix, who had framed photographs of sheep on every wall of his quarters. Rebecca, the spooky maid, was played by Jenny O'Hara. Also in the cast were Drs. Lester and Sanchez (David Byrd and Luis Avalos, respectively). They were attempting to sell their nefarious instructions for the "cloning of world leaders." They wanted Helen to leave so that they could continue their evil planning, but Helen didn't take hints very well—even when the doctors bought her new luggage and a one-way ticket to Brazil. Helen was also oblivious as her own impending doom was amplified by the reading of her husband's will—she got his Flash Gordon clock radio and also full control of The Blacke Foundation. Her days were definitely numbered.

Sitcom veteran Elinor Donahue, who was up for a part in the show told me, "I was fired from this show twice. Originally, I had the choice of a 'straight' role or a 'comedic' role. By the time I got back to them with my decision to take the 'straight' role, it had been given to my friend Shelley Fabares, so I took the 'comedic' role of Frances. The day after our first table reading, I got a call saying that I'd been replaced. Well, the person who replaced me didn't work out, so they invited me back again to assume the role. I agreed, and we had a run through for the network executives. I got the 'flop sweats,' and barely made it through. Needless to say, later that same day they called me yet again to tell me that they found someone else for the part."

The program was created by Robert Blees; the developers and writers of the show were Brad Buckner, Earle Doud, Rich Orloff, and Eugenie Ross Leming; and the director was Nick Havinga. The eerie theme song was written and performed by Frank DeVol.

Hiram Holliday (see *The Adventures of Hiram Holliday*)

His Honor, Homer Bell NBC Films/Gallahad Productions. First-run syndication. 1955. 38 black-and-white episodes were filmed in New York. Sponsors included Union Pacific Railroad and the Bavarian Brewing Company.

The father of June Lockhart, native Canadian Gene Lockhart, made the transition from the big screen to the small screen in this Western sitcom in which he portrayed the kindly Justice of the Peace Homer Bell of Spring City. Bell, a widower, had a good heart and would do almost anything for folks in need. Mary Lee Dearring played his young daughter, Casey, and Jane Moultrie played his housekeeper, Maude.

Some of the best episodes include "School Play," in which Homer helped Casey with her school play by portraying a knight in shining armor, only to find himself trapped inside the costume. In "Casey at the Bat," a real battle of the sexes began to brew when Casey was banished from the boys' baseball team. And in "Substitute Sitter," Homer did a favor for a niece and filled in on her babysitting job, with hilarious results.

The program was produced by Himan Brown; directors included Brown, Derwin Abbe, and Will Price. Gene Lockhart died less than two years after the show's demise.

Hizzoner The Huddleston Company. NBC. Thursday nights 8:00. May 10, 1979–June 14, 1979. Seven episodes were videotaped before a live audience.

Years earlier, David Huddleston had been an officer in the Air Force. As an actor, Huddleston guest starred in dozens of TV comedy and drama shows, and even starred in a couple of "limited run" sitcoms in the 1970s. After *The Kallikaks*, came this one, called *Hizzoner*. Not to be confused with *His Honor, Homer Bell*, this program featured Huddleston as the much adored, rather conservative yet open-minded Michael Cooper—the mayor of a small, unnamed Midwestern town. He adored the townspeople, but wasn't above doing a few underhanded things for political gain. He had an explosive temper and loved to sing barbershop quartet harmony as a release when stressed. He was a widower and had his hands full raising two kids—a feminist, very liberal 24-year-old daughter Annie (Kathy Cronkite—daughter of the legendary CBS News anchor), who was also a civil rights attorney; and free-spirited 18-year-old James (Will Seltzer), who was part of a hippie commune called "The Wilderness Cult." "Uncle" Donald Timmons (Don Galloway) was his chief of staff; Ginny Linden (Diana Muldaur) was his private secretary; Melanie (Gina Hecht, pronounced with a hard "G" sound) was another city hall secretary; and the klutzy Nails Doyle (Mickey Deems) was Hizzoner's childhood friend, bodyguard, chauffeur, and foil. Mickey Deems recalled, "Nails had no real first name—he was always just called Nails. How my character got that nickname was never really explained on the show."

Episodes include "Mizzoner," in which a girl named Jamie (Kim Richards), a habitual runaway, was named "mayor for a day" in an effort to set her on the straight and narrow. In "Nails Gets Kidnapped," the great physical comedian, Mickey Deems had the spotlight. Deems said, "That episode was originally intended to be a two-parter, but we wound up wrapping it up in just one week." Nails, much like Archie on *Duffy's Tavern*, often coined his own words. In one episode, he pinned a flower on Hizzoner's lapel and called it a "coronation." Deems also told me, "In each script, it would be designated for me to create some physical comedy in a few spots. For example, they wanted something funny at a Xerox machine, so I got my tie caught in it." Some of the clever episode titles were "Tea and Synthesizers," and "Daughter on Tenth Avenue."

The program was produced by Sheldon Keller, best known for his Emmy-nominated writing skills on *Caesar's Hour*; the executive producer was David Huddleston; writers included Sheldon Keller and David Huddleston; directors included Joan Darling, Will Mackenzie, and Howard Storm. The theme song, "Hometown Blues," was performed by Huddleston, and written by Huddleston and Keller. The program was loosely based upon the 1958 Spencer Tracy movie *The Last Hurrah*. Mickey Deems shared, "Huddleston was a good guy, but this was his show and he wanted to do things his way. He was constantly butting heads with NBC because of it." One episode is available for viewing at the UCLA TV Archives.

Holiday Lodge J and M Productions. Revue Studios, Inc. CBS. Sunday nights 9:30. June 25, 1961–October 8, 1961. 13 black-and-white episodes were filmed with a laugh track. Sponsors included Lever Brothers, Lipton, and State Farm Insurance.

This was the 1961 summer replacement for *The Jack Benny Show*. The Canadian comedy team of Johnny Wayne and Frank Shuster portrayed Johnny Miller and Frank Boone, respectively, in this sitcom about the social and recreational directors at a posh resort hotel in Lake Holiday, California, and the wide variety of guests who came to enjoy the golf, swimming, gourmet food, and fabulous entertainment. Wayne and Shuster incorporated a bit of their stage act into each and every episode. Also in the cast were Maureen Arthur as Dorothy Jackson, Johnny Miller's girlfriend; Charles Smith as the nerdy bookworm named Woodrow; and Justice Watson as J. W. Harrington, the blustery hotel manager who fired Johnny and Wayne on a regular basis.

Holiday Lodge—**Top to bottom, Johnny Wayne and Frank Shuster (CBS).**

Episodes included "Never Hit a Stranger," in which a famous boxer named Bobo Manning (Richard Bakalyan) challenged Johnny to a fight. However, reporters learned that Bobo intended to take a dive in the third round to increase his odds in upcoming bouts and suddenly all bets were off. Jackie Coogan played Bobo's manager, Harvey Silk, in that episode. There was a lot of expository information in the flashback episode titled "Wanted: Two Recreation Directors," which explained how Johnny and Frank came to get jobs at *Holiday Lodge*. Two other guys named Archie and Lenny were originally promised the job but, while disguised as bellboys, Johnny and Frank showed them the less desirable aspects of the lodge and got them to leave. In that episode, Johnny and Frank performed a clever song (written by Johnny Wayne) called *Holiday Lodge* at the amateur show.

The program was produced by Cecil Barker; the creator and director was Seymour Berns; and writers included Ed Simmons, Bob Fisher, Hal Goodman, Larry Klein, and Alan Lipscott. Music was provided by Cyril Mockridge. Several episodes are available for viewing in the UCLA TV Archives.

Holmes and Yoyo Heyday Productions/Universal City Studios. ABC. Saturday nights 8:00. September 25,1976–December 11, 1976. 13 color episodes were filmed with a laugh track.

In between *My Living Doll* and *Small Wonder* there was this sitcom about a very human-looking robot. Detective Alexander Holmes (Richard B. Shull) was a good cop. However, he was accident prone. In the series debut, Holmes's fourth partner was hospitalized. To avoid a fifth, Holmes's next partner was an indestructible one—a robot partner, specially programmed for police work, named Gregory Yoyonovich after his inventor. (He was called "Yoyo" for short, and played by John Schuck.) He was a mobile computer who weighed 427 pounds, had his very own power source, built-in trash compactor, and a photographic memory which could be printed out like a copier (the copy would pop out of his shirt pocket). He had a control panel on his chest

Holmes and Yoyo—Left to right, Richard B. Shull, John Schuck (photograph courtesy of Jean Cummings).

(tucked under his shirt). He did, however, have a few flaws—his circuits caused an elevator's doors to shut before he could get onto it, magnets adhered to his body and were very hard to remove, garage door openers caused him to do flips, and he always got stuck on the phrase "the bunco squad" and this would necessitate him giving himself a jolt to be able to move on to the next sentence. At first, only Captain Harry Sedford (Bruce Kirby) was in on the truth about Yoyo, but after a shootout with some car thieves in the debut episode, Holmes discovered that Yoyo was a robot, and the two cops bonded. Yoyo's status remained a secret from the other cops, however, especially Officer Maxine Moon (Andrea Howard), who was attracted to Yoyo, and continually made advances to no avail.

Episodes include the debut in which a rare automobile was reported stolen. Yoyo figured it all out—how a magnet was used to get into the garage, and how the car was disassembled and put into crates for overseas shipping. In the episode titled "Funny Money," a bevy of phony twenty dollar bills were turning up all over town—even in the wallets of the other policemen. In "Dental Dynamiter," Holmes and Yoyo figured out a connection between a chain of dental office bombings and the fact that all of them attended (at one time or another) Ohio State University. Through this connection, they were able to bring the man responsible (cleaning crew member Mr. Weston, played by James Callahan) to justice.

The program was created by Jack Sher and Lee Hewitt; the producer was Arne Sultan. The executive producers, Leonard Stern and Jackie Cooper, had really high hopes for this show, touting its stars as the next Laurel and Hardy. Writers included Bruce Taylor, Sher, Lee Hewitt, and Stern; directors included John Astin. A couple of previously unaired episodes of *Holmes and Yoyo* were burned off as a summer replacement on ABC during August of 1977. John Camper of *The Chicago Daily News* wrote,

"*Holmes and Yoyo* relies heavily on sight gags, which may wear thin after several shows, but it will be fun while it lasts." A few episodes can be viewed in the UCLA TV Archives.

Homer Bell (see *His Honor, Homer Bell*)

Honestly Celeste A CBS Production. CBS. Sunday nights 9:30. October 10, 1954–December 5, 1954. Eight black-and-white episodes were broadcast live. Sponsors included Bristol-Myers.

This show replaced *The Man Behind the Badge* on the CBS schedule. Celeste Holm had gained fame in *All About Eve*, and as Ado Annie in *Oklahoma*, but that success didn't translate well to television. Here she played Celeste Anders, a former Minnesota college journalism professor who sought some real-life journalism experience, and took a job at an east coast newspaper called *The New York Express*. She rented an apartment in Greenwich Village and instantly garnered the attention of the newspaper publisher's son, Bob Wallace (Scott McKay). The two quickly became an item. Bob's father, Mr. Wallace, was played by Geoffrey Lumb; Mary Finney played Mary, Mr. Wallace's secretary; and Mike Kellin, who was very adept at playing tough guys, played cabbie Marty Gordon (who had recently been released from prison). Celeste and Marty became friends from the moment she arrived at Grand Central Station.

Ratings troubles came quickly for this show, and so writers Larry Gelbart and Hal Collins were replaced by Ed Simmons and up-and-coming Norman Lear. That didn't help very much and the show disappeared after only eight episodes. Among those episodes, one is all about Celeste starting her new life in New York City; one revolved around her search for an apartment; and yet another explored Marty's boredom with driving a cab.

The program was originally produced and directed by Joseph Scibetta and later by Dave Alexander. Music was provided by Jerry Fielding. Celeste Holm would later try another sitcom, *Nancy*, with similar results. She is probably best remembered by TV audiences as the fairy godmother in *Rodgers and Hammerstein's Cinderella*, starring Lesley Ann Warren. At least one kinescope of *Honestly, Celeste* is alleged to have survived, but its whereabouts are unknown as of this writing. Celeste Holm died on July 15, 2012, at the age of 95.

The Honeymooners Jackie Gleason Enterprises, Inc./CBS. Saturday nights 8:30 (October 1, 1955–February, 1956), and Saturday nights 8:00 (February, 1956–September 23, 1956). 39 black-and-white episodes were filmed before a live audience. Sponsored by Buick.

Some will be astonished that *The Honeymooners* was a single season sitcom. Much like *The Bickersons*, many of *The Honeymooners* episodes were done live as a semi-regular feature on variety shows such as *The Cavalcade of Stars* on the DuMont Network (with Pert Kelton as the original Alice), then on CBS in various incarnations of *The Jackie Gleason Show*. The reason that *The Honeymooners* even became a regular series was Gleason's desire to forego the rigors of doing a live weekly hour-long variety show and instead do a filmed half-hour sitcom. He originally signed a contract for 78 episodes over two seasons, but opted out after the first season, believing the show had run its course. He couldn't possibly have known how treasured and beloved the "original 39" episodes would become in later years, because when first run, *The Honeymooners* did not fare well in the ratings and was beaten handily by *The Perry Como Show*. Gleason portrayed the blustery, scheming, gullible, and yet good-hearted Madison Avenue bus driver Ralph Kramden (who earned $62 a week); Audrey Meadows was his long-suffering, sarcastic but loving and forgiving wife Alice; Art Carney played the chipper "underground engineer" and best friend who lived upstairs, Ed Norton; and Joyce Randolph was Ed's wife, ex-burlesque star Trixie Norton (Alice's best friend). While most sitcom families of the era resided in beautiful homes in nice neighborhoods, the Kramdens had spent their last 14 years in the same ramshackle, barren, two-room apartment (with an icebox, a dinosaur of a sink, and a curtainless window) at 328 Chauncey Street in Bensonhurst in Brooklyn, with $12.83 in their savings account. The Kramdens had no phone and no TV set (except in one episode for each). Ralph's everyman quality, and his constant attempts at financial success, which invariably led to crushing failures, resonated in all of us who can recite every line of every episode by heart. Ralph and Ed were Laurel and Hardy for the TV generation.

Perhaps even more than *Seinfeld*, *The Honeymooners* gave us a wealth of memorable lines and phrases, such as, "Bang, zoom," "One of these days, Alice, pow, right in the kisser," "You're goin' to the moon, Alice," "Norton, you are a mental case," "You are a blabbermouth," "Hey, Ralphie boy," "Can it core a apple?," "A string of poloponies" (pronounced puh-LOP-uh-neez), "arterial monochromia," "Luu-luuuuuu," and, of course, at the end of every episode, "Baby, you're the greatest."

Actor/musician Van Dyke Parks recalled auditioning for the role of Tommy Manicotti on the show: "It was all very intimidating at first. Jackie Gleason's offices were in the Penthouse Suite of the Plaza Hotel in New York City. However, it turned out to be a wonderful and memorable experience."

The program was produced by Jack Hurdle; the executive producer was Jack Philbin. Every episode was directed by Frank Satenstein. The six unparalleled writers were Marvin Marx, Walter Stone, Leonard Stern, Sydney Zelinka, Herbert Finn, and A. J. Russell. Music was provided by Sammy Spear and the theme song, "You're My Greatest Love" was written by Jackie Gleason and Bill Templeton. The "original 39" episodes played every night for decades on WPIX-TV channel 11 in New York. The "lost" episodes are merely the erratically timed kinescopes taken from the live Gleason variety shows of the 1950s. What are now called "The Color Honeymooners" episodes are from the 1960s version of *The Jackie Gleason Show* (with Sheila MacRae as Alice and Jane Kean as Trixie). These episodes had more of a Broadway feel to them, as most contained at least one musical number. *The Honey-Mousers* was a cartoon spoof from Warner Brothers (1956), and featured mice named Ralph Crumden and Ned Morton; obviously, *The Honeymooners* had a huge impact upon *The Flintstones*, as well. Times, styles, television, technology, and mores have changed, but the timelessness and outright brilliance of the "original 39" episodes will forever remain intact (available on a DVD box set from Paramount).

Hot l Baltimore T. A. T./ELP Communications (Norman Lear). ABC. Friday nights 9:00. January 24, 1975–June 6, 1975. 13 color episodes were videotaped at the KTTV Studios before a live audience.

Every episode began with a disclaimer about "adult content" (a first for a sitcom). This sometimes very funny Norman Lear show experienced the same kind of furor and uproar as *Soap* a couple of years later. It was way ahead of its time and reveled in pushing the envelope. Based upon the award-winning Broadway play of the same name by Lanford Wilson, *Hot l Baltimore*, the series, took place in the lobby of a once grand hotel in Maryland. However, it was grand no longer—but rather run down. The neon letter "E" in "hotel" had long since burned out (and was never replaced). The hotel manager was Clifford Ainsley, played by Richard Masur, and the desk clerk, Bill Lewis, was played by James Cromwell. Several extremely diverse people took up residence there—and it's they who caused the furor. There were two "ladies of the evening"—Columbia-native Suzy Marta Rocket, played by Jeannie Linero, and April Green, played by Conchata Ferrell. April and desk clerk Bill were sometimes romantically linked. Also in attendance were TV's first regular gay characters, roommates George and Gordon (Lee Bergere and Henry Calvert, respectively). Add to that, a mean and cranky hypochondriacal septuagenarian named Mr. Morse (Stan Gottlieb); a dizzy, unemployed waitress named Millie (Gloria LeRoy); a tomboy named Jackie (Robin Wilson); a shady philosopher named Charles Bingham (Al Freeman, Jr.); an eccentric woman named Mrs. Bellotti (Charlotte Rae); and her unseen but even more eccentric son, Moose, who had some very exotic pets and had a penchant for mischief (such as recreating *The Poseidon Adventure* in his bathtub, and buttering the hallway). ABC had high hopes for this Norman Lear sitcom, and before cancellation seriously considered moving the show to a much later time slot.

Episodes include "Millie's Beau," in which one of Suzy's "clients" dropped dead in her bedroom, and suddenly she began having second thoughts about her chosen profession. In "George and Gordon," the elderly gay couple had a spat. Gordon was taking night classes in law school (he was tired of being just a shoe salesman). George then checked out of the hotel and the other residents made it their responsibility to get the couple back together. In "Mrs. Bellotti's Boyfriend," it seemed as though Mrs. Bellotti was about to walk down the aisle again—that is, until her fiancée found out about the wackiness of her son Moose. In "Ainsley's Secret," everyone was amazed when Ainsley, who was usually terrified of the opposite sex, suddenly had two girlfriends and a paternity suit.

The program was produced by Ron Clark, Woody Kling, and Gene Marcione; the executive producer was Rod Parker; writers included Kling; and directors included Burt Brinckerhoff and Tony Mordente. Music was provided by Marvin Hamlisch. A couple of episodes can be viewed at the Paley Center for Media.

Hot Off the Wife (see *The Jim Backus Show*)

Husbands, Wives and Lovers 20th Century–Fox. CBS. Friday nights 10:00. March 10, 1978–June 30, 1978. 13 hour-long episodes were videotaped with a laugh track at Golden West Studios.

The pilot was titled simply "Husbands and Wives," but that was expanded for the series. Sitcoms 30 minutes in length have flourished, but when expanded to 60 minutes something goes awry. *Husbands, Wives and Lovers* was another attempt to make the hour-long sitcom work, but it lasted only about three months. This was the story of five couples from the San Fernando Valley, near Los Angeles, who all knew one another—some were friends, some were relatives, and some were in-laws. Murray Zuckerman (Stephen Pearlman) was away a lot—he was a traveling salesman for a large pharmaceutical company; his love-starved wife, Paula (Cynthia Harris), reluctantly accepted his frequent absences; raspy-voiced Harry Bellini (Eddie Barth) was a tough, streetwise, self-taught waste management tycoon; and Joy was his much younger, dimwitted second wife (Lynne Marie Stewart). Joy was always bringing people her homemade cookies, fudge and caramels. Lennie Bellini (Mark Lonow) was Harry's younger brother, who was living with Rita DeLaTorre, played by Randee Heller. Together they ran Lennie's Denim Boutique (even their car seats were done in denim, with pockets for maps). Lennie's older brother Harry constantly urged the couple to get married, to no avail. All of the couples used the same dentist, Ron Willis (Ron Rifkin), who was separated from but still friends with his soon-to-be ex-wife, Helene (Jesse Welles). Ron's best friend and Helene's divorce attorney were the same person—Dixon Carter Fielding (Charles Siebert), and his wife was Courtney (Claudette Nevins) who spent his money as fast as he could make it.

One of the better episodes centered around Ron, who was unfairly charged with sexual assault by his sexy new patient, Carol Tyson (Trisha Noble). Through some trickery, the wives got Carol to admit that she had similar lawsuits in numerous other cities, and eventually the false charges against Ron were dropped before his spotless reputation had been sullied.

This program was produced by Don Van Atta; the executive producer was Hal Dresner; writers included Steve Kreinberg, Dresner, Joan Rivers, and Andy Guerdat; and directors included Marc Daniels, James Burrows, Alan Myerson and Bill Persky. The theme song was written by Ken and Mitzi Welch, and music was provided by Jack Elliott and Allyn Ferguson. The creator and executive story consultant was comedienne Joan Rivers.

Ichabod and Me A Kayro-JaM Production/Revue Studios. CBS. Tuesday nights 9:30. September 26, 1961–September 18, 1962. 36 black-and-white episodes were filmed with a laugh track. Sponsors included Quaker Oats, York Imperial-Sized Cigarettes, and Kent Cigarettes.

The character of Ichabod Adams originated in several episodes of *Robert Montgomery Presents* in the late 1950s. Adams then surfaced in an episode of *General Electric Theater* hosted by Ronald Reagan. Said episode, which served as the series pilot, was titled "Adam's Apples" and aired on April 24, 1960. Most of the pieces of the puzzle were already in place—George Chandler was Ichabod Adams and Christine White was his daughter Abigail Adams. However, Fred Beir portrayed Mr. Major (Terrence "Terry" Major, that is—he'd visited the previous summer and Abigail had taken a shine to him) in the pilot, but it was sitcom veteran Robert Sterling who would get the lead role in the series (as "Bob" Major). Sterling had previously been in two sitcoms (*Topper* and *Love That Jill*) with his real-life wife, Anne Jeffreys, but this time he was flying solo. Widower Bob Major and his six-year-old son, Benji (played by Jerry Mathers' little brother, Jimmy Mathers [in the pilot, Mr. Major had a dog named Fownes—named after his former boss, but no children]) are tired of big city life and settle in the small New Hampshire town of Phippsboro. Major took over the editing job of the *Phippsboro Bulletin* (a job previously held by Ichabod, who was also Phippsboro's long-time mayor). Major also eventually became romantically linked with Ichabod's daughter, Abigail. The pilot and the series were filmed at Revue Studios in Hollywood.

Episodes include "A Letter from Juliet," in which Mr. Major, who was wearing many hats at the *Phippsboro Bulletin*, gave a young couple some bad advice in the "Dear Debbie" column, thereby angering the girl's father. In "Bob's Redhead," an old girlfriend named Leona (Merry Anders) visited Phippsboro with designs on marrying Mr. Major. In "Election Fever," Ichabod had run for mayor unopposed for decades—that is, until his future son-in-law Bob Major threw his hat into the ring.

Guest stars included Rod Serling, who portrayed reclusive author Eugene Hollenfield in the episode called "The Celebrity"; Margaret Hamilton appeared in "The Purple Cow" as an artist who opted to live in obscurity rather than seek the limelight; and Irene Ryan and Mary Treen appeared in "The Old Stowe Road" as longtime residents of Phippsboro who didn't want to see growth in their small town, and offered a bevy of resistance when attempts were made to get Old Stowe Road open to prosperity and the twentieth century.

The program was produced by Irving Paley; the executive producers were Joe Connelly and Bob Mosher; writers included George Tibbles, the team of Joe Connelly and Bob Mosher, Allan Mannings, and the team of Bob Ross and Joseph Hoffman; and directors included Herschel Daugherty and Norman Abbott. The theme song was an updated version of the old fife and drum classic "The Girl I Left Behind Me." Christine White had been close friends with James Dean before their big breaks in the business. After the show was canceled, Sterling grew very disgusted with the business and appeared on TV very rarely. A few episodes can be viewed in the UCLA TV Archives.

I'm Dickens, He's Fenster Heyday Productions/Desilu Studios. ABC. Friday nights 9:00. September 28, 1962–September 13, 1963. 32 black-and-white episodes were filmed before a live audience. Sponsors included Crest Toothpaste, Tide, Crest, and El Producto Cigars.

Since they worked with tools, it was very clever that the "D" in "Dickens" was a c-clamp, and the "F" in "Fenster" was a monkey wrench in the opening credits. *I'm Dickens, He's Fenster* had good chemistry, good timing, and good slapstick—it just didn't have good ratings up against *Route 66* on CBS and *Sing Along With Mitch* on NBC. The original working title for the show was *The Workers*. This was the story of a pair of inept Los Angeles carpenters who were the best of friends and both started working for their boss, Mr. Myron Bannister (Frank DeVol), on the very same day nine years back. Arch Fenster (Marty Ingels) was single—a playboy (his little black book was legendary—several volumes—and he had the ultimate bachelor pad). Arch had been engaged nine times, but there were more than subtle hints that he had feelings for Kate Dickens. Arch was a bit of a moocher and yet extremely kindhearted—a true, loyal friend. He kept every tool and gadget in alphabetical order in the many pockets of his overalls. Fenster was the optimist and Dickens was the pessimist. Harry Dickens (John Astin) treated Fenster like the son he never had (the Dickenses were childless). Harry was 33 years old and his home was always a work in progress with splotches of mismatched paint on the walls, and cabinet doors which never opened and shut properly. He was somewhat pushy, sometimes overbearing, he gave bad advice, and he was rather insecure and subject to fits of jealousy—especially concerning his friendship (with Fenster) and his marriage (to Kate, played by Emmaline Henry). Kate was of Scottish descent and she was an extremely patient soul (considering all of the madcap goings-on). On the job, Dickens and Fenster's co-workers were Mel Warshaw (who had ten children) played by Dave Ketchum, Bob Dangerfield Mulligan (Henry Beckman), and Bentley (Noam Pitlik). They all worked for the most even-tempered man on earth, Myron Bannister (Frank DeVol).

Among the funniest episodes (and there were many) was the debut, "A Small Matter of Being Fired," in which Dickens was certain he wasn't getting the promotion he deserved because the boss continually forgot his name. He did, however get the promotion, only to find out that his first duty on the new job was to fire Fenster. In "Nurse Dickens," Kate got a part-time job as a nurse at a local hospital and the ever-jealous Harry was convinced that she was fooling around with the handsome doctors and male nurses there, so he and Fenster devised a plan to spy on her. Lee Meriwether guest starred in that episode and told me, "I was so nervous about this episode. I only had about five lines, and for me, a smaller role is more difficult than a larger role. And, the show was filmed before a live audience, making me even more nervous." In "Harry—The Father Image," Fenster's playboy ways came back to bite him when he forgot to let his many girlfriends know of his upcoming plans to wed, and they all showed up at the same time at the Dickens house. Future celebrities who made guest appearances include Ellen Burstyn (as Ellen McRae), Jim Nabors, Harvey Korman, Sally Kellerman, Peter Lupus, and Yvonne Craig.

The program was created and produced by Leonard Stern; writers included Stern, Don Hinkley, Mel Tolkin, Sheldon Keller, Howard Merrill, Jerry Davis, Frank Fox, Marty Roth,

Mel Diamond, Barry Blitzer, Walter Kempley, Ray Singer, Dick Chevillat, Fred Freeman, Garry Marshall, Wilton Schiller, Arthur Alsberg, and Bob Fisher; and directors included Arthur Hiller, Norman Abbott, Claudio Guzman, and Stern. The memorable theme song was written by Irving Szathmary (older brother of Bill Dana), who also wrote the legendary *Get Smart* theme. Stern was seeking a theme reminiscent of the old *Laurel and Hardy* theme song, and Szathmary, with that in mind, created "The Dickens and Fenster March." Dell released two *I'm Dickens, He's Fenster* comic books during the show's run; each sold for twelve cents. The program is now available on DVD from TV Time Machine Productions and Lightyear Entertainment.

In the Beginning T. A. T. Communications. CBS. Wednesday nights 8:30. September 20, 1978–October 18, 1978. Nine episodes were videotaped at Metrotape West Studios before a live audience; only five aired.

Even with a strong lead-in from *The Jeffersons*, this show failed to find an audience and disappeared from the CBS prime time lineup very quickly. It was the second of four ill-fated McLean Stevenson attempts at solo sitcom success after leaving *M*A*S*H*. *In the Beginning*, for all intents and purposes, was *Going My Way* revisited. McLean portrayed a conservative Irish priest named Father Daniel M. Cleary. His nemesis was a perky, energetic, street savvy, very liberal young nun named Sister Agnes (Priscilla Lopez) who was assigned to him. She wanted to set up a storefront mission in her home neighborhood in inner-city Baltimore, Maryland. She loved her job, working to help the downtrodden, the derelicts, the winos, the addicts, the hookers, and the ex-cons in the area. Conversely, Father Cleary hated it and tried everything within his power to get a transfer. Cleary had a nickname for Sister Agnes: "Attila the Nun." Others in the cast included Priscilla Morrill as Sister Lillian and Jack Dodson as Monsignor Francis X. Barlow. Some of the youngsters who frequented the mission were Bad Lincoln (Michael Anthony), Jerome Rockefeller (Bobby Ellerbee), and Willie (Olivia Barash). Barash told me, "What I remember most about those days is wanting to hang around the adults, like McLean Stevenson and Norman Lear. I was always being pulled away from conversations with these men, because of how colorful their discussions were. A word that I heard my mother say, when explaining why I shouldn't hang around them, was 'risque.' It was probably not the best arena for a little girl to be raised in." She also told me, "I really hit it off with Priscilla Lopez. We had a great New York City connection."

Episodes include "What's It All About?" with guest star Rick Springfield. Barash told me, "I loved working with Rick. I was very into music, and he was really on a roll at that time." Other episodes include "Cleary's Crisis," "The Good Thief," and "Aggie's Love Story." The show was canceled after only five airings. The four episodes left in the can were titled "The Poker Game," "The Kook," "Well-Heeled," and "Wedding for Three."

Barash remembered, "I loved that this show was videotaped before a live audience. It was much more like doing a play. I loved the live stage, and I got to work with some amazing people on Broadway such as Angela Lansbury and Ann Miller." She also said, "Somewhere in storage I have a wonderful memento of *In the Beginning*. I wore a gold satin baseball jacket with my

***In the Beginning*—McLean Stevenson and Priscilla Lopez (photograph courtesy of Olivia Barash).**

character's name, Willie, on the front, and a dragon on the back. I loved the jacket and I got to keep it."

The program was produced by Jim Mulligan and Rita Dillon; the executive producers were Mort Lachman and Norman Steinberg; the creators were Mulligan and Norman Lear; writers included Joseph Calvelli, Harriet Weiss, Pat Shea, Leonora Thuna, Joseph Bonaduce, Ron Bloomberg, Michael Morris, and Stephanie A. Miller; and directors included Doug Rogers, Jack Shea, Will Mackenzie, Marc Daniels, Bobby Lally, and Randy Winburn. The music was provided by Barry DeVorzon.

It's a Business? DuMont Network. Wednesday nights 9:00. March 19, 1952–May 21, 1952. Ten episodes were broadcast live.

Much like *Love and Marriage*, which would come a few years later, this short-lived sitcom focused upon the world of music publishing, but with a twist—the program was set in the Tin Pan Alley era. Leo DeLyon and Bob Haymes (brother of singer Dick Haymes) worked for the Broadway Music Publishing Company at a time when singers went directly to publishers for new material. The music and the comedy on this program were very Vaudevillian. Some old-time Vaudevillian performers visited the offices and there was quite a bit of singing in each episode. The secretary was an up-and-coming young actress named Dorothy Loudon, who was still studying at the Alviene School of Dramatic Arts at the time. Dorothy went on to become a big star and Tony Award-winner on Broadway. She attempted sitcom fame again more than 25 years later in *Dorothy*, which lasted just about as long as *It's a Business? It's a Business?* replaced *Famous Jury Trials* on the DuMont schedule.

DeLyon told me, "The shows were broadcast live from the old Adelphi Theater at 152 West 54th Street in New York City. Mort Lindsey, later of *The Merv Griffin Show*, was our musical director. Even though the show was broadcast live, I don't recall us having any on-camera mishaps. If we forgot any of the lyrics to any of the songs, we just threw in a few 'tra la las' to cover. One of the stars of our show, Bob Haymes, went on to write the classic song *That's All*, which became the theme song for American Airlines." Among the celebrity guests was actress Irene Dunne. DeLyon went on to provide the voice for several characters (Spook and Brain) on the classic *Top Cat* cartoon series.

The program was created by Bob Weiskopf; the producers were Paul Rosen and Charles Parsons; the director was Frank Bunetta; and writers included Norman Baer, Snag Werris, and Weiskopf. To my knowledge, no episodes of *It's a Business?* exist.

***It's a Business?*—The only known photograph from this live DuMont program. Leo DeLyon as a turn of the century song plugger (photograph courtesy of Leo DeLyon).**

It's a Man's World Heyday Productions/Revue Studios. NBC. Monday nights 7:30. September 17, 1962–January 28, 1963. 19 hour-long black-and-white episodes were filmed without a laugh track. Sponsors include Chesebrough Ponds, Inc., L and M Cigarettes, and Faberge.

Years later, shows such as *It's a Man's World* would be called "dramedies." This was the story of four guys living together on a houseboat called the *Elephant*, docked on the Ohio River in the small Midwestern town of Cordella (an idea attempted again years later on *The San Pedro Beach Bums*). Wes Macauley (Glenn Corbett) worked at Houghton Stott's Gas Station (Mr. Stott was played by Harry Harvey, Jr.) while going to college. Wes's busy schedule kept him from marrying his sweetheart, Irene Hoff, who wanted nothing more than to be a housewife and mother (played by Jan Norris). Wes, and his younger brother, Howie (Michael Burns), both lived on the houseboat and were orphaned when their parents were killed in an automobile accident. Also on the houseboat was the very brainy "Tom Tom" DeWitt (whose clever lines were referred to as DeWitticisms), played by Ted Bessell. He was a non-conformist and very socially conscious with aspirations of joining the Peace Corps. The fourth man rounding out the "man's world" on the houseboat was Vern Hodges of Bunkham County, North Carolina. Vern (Randy Boone) had a southern drawl, played the guitar, wore a leather jacket, worked in Dobson's Market, and was considered unaware, uninvolved, and apathetic by others (but really was more on the ball than he let on). Speaking of Dobson's, employed at that rundown emporium were Virgil Dobson (Scott White) who loved to fish; Virgil's portly wife, Iona (Kate Murtaugh), who had a very sunny disposition; and their daughter Alma Jean (Jeanine Cashell), who had a crush on Vern. When on land, the four "men" got around Cordella in a convertible Jeep. Also living on the houseboat were a dog and a cat.

Episodes include "A Drive to Exeter," in which Vern became a bad influence on impressionable young Howie when he took the youngster along on a road trip to Exeter—a nearby town with a bad reputation. In "The Man on the Second Floor," young Howie really wanted a job at Stott's Gas Station, but Mr. Stott wouldn't hire him. However, when Howie gave up on Stott and instead got a job at an insurance company, suddenly Mr. Stott was very jealous. In "The Macauley Profile," the "men" took a series of aptitude tests as a favor to Wes's girl, Irene, only to come back with results they didn't quite expect. In "Hour of Truth," Vern considered himself a "social dud," and tried to do something about it—tell people the truth. His frankness was at first refreshing and even amusing, but eventually led to many hurt feelings.

The program was created and produced by Peter Tewksbury and Jim Leighton; writers included Tewksbury, Leighton, David Duncan, James Menzies, Earl Hamner, Jr., John McGreevey, Ben Masselink, Williams Blinn, Elliott Simms, Michael Gleason, Hal J. Todd, Robert Bassing, and James Barnett; and directors included Tewksbury, Lamont Johnson, James Goldstone, and Hal J. Todd. Music (sometimes featuring only a banjo, a harmonica, or an organ) was provided by Jack Marshall. Many episodes are available for viewing in the UCLA TV Archives.

It's About Time Redwood/Gladasya Productions/United Artists. CBS. Sunday nights 7:30. September 11, 1966–August 27, 1967. 26 color episodes were filmed with a laugh track.

Even though *It's About Time* was a single season sitcom, everyone can sing its theme song. It's about two men in the strangest place—that place was planet Earth in the Stone Age. In their capsule (Scorpio EX-1), Captain "Mac" MacKenzie (Frank Aletter) and Lieutenant Hector "Hec" Canfield (Jack Mullaney) broke the time barrier and made a really rough landing in the middle of a pre-historic jungle rife with dinosaurs and cavemen. Luckily, they befriended a cave family after rescuing that family's son, Breer (Pat Cardi), who was hanging by a branch over a cliff. Breer's attractive older sister Mlor (Mary Graham Grace), father Gronk (Joe E. Ross) and mother Shag (Imogene Coca) were very grateful. Yes, in the very early episodes she was Shag with a "g," but somewhere along the way her name became Shad with a "d." This cave family protected "Mac and Hec" from the other cavemen who wanted the "evil spirits who dress funny" to be killed. The unfriendly (and extremely naïve) cavemen were the always suspicious "Boss" (Cliff Norton) and the bully "Clon" (Mike Mazurki). Mac and Hec attempted to stay on all of the cavemen's good sides while repairing their capsule, but that wasn't easy—the cavemen were fearful of that space capsule, of shaking hands, and of Hec's box of matches which "start fire with finger." Shad and Gronk helped find the materials needed, mainly copper, to fix the ship so that the astronauts could return to the 20th Century.

On January 22, 1967, Mac and Hec did just that: they left the pre-historic jungle to return to Los Angeles in the modern era and the lyrics of the show's theme song changed accordingly. However, the astronauts didn't leave the jungle empty handed. To prove to their commanding officer, General J. P. Morley (Frank Wilcox) that they indeed visited the Stone Age, they brought Shad, Gronk, Breer, and Mlor along with them. This format change led to many new "fish out of water" possibilities for the cave family (and for the show's writers as well). Everything was scary and new to the cave family—water faucets, rocking chairs (alive chair), TV sets, radios (box with sound), automobiles (strange animal), doors, and

It's About Time—Imogene Coca and Joe E. Ross, *lower right, l-r:* Frank Aletter and Jack Mullaney.

windows (hole in wall) just to name a few. To keep the cave family from creating a media circus, Mac and Hec kept them in their apartment (much to the dismay of their long-suffering building superintendent Mr. Tyler, played by Alan DeWitt). Mac and Hec told their landlord that their new roommates were from the small country of Nordania. The format change, however, did not lead to a ratings surge, and it was just a matter of time before *It's About Time* was no longer part of the CBS primetime lineup.

The program was produced by George Cahan; the creator and executive producer was Sherwood Schwartz; writers included Schwartz, Elroy Schwartz, David P. Harmon, Bruce Howard, Joel Kane, Michael Morris, Roland MacLane, Al Lewin, Herbert Finn, and Alan Dinehart; and directors included Richard Donner, Jerry Hopper, George Cahan, David McDearmon, Jack Shea, Bill Freedman, Ben Gershman, and Leslie Goodwins. Gold Key issued one *It's About Time* comic book (with Gronk and Shad on the cover) in 1967, selling for twelve cents each.

It's Always Jan Desilu Studios, Hollywood/A Janard Production. CBS. Saturday nights 9:30. September 10, 1955–June 30, 1956. 26 black-and-white episodes were filmed with a laugh track. Sponsored by Dreen Shampoo, Crest Toothpaste, and Dash Detergent.

This sitcom was somewhat of a *So This Is Hollywood* meets *How to Marry a Millionaire*. Jan Stewart (Janis Paige) was a nightclub singer who performed regularly in a place called Tony's Cellar in New York, but was always aspiring to bigger and better things (which, despite her talent, never panned out). Jan, in fact, got the opportunity to sing in almost every episode. She was a war widow with a ten-year-old daughter named Josie (Jeri Lou James). Jan and Josie had two other female roommates in their Manhattan apartment in the East 50s to help pay the bills—up-and-coming actress/model Val Marlowe (Merry Anders) and secretary to a theatrical producer, Pat Murphy (Pat Bright). The three adult women frequently quibbled over and competed for the attention of eligible bachelors. Speaking of bachelors, there were two of them in the regular cast—a young Arte Johnson played delicatessen delivery boy Stanley Schreiber and Sid Melton portrayed Jan's loyal agent and longtime friend Harry Cooper.

Episodes include "Guilty Conscience," in which Jan was lured by a big time show business agent who promised her the world. While this offer was indeed enticing, she remained loyal to good old Harry Cooper. In "Love Rings Bells," Jan and Pat had a big fight and Pat decided to move out, but young Josie devised a clever scheme to get them to patch up their differences.

The program was produced by Arthur Stander; Janard Productions was a combination of the names Janis Paige and Arthur Stander. The writers included Stanley Adams; directors included Norman Tokar. Music was provided by Spencer-Hagen.

Ivan the Terrible King Hitzig Productions. CBS. Saturday nights 8:30. August 21, 1976–September 18, 1976. Five episodes were videotaped before a live audience at CBS Broadcast Center, Studio 41 in New York City.

Unlike his namesake, this Ivan was not so terrible—in fact, he was a decent, hard-working guy. Ivan Petrovsky (Lou Jacobi) was the head waiter at the Hotel Metropole in Moscow. His wife Olga (Maria Karnilova) drove a truck and worked on a construction crew. They lived together with seven others and an unseen, vicious dog named Rasputin in a tiny apartment. Under the same roof were Vladimir—Olga's first husband (Phil Leeds), a chess champion; Tatiana (Despo), Ivan's mother-in-law who was a subway conductor; son Nikolai (Alan Cauldwell) who was a cosmonaut with a fear of heights; Nikolai's wife Svetlana (Nana Tucker—later known as Nana Visitor) was a ballerina; daughter Sonya (Caroline Kava); and young son Saacha (Matthew Barry), the only one without a job and the only one who could control Rasputin. The only non-family member was Raoul (Manuel Martinez) from Cuba, who had lived with the family for four years, but still spoke no Russian.

Episodes include "Ivan's Out of Work," in which Vladimir urged Ivan to demand a raise from his boss. Ivan followed the advice, only to find himself unemployed. In "The Very Loud Family," a smarmy American TV host tried to get the Petrovskys to be part of a documentary about "the typical Russian family."

The program was produced by Rupert Hitzig; the executive producer was Alan King (who also held that title on the short-lived series *The Corner Bar*); the creator was Herbert Sargent; writers included Michael Barrie, Jim Mulholland, and Sargent; and directors included Peter H. Hunt. The opening theme song tells of "beautiful Moscow" and how it gets better every day. *Ivan the Terrible* was one of only a small handful of sitcoms videotaped in New York City in the 1970s.

The Jean Arthur Show Universal City Studios. CBS. Monday nights 10:00. September 12, 1966–December 5, 1966. 12 color episodes were filmed with a laugh track. Sponsored by General Foods.

Actress Jean Arthur had previously gained acclaim in great movies like *Mr. Smith Goes to Washington*, *Mr. Deeds Goes to Town*, and *Shane*. In 1966, in semi-retirement, she was about to become 66 years old when CBS approached her with an idea for a sitcom. Jean needed a lot of convincing and reluctantly agreed. The original working title was *Mothers Word Is Law*, but to cash in on her star power, the eponymous title was selected. Jean portrayed a widowed and rather feisty seasoned lawyer named Patricia Marshall of the Marshall and Marshall law firm in Beverly Hills. The other Marshall was her 25-year-old son Paul (Ron Harper). Harper told me, "She looked so spectacular for her age there was some concern that I looked young enough to portray her son." He recalled, "Jean Arthur absolutely loved animals. She lived in Carmel, California, and I visited her. I had my German shepherd puppy, Ralphie in the car. She insisted that I bring the dog inside. She had several cats, and they were very frightened of the dog. Ralphie tore down a beaded curtain between two of the rooms in her house, and he jumped into her fish pond and tracked water through the house. She wasn't angry at all. She loved it. She was a wonderful and warm person." Similar to *Harrigan and Son*, parent and child often ended up on opposite sides of the courtroom. In the episode titled "My Client, the Rooster," Patricia was defending a young boy named Robby Fielding (Clint Howard), whose pet rooster named Brewster's crowing was disturbing a neighbor named Nelson Craig (Paul Reed). The younger Marshall was already representing Mr. Craig, a new and important client from Fidelity Chemicals and took on the additional duty of presenting Craig's side of the rooster case. In the episode titled "Lament of a Horse Player," Mickey Rooney guest starred as Eddie, an elevator operator with a gambling problem. Eddie had been secretly using Paul's phone to place his bets, and this led to Paul's arrest for bookmaking. Patricia then stepped in to help Eddie cure his gambling problem, and help Paul clear his name. In "A Slight Case of Music," Patricia defended the new girlfriend of her chauffeur Morton (Leonard Stone) in a rock and roll episode about copyright law.

The Jean Arthur Show—**Left to right, Ron Harper, Jean Arthur and Leonard Stone (photograph courtesy of Ron Harper).**

Harper remembered, "Richard Conte joined the cast midstream as an ex-gangster named Richie Wells, who liked my mother, Patricia. He was a brilliant dramatic actor, but what a great surprise it was that he was also great in a comedic role." Ron also said, "I think the time slot was the biggest reason our show wasn't more of a success. 10 p.m. was much too late for a family sitcom."

The producer was Si Rose; the executive producers were Richard Quine and Jay Richard Kennedy; writers included Steven Gethers, Ed James, John Fenton Murray, and Seaman Jacobs; and directors included Alan Rafkin and Mickey

Rooney. Quine and Kennedy also assisted Johnny Keating in writing the theme song "Merry-Go-Round." In the opening credits, Jean Arthur rode one of the painted ponies, and with each revolution of the carousel, she was sporting a totally different costume. A review by Aleene McMunn in the *Los Angeles Times* called the program "a class production in scenery, costume and talent." A couple of episodes can be viewed at the UCLA TV Archives. Harper recalled, "For our show and our sponsor, General Foods, Jean and I did a Jello commercial. Together we sang the 'J-E-L-L-O' jingle. We didn't sing very well, but it was fun and very memorable."

The Jean Carroll Show (see *Take it from Me*)

The Jim Backus Show (Hot Off the Wire) A RayDic Production. MGM Studios and Desilu Studios. 1960–1961. First-run syndication by California National Productions, Incorporated (CNP). 39 black-and-white episodes were filmed. Sponsors included Carling Beer and H. P. Hood and Sons, Inc.

In between *I Married Joan* and *Gilligan's Island*, Jim Backus starred in this syndicated sitcom as John Michael O'Toole, in charge of the Headline Press Service. O'Toole found it almost impossible to keep his company in the black and was constantly dodging all of his creditors while seeking that next big news scoop. His girl Friday was Dora Miles, played by the lovely Nita Talbot. Even though O'Toole was the boss, Dora had a lot of clout in the newsroom. Also on hand was the office boy Sidney (Bobs Watson). James Callahan was a semi-regular playing a reporter, but had two different character names—Bill Nichols and Lou.

Some of the more memorable episodes included "In the Rough," in which a new up and coming golfer was a gorilla named Arnold. Backus' real-life wife, Henny, played Henrietta Updyke in this episode, and golfer Jimmy Demaret made a cameo appearance as himself. In "The Woman's Touch," Dora had the notion that she could run things better than Mike, so she was briefly given the reins. There were immediate problems—the man Dora hired to be the new sales manager turned out to be a wanted polygamist. There was a holiday episode called "Sad Sack Santa," in which a man on the street (J. Pat O'Malley) dressed as Mr. Claus during the summer months turned out to be a department store Santa who had been out of work since the previous Christmas.

Writers included Stanley Davis, Elon Packard, Arthur Marx, Mannie Manheim, John L. Greene, Joe Quillan, and the team of Ray Singer and Dick Chevillat. Singer and Chevillat also produced the show—thus the name RayDic Productions. Directors included Christian Nyby, Johnny Florea, and Gene Reynolds. Singer, Chevillat, and Nyby had all previously worked together on *It's a Great Life*. A few episodes can be viewed in the UCLA TV Archives.

The Jimmy Stewart Show J. K. Ablidon Productions/Warner Brothers Television. NBC. Sunday nights 8:30. September 19, 1971–August 27, 1972. 24 color episodes were filmed without a laugh track. Sponsors included Procter and Gamble.

Josiah Kessel traveled from Pennsylvania to California during the gold rush. He found gold by selling whiskey and then purchasing quite a bit of land. He became extremely wealthy. Kessel couldn't read or write, but ironically his mansion in Easy Valley, California, became Josiah Kessel College years later. Kessel's grandson, James Kessel Howard (Jimmy Stewart), was a professor of anthropology at the college (he traveled to work each day by bicycle). He also played the accordion in his spare time. Howard had been married to the same youthful woman, Martha (Julie Adams), for 30 years, living at 35 Hillview Drive. Together they had a 29-year-old son named P.J. (Peter Jacob), played by Jonathan Daly, and a very bright eight-year-old son named Teddy (Dennis Larson). The elder son also had an eight-year-old son named Jake (Kirby Furlong). Teddy insisted that he be referred to as "Uncle Teddy" by Jake, even though they were born only five days apart. Jake's mom and Peter's wife was Wendy (Ellen Geer). Peter, Wendy and Jake lived ("lived" being the operant word) in their own house in Easy Valley until Jim accidentally burned it down. He'd been babysitting for grandson Jake and fell asleep with a lit cigar given to him by his best friend (Dr. Luther Quince, a chemistry professor played by John McGiver). Jim and Jake got out safely, but nothing was saved. With nowhere else to go, the kids moved in with Jim and Martha and the three generations of Howards were now all living under the same roof.

Episodes include "The Price of Plumbing Is Numbing," in which the single bathroom for six residents in the Howard household became troublesome, but adding one was deemed too expensive. In "Song of the Jailbird," Jim was the victim of a prank which landed him in jail—he played the accordion for a stripper at a stag party.

Jimmy Stewart's star power attracted many big name guest stars such as Cesar Romero, Jackie Coogan, Vincent Price, Regis Philbin, William Windom, and Gloria DeHaven.

The program was created and produced by Hal Kanter; writers included Kanter, John Lee Mahin, Fred S. Fox, and Seaman Jacobs; and directors included Kanter and Christian Nyby. Music was provided by Jeff Alexander. Jimmy stepped out of character at the beginning and end of each episode to address the audience as Jimmy Stewart. Sadly, Stewart was one of those huge motion picture stars who just couldn't make the successful transition to television (along with Henry Fonda, Mickey Rooney, Lana Turner, Debbie Reynolds, and Jean Arthur, to name but a few). *The Jimmy Stewart Show* was briefly rerun on the defunct Good Life cable network. Stewart tried again with a drama series titled *Hawkins*, but it suffered the same fate. Cecil Smith of the *Los Angeles Times* wrote, "Stewart is a highly-skilled and polished actor, but he's not a funny man. And the show runs more to whimsy and gentle humor than to laughter. It is also loaded with charm."

Joe and Mabel Kenco Films, Inc. CBS. Tuesday nights 9:00. June 26, 1956–September 25, 1956. 13 black-and-white episodes were filmed using a laugh track. Sponsored by Pharmaceuticals, Incorporated (Geritol, Serutan, Sominex) and Carter Products (Arrid and Rise).

The program was originally slated for the 1955 fall schedule but was delayed and used as a summer replacement show in 1956 instead. This was the story of cab driver (cab number 124) Joe Spartan (Larry Blyden). Each episode began and ended with Joe, in his taxi, addressing us as if we were sitting in the backseat (we would see his face in the rear view mirror, conveniently placed next to a picture of his girlfriend Mabel). At the beginning of the show he'd set up the episode, and at the end he'd give a preview of next week's show. Joe was the jealous type. He was very much in love with manicurist Mabel Spooner (Nita Talbot), but had cold feet about the responsibilities associated with marriage. On the other hand, Mabel (who lived in apartment 3H on Bushwick Avenue in Brooklyn) was ready and very eager to tie the knot. Mabel had a very strong New York accent. She lived with her widowed mother, Adele Spooner (Luella Gear), and her younger brother, Sherman (Michael Mann). Mabel's best friend was Dolly Armstrong (Shirl Conway). Joe's best friend was fellow cabbie Mike (Norman Fell). Joe and Mike would frequently hang out at the counter of Mac's Diner and try to figure ways out of predicaments over coffee. John Shellie portrayed Harry, who worked behind the counter. The program was based upon characters created in stories written by Irving Gaynor Neiman. Actor Marvin Kaplan recalled, "CBS's New York office wanted to cancel the series I was on, *Meet Millie*, to put *Joe and Mabel* on the schedule, but our loyal fans kept bringing us back. When it did finally air, it replaced *Guy Lombardo's Diamond Jubilee Show*."

Episodes include "The Line-up," in which Joe's fare greatly resembled a wanted criminal. He was reluctant to tell the police—fearing for his life, but Mabel urged him to do the right thing. In "Mabel's Voice," Mabel noticed Joe's infatuation with a female singer on TV and dis-

Joe and Mabel—**Nita Talbot and Larry Blyden (CBS).**

creetly decided to take voice lessons herself. Comedy ensued when Joe was led to believe that Mabel was seeing another man, but that other man was really her elderly vocal coach. In "Mabel's Legacy," Mabel's old love letters revealed that she was once involved with an older millionaire named Stanley. When Stanley kicked the bucket, it was thought that Mabel might be an heiress.

The program was produced by Alex Gottlieb and Paul Bogart; the executive producer was Marlo Lewis; writers included Lucille Kallen, Phil Sharp, Aaron Ruben, Harvey Orkin, Jerry Ryan, Harold Flender, Irving Gaynor Neiman, and James Lee; and directors included Daniel Petrie, Bogart, and Ezra Stone. The show was packaged by David Susskind, and the opening credits were animated, with Joe and Mabel riding together in Joe's cab, and the show's title, *Joe and Mabel* was carved in a heart on a tree.

Joe and Sons A Douglas S. Cramer/Kukoff-Harris Production. CBS. Tuesday nights 8:30. September 9, 1975–January 13, 1976. 15 color episodes were videotaped before a live audience.

Richard S. Castellano got another shot at blue collar sitcom stardom after his short-lived *The Super* in 1972. This time around, he was Joe Vitalie, an Italian-American widower, living in Hoboken, New Jersey (the city of Frank Sinatra's birth). He worked for the Hoboken Sheet and Tube Company, and his best friend and co-worker was Gus Duzik (Jerry Stiller). Joe also had two boys to look after. The eldest was Mark (Barry Miller); Nick (Jimmy Baio) was his 12-year-old brother. Also in the cast was Estelle (Bobbi Jordan), the cocktail waitress who lived down the hall and cared for the boys while Joe was at work, and Josephine Molonaire (Florence Stanley) played Joe's meddling sister. The pilot episode ran as a comedy special on CBS on April 18, 1975, but it didn't become a series until fall.

In just a few episodes, this program managed to cover quite a few topics which were new to television—Mark doubted the existence of God; Nick's school biology book contained

***Joe and Sons*—Left to right, Jerry Stiller, Richard S. Castellano, Jimmy Baio from the episode "Nick's Book" (photograph courtesy of Jean Cummings).**

some unusually explicit pictures in its sex education section; Mark was dating a girl whose mom had a "reputation"; Nick wanted to study ballet, which caused Josephine to doubt his masculinity; a long-haired friend of Mark's gave the Vitalies a gift house plant which had an uncanny resemblance to marijuana; Nick made continued attempts to hide his bedwetting problem, and so on. The edgy material seemed to repel rather than attract viewers and *Joe and Sons* was gone from the CBS prime time lineup early in 1976.

The program was produced by Bernie Kukoff and Jeff Harris; the executive producer was Douglas S. Cramer; writers included Bob Iles and Mike Milligan; and the director was Peter Baldwin. Music was provided by David Shire. Many of the co-stars on this program went on to other TV sitcoms: Florence Stanley moved on to *Fish*, Jerry Stiller did both *Seinfeld* and *The King of Queens*, Jimmy Baio went to another topical show named *Soap*, and Barry Miller co-starred with Ned Beatty on *Szysznyk*.

The Joe Palooka Story Guild Films. First-Run Syndication 1954–1955. 26 black-and-white episodes were filmed without a laugh track.

Based upon the comic strip character created by Hammond E. "Ham" Fisher in 1921, the very moral, honest, kind-hearted, somewhat naïve boxing champion Joe Palooka briefly came to television in this very low-budget syndicated comedy/drama series during the 1954–1955 season. Appropriately, Joe Palooka was portrayed by an actor named "Joe" Kirkwood, Jr., who also co-produced the series. Kirkwood was already very familiar with the character—he had portrayed Palooka in a series of films beginning in 1946. Joe Palooka was one of the most popular comic strip characters of the day and this led to a series of Palooka products such as watches, board games, and lunchboxes. Joe had a patient, understanding society girlfriend—the lovely Ann Howe (Cathy Downs)—and a manager named "Knobby" Walsh (Sid Tomack in the first 13 episodes, and Luis Van Rooten in the rest). Joe's trainer, Clyde, was played by boxing great "Slapsie" Maxie Rosenbloom. A young Charles Bronson (still using his real name Charles Buchinski) appeared in a few episodes as Eddie Crane.

Episodes include "A Career for Ann," in which Joe hired a maid named Hilda (Florence Auer), leaving Ann very bored, so she took a job as a sales clerk. In "A Turkey for Terry," a practical joke played on Knobby (he was given a gag gift of a very realistic looking rubber turkey) backfired when Joe Palooka, who was not in on the joke, gave away the turkey to a poor neighborhood boy for his Thanksgiving dinner. In "And Still Champ," Joe's birthday led to a lot of worry over the champ's age—especially as he was about to fight a much younger challenger.

The program was initially produced by Richard Baer, but after 13 weeks he was replaced by William Berke. Writers included Charles R. Marion; directors included William Berke, Richard Baer, and Erle C. Kenyon. The show was produced by Guild Films, which also gave us the popular *Life with Elizabeth* and *Liberace*. In the fall of 1954, Joe Kirkwood received a special award from the Honor League of New York's Police Department for his portrayal of Joe Palooka on television, for which a special unaired segment of the show was filmed. *Variety* called the program "a good sponsorship bet" and *Billboard Magazine* said it had "broad appeal for viewers of all ages." One episode of *The Joe Palooka Story* is available for sale from Marathon Music and Video.

Joe's World T. A. T. Communications . NBC. Friday nights 10:00 (December 28, 1979), and Wednesday nights 9:30 (January 2, 1980), and Saturday nights 9:30 (May 10, 1980–July 26, 1980). 11 episodes were videotaped before a live audience.

This show just made it into this book by one week. *Joe's World* certainly moved around a lot. It debuted on the final Friday of 1979, then moved to Wednesdays for one week in January of 1980 before going on hiatus until May when it was seen on Saturday nights. It was the story of everyman Joe Wabash (Ramon Bieri), the foreman of a union painting crew. Joe lived in Detroit with his wide-eyed, ponderous wife Katie (K. Callan) and their five children. Girl-and-baseball-crazy Steve was the oldest (Christopher Knight) and he worked as a painter with his dad; Melissa Sherman played boy-crazy teenage daughter Maggie; Michael Sharrett played Jimmy; Missy Francis played Linda; and Ari Zeltzer was Rick, the youngest. Whenever Joe wanted privacy, he'd say one word to the kids: "evaporate." They often recited it with him.

On the painting crew were the very macho Brad Hopkins (Russ Banham); Joe's longtime friend, Andy Kinski (Frank Coppola); and in the episode titled "The Woman Painter," Joe added a very attractive young female painter to his crew named Judy Wilson (Misty Rowe). Judy's husband had left her for a stewardess and she instantly became a major distraction for the guys on the crew (especially Brad and Joe's son Steve). Initially, Joe's wife Katie was all for the decision and Joe's open-mindedness, until she got to see the stunning, single mother breastfeeding her baby on the job.

The creators and executive producers were Mel Tolkin and Larry Rhine; the producer was Herbert Kenwith; writers included Rhine, Tolkin, Albert A. Schwartz, Ray Singer, Jeremy Stevens, Tom Moore, Gordon "Whitey" Mitchell, Chuck Stewart, Jack Elinson, Joseph Bonaduce, Ann Gibbs, Joel Kimmel, and Bill Daley; and directors included Herbert Kenwith, John Bowab, Jim Drake, and Gerren Keith. The theme song was written by Hal Hidey, Tolkin, and Rhine. Several episodes of *Joe's World* are available for viewing at The Paley Center for Media.

The John Forsythe Show A Universal-Forsythe Production. NBC. Monday nights 8:00. September 13, 1965–August 29, 1966. 30 color episodes were filmed with a laugh track. Sponsors included Ajax Detergent and Colgate.

John Forsythe starred in this eponymous sitcom which was actually two sitcoms—it altered its format midseason. Here he portrayed U.S. Air Force Major John Kendall Foster. The major's friend in the Air Force, Ed Robbins, portrayed by Guy Marks, alerted him to some important news which came in a telegram (which Ed opened without permission). The major's Aunt Victoria Foster had passed on. John was her sole heir and thus inherited her struggling Foster School for Girls in San Francisco. The major's initial inclination was to sell the school, but after a visit, the girls won his heart and he decided to stay on (to get the school back in the black).

The comedy revolved around him being the only male in this all-female environment. This initial format failed to catch on, even with a lot of very familiar names and faces in the cast—Elsa Lanchester was the principal, Miss Margaret Culver; and Ann B. Davis played Miss Wilson, the gym teacher. The schoolgirls included Peggy Lipton as Joanna; Darleen Carr as Kathy; Pamelyn Ferdin as Pamela; and two of John Forsythe's real-life daughters, Brooke and Page (who played Norma Jean and Marcia, respectively).

The John Forsythe Show—Left to right, Ann B. Davis, John Forsythe and Elsa Lanchester (NBC).

In episode number 21, "Funny, You Don't Look Like a Spy," the format was altered. John and Ed were still based out of the school, but the girls were rarely seen, and the roles of Elsa Lanchester and Ann B. Davis were greatly diminished. Every week, John and Ed were now U.S. government undercover agents, and their weekly mission took them around the globe. In "Mission to Italy," John and Ed pretended to be attending a seminar for school directors in the small Italian village of Morasco, but in reality were trying to deliver important plans for a tracking site for the next billion dollar space shot. Comedy ensued when their car broke down, and John got arrested after a brief affair and a misunderstanding with a beautiful girl. Much like his role of Bentley Gregg in *Bachelor Father*, in *The John Forsythe* Show, he was still quite the womanizer. It should be noted that only a few years later, Forsythe would again find himself in Italy in the two-season sitcom, *To Rome with Love*.

The program was produced by Peter Kortner; writers included Joel Kane and Joseph Bonaduce; and Earl Bellamy directed most of the episodes. Music was provided by Lyn Murray.

Just Friends (see *Stockard Channing in Just Friends*)

The Kallikaks A Neila Production. NBC. Wednesday nights 9:30. August 3, 1977–August 31, 1977. Five videotaped episodes aired.

Conniving, greedy Jasper T. Kallikak (David Huddleston) left his job as a coal miner in his native Appalachia and, along with his family, found his future out west in a town called Nowhere, California. In tow were his gushingly affectionate wife, Venus (Edie McClurg); his status conscious teenage daughter Bobbi Lou (Bonnie Ebsen, daughter of Buddy); and his pre-teen technical genius of a son Junior (Patrick J. Peterson). The family had inherited a small dual-pump gas station and now Jasper got to be his own boss, making it easier to "beat the system"—which just happened to be the very apt title of the theme song for *The Kallikaks*. Jasper had a hired hand from Germany named Oscar Heinz (Peter Palmer). Oscar spoke very little English. Because of his limited grasp of the language, often got a lot of things mixed up.

Episodes include "The Bells Are Wronging," in which a clerical error netted the Kallikak family a $140,000 refund from the telephone company. In the cleverly-titled "Swami, How I Love Ya," a hired medium (Jay Robinson) tried to determine if Venus's late brother intended to leave her any kind of inheritance; in "I Coulda Been a Contender," the mob took an interest in putting Oscar in the ring as a prizefighter.

The program was produced by Stanley Ralph Ross and George Yanok; the creators were Ross and Roger Price; writers included Price, Ross, and Ron Kantor; and directors included Kantor, Bob LaHendro, and Dennis Steinmetz. Music was provided by Tom Wells, and the theme song was written by Stanley Ralph Ross, and performed by Roy Clark. A few episodes are housed in the Paley Center for Media.

Karen A Kayro-Vue Production/Universal. NBC. Monday nights 7:30. October 5, 1964–August 30, 1965. 28 black-and-white episodes were filmed with a laugh track. Sponsors included Bufferin, Bravo Floor Wax/Johnson's Wax, Lady Schick, Purina Cat Chow, Gerber, and Coca-Cola.

Once upon a time, there was a 90-minute block of 30-minute sitcoms on Monday nights under the umbrella title *Ninety Bristol Court*. Here was the story of three different Southern California families who all lived in the same apartment complex. They all shared the same handyman, Cliff Murdock (Guy Raymond). In this triumvirate were *Harris Against the World*, with Jack Klugman, *Tom, Dick and Mary*, with Don Galloway and Joyce Bulifant, and getting everything started on Monday nights was *Karen* (not to be confused with the Karen Valentine sitcom of the same name). This *Karen* starred Debbie Watson as 16-year-old Karen Scott. Debbie's only previous experience had been in a local Southern California production of *Bye Bye Birdie* and as a performer at the Knott's Berry Farm Amusement Park. Harvey Korman was originally considered for the part of her lawyer dad, but Richard Denning won the Steve Scott role; Mary La Roche played Karen's mom, Barbara Scott; and Gina Gillespie was her tomboy sister, Mimi.

Karen **(1964)—Debbie Watson as "Karen." NBC.**

If Mimi seemed like the female equivalent of Beaver Cleaver, it could be the influence of the creators and producers they had in common—Joe Connelly and Bob Mosher. A very young Richard Dreyfuss appeared occasionally as David Rowe III and Teddy Quinn played Mimi's friend, Peter. At Steve's law office was secretary Miss Skinner portrayed by Barbara Werle. Another character, basketball player Wilbur "Spider" Gibson (Murray MacLeod), was added very late in the series' run. MacLeod told me, "This was originally intended to be little more than a walk-on role, but I conjured up a pretty funny character on my own, and director Ezra Stone expanded the part (albeit, for only the final three episodes). I had just gotten out of the army in real-life, and I based the Spider character on a guy I knew in the army." Regarding the star of the show, Debbie Watson, MacLeod said, "She was wonderful—extremely mature for her age. She had very poor vision, however. As Karen, she didn't wear glasses or contact lenses, and honestly couldn't see two feet in front of her, but you'd never know it when watching the show."

After 13 weeks, there were some changes in the neighborhood at *Ninety Bristol Court. Harris Against the World* and *Tom, Dick and Mary* were canceled, but the anchor *Karen* got to stay for the remainder of the season. The *Ninety Bristol Court* umbrella was closed.

Episodes include "Beethoven or Baseball," in which Mimi suddenly wanted to take up the cello. She confided in big sister, Karen, that it was all to get closer to a boy named Harold Osterstock (Scott Lane). The problem was that by only confiding in Karen, she greatly upset her mother. In "The Formal," Steve did a good deed and bought a new dress for Karen to wear to her upcoming dance. However, the dress he brought home was a bit too flashy and mature for a 16-year-old girl, and Karen was embarrassed to wear it.

Writers included Joseph Hoffman, George Tibbles, Ben Fox, Dale and Katherine Eunson, Richard Conway, and Roland MacLane; and directors included David Alexander, Jack Arnold, and Norman Abbott. Music was provided by Jack Marshall. The theme song was performed by an up-and-coming rock and roll group known as The Beach Boys (who had yet to achieve superstardom). This title song, "Karen," was never released by The Beach Boys on 45 rpm records or LP.

***Karen* (1975)** 20th Century–Fox. ABC. Thursday nights 8:30. January 30, 1975–June 19, 1975. 13 color episodes were filmed with a laugh track.

Not to be confused with the other single season sitcom called *Karen*, which was part of *Ninety Bristol Court* in 1964, this *Karen* starred Karen Valentine as Karen Angelo. The program debuted on Thursday nights along with another ABC show which became a bit more famous—*Barney Miller*. Karen Angelo lived in the Georgetown area of Washington, D. C. at 1460 Cambridge Street and served as a lobbyist for a citizen's action group called "Open America." Her target was crooked politicians and her goal was citizen's rights. These were things she felt strongly about since her youth. She was bright, energetic, and she was intended to be ABC's answer to Mary Richards of *The Mary Tyler Moore*

Karen—**Will Seltzer, Karen Valentine (photograph courtesy of Jean Cummings).**

Show. However, that didn't quite pan out. The show tried to be very topical, with subject matter such as illegal surveillance, mysterious government defense contracts, consumer protection, and shoddy aeronautics design. It was a concept show that had a few too many concepts.

Karen's boss, the cranky Dale Busch, in the pilot, was played by Denver Pyle, but in the series was played by the equally cranky Charles Lane. Actress/talk show host Stephanie Edwards portrayed herself in the pilot episode. She told me, "The cast was delightful, but I had a terribly embarrassing moment. Denver Pyle played Karen's boss in the pilot, and after we'd wrapped up filming for that week I mistakenly called him Gomer Pyle instead of Denver Pyle." The ever-cynical Dena Madison was portrayed by Dena Dietrich (of those "mother nature" commercials for Chiffon Margarine). Also in the cast was Will Seltzer as a young volunteer at the organization named Adam Cooperman; Aldine King played Cissy Peterson (Karen's roommate who was also an FBI agent); Joseph Stern played her good friend Ernie; and Edward Winter played her sometimes beau, Representative Bob Hartford. There were also two tenants in Karen's rooming house, Jerry and Cheryl Siegel (Oliver Clark and Alix Elias, respectively). Alix told me, "They were always testing things—that's how I got the job. They hired me to do one line, and in a weak moment asked me to improvise a few more (I'd been in an improv company in New York City), and when they tested the scene in front of an audience, I tested off the charts, so they decided to throw me in as a regular." Alix joined the show already in progress. She recalled, "They had Oliver Clark already, so they decided to give him a wife. We were newlyweds, and always having (implied) sex all over the house, which Karen would stumble into and be embarrassed. The episode I remember most vividly was when Oliver and I were in the shower together. Oliver had been hugely overweight and had lost an enormous amount of that weight. The poor guy was extremely embarrassed to be semi-nude with me in the shower. Because of the weight loss, his skin was kind of hanging off his body, so I promised him I wouldn't look (all right, I peeked)."

Guest stars included Marty Feldman as Mr. "X" in the episode titled "Them"; Bert Convy was Steve Hunter in the episode called "Love and Other Issues"; both Fred Willard (as Ritter) and William Christopher (as Andrew) appeared in the episode called "Whistle Blowing"; and *Dobie Gillis'* Dwayne Hickman portrayed the houseguest's husband in the episode titled "The Visitors." Karen Morrow, who guest-starred on an episode called "A Day in the Life" remembered, "My character, Cerita, and the characters portrayed by David Doyle and Dick Patterson were zany guests alongside Karen Valentine on a TV talk show. Karen was on that talk show to talk about consumer protection, but was overwhelmed by the madcap antics going on around her. It was so much fun. I can still envision the director, John Erman, doubled over—he was laughing so hard." Alix Elias recalled that episode with Karen Morrow: "She was wearing huge false eyelashes, caked with big globs of mascara, and they let her get away with it. She was simply hilarious. We later did a commercial together playing housewives (however, two less likely housewives I can't imagine)."

Several episodes were written by John D. Hess; and directors included Gene Reynolds, Hy Averback, Jerry Paris, John Erman, and Mel Ferber; the executive producers were Reynolds, Larry Gelbart and Carl Kleinschmidt—some of the very best in the business. Elias told me, "I thought with all of those important people at the helm, we'd keep going at least for a second season, but in retrospect, maybe it was a question of too many cooks." The show's theme song was written by Benny Golson. During that theme song in the opening credits, Karen was on a bicycle taking in all of the sights of our nation's capital. After the program was canceled, Elias recalled, "Karen Valentine was under a huge amount of pressure, but I think it was her nature to be removed and pleasant at all costs. I never saw her be anything but pulled together and courteous to everyone around her." Several episodes can be viewed in the UCLA TV Archives.

Kentucky Jones A Buzz Kulik Production/Desilu. NBC. Saturday nights 8:30 (September 19, 1964–December 27, 1964), and Saturday nights 8:00 (January 2, 1965–September 11, 1965). 26 black-and-white episodes were filmed. Most episodes have a laugh track. Sponsors included Timex.

Dennis Weaver left *Gunsmoke* to star in this single season comedy/drama as race horse trainer/veterinarian Kenneth Yarborough Jones. Because his initials were K.Y. Jones, folks often called him "Kentucky Jones." Shortly after the untimely death of his wife, Kentucky was reminded that he and Mrs. Jones had applied to adopt a nine-year-old Chinese child. Now a widower, Kentucky was unsure that he still wanted to go through with the adoption, but it couldn't be undone. The new addition to the Jones household was named Dwight Eisenhower Wong, nicknamed "Ike" (Ricky Der). Ike had plenty of room to play and grow up, as Jones owned a 40-acre ranch in Southern California. Jones' ranch hand was a former jockey named Seldom Jackson (Harry Morgan). Edith Thorncroft (Nancy Rennick) was the social worker who occasionally stopped by to check up on young "Ike." Also in the cast were Keye Luke as Jones's friend Thomas Wong; Cherylene Lee as Ike's friend Annie Ng; and Arthur Wong as Mr. Ng, Annie's dad.

Guest stars included Yvonne Craig in the episode titled "Kentucky's Vacation"; Spring Byington in "Feminine Intrusion"; Pat Harrington in "Ike's Song"; and Dennis Weaver's real-life son Robby in "The Music Kids Make."

The program was produced by Albert Beich; the executive producer was Buzz Kulik; the creators were Beich and William H. Wright; directors included Kulik; and writers included Douglas Morrow. The theme song was written by Vic Mizzy. To increase bleak early ratings, a laugh track was added after a few episodes had aired. One episode can be viewed in the UCLA TV Archives.

The Kids from C.A.P.E.R. An Alan Landsburg/Don Kirshner Production. NBC. Saturday mornings September 11, 1976–November 20, 1976, and April 9, 1977–September 3, 1977. 13 episodes were filmed with a laugh track.

This was a Saturday morning live action musical sitcom which focused upon a group of kids who, through the 927th Police Precinct in mythical North South Weston, formed C.A.P.E.R. (the Civilian Authority for the Protection of Everybody Regardless). P.T. (Steve Bonino) was the group's leader. P.T. had an extremely keen sense of smell, and his nose was named "Seymour." He also served as the narrator who often reviewed specific scenes for the audience's clarification. Bugs (Cosie Costa) had unexplained superhuman strength. The word "bananas" made him go bananas. Doomsday (Biff Warren) was the naïve one who had the unique ability to communicate with animals. He also sang in many of the episodes. Doc (John Lansing) was the brains of the outfit. He was also a "babe magnet," but was totally unaware of his good looks. Mr. Featherstone, who was a shark puppet and had a tank inside the "Big Bologna," served as their guide and navigator. Each of the kids had a special walkie-talkie on which was emblazoned a big letter "C" for Caper.

Episode titles include "The Uncanny Nanny," "King Cone," "The Post Monster General," "Dunga Gin," "Mummy's the Word," and "The Goodfather."

The program was created and written by Romeo Muller; the producer and director was Stanley Z. Cherry; and the executive producers were Alan Landsburg and Don Kirshner. *The Kids from C.A.P.E.R.* theme song was written by Ron Dante (of The Archies, Cufflinks and Detergents) and Jake Holmes. Dante told me, "I wrote and produced that theme with my pal, Jake Holmes. He was a top jingle writer in New York at that time, and is credited with writing hundreds of the most popular TV and radio commercials during those years. Don Kirshner brought me in to be part of the show. Originally, I auditioned for the role of P. T., and got it, but turned it down. I didn't wish to be tied down to a TV series—I wanted to focus on my music. " Other music used on the show was provided by Wally Gold (who had written hits for Elvis Presley) and Jay Siegal (of The Tokens). A vinyl LP was released during the program's brief run, featuring music performed on the show.

The Krofft Supershow A Sid and Marty Krofft Production. ABC. September 11, 1976–September 2, 1978. The programs were videotaped with a laugh track.

The Krofft Supershow aired for two seasons and consisted of several 15-minute segments, a few of which were kid's sitcoms. However, the two mentioned below are single season sitcoms.

Dr. Shrinker Jay Robinson portrayed Dr. Shrinker—a borderline evil scientist who, along with his assistant Hugo (Billy Barty), had the ability to shrink anything with his patented shrink ray (long before *Honey, I Shrunk the Kids*). He used this ray on three young people: Brad Fulton (Ted Eccles), B. J. Masterson (Susan Lawrence), and her younger brother Gordie (Jeff MacKay). Most of their time was spent attempting to find a way to return to normal size. Sixteen episodes aired.

Magic Mongo told of the zany adventures of three teenagers: Donald (Paul Hinckley), Lorraine (Helaine Lembeck), Kristy (Robin Dearden), and their genie friend Mongo (Lennie Weinrib). It was basically, a kid's version of *I*

Dream of Jeannie with a male genie, whose powers sometimes caused a lot of trouble. Seventeen episodes aired. *Wonderbug* was the other comedy segment (lasting two seasons); non-comedy segments were *Bigfoot and Wildboy* and *Electra Woman and Dyna Girl.*

The Last Resort MTM Productions. CBS. Wednesday nights 8:00 (September 19, 1979–October 3, 1979), and Monday nights 8:30 (December 17, 1979–March 17, 1980). 15 color episodes were filmed before a live audience.

This show got off to a really rocky start on Wednesday nights up against *Eight Is Enough* on ABC and *Real People* on NBC. The program which followed *The Last Resort* on Wednesday nights didn't help any either (*Struck by Lightning*, starring Jack Elam). Luckily, after a hiatus, this funny little show was returned to the line-up in December of 1979, but this time on Monday nights where it at least had a four-month run. It was the story of five college kids who earned a living as waiters at a resort hotel during their summer vacations. The four guys all lived together in the same dorm. Larry Breeding played pre-med student, Michael Lerner; Zane Lasky played science major Duane Kaminsky; Walter Olkewicz portrayed Zach Comstock, who often made light of his own weight issues; and Ray Underwood played the narcissistic rich kid, Jeffrey Barron. Stephanie Faracy portrayed the only female student, Gail Collins, working at the resort. She was the pastry chef. Others in the cast included John Fujioka as Kevin, the temperamental cook, and Robert Costanzo as Murray, the maître d' who had quite a hard time keeping his wait staff in line.

Among the best episodes were "Dorm Window," a take-off on *Rear Window*, in which Michael was convinced he saw a murder being committed. In "Not a Prayer," Zach had a blind date with a very mysterious woman who turned out to be a nun. Judd Hirsch made a guest appearance in the final episode, "Zegelmania," as Dr. Alan Zegelman, a mentor to Duane who faked test results (involving mice being forced through a maze by soundwaves) in order to get a $50,000 research grant.

The show was created and produced by Gary David Goldberg; all episodes were directed by Asaad Kelada; and writers included Goldberg, Jeannie Pagliaro, Donald Reiker, Rich Reinhart, Patricia Jones, Lloyd Garver, and Marty Nadler. The theme song was by Pat Williams. Frank Torrez of the *Los Angeles Herald-Examiner* reviewed the show this way: "the strength of *The Last Resort* is some occasionally snappy dialogue, delivered by a few standouts in an otherwise adequate cast."

The Laytons DuMont Network. Wednesday nights 8:30. August 11, 1948–October 27, 1948. Broadcast live. Sponsored by John Wanamaker Department Store.

This series is perhaps the most difficult program on which to not only compile information, but also to determine whether it is indeed a network program (or merely a local New York program). While most other reference books list it as being both local New York and network (DuMont), there are no reviews in any of the trade papers (such as *Weekly Variety* and *Daily Variety*) nor is the program listed in *TV Guide* outside of the New York City edition. This is a clear indication that the program was likely local.

Copies of the program, as well as press material, also appear to be non-existent. There are no records at the Library of Congress, the Paley Centers for Media, or the UCLA TV Archives. But to present a fair evaluation of the program, there is always that doubt—it could have been a network program (possibly only a one-episode test in other markets which leads some researchers to believe it was a full-fledged network program, not just seen locally on WABD, Channel 5 in New York City).

Cast information is virtually non-existent, with only Vera Tatum and Amanda Randolph receiving recognition. Based on what is known, Vera played the head of the family, with Randolph (who also appeared in a live daytime variety series on DuMont at this same time called simply *Amanda*) as her maid, kindly referred to as "Aunt Martha." It has also been speculated that Amanda sang and played piano on *The Laytons.*

As for credits, only the writer (Barbara Boothe) and director (Pat Fay) of the only known episode title, "The Moose Hangs High," are known.

Leave It to Larry CBS. Tuesday nights 8:00. October 14, 1952–December 23, 1952. Broadcast live.

One year before being nominated for a Best Supporting Actor Oscar in *Roman Holiday*, Eddie Albert starred in the short-lived sitcom *Leave It to Larry* (originally to be called *Leave It to Lester*). Larry Tucker was a bumbling store clerk who worked at his father-in-law Mr. Koppel's shoe store (played by Ed Begley, Sr.). Koppel lived with his son-in-law and daughter, Amy (Betty Kean), in a two-story house, making life rather hectic for Larry. The Tuckers also had two children, Stevie (Glenn Walken) and Harriet (Lydia Schaeffer). The program was absolutely pummeled in the ratings up against Milton Berle, and shortly before Christmas of 1952, *Leave It to Larry* had to leave the airwaves. To my knowledge, no episodes exist. Albert went on to do two highly successful TV series years later—one originally to be called *Country Cousins*, then *The Eddie Albert Show*, and finally *Green Acres* with Eva Gabor, and a few years later, *Switch* with Robert Wagner.

The program was produced by Leo Solomon; the directors were Alan Riesner, Mervyn Nelson, and Ashmead Scott; and writers included Solomon, Vinnie Bogert, William Glickman, and Billy Friedberg.

Leave It to Papa First-run syndication. 1950. Thursday nights 7:30. Originating from WPIX-TV, New York. Sponsored by Ronzoni Macaroni and Torino Foods. Broadcast live.

This short-lived sitcom starred William Edmunds (Papa), Aristide Sigismundi, Carlotta Sherwood, Augusta Ciolli, Frank Puglia, Mabel Tagliaferro, and 23-year-old Peter Fernandez. Fernandez was making $30 an episode. At the time, unemployment was $35, so Fernandez asked for a raise, but was turned down. He asked to be released from the show, albeit briefly, and was replaced in the role of the son by Richard Seff. After his unemployment ran out, Fernandez asked for his job back and got it. He stayed for the rest of the show's brief run. *Leave It to Papa* told the tale of the Lombardi family in a manner much like *The Goldbergs*, only with a lot less polish. One of their sons was abandoned by his birth mother and taken in and raised by the Lombardis.

The producer and writer was Nicolas Cosentino; the directors were Al Hartigan and Bob Birch. Fernandez later had a successful career in cartoons, writing for and providing voices for *Astroboy*, *Gigantor*, *Speed Racer*, and *Kenny the Shark*. Fernandez died in 2010 at the age of 83. For some reason, the show was also briefly known as *They Live in Brooklyn*. To my knowledge, no episodes exist.

The Life of Riley Irving Brecher Productions. Produced at Filmtone. NBC. Tuesday nights 9:30. October 4, 1949–March 28, 1950. 26 black-and-white episodes were filmed—a laugh track was added in syndication. Sponsors included Pabst Blue Ribbon Beer.

William Bendix had originated the role of Chester Alphonse Riley on radio in 1943. When time came for the TV version in 1949, Bendix had film commitments, so a young and thinner Jackie Gleason was selected for the role (his first on TV). Along with *The Hank McCune Show*, this incarnation of *The Life of Riley* was a filmed comedy in an era when most were done live. Riley was a riveter for Stevenson Aircraft and Associates in Southern California and earned $59 a week. The blue collar Riley lived at 1313 Blueview Terrace. He was a lovable oaf with a good heart who unintentionally incited chaos wherever he went. Riley was married to the unbelievably patient and loving Peg Riley (Rosemary De-Camp). They had two children, a teenage girl named Babs (Gloria Winters) and the slightly younger Junior (Lanny Rees). Riley had a couple of friends, too; Bob Jellison was Waldo (with a voice reminiscent of cartoon character Droopy Dog) and Sid Tomack was Riley's clever, nosy neighbor and co-worker Herbert T. Gillis. The only holdover from the cast of the radio version was John Brown as friendly local undertaker Digby "Digger" O'Dell, who always left a scene by saying, "Guess I'll be shovelin' off."

Episodes include "Nervous Breakdown," in which Riley spent his entire paycheck on a diver's helmet. Peg was uncharacteristically outraged, prompting Riley to think she was having a nervous breakdown. Meanwhile, Peg was thinking the exact same thing of Riley. In "The Five Dollar Bill," Riley accused Junior of stealing five dollars out of the cream jug, only to realize later that the missing money was in his own pants pocket. In "The Prom Dress," Riley hocked his bowling ball so that he could buy a formal dress for Babs's upcoming dance. However, the dress was a second-hand dress made originally for a wealthy acquaintance of Babs who recognized the dress immediately as her hand-me-down. In "Riley's Birthday Gift," Riley thought Junior had forgotten to buy him a gift for his birthday so he bought himself the bathrobe he wanted and made it look like it came from Junior. However, Junior hadn't forgotten, and Riley ended up with more than one identical robe.

The program was produced by Reuben Ship, Alan Lipscott, and Irving Brecher (Brecher would later go on to produce *The People's Choice*); writers included Ship, Lipscott, Brecher, and

Ashmead Scott; and directors included Herbert Leeds. The show won an Emmy Award on January 27, 1950, for Best Film Made for and Viewed on Television, even though this version of Riley was not a success. Almost exactly three years later, NBC assembled a totally different cast, secured William Bendix back in the Riley role, and that version of *The Life of Riley* ran from January of 1953 until August of 1958. The 26 episodes of the original Gleason version went into syndication in the 1980s because of the popularity of reruns of *The Honeymooners*, particularly on WPIX-TV channel 11 in New York City. The theme song was performed by an acapella whistler. The entire series is available on DVD very inexpensively from TGG Direct.

Life with Buster Keaton (see *The Buster Keaton Show*)

Life with Luigi A Cy Howard Production. CBS. Monday nights 9:30 (September 22, 1952–December 29, 1952), and Thursday nights 8:00 (April 9, 1953–June 4, 1953). Broadcast live in front of a studio audience. Sponsors included Instant Maxwell House Coffee and Wrigley's Gum.

Years later, *Bridget Loves Bernie* would suffer a similar fate—a hit show which was canceled because of a backlash from a certain ethnic group. In *Bridget Loves Bernie*, it was the Jewish community, and in *Life with Luigi*, it was the Italian-American community. *Life with Luigi* had its origins in radio beginning in 1948 with J. Carroll Naish in the title role. When the series went to television in the fall of 1952, Naish went with it. It was the story of Luigi Basco, who recently came to America from Canto Loma, Italy (he often referred to himself as "the little immigrant"). His sponsor in America was an old friend, Pasquale (Alan Reed), who paid for Luigi's fare from Italy with a sly ulterior motive—he wanted Luigi to marry his 250-pound daughter, Rosa (Jody Gilbert). Pasquale owned Pasquale's Spaghetti Palace at 19 North Halstead Street in the Little Italy section of Chicago. Pasquale also set up Luigi with his own business right next door at 21 North Halstead—an antique shop simply called Luigi Basco. Luigi came to America with only three dollars in his pocket, but eventually had enough money to open a checking account at the Case National Bank. Luigi was a sweet, gentle, gullible soul who often took things a bit too literally. He opened and closed each episode writing a letter to his "mama mia." *The Red Buttons Show* and *Life with Luigi* were the biggest new shows on CBS that season, but despite its success, *Life with Luigi* left the airwaves on December 29, 1952. The show was retooled and softened and returned with a new cast as *The New Life with Luigi* on April 9, 1953, with new episodes (now on Thursday nights at 8:00). However, this new version with Vito Scotti as a less naïve and less insecure Luigi Basco (he no longer owned an antique shop, but rather worked in Pasquale's Spaghetti Palace); Thomas Gomez as Pasquale; and Muriel Landers as Rosa just didn't have the same chemistry or charm. It only lasted a matter of weeks before it was canceled for good this time.

At least three kinescopes have survived. From the original format, there's "The Phone Booth," in which Luigi tried to lure more customers into his antique shop by installing a phone booth inside. What he lured was trouble from a pushy plastic products salesman who moved in and tried to take over. In "Citizenship," Luigi was very proud and excited to be one step away from his dream of becoming a U.S. citizen. That dream was almost crushed by Pasquale who attempted to make it look as though Luigi were offering the judge a bribe for his citizenship. This was a ploy to get Luigi to finally marry his daughter, Rosa (to get to stay in the U.S.), but luckily Luigi's night school English teacher, Miss Spalding (Mary Shipp), was present and straightened things out. From the second format with the new cast, there was "The Dance," in which both Luigi and Rosa needed money for new clothes for an upcoming formal dance, but neither had any. Against his better judgment and everything he believed in, Luigi signed up for his first credit card, but unselfishly didn't get himself the blue suit he needed, but rather a dress (size 50) for Rosa.

The original version was created and produced by Cy Howard. Norman Tokar produced the second format. The directors for the first format were Tokar and Mac Benoff, and for the second John Claar. Writers for the first format were Benoff and Lou Derman, but Lou Derman was on his own for the second format. Music was provided by Lud Gluskin. The theme song, the Italian classic "Maria Mari" (Way Marie), was written by Eduardo DiCapua.

Lotsa Luck Concept II Productions. NBC. Monday nights 8:00 (September 10, 1973–January 7, 1974), and Friday nights 8:30 (January 11, 1974–May 24, 1974). 22 episodes were videotaped before a live audience.

Each episode began with the catchy little ditty, "I used to buy a pickle, it only used to cost a nickel." *Lotsa Luck* was a blue collar show about bachelor Stanley Belmont (Dom DeLuise), who was a clerk in the lost-and-found department of a New York City bus company. The one thing Stanley wanted more than any other in this world was a color TV set, but his little nest egg to fulfill that dream was constantly being depleted by broken furnaces and water heaters, as well as mooching relatives. Some of the action took place at Stanley's place of business, but most of the focus was on Stanley's harried home life in Brooklyn where he cared for and supported his bossy widowed mother Iris (Kathleen Freeman). She could always get her way by uttering the words "Do I have a son?" to which Stanley would invariably respond, "You have a son, Ma," and he would acquiesce. Also living in Stanley's house and on his dime were his plain Jane, naïve, nearsighted and love-struck younger sister, Olive Swan (Beverly Sanders), and her slovenly, ne'er-do-well, motivationally-challenged husband of seven years Arthur Swan (Wynn Irwin), who was almost always seen unshaven and in his bathrobe (he had quite an appetite, too). Beverly Sanders told me, "They wanted me to be fat on the show. I auditioned for the part of Olive while wearing several layers of clothing. They wanted me to gain a few pounds, and with all of the eating we did on-camera, that came easily. In fact, at one point I was called into the office where I was told, 'You can stop now, you've gained enough.'" Many scenes took place at the kitchen table. Stanley's best friend was neighbor and bus driver Bummy Fitzer (Jack Knight). Bummy was quite the ladies' man and wore the loudest and most outrageous sport jackets on his many dates. The program was loosely based upon the British series, *On the Buses*.

Lotsa Luck—**Back row left to right, Wynn Irwin, Jack Knight, Kathleen Freeman. Front row left to right, Beverly Sanders, Dom DeLuise (photograph courtesy of Jean Cummings).**

There were some very funny and memorable moments in this short-lived series (which was pummeled in the ratings on Monday nights by *Gunsmoke* on CBS and *The Rookies* on ABC). Among the best episodes was the debut, "Olive's Present," in which Olive got a new toilet as a birthday gift from Stanley. She'd broken the old one and to save a few bucks, Stanley bought one in an off color—orange with a purple seat. Comedy ensued when he again cut corners, didn't call a plumber, and installed it himself with disastrous results. In "The Bare Facts," everyone thought Arthur was cheating on Olive with another woman, but he was actually posing nude for an art class to raise money for a special gift for Olive. In "Stanley and the Librarian," Jackie Joseph played against type as a part-time librarian named Millie who was also, unbeknownst to Stanley, a hooker. Jackie Joseph remembered, "It was my idea to have Dom accidentally take my wig off in the episode and then try to put it back on. Such a wonderful role to play. It was really different for me, but no one was shocked." Sanders told me, "The sponsor was up-in-arms about this episode. They didn't want to sponsor a show about a prostitute."

The program was created by Bill Persky, Sam Denoff, and Carl Reiner. Jackie Joseph told me, "I knew Carl Reiner from working on his shows so much. It's a good thing I didn't know what a giant he truly is/was, because I would have been trembling in his presence. Carl never acted like a big deal. He was a warm, fuzzy, funny gentleman. He was and is beloved." Persky and Denoff were the producers; writers included Saul Turteltaub, Persky, Denoff, Reiner, Norman Barasch, Carroll Moore, Roy Kammerman, Bill Manoff, Ron Friedman, Gordon Farr, Arnold Kane, Steve Gordon, John Boni, and Arnie Kogen; and directors included Bill Foster, Persky, and for the majority of episodes, Alan Rafkin. The theme song was written by Jack Elliott, Allyn Ferguson, Persky and Denoff. Beverly Sanders recalls, "It was my first sitcom as a regular, and at one of the run-throughs with all of those wonderful creative people, I said to myself, 'I can't believe I am getting paid to learn and have so much fun.'" Jackie Joseph told me about her many associations with Kathleen Freeman: "I knew Kathleen since I was 15. I thought she was much older, but she was a young woman who looked the same age most of her life. She was a real performer—she played old and dour parts, or really funny 'out there' roles." Jackie said the nicest thing about Dom DeLuise: "He was like a walking hug. I miss Dom and loved doing *Lotsa Luck* with him." Most episodes are available in a DVD box set from S'more Entertainment.

Love and Marriage Louis F. Edelman Enterprises. NBC. Monday nights 8:00. September 21, 1959–January 25, 1960. 26 black-and-white episodes were filmed with a laugh track, only 18 aired. Sponsors included the Noxzema Chemical Company.

Not to be confused with the 1996 Fox network show of the same name, this *Love and Marriage* focused upon the Harris Music Publishing Company of Los Angeles, which was down on its luck. In fact, it was practically bankrupt, mostly because one of its partners, the very conservative William Harris (William Demarest), didn't think rock and roll was melodious. However, citing the company's financial woes, Harris' daughter and business partner, Pat Baker (Jeanne Bal), continually tried to change her father's stubborn ways and bring in new music and new talent. Pat was also the frequent referee between her dad and her husband, Steve Baker (Murray Hamilton), who practiced law. They had a couple of daughters, Susan (Susan Reilly) and Jennie (Jeanne Lynn). The company's secretary was Sophie (singer Kay Armen) and the company's song plugger was named Stubby Wilson (Stubby Kaye). Stubby got to sing the songs he was plugging in many of the episodes. The program added a couple of characters late in 1959—a Chinese songwriter named Jimmy Chang (Robert Kino) and a housekeeper for the Bakers named Han Cho-Yee (Judy Dan). Jimmy and Han fell madly in love, even though Han's very strict and traditional father Mr. Cho-Yee (Benson Fong) had "arranged" for her to marry someone else.

Episodes include "Stubby Picks a Winner," in which an unemployed songwriter gave Stubby one of his songs in exchange for a loan. Stubby then devised a plan to get the song published. In "Sophie's Engagement," when Sophie made her engagement announcement at the office, William made plans to publish a song that her new fiancée wrote.

The program was produced by P.J. Wolfson; the executive producer was Louis F. Edelman; writers included Melville Shavelson; and directors included Bob Sweeney and Norman Abbott. The theme song was written by Earle Hagen and Herbert W. Spencer.

Love on a Rooftop Screen Gems. ABC. Tuesday nights 9:30 (September 6, 1966–January 10, 1967), and Thursday nights 9:30 (January 12, 1967–August 31, 1967). 30 color episodes were filmed with a laugh track. Sponsors included Certs, Top Job, Warner Lambert, and Salem Cigarettes.

The couple in our story got together when the guy accidentally dropped his liverwurst on pumpernickel sandwich into the girl's purse, their eyes met, and, well, you get the picture. After five days of dating, in a surprise move, she proposed to him (even though he had already written up a long list of reasons never to get married). They married and the newlywed Willises then spent their first night together in a tent on a rooftop. They had taken up residence in a very small apartment on the top floor at 1400 McDoogal Street in San Francisco, which had a staircase that led to the rooftop. It was all they could afford on his meager salary of $85.37 a week as an apprentice architect for Bennington and Associates. The Willises consisted of the orphaned David (Peter Deuel) and 21-year-old Julie (nee) Hammond (Judy Carne), an aspiring artist who gave up wealth for love. Her side of the family was quite well-to-do. Her dad (Fred Hammond, played by Herb Voland) owned nine very successful automobile dealerships and he was not the biggest fan of his new son-in-law. Julie's mom (Phyllis, played by Edith Atwater) was the peacekeeper between Fred and David. It was never explained, however, why Fred and Phyllis Hammond's daughter, Julie, had a British accent but they did not. The Willis' cramped apartment (above Loomis' Gift Shop) had no windows, so to make it more like home, Julie painted a picture of a window and placed it where the window should be. However, as a wedding gift, Julie's dad hired construction workers to put in two windows. There were also some busybody neighbors (Stan and Carol Parker, played by impressionist Rich Little and Barbara Bostock, respectively) who were in the same financial predicament as the Willises. Stan was, as Carol put it, "a freelance genius," a would-be-inventor who also wrote menus for a living. Stan was constantly barging in, uninvited to the Willis' apartment to borrow their coffee pot and other appliances or to get to the rooftop (the only access was through the Willis' apartment). The Parkers also imposed upon the Willises to babysit for chinchillas (in "Chinchilla Rag") and pigeons (in "War on a Rooftop"). Stan also spent Dave's $50 bonus check on art supplies without asking first (in "The Fifty Dollar Misunderstanding"). However, Stan did reciprocate in the episode titled "Shotgun Honeymoon," in which he got David and Julie (who, after eight months of marriage, still hadn't gone on a honeymoon) the bridal suite at The Lodge Inn (where he and Carol had their own honeymoon five years earlier) for free after convincing the hotel clerk that he was John Wayne (on the telephone) making reservations for the newlywed couple. The Inn was fond of good relationships with celebrities, and the Willises were treated like royalty.

Love on a Rooftop—**Left to right, Peter Deuel, Judy Carne, Rich Little, Barbara Bostock (photograph courtesy of Jean Cummings).**

The program was produced by E.W. Swackhamer; the executive producer was Harry Ackerman. The program was created by Bernard Slade, who told me, "Of all of the Screen Gems shows I did—*The Flying Nun*, *Bewitched*, *The Partridge Family*—my personal favorite is *Love on a Rooftop*." Writers included Slade,

James Henerson, Marty Roth, Richard Baer, John McGreevey, Barbara Avedon, Dorothy Cooper Foote, Tom and Helen August, and Ron Friedman; directors included Swackhamer, Robert Rosenbaum, Claudio Guzman, Jerry Bernstein, Alex Grasshoff, Robert Ellenstein, Richard Kinon, Mack Bing, Russell Mayberry, and Lee Phillips. Music was provided by Mundell Lowe, and Don Kirshner served as musical consultant. Reruns of the show aired in primetime on ABC during the summer of 1971. The program was reviewed by Jack Gould of *The New York Times* as "a show which displayed a thread of potential." Several episodes are available for viewing in the UCLA TV Archives.

Love That Jill Hal Roach Studios. ABC. Monday nights 8:00. January 20, 1958–April 28, 1958. 13 black-and-white episodes were filmed with a laugh track. The sponsor was Max Factor.

They had previously been the Kerbys (the ghosts) on *Topper*. This time, in *Love That Jill*, real-life husband and wife Anne Jeffreys and Robert Sterling were teamed in another sitcom. Here they were competing modeling company agents on New York City's Madison Avenue. Bob Sterling, as he was called for this show, played Jack Gibson of Gibson's Girls; Anne Jeffreys was Jill Johnson of Model Girls, Incorporated. Even though they were fierce competitors on the job, they were actually very much in love. The fact that their names were Jack and Jill made for a cute gimmick. Others in the cast included Barbara Nichols as Ginger; Jimmy Lydon as Jill's male secretary, Richard; and Betty Lynn as Jack's female secretary, Pearl. Every episode of the show ended with Jack saying the words "Love that Jill."

In the episode titled "They Went Thataway," Jack and Jill were both pitching commercial ideas to the Peterson Potato Chip Company. Jack wanted to go with a sputnik theme, but Jill wanted a western motif. They both ended up in Arizona for the filming of the commercial, where Jill had Jack believing that a tall, handsome cowboy named Cliff (Chuck Connors) wanted to marry her. In reality, he wanted to marry Sandy, the hotel desk clerk. In this episode, Jack and Jill sing a duet, "There's Silver on the Sage Tonight." In the episode titled "Hug That Hillbilly," Jack was giving a new model named Lulubelle (Barbara Wilson) so much attention, jealous Jill forged a letter from the model's hillbilly daddy stating that he wanted her back home. Laughter ensued when Lulubelle's father showed up at the modeling agency unannounced. When daddy found out that Lulubelle had fallen for Jack, he demanded that she and Jack get married.

Writers included Larry Rhine, Bill Freedman, and Alex Gottlieb; the creator and producer was Gottlieb; the executive producer was Hal Roach, Jr.; and the director was William A. Seiter. Music was provided by Leo Klatzkin. *Love That Jill* replaced *The Guy Mitchell Show* on ABC's prime time schedule. A few episodes of the show can be viewed at the UCLA TV Archives.

Love Thy Neighbor Herman Rush Productions. ABC. Friday nights 9:30 (June 15, 1973–July 20, 1973), and Wednesday nights 8:00 (August 15, 1973–September 19, 1973). 12 episodes were videotaped before a live audience at ABC Television Center in Los Angeles.

This American sitcom was based upon the long-running British TV series of the same name. Harrison Page, who portrayed Ferguson said, "I remember them screening a British episode as we were getting started." *Love Thy Neighbour* became *Love Thy Neighbor*, a 1973 summer replacement sitcom on ABC. The action took place on Friar Tuck Lane in the Sherwood Forest Estates in California's San Fernando Valley. What had long been a very Caucasian blue collar neighborhood was suddenly integrated by an African American couple named Ferguson and Jackie Bruce (Harrison Page and Janet MacLachlan, respectively). Living right next door were the Wilsons—Charlie and Peggy (Ron Masak and Joyce Bulifant, respectively). Charlie worked at and was shop steward for Turner Electronics, where, coincidentally, his new neighbor, Ferguson, was newly employed as an efficiency expert. Also employed there was Murray Bronson, played by stand-up comic Milt Kamen. Episodes focused upon how the Fergusons and Wilsons adjusted to this wholly new territory in race relations. Ron Masak told me, "I think my on-screen kiss with guest star Annazette Chase was one of television's first interracial kisses."

Episodes include the cleverly-titled "Guess Who's Coming to Dinner," in which both Charlie and Ferguson competed for the attention of their boss Roger Turner (John Fink) at the dinner table. Ferguson one-upped Wilson by asking for a raise. In "The Grass Is Always Greener," the Wilsons had to explain to a detective named Palmer (Jed Allan) why a marijuana plant was

Love Thy Neighbor—Top left to right, Ron Masak, Joyce Bulifant. Bottom left to right, Harrison Page, Janet MacLachlan (photograph courtesy of Jean Cummings).

growing in their backyard. Masak recalled, "Co-producer Arthur Julian was constantly in talks with the censors. So much has changed. We weren't allowed to say, 'let's go into the bedroom'—instead we had to say, 'let's go into the other room.'" Joyce Bulifant recalled an odd bit of censorship: "We weren't allowed to say the approaching hurricane had petered out, but we were allowed to say it pooped out. That was very odd."

I asked Harrison Page if there was any flak about an episode called "The Minstrel Show," in which Ron Masak was in black face and he was in white face, and he replied, "Not that I recall, but this was 1973 and everyone was focused on Watergate. Humor was kind of infantile on TV in those days, and a minstrel show was just silliness that the audience loved." Bulifant recalled a funny line from the show: "Jackie (Janet MacLachlan) and I were going to share a maid in one episode. We didn't know whether to hire a black maid or a white maid, so I said that we should compromise and split a Puerto Rican." Joyce also recalled a slapstick moment: "We had invited the Bruces over for dinner. Ron Masak's character, Charlie, had bought a couple of watermelons for dessert. My character was very embarrassed when the Bruces came to the door, and I attempted to cover the melons with my body so they wouldn't be offended."

The program's directors included Hal Cooper and Jack Donohue; writers included Arthur Julian, Lloyd Turner, and Gordon "Whitey" Mitchell; the producers were Julian, Ted Bergman, and Herman Rush. Masak remembered, "I went into Herman Rush's office to ask what night of the week the show would be on in the fall, and was told that ABC had instead opted for *The New Temperature's Rising* with Paul Lynde, which quickly bombed." This is an interesting coincidence, because *The New Temperature's Rising* was a program directed and produced by William Asher. Asher became Joyce Bulifant's third husband a few years later. Little did she realize Asher's show replaced *Love Thy Neighbor*. Page recalls, "Ron Masak and I had just gone to Bakersfield as part of a promotional tour for the show, and when I got back I heard we were not picked up for the fall." The *Love Thy Neighbor* theme song (complete with the lyrics, "Love thy neighbor, follow the golden rule, love thy neighbor, you'll find it's really cool") was sung by soul music legend Solomon Burke. One of Bulifant's fondest memories of the show is when she "got to use Julie Andrews's dressing room. That was incredible." Coincidentally, Bulifant's fourth husband, Roger Perry, starred in a made-for-TV movie in 1984, also called *Love Thy Neighbor*. The entire run of this series is housed in the UCLA TV Archives. The show was rerun briefly on the BET network

Loves Me, Loves Me Not Witt/Thomas/Harris Productions/20th Century Television. CBS. Sunday nights 10:30 (March 20, 1977), and Wednesday nights 8:30 (March 23, 1977–April 27, 1977). Six filmed episodes aired.

In between *The Partridge Family* and *L. A. Law*, Susan Dey starred in this short-lived CBS sitcom called *Loves Me, Loves Me Not*. This was the story of Dick and Jane. Susan was Jane Benson, a single California schoolteacher, and Kenneth "Kip" Gilman was Dick Phillips, a hard-working but awkward single newspaper reporter. At first, Jane wanted nothing to do with Mr. Phillips. When Dick and Jane started dating, each was very unsure of where the relationship was going. Dick was head-over-heels for Jane, but Jane was a little less certain, and thus hesitant to reciprocate his affection. Dick's boss, Tom (Art Metrano), was also his best friend. Tom was married to Sue (Phyllis Glick), who became a friend of Jane's.

Episodes include "Jane's Parents," in which Dick was scheduled to meet Jane's very persnickety parents. In "Walter Comes Back," Jane's ex-fiancée returned to town and made Dick feel very insecure. In "Dick's Novel," Dick took a leave of absence from work to finish up his writing.

The program was produced by Paul Junger Witt and Tony Thomas; Susan Harris was the creator and writer; and directors included Jay Sandrich.

Mack and Myer for Hire Sandy Howard Productions/Trans-Lux Television. First-run syndication 1963. 202 fifteen-minute black-and-white episodes were filmed with a laugh track.

Mack (Mickey Deems) was a pessimist and Myer (Joey Faye) was an eternal optimist. They were friends and New York roommates who made a living working odd jobs. Mack and Myer were both very kindhearted guys, but their good deeds almost invariably backfired. They were just Mack and Myer, as Mickey Deems told me: "We never had full names—it was always simply Mack and Myer through all 202 episodes." The two stars had deep roots in Vaudeville, and those roots were very apparent in this series of slapstick shorts, very much in the same vein as Laurel and

Hardy or Abbott and Costello. Joey Faye was selected for the show first by Trans-Lux Television of Norwalk, Connecticut (Trans-Lux had previously produced *Felix the Cat* and *The Mighty Hercules* cartoons), and Joey recommended his old friend Deems to be his on-screen partner. Joey and Mickey were long-time friends and had most recently worked together on Broadway in Sid Caesar's show, *Little Me*. The two actors were very comfortable working with one another and never really rehearsed. They did a basic read-through while in the make-up chair, and then the filming commenced. The budget for the show was extremely small, so there weren't a lot of big name guest stars, there were very few scene changes. As Deems recalled, "I don't recall ever doing a retake." He added, "There weren't pages of dialogue—that was made up on the fly. Sometimes our budget was so tight, Joey and I played multiple roles so that we didn't have to pay other actors. Those episodes, like our parody of Charles Dickens's *A Christmas Carol*, were probably the most fun."

Episodes available include "Friendly Enemies," in which the boys were hired to build a fence between the homes of two feuding neighbors and everyone involved got a black eye. In "Finders Weepers," Mack and Myer found a wallet full of money and returned it to its owner, only to be accused of being pickpockets. In "Dueling Fools," Mack and Myer performed a parody of *Cyrano De Bergerac* with Mack as Cyrano, donning a long rubber nose, seeking the hand of the fair Lady Rocksalt.

The executive producer was Sandy Howard; most episodes were written by Mickey Deems and directed by Ted Devlet. Music was provided by Ross-Gaffney. The program was filmed at the Hempstead Film Studios, and the same laugh track used for *The Patty Duke Show* was used on this show. Two fifteen-minute episodes were shown back-to-back to equal a half hour. Six episodes are available on DVD from Alpha Video. The program has a cult following, especially in Germany and Japan.

Make Room for Granddaddy Danny Thomas Productions/Paramount Studios. ABC. Wednesday nights 8:00 (September 23, 1970–January 1971), and Thursday nights 9:00 (January 1971–September 2, 1971). 24 color episodes were filmed with a laugh track. Sponsors include General Foods, Lever Brothers, Sterling Drug, and Warner Lambert.

The original *Make Room for Daddy/The Danny Thomas Show* ran from 1953 to 1964. It was an attempt at a sequel, but this update only lasted a single season. Danny Thomas was still Danny Williams, the nightclub entertainer, and he was still married to Kathy (Marjorie Lord). Terry (Sherry Jackson), the daughter who left the original show back in 1958, reluctantly agreed to appear in the hour-long pilot episode only (which aired on CBS and was sponsored by FTD Florists), so that the "Granddaddy" part of the new show could be established. In the original series, Terry had married a guy named Pat Hannigan (Pat Harrington, Jr.), but here her husband's name was Bill Johnson (he was stationed in Japan so we never got to see him). Terry was to join Bill overseas, so her six-year-old son, Michael (Michael Hughes), moved in with his grandparents. Occasionally we saw 23-year-old Rusty (Rusty Hamer) who was now in medical school and married to a colonel's daughter named Susan (Jana Taylor). Linda (Angela Cartwright) was now 17 years old, still lived at home with Danny and Kathy, and was a regular. Uncle Charley Halper (Sid Melton) was still Danny's

Make Room for Granddaddy—**Left to right, Danny Thomas and Michael Hughes (ABC).**

manager, and on a couple of occasions we again got to see Uncle Tonoose (Hans Conried). New to the cast were football star/singer/actor Roosevelt Grier as Rosey Robbins (Danny's musical arranger and pianist) and Stanley Myron Handelman (as Henry, the neurotic elevator operator).

The best episodes are those with very special guest stars. Diana Ross portrayed egotistical diva Diana Hendricks in the episode titled "The Star." We found out later in the episode that she wasn't such a prima donna after all. In "A Hamburger for Frank," Frank Sinatra guest starred as himself, paying a visit to the Williams household. While there, he asked Danny to play in the famous Bob Hope Classic Golf Tournament in Palm Springs (nowadays known as the Humana Challenge). Danny agreed, but he had to stay at Frank's bachelor pad for a few days. Because Kathy had heard about Frank's alleged harem of women followers, she became nervous that Danny might be tempted. In "Lucy Carter, Houseguest," Lucille Ball, in character from her popular *Here's Lucy* series, wreaked havoc as a guest in the Williams household. Lucy also guest starred on Danny's next TV series, the very funny but short-lived *The Practice* in October of 1976 in an episode titled "The Dream."

Danny Thomas was the executive producer of *Make Room for Granddaddy*; writers included David Adler, Erik Tarloff, and Bernie Kahn; and directors included John Rich and Amos Jacobs (the latter was an alias for Thomas—a name he used when first starting out in show business—an Anglicized version of his real name, Amos Yakhoob). Music was provided by Earle Hagen and Carl Brandt. Just like its predecessor, the theme song was an updated version of the Irish standard, *Danny Boy*, written by Frederic Weatherly. Even nestled between two hit ABC shows (*The Courtship of Eddie's Father* and *Room 222*) this updated show failed to catch on. Thomas was never again able to attain the success of the original *Make Room for Daddy*. His last two shows, *I'm a Big Girl, Now* and *One Big Family*, were both single season sitcoms. Ben Gross of *The New York Daily News* reviewed *Make Room for Granddaddy* this way: "If you're in the market for a wholesome escapist family type of entertainment, this is it."

Makin' It Henderson Production Company, Inc./The Stigwood Group, Ltd/Miller-Milkis Productions/Paramount Studios. ABC. Thursday nights 8:30 (February 1, 1979), and Friday nights 8:00 (February 9, 1979–March 23, 1979). Nine color episodes were filmed with a live audience, only eight aired. Sponsored by General Foods.

Inspired by *Saturday Night Fever* (there was a Travolta in the cast; Robert Stigwood who produced the movie was involved; and plenty of Bee Gees songs were part of the soundtrack), this was the story of the Manucci family of King Street in Passaic, New Jersey. Billy Manucci was played by David Naughton (later of *An American Werewolf in London* and some very popular Dr. Pepper commercials). Billy was trying to do well in college (he wanted to be a schoolteacher), but there were many distractions—his daytime job at the Tasty Treats ice cream parlor (on an undetermined street with the address 3519); his passion for disco music and the Inferno nightclub; and his two dimwitted best friends, Al "Kingfish" Sorrentino (Ralph Seymour), who carried a boom box with him everywhere, and tow-headed numbskull Bernard Fusco (Gary Prendergast). Billy was the middle child—he had a younger sister named Tina (Denise Miller) and an estranged-from-his-dad older brother Tony Herbert Manucci (Greg Antonacci). Prolific director Joel Zwick remembered, "I had directed Antonacci on Broadway in a show called *Dance with Me* at the Mayfair Theater. We had also worked together on a series called *Busting Loose*." Lou Antonio played the bumbling dad, Joseph, and Ellen Travolta played the Pollyanna-esque mom, Dorothy. Zwick remembered, "I directed Ellen Travolta as the mother of an Italian-American family on three different sitcoms."

Episodes include one taken directly from the *Saturday Night Fever* songbook titled "Stayin' Alive," in which Billy opted out of his church's bishops dinner to study, but was talked into going to the Inferno instead by his influential buddies, and of course, got caught in the lie. In "Something for Ma," it was Dorothy's birthday, and Billy wanted to get something extra special for her. His gift was a visit from the estranged Tony (against his father's wishes). Tony's own gift of stolen earrings mistakenly got Dorothy arrested.

The show was produced by David W. Duclon, Deborah Leschin, and Jeffrey Ganz; the executive producers were Lowell Ganz and Mark Rothman; the creator was Garry Marshall; writers included Babaloo Mandel, Ganz, and Rothman; and directors included Ganz and Joel Zwick. Zwick told me, "This was a show about dancing, but we really didn't have any dancers. We had to keep it simple for Greg Antonacci in the dancing sequences. Now, David Naughton was a good dancer, but he didn't have the role of a dancer on this show."

The most memorable part of this show was the theme song, "Makin' It," performed by Naughton and written by Freddie Perren and Dino Fekaris (also the writers of *I Will Survive*). Strangely, the theme song became a top five hit on the charts a full two months after the series had been canceled. It was also later used in the soundtrack of Bill Murray's classic comedy film *Meatballs*. Several episodes can be viewed at the UCLA TV Archives.

Mama Rosa A Rockett-Lauritzen Production/ABC. Sunday nights 9:30. April 23, 1950–June 11, 1950. Episodes were broadcast live without an audience and without a laugh track. The sponsor was Sun Vista Pinto Beans in Chili Sauce.

Matronly Mama Rosa (Anna Demetrio) ran a boarding house, mostly for "theatrical types" in Hollywood. She was the voice of reason amidst a lot of insanity going on around her. Looking at Mama Rosa, one can't help but make comparisons to Gertrude Berg's Molly Goldberg. Helping out at the boarding house was Mama's daughter Nina (Beverly Garland, with dark hair, in her first sitcom, here known as Beverly Campbell). Nina worked as a stenographer for an insurance company run by the unseen Mr. Dennis Campbell. Among the boarders, Roberto Novello (Jack Bernardi) was an actor who had trouble finding steady work in the movie industry; Nicoli (Vito Scotti, miscast as a Frenchman) was a violinist, but also a gardener for Mama to help pay his rent. He often got things backwards—the word "bookworm" to him was "wormbook" and "okay" was "kayo." Another of the boarders, Italian immigrant Crispino (John Romano), experienced major character changes on the show. In the early episodes, he spoke almost no English, but his proficiency with the English language grew exponentially during the show's brief network run. Crispino also removed his pince-nez glasses every time he spoke. The most colorful character of the bunch, known only as "Shakespeare" (Frank Pucci), was somewhat of a schemer/prankster, an amateur inventor, and one who latched onto many different "get rich quick schemes" with little success.

Episode titles are unknown, but among them is one in which Nina's steady boyfriend Tommy (Bob Knapp) greatly curtailed his dates with Nina so that he could study hard for medical school. Mama Rosa suggested that Tommy could do his studying at the boarding house so that he and Nina could still be together. It sounded like a great idea on paper, but there proved to be too many distractions there. When this didn't work out, Tommy stated that he did his best studying with someone named "Molly." Well, all of the busybodies at the house, including Nina, thought Molly was another woman, but it turned out to be a plastic skeleton Tommy used for studying anatomy. In the show's final network episode, Roberto finally landed a major role in a motion picture about the explorer, Cortez, and was to board a plane the next day. His enthusiasm led Nina and her friend and co-worker Estelle Granite (Alix Talton) to ponder leaving their jobs at the insurance company to pursue an acting career. That all changed, however, and Roberto's bubble burst, when at the last minute, the movie lost its backer and was postponed indefinitely. After seeing the ups and downs of show biz, Nina and Estelle gladly returned to their boring jobs as stenographers.

The program was produced by Alan Armer, Walter Grauman and Walter King; writers included Armer, Grauman and King, Ted Byron, and Louella MacFarlane; and the director was George M. Cahan. The theme song was "O Sole Mio," played on the organ by Rex Koury. In fact, all of the scoring consisted solely of organ music. The premise for the show, a boarding house for "show biz folk," was very similar to that of another single season sitcom, *Actor's Hotel*. Surprisingly, most 1950 ABC Network episodes of this live show exist on kinescope, and several are available for viewing in the UCLA TV Archives. The program began as a local Los Angeles sitcom in 1948 on KFI-TV.

Many Happy Returns A Lindabob Production. MGM Studios. CBS. Monday Nights 9:30. September 21, 1964–April 12, 1965. 26 black-and-white episodes were filmed with a laugh track. Sponsored by General Foods.

This was the story of Krockmeyer's Department Store on Avalon Street in Los Angeles. The new head of the Adjustments and Refunds Department arrived in the debut. His name was Walter Burnley (John McGiver), a widower of ten years who had been the head of the refunds department at the New York City Krockmeyer's for twelve years. He was a business school graduate and had just taken up residence at 609 North Elm Street with his daughter Joan Randall (Elinor Donahue), his lawyer son-in-law Bob Randall (Mark Goddard), and four-year-old granddaughter Laurie Randall (Andrea Sacino). Mr. Burnley also has a nephew named Martin Braddock (Ralph Conway) who lived right down the street at 629 North Elm, along with his wife Ellen (Ina Victor) and their son Jimmy (Bobby Buntrock). The show's large cast grew exponentially when the staff at Krockmeyer's was factored in. Employed in the Adjustments and Refunds Department (the complaint/refunds desk) were some very unique individuals. There was Lynn Hall (Elena Verdugo), who had been employed at the store for eight years between ladies apparel, sportswear, and the complaint department, and she was unhappily unmarried; Harry Price (Richard Collier) had been with the company on-and-off for 17 years (most of those years spent in the bargain basement)—he was a league bowler, and married with eight children; and Wilma Fritter (Jesslyn Fax) had previously spent seven years as the company's fashion model. In her own words, "My figure changed faster than the fashions." Joe Foley (Mickey Manners) was a real piece of work. He was 30 years old and single. He spent four years at Columbia Medical School—not as a student, but rather as a parking attendant. Joe had a unique problem which kept him from advancing—the English language. His grammar and diction were a unique mixture of Chester A. Riley, Norm Crosby, and Archie Bunker. Then there was the store's manager, J.R. Fox (Jerome Cowan) who took an instant dislike to Walter Burnley. Fox called him a "maverick." Fox was a stickler for rules and regulations, while Burnley was not. Cranky Owen Sharp (Russell Collins) was the owner of the store and his conniving nephew, Virgil Slamm, was played by a young Arte Johnson.

Many Happy Returns—**Elinor Donahue and John McGiver (photograph courtesy of Elinor Donahue).**

Elinor Donahue told me, "This was not a happy experience for me. The cast was delightful, but my character was very blah and bland, and never went anywhere. At the time, my young family was more important, and I was initially assured that I wouldn't be included in every episode, allowing me more time with my family. However, I'd often get frantic calls asking my whereabouts after being promised that I wouldn't be needed for a couple of weeks, and this happened over and over again. I really wasn't terribly disappointed when it ended."

It was the policy of Krockmeyers to avoid having to give refunds to the best of its ability. This policy gave Mr. Burnley fits in the debut episode as he tried to get a groom's mother to change her mind about her son's upcoming nuptials so that the bride (Cynthia Pepper) wouldn't have to be refunded a fortune for her trousseau. In "Krockmeyer's On Avalon," the employees staged a rather shaky interpretation of Shakespeare's *Romeo and Juliet*. In "House Divided," a customer took a spill in Krockmeyer's and decided to sue the store. Comedy ensued when Mr. Burnley's son-in-law Bob was hired to represent the plaintiff.

The program was created and produced by Parke Levy; writers included Sid Dorfman, Burt Styler, Albert E. Lewin, Harvey Helm, Phil Green, Hannibal Coons, Harry Winkler, Earl Barret, Norman Paul, and Parke Levy; and directors included Sherman Marks, Theodore J. Flicker, and Stanley Z. Cherry. The theme song was written by David Rose (*The Stripper*) and Levy. The debut episode had an animated open, but the opening credits for the remaining episodes had Mr. Burnley opening the doors to Krockmeyer's, with an immediate barrage of customers filing in from every direction.

Some members of this extremely large cast went on to bigger and better things. John McGiver did *Mr. Terrific* and *The Jimmy Stewart Show*; Mark Goddard became Don on *Lost in Space*; Elena Verdugo portrayed Consuelo Lopez on *Marcus Welby, M.D.*; and Arte Johnson had a long run on *Rowan and Martin's Laugh-In*.

The Marge and Gower Champion Show J and M Productions. CBS. Sunday nights 7:30. March 31, 1957–June 9, 1957. 11 black-and-white episodes aired, some live, some filmed. Sponsored by Hit Parade Cigarettes.

Real-life husband and wife dance team, Marge and Gower Champion, attempted sitcom stardom in 1957 playing themselves, on alternating weeks with *The Jack Benny Program*. Plots focused upon the couple's attempts to find a normal life within the showbiz world. Gower played a choreographer, and Marge his dance partner. Many of the situations were based upon real-life experiences. As you would expect, each episode had at least one song and dance number worked into the script. The legendary Buddy Rich was Cozy, their drummer. Others in the cast included Jack Whiting as Marge's dad (also their manager); Peg LaCentra was Marge's best friend, Amanda, the interior decorator; and Barbara Perry was Miss Weatherly.

One untitled episode flashed back to a time when the Champions lived in a tiny rundown apartment and had no money. That is, until Marge's father got them connected with a backer named Feets Fortunata, who offered them a small fortune for a show Gower had written. There was one important stipulation—the backer wanted to rename the show *Wildflower Girls of 1926*, but Gower had his heart set upon the title *Requiem of Rhythm*. To keep from blowing the deal, however, Gower eventually gave in.

The program was produced by Paul Harrison; the executive producer was Jack Benny; directors included James Sheldon; and the writers were Joe Connelly and Bob Mosher. Music was provided by Richard Pribor. Marge and Gower Champion divorced in 1973. One episode can be viewed at the Paley Center for Media.

Marge and Jeff DuMont Network. Monday thru Friday nights 7:15. September 21, 1953–September 24, 1954. 15-minute episodes were broadcast live with no laugh track and no live audience.

Marge was Marge Greene and Jeff was Jeff Cain. In this live nightly 15-minute sitcom, written by Greene, *Marge and Jeff* were newlyweds getting through life together in their New York City apartment. Marge's maiden name on the show was McCaffrey. There were occasional sightings of their cocker spaniel Paisley. Paisley didn't do any tricks, but rather just sat there unfazed by any of the goings-on. Jeff was rarely seen without his pipe and black horn-rimmed glasses. Jeff Cain's real first name was Jess, but he had that changed legally to lessen confusion. Jeff's boss was always referred to as E.W.

In one episode, Marge tried to earn some extra money for a trip to Bermuda by selling *The Book of Knowledge* (basically, a set of encyclopedias), only to find that Jeff had just bought a set on the installment plan from the boss' nephew Monty. In another episode, the newlyweds had just too many plans for one night—four tickets to a show, friends named the Dubins coming to visit, and Marge's old friend Stephanie Lime in town for a reunion.

Marge and Jeff was called a "strip show"—a show seen Monday thru Friday at the same time. This strip show benefited from its lead-in, *Captain Video and His Video Rangers*. *Captain Video* was one of DuMont's few success stories, and having the show as a lead-in garnered great ratings for *Marge and Jeff*. It should be noted that this is also the reason that numerous kinescopes of *Marge and Jeff* have survived. A goodly amount of episodes are available for viewing at both The UCLA TV Archives, and The Paley Center for Media.

The program was produced by Ernest Walling and directed by Leonard Valenta.

Margie 20th Century–Fox Television. ABC. Thursday nights 9:30. October 12, 1961–August 31, 1962. 26 black-and-white episodes were filmed with a laugh track. Sponsors included Prell Shampoo, Crest Toothpaste, and Ralston Purina.

This period piece had absolutely no relation to *My Little Margie*, but rather was loosely based upon the Jeanne Crain and Alan Young film called *Margie* from 1946 (although the surname was McDuff in the movie and Clayton in the series). The show's star, Cynthia Pepper told me, "They even used some of the same furniture from the Jeanne Crain movie. In fact, I found a fan letter, addressed to Miss Crain, in one of the

Margie—**Left to right, Cynthia Pepper and Penny Parker (photograph courtesy of Cynthia Pepper).**

drawers of a dresser on our set." This became ABC's third show on their 1961 fall schedule based in the 1920s (along with *The Untouchables* and *The Roaring Twenties*). Being part of a period show was just fine with Cynthia, who said, "I am a big fan of that era—I felt like I belonged there." Cynthia Pepper as Margie (previously Jean Pearson on season one of *My Three Sons*) had long braided pigtails on the show, but told me, "It was a fall. My hair was actually very short." Even though the world was a vastly different place in the 1920s, teenagers still faced the same dilemmas—acne, love, parents, school, friends, jobs, money, and life. Margie attended Madison High School and lived in a nice house in the small town of Madison (somewhere in New England) with her rather old-fashioned parents (Harvey and Nora, played by Dave Willock and Wesley Marie Tackitt, respectively), along with her mischievous little brother Cornell (Johnny Bangert) and her Aunt Phoebe (Hollis Irving). Margie had a boyfriend named Heywood Botts (Tommy Ivo). Cynthia said, "Tommy Ivo became a world-famous drag car racer—not at all what one would expect from his rather nerdy Heywood character on our show." Margie also had a best friend named Maybelle Jackson (Penney Parker) who was a flapper. Maybelle's boyfriend was Johnny Green (Richard Gering).

Episodes include "The Jazz Band," in which Margie and her friends put together a jazz band called "Margie and the Connecticut Yankees," which was starting to get some attention. They even had an agent (Eddie Foy, Jr., as J. J. Burton), who got them booked into a speakeasy, much to their parent's dismay. Cynthia said, "'The Jazz Band' is my favorite episode. I got to sing several numbers in that one." In "Flaming Youth," when Margie's parents saw a new movie about the loose morals of modern teenagers, they pulled the reins in tighter on Margie (just after she had the hems on all of her dresses raised). While having her hems lowered again, her parents saw her empty closet and were led to believe that Margie and Heywood had run away and eloped. In "A Woman Scorned," Margie began taking Heywood for granted, treating him badly, prompting her dad to have a man-to-man talk with the lad, urging him to be more assertive and more of a cad. Cynthia recalled the most memorable guest stars to be "a young and yet-unknown James Brolin, the great Eddie Foy, Jr., Yvonne Craig, Jack Albertson, and the wonderful J. Pat O'Malley."

Cynthia remembered one very funny outtake which occurred during filming on her 21st birthday: "I was wearing heels, and while walking down the staircase, I tripped and said a bad word. This was very odd for me because I never swore, but it just slipped out. Needless to say, that clip made the funny outtakes reel we would watch every Friday night after wrapping up that week's filming."

Margie was a relatively successful sitcom, but wasn't renewed for a second season. Cynthia admits, "We were all rather surprised at that. However, we were up against *Hazel*, which was beating us in the ratings and our sponsor jumped ship and went over to *Hazel* on NBC. This was a major factor in our not being renewed."

The program was produced by Hal Goodman and Larry Klein; writers included Albert E. Lewin, Burt Styler, Ben Freedman, Ralph Goodman, Robert Van Scoyk, Ray Brenner, John Bradford, Larry Rhine, Milton Pascal, Mel Tolkin, Leo Rifkin, Barbara Hammer, Arnold Horwitt, Walter Kempley, Alan Woods, Alan Lipscott, and Bob Fisher; and directors included Jack Sher, Don Richardson, Gene Reynolds, Jack Donohue, Rod Amateau, and James Sheldon. Music was provided by Warren Barker and Lionel Newman. The theme song, "Margie," was written about Eddie Cantor's five-year-old daughter by Con Conrad, J. Russel Robinson and Benny Davis (Cantor was the first to popularize the song). Cynthia Pepper sang in several episodes, and even had a 45 rpm record called *Baby Blues/A First Time Love* on the Felsted record label (Felsted 8651 in 1962). Two issues of *Margie* comic books were released by Dell during the run of the series, each originally selling for 12 cents. Cynthia told me, "*Margie* was my baby. I loved doing the show. I never told the guys in charge, but I would've paid them to let me do *Margie* instead of the other way around." A few episodes are available for viewing in the UCLA TV Archives.

The Marriage Ted Ashley Productions/NBC. Thursday nights 10:00. July 8, 1954–August 19, 1954. Eight episodes were broadcast live with a small studio audience.

This live sitcom had also been on radio and was set in the Gramercy Apartments in New York City. As a summer replacement for *Martin Kane, Private Eye*, it starred real-life married couple Hume Cronyn and Jessica Tandy as Ben and Liz Marriott, respectively, who had been married for 17 years. Ben had a fairly successful law practice and Liz was a former buyer for a department store chain, but she became a housewife when the kids, ten-year-old Pete and 15-year-old Emily (Malcolm Broderick and Susan Strasberg, respectively), came along. This show may have been extremely short-lived, but it was very historically significant. It was among the first programs broadcast in color—in fact, much ado was made about this in the opening and closing with the announcement that "this program was broadcast live in color using the RCA compatible color

TV system." It should also be noted that Ben and Liz (Hume and Jessica) slept very closely in the same double bed on this show—likely the first sitcom couple to do so (perhaps because they were a real married couple).

Episodes include the untitled debut in which young Pete came home from the first day of school very upset because his teacher, Miss Whitman (Vera Allen), had decided to teach the class the exact same lessons as the year before. When Ben attended a PTA meeting to get to the bottom of this bizarre lesson plan, he was instead tricked into hosting a fiesta meeting for the Hispanic fathers. In the episode titled "Inside Bobby Logan," Emily's boyfriend Bobby (William Redfield), whose family owned a cheese shop, discovered what an understanding person and good listener Liz was, and began to develop a mad crush on her. In the final episode, "The Dreamer," while out on a picnic with Liz, Ben took a nap and had several odd dreams, including one about being a big game hunter, and another about being a participant in a duel to earn the hand of his beloved, Liz. At the end of the episode, Hume and Jessica addressed the audience and announced that it would be the final show of the series because they had a prior commitment to go on tour in a play titled *Face to Face*. They also stressed that the joys of married life should be experienced by all.

The program was produced by Hume Cronyn; writers included Ernest Kinoy; and directors included Edward S. King, Jack Garfein, Marc Daniels, and Paul Bogart. Music was provided by Morris Mamorsky. Even though the program was broadcast in color, only black-and-white kinescopes exist, and are available for viewing at both the Paley Center for Media and the UCLA TV Archives. The program was to have begun its run on July 1, 1954, but Jessica Tandy was ill, so the debut was delayed one week. Cronyn and Tandy made a brand new filmed pilot episode in 1957, attempting to bring the series back to prime time but to no avail. This new pilot aired on June 8, 1957 on NBC at 10PM.

Mayor of the Town A Rawlins-Grant Production/Gross-Krasne Production/Distributed by MCA TV. First-run syndication. 1954–1955. 39 black-and-white episodes were filmed without a laugh track.

Thomas Russell (Thomas Mitchell) had first been a lawyer before becoming a long-time fixture as *Mayor of the Town*. That "town" was Springdale (however the state was never mentioned). The mayor was a widower and his nephew Butch (David Saber) was his ward. As she was wont to do, Kathleen Freeman portrayed a housekeeper (named Marilly, pronounced Muh-RIHL-lee) and she also kept mischievous young Butch in line. The mayor had a secretary named Minnie (Jean Byron, later Natalie on *The Patty Duke Show*). Speaking of Natalies, future star Natalie Wood appeared in several episodes as the mayor's niece, June.

Episodes include "Take Me Out to the Ballgame," in which a local baseball great (John Lupton) had a huge decision to make—play ball for the New York Giants or tie the knot with his fiancée. In "The Farmer," Minnie's cousin David Lewis (Robert Patten) lost job after job, and the mayor sought to get him back to his farming roots where he belonged. In "His Honor, Butch," the mayor's young ward got to experience being "mayor for a day," and, as complications arose he soon realized how tough his uncle's job was.

The program was produced and directed by John Rawlins and Marshall Grant; writers included Erna Lazarus. *Mayor of the Town* had been a successful radio program in the 1940s (starring Lionel Barrymore). Gross-Krasne Productions also gave us the private eye adventure series, *The Lone Wolf*.

McDuff, the Talking Dog D'Angelo/Bullock/Allen Productions. NBC. September 11, 1976–November 20, 1976. Thirteen episodes were videotaped with a laugh track, but only eleven aired.

This was a live-action Saturday morning kid's sitcom—one of the few which did not come from the studios of Sid and Marty Krofft. McDuff was a 100-year-old English sheepdog's ghost (featuring the voice of Jack Lester). McDuff haunted the home of veterinarian Dr. Calvin Campbell (Walter Willison), who lived with his little sister Kimmy (Michelle Stacy), and his housekeeper Mrs. Osgood (Monty Margetts). Gordon Jump in his pre-*WKRP in Cincinnati* days portrayed neighbor Amos Ferguson. Squeaky (Johnnie Collins III) was his nephew.

Calvin, not unlike Wilbur Post in *Mister Ed* and David Crabtree in *My Mother, the Car*, was the only one who could hear McDuff speak (besides other animals, that is). *McDuff, the Talking Dog* was briefly part of a three-hour block of live-action programming on the NBC Saturday morning schedule.

McKeever and the Colonel Four Star Studios. NBC. Sunday nights 6:30. September 23, 1962–June 16, 1963. 26 black-and-white episodes were filmed with a laugh track. Sponsors included Chesebrough Ponds, Inc., Texaco, Milton Bradley, and Mentholatum.

It was rarely mentioned during the show's brief run, but McKeever did have a first name—Gary. However, most people simply called him McKeever. Adults usually called his name in loud exasperated tones. McKeever (Scott Lane) was enlisted in the Westfield Academy for Boys in the notorious "Squad C." The letter "c" might have stood for chicanery, conniving or cunning. McKeever was the master of monkeyshines, but he wasn't evil—he had a good heart. *McKeever and the Colonel* should not be confused with the animated *Calvin and the Colonel*, which ran in prime time the previous year.

McKeever's partners in crime were Keith Taylor as the calorically-challenged, bespectacled "Tubby" Anderson and the red-haired straight man of the triumvirate, John Eimen as Cadet Monk Roberts (although his surname of Roberts rarely came up). Eimen told me, "I was the foil to Tubby and McKeever. My character was less developed than theirs. Monk's talents did come out in one episode called 'The Cookie Crumbles.' McKeever and I were trying to raise money so Tubby could stay on at Westfield, and I mentioned that I knew how to bake cookies." The machinations of this trio became a huge thorn in the side of Harvey Blackwell (Allyn Joslyn), their commanding officer. His aide, Sergeant Claude Barnes, was played by former child star Jackie Coogan. Coogan benefited the most from the single season status of *McKeever and the Colonel*, as he had a more memorable role awaiting him—Uncle Fester on *The Addams Family*. Eimen recalls working with Coogan: "He made the greatest effort to help us kids (although he was the strictest). He taught us how to do our ties, and all of the proper military maneuvers associated with marching and rifles." Coogan had prior experience with military sitcoms, as he had been in charge of staging the live 1955 NBC sitcom, *The Soldiers*. Elisabeth Fraser played Academy dietician, Miss Frances Warner, who dated Sergeant Barnes on occasion.

McKeever and the Colonel—**Left to right, Johnny Eimen, Scott Lane and David Kent (photograph courtesy of John Eimen).**

Many have compared the McKeever character to *Dennis the Menace*, but Eimen says, "If anything, he seemed to me more of a pint-sized Sergeant Bilko." Not only were the kids mischievous when the cameras were rolling, but also when they were off. Eimen told me, "Scott, Keith and I found out about a movie being filmed on the far side of the Four Star lot with people in a boat on the water. We heard that the women on the boat would be topless. For twelve-year-old boys, this was the chance of a lifetime. We hid in the bushes and watched the boat approach, and sure enough, there were half-clad babes. And then we heard the director yell, 'Cut.' We got busted."

Among the most memorable episodes are those which boasted famous guest stars, such as Jim Backus in "The Neighbor"; Soupy Sales played a former Westfield cadet who was very much like McKeever in his day in an episode called "The Old Grad"; Ann B. Davis was strict Sergeant Gruber in "Too Many Sergeants"; and Mel Blanc was the voice of Stanley the bird in "All Quiet on the Westfield Front." Eimen recalls, "We were thrilled when Mel Blanc did some of his most famous voices for us off camera—Porky Pig, Bugs Bunny,

Yosemite Sam. He did them from a page in our script as if those characters were acting out a scene from our show. It was hilarious." The unaired pilot episode was later retooled into an aired episode called "Blackwell, the Retread," in which Blackwell left the Academy to work as plant manager for Tubby's dad's electronics company. When the new colonel proved to be too strict, the boys schemed to get Blackwell to come back. In the original pilot version of this episode, McKeever had an older brother named Donald (David Kent) who was also enrolled in the Academy.

Quite a few episodes involved animals. In "The Army Mule" the cadets babysat for the general's pet mule; in "The Mascot," the cadets grew fond of an escaped baby elephant; in "McKeever Meets Munroe," the boys attempted to rid a dog of his fear of cats; in "McKeever's Astronaut" a visiting hero from a space mission turned out to be a chimpanzee; and in "The Old Grad," a calf was put in the Colonel's bed as a joke. Eimen adds, "The directors worked well with us kids and often had to deal with that additional wild card—animals. Obviously, when veterans of the biz said don't work with animals or kids, these directors weren't paying attention."

Even with favorable reviews and many young fans, the show was cancelled after one season. Eimen remembers, "We were all devastated when the show wasn't picked up. It was like having the floor fall out from under us." The fun may have been short-lived, but Eimen has "no regrets whatsoever. All the great experiences, people, opportunities, twists and turns. What a ball!"

The program was produced by Tom McKnight; the creators were R. Allen Safian and Harvey Bullock; writers included Sam Locke, Joel Rapp, Lou Derman, Max Wilk, Jerry Seelen, Leo Rifkin, Dean Riesner, Allan Manings, Arthur Marx, Ray Allen, Harvey Helm, Bob Marcus, John Bradford, Barry Blitzer, Elroy Schwartz, Austin Kalish, Burt Styler, Al Lewis, Bob Fisher, and Howard Leeds; and directors included Jeffrey Hayden, Stanley Z. Cherry, Don Weis, Christian Nyby, Richard Whorf, and Norman Abbott. The opening credits featured clay figurines resembling McKeever and Tubby, performing some very clumsy sentry duty. It should also be noted that Dell published two *McKeever and the Colonel* comic books, each selling for twelve cents, during the show's single season run. A few episodes can be viewed in the UCLA TV Archives.

The McLean Stevenson Show McLean Stevenson Enterprises, Inc./Monty Hall Enterprises, Inc. (M & M). NBC. December 1, 1976–March 9, 1977. Wednesday nights 8:30 (December and January), and 9:30 (February and March). 13 color episodes were videotaped before a live audience.

He had been Mr. Nicholson on *The Doris Day Show*, and, more notably, he had been Henry Blake on *M*A*S*H*. McLean Stevenson was then poised for super-stardom in his own show. If only he could have found one that worked. In this eponymous and short-lived sitcom, he portrayed Mac Ferguson, who owned a hardware store. The show was created by Monty Hall, who told me, "The concept was one to which people could relate. The show was to be about a longtime married couple who finally had the money and the time to enjoy life, and travel. However their daughter, son, and his mother-in-law moved in and changed everything. The original pilot was called *Prime of Life*, and the wonderful William Windom was the star. However, NBC gave me an ultimatum—they would either get to put McLean Stevenson in the starring role or there would be 'no deal.' Unfortunately, McLean was very difficult to work with, and he replaced most of the cast from the pilot, and the series never had the same spark the pilot had. I had the misfortune of having to break the news to William Windom." Most of the action took place in the Ferguson's Evanston, Illinois, home. Mac resided there with his wife, Peggy (Barbara Stuart), and her sarcastic, wise-cracking mother (Madge West). As if that weren't enough, Mac and Peggy's two adult children had just returned—their lothario son, Chris (Steve Nevil), who lived in the basement and was trying to "find himself," and their newly-divorced daughter, Janet (Ayn Ruymen), and her two little boys, David and Jason (David Hollander and Jason Whitney, respectively).

In the debut, Mac confronted a burglar named Lenny (Jerry Houser) in the house. However, the burglar turned out to be a pretty nice guy who was just down on his luck and desperate. He, and his pregnant wife, had been living in a van and were on their way to California. In fact, the wife was taken aback when she learned what Lenny had been up to. Lenny apologized profusely and the Fergusons offered some financial assistance from Peggy's "emergency fund" (she had been secretly putting away five dollars every time she and Mac made love). The episode titled

"Who Do You Trust?" was written by Mark Evanier and Dennis Palumbo. Dennis told me, "The title of the episode was inspired by the classic game show of the fifties and sixties which starred Johnny Carson."

The program was created by Norman Barasch and Carroll Moore; writers included Mark Evanier, Dennis Palumbo, and Lloyd Garver; and most episodes were directed by Alan Myerson. The producers were Arnold Margolin and Don Van Atta; the executive producer was Monty Hall. The theme song was composed and performed by Paul Williams. A couple of episodes can be viewed in the UCLA TV Archives.

This show was canceled after 13 weeks. McLean kept trying for sitcom success, but floundered in *In the Beginning*, *Condo* and *Hello, Larry*. A sitcom which debuted on the same night as *The McLean Stevenson Show* titled *Sirota's Court* met a similar fate.

Me and the Chimp Paramount Television Productions. CBS. Thursday nights 8:00. January 13, 1972–May 18, 1972. 13 color episodes were filmed with a laugh track.

The premise had failed a decade earlier in *The Hathaways*, but apparently it was still believed that a sitcom about a family with a mischievous chimp could catch on. It didn't. This time around it was the Reynolds family of San Pascal, California. The head of the Reynolds household was Mike Reynolds played by Ted Bessell, who had a successful dental practice. His wife Liz, played by Anita Gillette, was a stay-at-home mom. They had two adorable kids—Scott, played by Scott Kolden, and Kitty, played by Kami Cotler. One day, while visiting the local park, they encountered an abandoned chimpanzee, which they brought home with the intention of finding its rightful owner. They contacted all of the zoos in California. They also placed newspapers ads, but all of their ads went unanswered. Even though Mike objected, Buttons became a member of the family. They called him "Buttons" because of his fascination with anything that had buttons (appliances, adding machines, telephones, etc.). Buttons was played by a three-and-a-half-year-old chimpanzee named Jackie.

Episodes include "Mike's Day with Buttons," in which the family recommended that Mike spend an entire day with the primate, because he still had misgivings about keeping Buttons. Mike made the mistake of bringing the chimp to his dental office, where a new patient (Reta Shaw) was frightened half out of her wits just as her laughing gas was wearing off. In "Hoopla," Scott was upset when his basketball coach (Henry Beckman) gave all of the playing time to a very tall new player named Claude Mingo. When Mike arranged a meeting between Coach Pitts and the other players' parents, the coach quit, leaving Mike to coach the team. When one of the young players took ill during the game, Buttons got to fill in for him, and the team almost pulled out a victory.

The program was created by Garry Marshall and Thomas L. Miller; the producer was Alan Rafkin; the executive producer was Marshall; writers included Marshall and Ron Friedman; and directors included Rafkin and Gary Nelson. TV Land reran a couple of episodes in the 1990s.

Menasha, the Magnificent Martin Goodman Productions/NBC. Monday nights 8:00. July 3, 1950–September 11, 1950. Broadcast live.

Great Yiddish comic Menasha Skulnik, who had played Uncle David on the radio version of *The Goldbergs* for 19 years, made the transition to television in this live short-lived summer replacement series. The pilot episode was called "The Magnificent Menasha," and aired February 20, 1950, but the actual series debuted on July 3, 1950. Menasha was known for his unusual gait (he had a hop in his walk), and he began each episode singing the classic "Oh, What a Beautiful Morning" from *Oklahoma*, but his beautiful morning always went awry with situations at his place of employment. Menasha was the manager of a rundown restaurant, owned by the very tall, very bossy, very pushy Mrs. Davis (played by Jean Cleveland in the pilot episode, and Zamah Cunningham in the series). The show began each week with a woman yelling, "Menasha, Menasha." Skulnik's grandson, Dennis Wilson told me, "He did a regular thing on the program to show that he was only a 'little manager.' He'd hold his hands far apart and say, 'I am not a manager,' and then bring his hands together and say, 'I am a manager.'"

The program was produced by Martin Goodman; the director was Alan Neuman; and writers included Louis Quinn and Matt Brooks. To my knowledge, no episodes exist. Because of other commitments, Menasha recommended Eli Mintz for the Uncle David role on stage and then in the TV version of *The Goldbergs*.

Mickey Selmur Productions/Four K's, Inc/ MGM Studios. ABC. Wednesday nights 9:00. September 16, 1964–January 13, 1965. 17 black-and-white episodes were filmed with a laugh track. Sponsors included Clairol and Ajax Laundry Detergent.

In between *Hey, Mulligan* and *One of the Boys*, Mickey Rooney also had this unsuccessful sitcom. He was just one of those movie stars who couldn't make the transition to television. Here he played Mickey Grady, a retired Coast Guard recruiter from Omaha, Nebraska, who inherited the Marina Palms Hotel at the Newport Palms Marina in California from his late uncle from where, on a clear day, it was alleged one would be able to see Catalina Island. The Grady family consisted of wife, Nora (who was taller than Mickey), played by Emmaline Henry, and sons Timmy (Mickey's real-life son, Tim Rooney) and Buddy (Brian Nash). All four moved to California and instantly had their hands full trying to make a profit on the hotel, which came with a manager named Sammy Ling (Sammee Tong) who had a lifetime contract which couldn't be broken. Ling's family was very much involved in the operation as well, and in fact the mortgage for the hotel was held by the Ling Savings and Loan. Once the Gradys took over the operation, Nora's ne'er-do-well brother Bobby Wilson (song and dance man and game show host Bobby Van) was hired as lifeguard and night manager. Mickey was always brainstorming new ideas to bring more vacationers to the hotel, while his inept helpers Bobby and Sammy always seemed to drive those same vacationers away.

Episodes include "Somebody's Been Sleeping in My Bed," in which Mickey was attempting to get shoe magnate Elroy Smight (Willard Waterman) to have his shoe convention at the hotel. While The Gradys went looking for Mr. Smight, he was already staying at the hotel in the Grady's suite, trying to get some much needed rest. In "The Elephant Mickey Won't Forget," Mickey thought his eyesight was failing him—he thought he'd seen an elephant water-skiing. Mickey's eyesight was just fine, and because of a misunderstanding about the hotel accepting pets, the elephant named Bimbo was staying in one of the rooms in the hotel. In "For the Love of Grandpa Toddie," Walter Burke portrayed Mickey's Irish grandfather who dropped in unexpectedly, and reunited with an old flame named Molly (Kitty Kelly) who lived in Laguna. They were wed a short time later and decided to stay on at the hotel for six months, much to Mrs. Grady's chagrin.

The program was produced by Bob Fisher and Arthur Marx; the executive producer was Selig J. Seligman; writers included John Fenton Murray, Bob Fisher, and Marx; and directors included Richard Whorf. Music was provided by Bobby Hammack. A few episodes can be viewed in the UCLA TV Archives.

The Mickey Rooney Show (see *Hey, Mulligan*)

Miss Winslow and Son T. T. C. Productions. CBS. Wednesday nights 8:30. March 28, 1979–May 2, 1979. Six episodes were videotaped before a live audience.

A few years before *Murphy Brown*'s unwed mother status caused an uproar, there was *Miss Winslow and Son*, which was based upon a British show called *Miss Jones and Son*. Susan Winslow (Darleen Carr) was a freelance art designer and Mr. Joseph X. Callahan (William Bogert) was her boss. Susan was pregnant, but decided not to marry the father of the child because she didn't love him. He moved to Brazil and she was left to fend for herself. Susan's father Warren (Elliott Reid) was a pharmacist, and her socially prominent mother, Evelyn (Sarah Marshall), tried to keep her daughter's "situation" a secret from those in her circle. Both parents continually tried to get her married. Many friends and other members of her family shunned her. Susan lived in apartment number 36, while her neighbor in apartment 35 was cranky, sarcastic Harold Devore Nelstadter (Roscoe Lee Browne) who, despite his gruff exterior, really had a heart of gold. He watched the baby while she was at work. Harold created crossword puzzles for a living.

In the debut, Susan gave birth to a baby boy whom she named Edmund Hillary Winslow (named after Sir Edmund Hillary, who was the first to scale Mount Everest). In "A Visit from Aunt Victoria," when Susan's conservative, judgmental Aunt Victoria (Irene Tedrow) came by for a visit, Susan pretended she was married to her neighbor Harold. In an untitled episode, when the baby developed a rash, Susan was confident that the child's regular doctor's diagnosis was correct. However, after being badgered by both her mother and Nelstadter, she got a second opinion from a recommended pediatrician. That second opinion, an allergy to the formula, proved correct and Susan had to swallow her pride and admit that she was in the wrong.

The program's executive producers were Ted Bergman and Don Taffner; writers included Liz Coe, and Alan J. Levitt; and directors included Jack Donohue and George Tyne. One episode of the program is available for viewing at the UCLA TV Archives.

Mr. Deeds Goes to Town Screen Gems. ABC. Friday nights 8:30. September 26, 1969–January 16, 1970. 17 color episodes were filmed without a laugh track, only 16 aired. Sponsors included Warner-Lambert, General Foods, and S. C. Johnson and Company.

Liberally based upon the 1936 Frank Capra movie of the same name (which starred Gary Cooper and Jean Arthur), this was the story of a tuba player named Longfellow Deeds (Monte Markham) of the small town of Mandrake Falls, who was an unaware heir to his late Uncle Alonzo P. Deeds (of the multi-million dollar corporation known as Deeds Enterprises). The problem was, Longfellow had been the news editor for a small newspaper and was now overwhelmed in his new position as president of his uncle's New York City empire. He had very little experience in the business world, and his assistant Tony Lawrence (Pat Harrington, Jr.) and Deeds Enterprises chairman of the board Henry Masterson (Herb Voland) tried their level best to keep this information under wraps. However, in the second episode, "The Education of Longfellow Deeds," that news got out when Deeds' young business and stock market-savvy tutor, Jeff (Bud Cort), had a slip of the tongue (to a gas station attendant). Soon it made headlines. The ever-honest Deeds then told the truth at a stockholders' meeting and regained their confidence. Longfellow also tried to undo and correct some of his uncle's less savory business deals—much to the chagrin and amazement of Chairman Masterson. In "The Improbable Mr. Deeds," Longfellow wanted to buy a used tuba in a second-hand store, but the owner, played by Ned Glass, wouldn't take a check. A passer-by named Charlotte (Arlene Golonka) didn't recognize him, thought he was hocking the tuba, and feared that he was a pauper. She didn't believe he indeed was Longfellow Deeds until she saw his limousine and driver named George (Ivor Barry).

The program was developed for TV by Bernard Slade. I asked Slade why the movie was such a success, but the TV incarnation was not, and he simply said, "Gary Cooper." The producer was Bob Sweeney; writers included William Raynor, Myles Wilder, Michael Morris and Slade; and directors included Harry Falk and Herbert Kenwith. Music was provided by Shorty Rogers. This program was pummeled in the ratings by *Hogan's Heroes* on CBS and *The Name of the Game* on NBC, and disappeared very early in 1970. Adam Sandler starred in an extremely loose 2002 Columbia Pictures interpretation of the original, called simply *Mr. Deeds*. Cecil Smith of the *Los Angeles Times* said of the TV version: "There's a sense of quality, of intelligence in approach, of an attempt to offer literate restrained comedy."

Mr. Roberts Warner Brothers Television. NBC. Friday nights 9:30. September 17, 1965–September 2, 1966. 30 color episodes were filmed with a laugh track. Sponsors included Lever Brothers, and Liggett and Myers Tobacco.

First *Mr. Roberts* was a play by Thomas Heggen and then it was a very successful movie with a bevy of celebrities (Henry Fonda, Jack Lemmon, James Cagney, and William Powell). It didn't seem to translate as well to television, however, and became a single season sitcom. This was the story of Lieutenant Douglas Roberts, played by Roger Smith, and his quest for more participation in the war effort (World War II). Frankly, he was bored aboard the cargo ship known as the *USS Reluctant* (nicknamed "the bucket"), and wrote many letters requesting reassignment. However, those letters were never delivered to the proper channels because they were intercepted by his commanding officer, Captain John C. Morton (Richard X. Slattery). Morton was not one to bend the rules even slightly, but the shenanigans of the men aboard his ship threatened his sanity—especially those of one Ensign Frank Pulver (Steve Harmon). Pulver wanted to spice things up aboard this less-than-exciting vessel (as long as no real work was involved, of course). Also on board were George Ives as Doc; John McCook as Stefanowski; Dennis Robertson as "Cookie" Pike; and Henry Gibson as Insigna.

Episodes include "Liberty," in which Pulver had Captain Morton thinking that the crew had sunk a Japanese submarine, when in reality it was merely part of a washtub. In "Love at 78 RPM," the girlfriends of many of the crew members had sent love messages on phonograph records and Pulver was then sent ashore to attempt to find a phonograph on which to play them. In "Unwelcome Aboard," the crew began to think that Roberts had been at sea too long when he reported having seen a woman (Barrie Chase) on board, numerous times.

The program was produced by James Komack, who had previously been involved with two other military sitcoms—*Ensign O'Toole* and *Hennesey*; the executive producer was William T. Orr; writers included Ed Jurist, James O'Hanlon, Douglas Morrow, Herman Groves, Leo Rifkin, and Ken Pettis; and directors included Komack, Fielder Cook, Robert Butler, Gene Reynolds, Lawrence Dobkin, Douglas Morrow, Seymour Robbie, Allen Baron, William Wiard, Leslie Martinson, Bobby Bell, and Bill Lee. Music was provided by Johnny Mandel, and the theme song was by Frank Perkins. *Gomer Pyle, USMC* broadcast its first episode in color (now in its second season) on the same day *Mr. Roberts* debuted in color.

Mr. Smith Goes to Washington A Starstan/Fespar Production. ABC. Saturday nights 8:30. September 29, 1962–March 30, 1963. 24 black-and-white episodes filmed with laugh track. Sponsors included U.S. Royal Tires, Camel Cigarettes, and Metrecal.

The "Starstan" in Starstan/Fespar Productions came from creator and producer Hal *Stan*ley. The "Fespar" part came from its star, *Fess Par*ker. This show came in between Parker's greatest successes, *Davy Crockett* and *Daniel Boone*. His first attempt at a sitcom was the unsold pilot called *White Collar Girl* from Hal Roach Studios. *Mr. Smith Goes to Washington* (based upon the classic Jimmy Stewart movie) got a spot on ABC's fall schedule for 1962. Fess played Senator Eugene Smith from an undetermined, rural state. He was elected to the Senate after the sudden death of the incumbent. The number on his office door was 514. His wife Pat (he called her Patricia) Smith was played by Sandra Warner; his guitar-strumming, philosophizing Uncle Cooter was played by Red Foley (who sang a tune on the front porch in most episodes); his secretary Miss Kelly was played by Rita Lynn; and his womanizing chauffeur Arnie was portrayed by Stan Irwin.

Some of the best episodes involved big name stars of a bygone era—Harpo Marx was mistaken for famous French pianist Pierre LeGrand in "The Musicale;" Buster Keaton was an up-and-coming mink rancher named Sy Willis in "Think Mink;" Leo Gorcey of those *Bowery Boys* movies portrayed Windy, a hobo, whom the Senator tried to rehabilitate in "But What Are You Doing for Your Country?" Singer Kay Starr played a would-be socialite in the debut episode, "Washington Hostess."

Writers included Earl Hamner, Howard Snyder, and Jack Harvey; directors included Oscar Rudolph and Claudio Guzman. The program's theme song and lyrics were written by Hal Stanley and Irving Taylor. A few episodes are available for viewing in the UCLA TV Archives.

Mr. T. and Tina The Komack Company. ABC. Saturday nights 8:30. September 25, 1976–October 30, 1976. Nine color episodes were videotaped before a live audience, only five aired. Sponsors included All-Tempa-Cheer Detergent.

Executive Producer, James Komack, had a great track record for hit TV shows—*Hennesey*, *The Courtship of Eddie's Father*, *Welcome Back, Kotter*, and *Chico and the Man*. Along the way, however, he did have a few missteps, and *Mr. T. and Tina* was among the biggest. Pat Morita had garnered great popularity portraying Arnold on *Happy Days*, so it seemed like a good idea for him to get his own TV series—at least on paper. Here he played Taro Takahashi (Mr. T., for short), a widower with a very technology savvy mind. Because of his many inventions, the Japanese company for which he was employed, Moyati Industries, sent him to Chicago to set up a branch. Along for the ride were Mr. T.'s two children, Sachi and Aki (June Angela and Gene Profanato, respectively). Taking care of the motherless children was bubbly, klutzy, well-meaning Nebraska native Tina Kelly (Susan Blanchard); Pat Suzuki was the sarcastic Michi (his sister-in-law); "Jerry" Hatsuo Fujikawa was the very set-in-his-ways Uncle Matsu; Miriam Byrd-Nethery was scatterbrained Miss Llewellyn (the landlady); and Ted Lange was a hipster named "Harvard the Handyman" (similar to his "Junior" character on *That's My Mama*). Plots for the few shows produced focused upon Mr. T.'s inventions and the unintentional Americanization of the Takahashi children (mostly at the hands of Tina, who taught them words and phrases such as "cool," "the pits," and "neato," much to Mr. T.'s chagrin).

The show struggled from the get go. As a last resort, James Komack got the four "sweathogs" from *Welcome Back, Kotter* to open the episode titled "Tina Really Truly Gets Fired," which aired on October 23, 1976. It didn't help very much. Two weeks later, Tina (and Mr. T.) really, truly did get fired. The show was an early casualty of the 1976 TV season with four episodes left in the can.

The program was produced by Bob Carroll, Jr., and Madelyn Davis; directors included Rick Edelstein and James Sheldon; and writers included Rowby Goren, George Tibbles, and the team of Carroll and Davis. The theme song was an instrumental version of *Chicago* (written by Fred Fisher in 1922), performed here with an Asian flair. A few episodes can be viewed at the Paley Center for Media. Pat Morita rebounded nicely in the 1984 classic film, *The Karate Kid*, as Mr. Miyagi.

Mr. Terrific Universal Television. CBS. Monday nights 8:00. January 9, 1967–August 28, 1967. 17 color episodes were filmed with a laugh track. Sponsors included Procter and Gamble.

It was 1967 and superheroes were huge. ABC had *Batman* and *The Green Hornet.* NBC and CBS both tried to cash in on the craze with superhero parodies. NBC had *Captain Nice* and CBS had *Mr. Terrific*—both debuted on January 9, 1967, and both left the airwaves on August 28 of that same year. Allegedly, Stephen Strimpell auditioned for both roles, but was selected to be Mr. Terrific. He wasn't the first choice for the role—Alan Young, who had been Wilbur Post for many years on *Mister Ed*, was and here he was almost cast in another "Mister" show (he starred in the unaired pilot with a completely different cast). The program's opening credits told the whole story in an almost Dr. Seuss-like manner, with a lot of clever rhymes. *Mr. Terrific* was Stanley Beamish, born July 17, 1939 (weighing four pounds, three ounces). He was the meek, mousey co-owner of Hal and Stanley's Service Station ("Capital Service in the Nation's Capital") at Northwest and Wyoming Streets in Washington, D.C. Hal and Stanley frequented a local establishment called The Hungry Nose, and Stanley's favorite food was peanut butter and jelly. Stanley, however, had an alter-ego about which even business partner, roommate (in Apartment 2A), and suave ladies' man Hal Walters (Dick Gautier) didn't know. Stanley was the only person on whom a scientifically engineered pill worked without his becoming ill (it had been tested unsuccessfully on many). Upon ingesting the pill, Stanley repeatedly went through a series of painful red-faced expressions until he'd fully morphed into Mr. Terrific who could crash through brick walls, lift automobiles as if they were toys, and soar like an eagle (by flapping his arms while bedecked in his metallic silver cape and goggles). He worked for "The Bureau of Secret Projects" to assist the government in catching wanted felons. His contacts at the Bureau were the very pro-Mr. Terrific, Barton J. Reed (John McGiver) and the very anti–Mr. Terrific, Harley Trent (Paul Smith). Whenever Stanley's services were needed, Mr. Reed would spring into "a-c-t-i-o-n" (he'd always spell it out) and issue a "purple alert," which would invariably bring about a "do we have to?" from Mr. Trent. Trent had his reasons—you see, Stanley never did fully get the hang of landing on his flights, and would often crash through doors and windows, necessitating costly repairs. He would also kick up a huge

Mr. Terrific—**Left to right (back row)—Dick Gautier, Stephen Strimpell. Left to right (front row)—John McGiver, Paul Smith (photograph courtesy of Dick Gautier).**

cloud of dust on take-offs, which invariably ended up in Mr. Trent's face. Stanley would be given one large pill (for an hour), and two ten-minute booster pills (which cost $10,000 each). When these ran out, a buzzer would sound and Stanley would instantly lose his superpowers, always at the most inopportune time (usually mid-flight or while taking down the bad guys). Stanley was a busy boy in the show's 17 episodes—he rescued a crippled airplane, captured his exact double—a notorious safe cracker, rescued a defecting ballerina, became a circus performer to retrieve a stolen code book, captured the infamous Mr. Big (who turned out to be a woman), captured jewel thieves, and put a jail breaker back behind bars. In the episode titled "The Formula Is Stolen," Hal was hypnotized and was supposed to get on all-fours and act like a dog, but Gautier cleverly changed that: "I asked if I could make it a pigeon instead. At least that way I could stand erect. I even had a payoff for the pigeon—I ended up on a statue. It worked really well."

Gautier remembered, "I never had to audition or read for this show. Universal had seen me in another recent role, and wanted me to play the part of Hal in the series." Regarding the cast, Gautier told me, "Paul Smith and John McGiver were absolutely delightful. Stephen Strimpell, however, had his moments. He could be difficult. On several occasions, Stephen was unhappy with the material and had a hissy fit and holed up in his trailer. I kept telling him that this wasn't Ibsen, it was a show targeted to kids."

The program was produced by Budd Grossman; the executive producer was Jack Arnold; writers included Harvey Bullock, R. S. Allen, David P. Harmon, Arnold Margolin, Jim Parker, William Raynor, Miles Wilder, Grossman, and Martin A. Ragaway; and directors included Arnold, Tony Leader, Byron Chudnow, Arthur Lubin, Jerry Hopper, Sidney Miller, and Alan Rafkin. Gautier loved working with Rafkin and said: "Alan was an amazingly funny guy. Working with him really sticks out in my memory. He should've been in front of the camera, he was that funny." Music was provided by Gerald Fried. This program has a dedicated cult following, and recently, all 17 episodes were released on a DVD set in Germany from Universal Video Germany, where the show is called *Immer Wenn Er Pillen Nahm* (*When He Took Pills*). Several episodes of the show were also edited into a movie called *The Pill Caper* in 1968. Gautier reflected, "I found out about that movie quite by accident. It was advantageous that I did, or I may not have been paid for it."

Mrs. G. Goes to College/The Gertrude Berg Show Jahfa Productions/Four Star Studios. CBS. Wednesday nights 9:30 (October 4, 1961–December 27, 1961), and Thursday nights 9:30 (January 11, 1962–April 5, 1962). 26 episodes were filmed with a laugh track. Sponsors included General Foods.

In television's infancy (as well as on radio), she had been Molly Goldberg on *The Goldbergs*. In 1961, Gertrude Berg had the opportunity to star in yet another TV sitcom. This one was far less successful. The original working title was *Mother Is a Freshman*, and later simply *The Freshman*. This was the story of a matronly widowed grandmother named Sarah Green who, now that her children were married and on their own, wanted to get the college education she never had. Getting started wasn't easy—her daughter Susan (Marion Ross) attempted to talk her out of it. Her professors (Cedrick Hardwicke as English Professor W. W. Crayton and Peter Lorre as chemistry Professor Kessner) tried to dissuade her, and the comments from fellow freshman who were much more than 40 years her junior threatened to break her spirit, but her thirst for knowledge prevailed. Berg and Hardwicke had previously worked together on Broadway very successfully in *A Majority of One*. Sarah Green became affectionately known as Mrs. G. Among her best friends were Winona Maxfield (Maxie for short) played by the ubiquitous Mary Wickes who ran the boardinghouse where Mrs. G. lived (in apartment 2-I); and fellow freshman Joe Caldwell (Skip Ward), whom Mrs. G. encouraged to take tougher and more worthwhile courses than home economics and physical education; and Joe's girlfriend Carol (Karyn Kupcinet, daughter of Chicago talk show host Irv Kupcinet). Others in the cast included Paul Smith as psychology professor George Howell. Howell and his wife Irma (Aneta Corsault) had a baby, and lived among the students in the boarding house. There was constant competition for the only pay telephone in the hallway of the boarding house. When Mrs. G. got to use the phone, she was either talking to her daughter, Susan, or her sister, Dora, in Daytona.

Episodes include the crossover titled "Mrs. G. Meets Dr. Hennesey," in which Joe Caldwell, because of a poor grade from Professor Crayton, decided to join the navy. Jackie Cooper, who portrayed navy doctor Chick Hennesey on his own sitcom called *Hennesey*, appeared in character and helped talk Joe out of his impetuous decision. In "Mrs. G. Versus the Kingston Trio," the legendary folk trio competed with a faculty string concert which Mrs. G. was promoting. In "Peace Corps," actor/teen idol Fabian portrayed Paul Volk who wanted to join the peace corps, but had to change his mind after receiving much flak from his father.

The program was produced by Hy Averback; writers included Gertrude and Cherney Berg, Howard Merrill, Richard Baer, Arthur Stander, Bill Davenport, Jim Fritzell, Everett Greenbaum, Sheldon Keller, James Allardice, and Tom Adair; and directors included Averback, Robert Butler, Richard Kinon, and Marc Daniels. Music was provided by Herschel Burke Gilbert and Rudy Schrager. The show had anemic ratings in its original timeslot, and so it was moved from Wednesday nights to Thursday nights early in the new year, 1962. The program was then retitled *The Gertrude Berg Show*, but these changes didn't help much, and the show disappeared in early April. Gertrude Berg passed on only four years after the show's demise at the age of 67. A biopic about the life of this amazing TV pioneer, *Yoo Hoo, Mrs. Goldberg*, was released in 2009. The exterior scenes of *Mrs. G. Goes to College* were filmed at the University of Southern California. The program was briefly rerun on the Performance Channel in the UK.

Mona McCluskey McCadden Enterprises, Inc./United Artists. NBC. Thursday nights 9:30. September 16, 1965–April 14, 1966. 26 color episodes were filmed with a laugh track. Sponsors included R. J. Reynolds Tobacco.

The original working titles for this series were *McCluskey*, *Presenting McCluskey* and even *Meet Mona McCluskey*. They settled upon *Mona McCluskey*. Tall, leggy Juliet Prowse had found success in the movies (such as *Can-Can*, and *G. I. Blues*) and especially on the stage, so a starring role in a hit situation comedy seemed like shoe-in. Why, Juliet would even get to dance in some of these episodes, so it couldn't miss, right? Juliet portrayed actress/dancer Mona Carroll (which sounded so much better than her married name, McCluskey). Carroll made great money as an actress, too ($5,000 a week). However, there was one drawback—she wasn't allowed to spend it. Juliet's "Romeo"—her husband, Sgt. Michael J. McCluskey (Denny Miller)—would only allow her to spend his Air Force salary (a meager $500 a month) so that he would feel less emasculated and more like the breadwinner of the family. They lived in a small two-room Hollywood apartment.

In one of the few episodes available, "All Dough and No Place to Go," Mona wanted to vacation in Acapulco, but frugal and stubborn Mike wouldn't let Mona use her own money. He had a more sensible and cost-effective vacation in mind—a camping trip to Lake Wattatoma, somewhere in the San Bernardino Mountains. Mona then tried scheme after scheme to put enough money for a trip to Acapulco in Mike's wallet, but to no avail. Then, when a real windfall came his way via a long-lost Aussie cousin named Alfred who left him $3,000 in his will, Mike was again convinced that this was another of Mona's schemes and tore up the check.

Denny Miller told me, "It was such a happy

Mona McCluskey—**Juliet Prowse and Denny Miller (photograph courtesy of Denny Miller).**

set. We all got along so well. Juliet was an absolute delight. She was used to being on stage in front of a live audience. Our show was filmed without an audience—with a laugh track, and while she hit her mark consistently, the director, Richard Whorf was always joking that to make her stay on her mark he was going to nail her feet to the floor. Juliet was also a wonderful cook, and had a passion for garlic, and this used to drive her make-up man, Ray Stork, out of his mind."

Also in the cast were Bartlett Robinson as Frank Caldwell, Mona's producer; Herb Rudley as General Windy Crone; Robert Strauss as Sgt. Stan Gruzewsky; and Elena Verdugo as Alice Henderson, Stan's girlfriend.

George Burns was the executive producer. Miller remembered, "George Burns did one of his routines for us every Monday. We were supposed to be working, blocking the scenes, but nothing got done—we laughed all day. However, we made up for goofing off when Tuesday came around." Directors included Stanley Z. Cherry and Richard Whorf; writers included Don McGuire, Fred S. Fox, Iz Elinson, Bob Fisher, Arthur Alsburg, Henry Garson, Edmund Beloin, Norman Paul, Elon Packard, and William Burns. The theme song was the old standard, "Yessir, That's My Baby," written by Gus Kahn and Walter Donaldson, and music was provided by Sonny Burke. Characters were based upon those originated by Sumner Long. In an attempt to boost ratings, NBC incorporated more and more dancing in the show, but it didn't help. Miller recalled, "We had a terrible time slot—up against *Peyton Place* on ABC and *The CBS Thursday Night Movie*. We were doomed from the beginning—CBS' first movie that fall was *The Manchurian Candidate*. We were oddly sandwiched between *Laredo* and *The Dean Martin Show*. Herbert Rudley was so very upset when we got word that we were canceled, he absolutely cried like a baby. None of us wanted it to end. Those 26 weeks were among the most fun of my entire career."

The Monster Squad D'Angelo/Bullock/Allen Productions. NBC. September 11, 1976–September 3, 1977. 13 episodes were videotaped with a laugh track.

Walter (Fred Grandy) was a university student who majored in criminology. He also worked part-time at a wax museum to help pay his tuition. Somehow, his special "crime computer," caused the wax statues to become live monsters who became his assistants in fighting and solving crimes. Among the creatures were Dracula (Henry Polic III), Frank N. Stein (Michael Lane), and Bruce Werewolf (Buck Kartalian). This show was part of a three-hour live-action Saturday morning programming block on NBC.

The Montefuscos Persky/Denoff Productions—A Concept Plus II Production. NBC. Thursday nights 8:00. September 4, 1975–October 16, 1975. 13 episodes were videotaped before a live audience, only eight aired.

The Montefuscos was part of a heavily hyped NBC Thursday night lineup fiasco which also included *Fay*. Originally to be called *Family Dinner*, *The Montefuscos* were a large Italian-American family in Connecticut who got together every Sunday night (even though the program was on Thursday night) for dinner. The problems discussed at the dinner table were fodder for each episode. Tony "Papa" Montefusco (Joe Sirola) sat at the head of the table; his wife was named Rose (Naomi Stevens), who was a worrywart; their son Frank was a dentist (Ron Carey) and he was married to the perennially-pregnant Teresa (Phoebe Dorin). Another son, Nunzio (Sal Viscuso), was a Casanova, drove a motorcycle, and was an out-of-work actor. His dad sarcastically called him "Mr. Show Business." A third son, Joseph (John Aprea), was a priest. Tony and Rose also had one daughter, Angelina (Linda Dano), who was married to the family's only Protestant member, Jim Cooney (Bill Cort). Angelina and Jim's only child was Anthony Patrick (Damon Raskin). Frank and Teresa's kids were Gina, Carmine, and Jerome (Dominique Pinassi, Jeff Palladini and Robby Paris, respectively).

Episodes include "Behind Papa's Behind," in which the family became convinced that Papa was dying. It turned out to only be a hernia, but Papa let everyone in the family know what they were getting in his will anyway. After his reading, family members began to trade willed items with one another in a rather macabre version of *Let's Make a Deal*. In "Last of the Red Hot Dinners," Jim, the token Protestant, caused a clamor when he opted to attend a football game instead of Sunday dinner. In the episode titled "Nunzie's Girl," guest star Candy Azzara, who played Blossom Bazussi recalled, "Ron Carey (Frank) was such a talent—and many people don't realize what an amazing stand-up comic he was. He played at the legendary Improv a lot. We were great friends."

The program was produced by Don Van Atta and Bill Idelson; the executive producers were Bill Persky and Sam Denoff.

Mulligan's Stew Christiana Productions/ Paramount. NBC. Tuesday nights 9:00. October 25, 1977–December 13, 1977. Seven episodes were filmed without a laugh track.

Not to be confused with the educational children's program, *Mulligan Stew*, *Mulligan's Stew* was set in the mythical Southern California town of Birchfield at 1202 Circle Drive. It was an hour-long comedy/drama—the kind of program which would later be coined a "dramedy." It began as a TV movie with a very large cast. For the most part, it was like *Room for One More* meets *The Brady Bunch* meets *Eight Is Enough*. Jane Mulligan (Elinor Donahue)—a school nurse, was married to Michael Mulligan (Lawrence Pressman)—a high school teacher and football coach. Together they had three natural children: ten-year-old son Jimmy (K. C. Martel); 12-year-old daughter Melinda (Julie Anne Haddock); and 15-year-old son Mark (played by Johnnie Whitaker in the TV movie, but by Johnny Doran in the series). The Mulligans also welcomed in four nieces and nephews after their own biological parents died in a plane crash—nine-year-old Adam "Moose" Friedman (Christopher Ciampa); 14-year-old daughter Stevie (Suzanne Crough); Polaris, a.k.a. "Polly" (Lory Kochheim); and eight-year-old Kimmy Nguyen Friedman (Sunshine Lee), a Vietnamese orphan whom the Friedman's had adopted.

Mulligan's Stew—**Lawrence Pressman and Elinor Donahue (photograph courtesy of Elinor Donahue).**

The TV movie, which served as the pilot, aired on June 20, 1977. Elinor Donahue told me, "It got almost no promotion. I wasn't even home to watch it the night it aired. To our surprise, the overnight ratings were huge and my phone wouldn't stop ringing. We thought it might be considered as a midseason replacement show, but NBC wanted it to begin that fall. The show's creator and producer, Joanna Lee, just couldn't say no to the network, so we immediately got to work. This wasn't a particularly good time in my life—my husband Harry Ackerman and I were losing our house in Sherman Oaks. The night before we began shooting the first episode, I had been up most of the night crying and had gotten very little sleep. The series came about so suddenly it led to us always being under the gun—a mad rush to complete another episode each week. They were literally editing the show up until the eleventh hour. To add to the pressure, I was also doing a series of *Father Knows Best* 'reunion shows' at the time."

There was one minor difference of opinion on the show, however, between Elinor and Joanna Lee. Elinor recalled, "Joanna wanted my character to wear a lot of makeup, including this bright red lipstick. I was very much against it, but I eventually gave in to the lipstick."

On the day the series made its debut, Elinor had another important task: "My son was unable to complete his paper route that morning, so I did it, and inserted promotional fliers for *Mulligan's Stew* in each copy I delivered to Studio City, California." Sadly, it didn't help. The series failed to catch on. Elinor remembered, "There were telltale signs that the end was near. Each week, the crew got smaller and smaller. We were eventually down to a skeleton crew."

Episode titles were, "The Biggest Mansion You've Ever Seen," "The Melinda Special," "A New Grandpa," "The Little Grey Bird," "Ah, Wilderness," and "Winning the Big One."

The program was created and produced

by Joanna Lee; writers included Nancy Sackett, Elroy Schwartz, and Lee; and directors included Hollingsworth Morse, Noel Black and Lee. The opening credits were narrated by Donahue. The theme song, "We're Gonna Stick Together," was written by Steve Barri, Michael Price and Daniel Walsh, and performed by Michael Lloyd. Exterior scenes of the Mulligan's house were shot in Brentwood, California. Elinor said about the show's demise: "We were devastated. It was a surprise because the TV movie had done so well. We really thought we had something going there." A few episodes were rerun on TV Land.

My Hero Official Films. NBC. Saturday nights 7:30 (November 8, 1952–April 1953), and Saturday nights 8:00 (April 1953–August 1, 1953). 33 black-and-white episodes were filmed with a laugh track. Sponsored by Dunhill Cigarettes.

This was the first of four situation comedies for Bob Cummings (three of which are included in this volume). In this early filmed show, he portrayed Robert S. Beanblossom, the lowest-ranking, lowest-performing salesman for the Thackery Realty Company in Los Angeles. He often referred to his boss as "old blubberjowls." The only reason "old blubberjowls," a.k.a. Willis Thackery (John Litel) kept him on the payroll was because three years earlier Mr. Thackery had taken ill. Beanblossom was the only person around with the same blood type, and his donation saved Mr. Thackery's life. Beanblossom also frequently got lucky (it wasn't skill) and managed to get rid of some hard-to-sell properties. Beanblossom's office was, for all intents and purposes, a small supply closet awkwardly converted into an office (he was always knocking over the water cooler). To instill more confidence in his abilities as a salesman, Beanblossom had several inspirational messages on his office walls, such as, "Never Take No for an Answer," "Retreat Is Defeat," and "Is Your Foot in the Door?" Whenever things went awry (which was every week), the office secretary/Beanblossom's girlfriend, Julie Marshall (Julie Bishop) defended him, came to his rescue, and plotted his escapes from sticky situations. Almost every episode ended with Julie referring to Beanblossom as "My Hero." They'd then kiss and steam would escape from his ears.

Episodes include the debut, "Oil Land," in which the underperforming Beanblossom was suddenly on a hot streak and sold all of the "Haven-Myer" lots. He was immensely proud of his achievement—that is, until he found out that Mr. Thackery didn't want to sell that land because of the likelihood of an oil strike on the property. In "Horse Trail," Beanblossom managed to get rid of an undesirable piece of land by making a trade for a horse. This trade proved unpopular when the animal activated Mr. Thackery's allergies. It also got Beanblossom arrested because the horse had been stolen from a racetrack. Until things were sorted out, the horse got to stay in Beanblossom's tiny office.

Producers included Mort Green, Edmund Beloin and Bob Cummings; writers included Dick Conway, John Conway, Roland MacLane, Jack Elinson, Norman Paul, and Cummings; and directors included Oscar Rudolph, Leslie Goodwins, Mort Green, and Harold Daniels. Music was provided by Leon Klatzkin. Reruns were shown on Family Net in the 1990s.

My Living Doll Jack Chertok Productions/ Desilu Studios. CBS. Sunday nights 9:00 (September 27, 1964–December 13, 1964), and Wednesday nights 8:00 (December 16, 1964–September 8, 1965). 26 black-and-white episodes were filmed with a laugh track. Sponsors included Alberto VO-5, Pepto-Bismol, and The American Tobacco Company.

This was the fourth and final starring role on TV for Bob Cummings. The original working title was *The Living Doll*, but Cummings insisted on *His Living Doll*. The producers compromised with *My Living Doll*. This time, Cummings portrayed Dr. Robert McDonald, a Los Angeles psychiatrist. His whole world was turned upside down when his friend, Dr. Carl Miller (Henry Beckman), had to leave suddenly for an important mission in Pakistan and left behind, in Bob's care, a beautiful, intelligent, extremely lifelike (although made of poly-ethylene plastic) female robot (Julie Newmar) who would obey any and all orders. The robot's lab name was AF709 (a number which would influence the Borg Girl "Seven of Nine" on Star Trek). She was an important part of Project Orion (destined for outer space), but Bob simply called her Rhoda Miller (and no one, except Bob, was to know that she was "a living doll"). Since Rhoda now resided in Bob's apartment on Wilshire Boulevard, Bob's sister, Mrs. Irene Adams (Doris Dowling), agreed to live there temporarily, too, to act as chaperone (mind you, this was 1964). Bob's co-worker, friend and neighbor, physicist Dr. Peter Robinson (Jack Mullaney), found Rhoda to be extremely attractive and continually attempted to get her to go out on dates with him (but this wasn't allowed, lest he find out her secret). Rhoda's on-and-off switches were the moles on her back. She could also be turned off when her light source was removed (usually accomplished by placing a towel over her eyes). Newmar told me, "I designed all of my own clothes for the role in order to accentuate the unwontedness of being a robot." She also said, "I was saying 'that does not compute' long before the *Lost in Space* robot did." Rhoda became Bob's secretary (typing a flawless 240 words per minute).

Episodes include "Beauty Contest," in which Bob's sister Irene, against his wishes, entered Rhoda into a televised beauty contest with Bob as one of the judges. Not only was Rhoda a shoe-in for her beauty, she also became a concert pianist by watching only one piano recital on TV. She was bound to win the talent portion of the contest as well—that is, until Bob disrupted her circuits with a TV remote control. Newmar told me, "That was really me playing the piano in that episode." In "My Robot, My Warden," Bob asked Rhoda to make certain that he stayed home all night to work on his book. She was not to let him leave until 8 in the morning. When he was unexpectedly asked by his publisher to attend an urgent meeting, Rhoda forced him to stay in the apartment because her timing circuits were set for 8 a.m. and couldn't be changed.

The program was created by Al Martin and Bill Kelsay, based upon an idea by Leo Guild; the producer was Howard Leeds; the executive producer was Jack Chertok; writers included Martin, Kelsay, Arthur Dales, Tom Koch, Louis Kamp, Bernard Slade, and Roland Wolpert; and directors included Larry Dobkin and Ezra Stone. Abruptly, Cummings was "let go" by Chertok and CBS late in the season. Bernard Slade added, "Bob Cummings was very talented. Talented, but very difficult." With Cummings gone, the whole dynamic of the program had changed (Jack Mullaney's character, Peter, was put in charge of the robot), and *My Living Doll* became a single season sitcom. Eleven of the 26 original black-and-white episodes of the program are available on a limited-edition DVD set (the whereabouts of the other fifteen filmed episodes is a mystery). The program initially had two different openings—one featured "the doll" in an evening gown, and the other had her in a nightgown. The opening changed yet again after Cummings was gone.

My Mother, the Car Cottage Industries, Inc./United Artists Television. NBC. Tuesday nights 7:30. September 14, 1965–September 6, 1966. 30 color episodes were filmed with a laugh track. Sponsors include Pepsi-Cola.

Small town lawyer Dave Crabtree (Jerry Van Dyke, a Sagittarius) earned $5,000 a year (his father had also been a lawyer) and lived at 485 Maple. He lost his mother on August 23, 1949. On September 14, 1965, Dave and his mother (featuring the voice of Ann Sothern) were reunited. Dave had gone shopping for a station wagon on a used car lot, but instead was inexplicably drawn to a decrepit 1928 Porter (California license number PZR 317). Once behind the wheel of the eyesore, the car began carrying on a conversation with him. It was Dave's mother reincarnated (or is that rein-CAR-nated?) She said she'd come back because "David needed her help." Dave then purchased the old car for $200, but was immediately faced with two huge obstacles—his wife, Barbara (most people called her "Barbs," maiden name Netwick—born under the sign of Cancer), played by Maggie Pierce who wanted a station wagon and wanted Dave to sell the Porter. That other huge obstacle was a persistent car collector named Captain Bernard Manzini (Avery Schreiber) who wanted to purchase the candy apple red Porter as the crown jewel for his collection (it seemed as if money were no object, and the word "no" was unacceptable). Manzini could never get Dave's last name right and called him Crabgrass, Cranberry, Crabcake, Criswell, Crenshaw, and a myriad of other similar surnames. Oh, and there was one other wrinkle—much like *Mister Ed* only talking to Wilbur, the 1928 Porter only talked to Dave (although, in episode number 28, called "Blabbermouth," Dave had a nightmare in which the entire family and even Manzini were let in on the secret). In the series, Mother spoke whether the radio was on or off, but in the unaired pilot, Dave had to keep turning on the radio to have a conversation. Dave and Barbara also had two young children—towheaded young Cindy (Cindy Eilbacher) and the even younger Randy (Randy Whipple). In the unaired black-and-white pilot, the Crabtree's son was named Harry and was played by Harry Moses. There was also the family dog named Moon (a different, smaller dog portrayed Moon in the unaired pilot). The Crabtrees had a recurring neighbor named Phil Durkin (played in the early episodes by Bill Daily, and in later episodes by Dave Willock) who raised homing pigeons. Most of the 30 episodes of *My Mother, the Car* concerned the evil Manzini's continual scheming to get his hands on the Porter, Barbara's growing impatience at not having a station wagon, and the situations incited by Dave's meddling mother, the car. We'd find out that mother's favorite actor was Sonny Tufts (in the episode titled "And Leave the Drive-In to Us"), and that mother's maiden name was Gladys Brown (in the episode titled, "I Remember Mama, Why Don't You Remember?").

Several episodes had very clever titles—"What Makes Auntie Freeze," in which the alcohol in anti-freeze had an inebriating effect upon mother; "The De-Fenders," in which Dave was apprehensive about leaving mother alone in the garage because of a series of car-stripping crimes in the neighborhood, so he slept in the garage; and "When You Wish upon a Car," in which mother pretended she was like Aladdin's Lamp and could grant any wish to her grandchildren when they polished her with a "magic cloth."

The program was created by Allan Burns and Chris Hayward; the producer was Rod Amateau; writers included Phil Davis, James L. Brooks, Gordon "Whitey" Mitchell, Mitch Persons, Burns, George Kirgo, Robert C. Dennis, Earl Barret, Frank Fox, Tom Koch, Jim Parker, John Barbour, Lila Garrett, and Arnold Margolin; and directors included David Davis, Thomas Montgomery, and Sidney Miller. The theme song was written and performed for the series by Paul Hampton, but was performed by Jerry and Myrna Music in the unaired pilot. Hampton had a small role as the second attendant at the car wash in the unaired pilot episode. This much-maligned series was briefly rerun in June of 2004 on the now-defunct Trio cable channel as part of their "Famous Flops" month. Jerry's first starring role was as emcee of the 1963 prime time game show *Picture This*, produced by Art Baer and Ben Joelson for CBS—one episode of which is available for viewing in the UCLA TV Archives.

My Sister, Eileen Screen Gems. CBS. Wednesday nights 9:00. October 5, 1960–April 12, 1961. 26 black-and-white episodes were filmed with a laugh track. Sponsors included Colgate- Palmolive and Pillsbury.

The story of *My Sister, Eileen* began with a series of short stories and then a book written by Ruth McKenney. The book then became a stage play in 1940. Rosalind Russell starred in the 1942 movie adaptation. Then came the 1955 musical comedy version with Jack Lemmon and Janet Leigh.

The pilot for the television show came as part of the anthology series *Alcoa Theater*. Here it was called "You Should See My Sister," and it aired on May 16, 1960. The pilot looked very much like what would become the series—two sisters sharing a basement apartment in Greenwich Village while pursuing their respective dreams. They had moved there from Ohio to seek fame and fortune. Ruth Sherwood (Elaine Stritch) was the older sister who wanted to be a writer, but was having trouble getting her first story published. To help pay the rent, she worked as a reader for the McMahon Publishing House. Her sister, Eileen, was portrayed in the pilot by Anne Helm (later with Elvis Presley in *Follow That Dream*). Eileen wanted to be an actress and a model. She had the looks and the talent, but simply wasn't getting the breaks. The girls were always late paying their rent which raised the ire of their landlord Mr. Spivak (Henry Corden).

The pilot was directed by Oscar Rudolph, produced by Winston O'Keefe, and written by Dan Beaumont. Harry Ackerman was executive producer. Dick Wesson played Ruth's date, Ernie, in the pilot, but Wesson played a much larger role behind the scenes for the series—writer and producer. Speaking of Wesson, Rose Marie, who portrayed proofreader Bertha Bronsky in the series told me, "I had worked with Dick Wesson on *The Bob Cummings Show*, and he brought me over to do *My Sister, Eileen*." Rose also recalled, "Elaine Stritch is an enormous talent, but we never became friends. We had a pretty good working relationship, but Elaine could be rather difficult—she could be a bit caustic at times. She had her own way of doing things. She was very hard to get close to."

Well, when the pilot became a series, it debuted on the first Wednesday in October of 1960. Stritch was still there, but now playing Eileen Sherwood was the lovely Shirley Bonne. Screen Gems thought Bonne was more bubbly than Anne Helm. Rose Marie remembered, "Shirley was sweet and wonderful. She was a novice and she was very agreeable and did whatever was asked of her." The girls' landlord was now Mr. Appopolous, played by Leon Belasco, and Stubby Kaye made frequent appearances as Marty Scott, the agent for both Sherwood sisters. Ruth now worked for Parkview Publishing.

Episodes include the debut titled "The Photography Mix-up," in which the publishers of a girly magazine named "Bon Vivant" took pictures of Eileen sunning herself in her bikini on the roof of the apartment without her knowing it. Here's the mix-up—the publishers thought the pictures were of Ruth and they wanted to pay her a great deal of money for her story and a photo shoot. Ruth had a mix-up of her own—she didn't realize what "Bon Vivant" was all about and wasn't cognizant of the fact that the photo shoot was to be done au naturel. In "Marty's Best Friend," Marty's friend Frank Marshall (Bill Williams) came to town for a visit. This alleged best friend continually belittled Marty in public, and the girls came to Marty's rescue.

Writers included Richard Baer, Dick Wesson, Philip Shuken, John L. Greene, Shirl Gordon, Dan Beaumont, Fred S. Fox, Iz Elinson, Dean Riesner, Arthur Dales, Nate Monaster, Jay Sommers, Don Nelson, Ben Gershman, Robert White, John Bradford, Leo Solomon, Peggy Phillips, and Ralph Goodman; directors included Oscar Rudolph, Fred De Cordova, Paul Harrison, Wesson, Jeffrey Hayden, Gene Reynolds, and William D. Russell. Music was provided by Herbert Spencer. The show had two different opens—the early ones were animated, but later on, a piece from the opening credits of the pilot was resurrected (an attractive pair of legs were walking down a New York street. We were led to believe that they were Eileen's legs, but we never saw her face. She was followed immediately by two pairs of legs belonging to sailors who were eagerly following her home). Even though *My Sister, Eileen* lasted only the one season, Rose Marie had something much bigger awaiting her—*The Dick Van Dyke Show*, which she calls "the best five years of my life. That wasn't work, that was playtime each and every day." Also moving on to bigger and better things after the cancellation of *My Sister, Eileen* was Raymond Bailey who played Ruth's boss, D. X. Beaumont. Bailey became Mr. Drysdale, the banker on *The Beverly Hillbillies*.

My Son, Jeep Rockhill and Jeep Productions. NBC. Saturday nights 7:30 (July 4, 1953–August 29, 1953), and Tuesday nights 8:00 (September 1, 1953–September 22, 1953). 13 episodes were broadcast live before a live audience. Sponsors included Beacon Wax.

My Son, Jeep had a brief run on NBC and also on NBC Radio with a slightly different cast. Common to both were Leona Powers as Mrs. Bixby, the sassy housekeeper, and Martin Huston as that unpredictable 10-year-old rascal, Jeffrey "Jeep" Allison. The nickname "Jeep" came about during a parade. Jeffrey was infatuated with a Jeep riding in that parade and afterwards, for the rest of that day, he pretended to be a Jeep, and thus the nickname. "Jeep" had a sister named Peggy (Betty Lou Keim on TV, Joan Laser on radio), who preferred to be called Margaret to sound more grown-up. She was 13 going on 30. Their father, Dr. Robert Allison (Jeffrey Lynn on TV, Donald Cook on radio), was a widower who had the responsibility of being both dad and mom to his offspring. The program was set in the mythical small town of Grove Falls, and Dr. Allison's offices were part of the house. The good doctor served as narrator, and set up and closed every episode. Other characters were Barbara Miller (Anne Sargent on TV, Lynn Allen on radio), who was initially Jeep's substitute teacher. Jeep and the rest of the family became fond of pretty Barbara so quickly, that the Doctor asked her to be his secretary, and soon she became his romantic interest. Jeep's best friend and partner in crime was nicknamed "Boots," and was played by Richard Wigginton.

One episode of the TV version exists in the Library of Congress, and many episodes of the radio version have survived. Episodes centered around Jeep's good intentions gone awry. In one instance, he performed numerous good deeds to move up in rank in his Boy Scout troop, but every intended good deed turned to disaster. In another episode, Jeep came down with the measles and was quarantined in his bedroom. Itching for human contact, Jeep played a game with his friend "Boots" through an open window involving a pretend kidnapping and a ransom note. Somehow the note ended up in the hands of the police and comedy ensued. On the TV version, in one untitled episode Jeep strived for independence by getting a paper route, and in another Jeep and the Doc's good intentions threatened to ruin Peggy's first date with a new boy in town.

The program was created and written by Walter Black and William Mendreck; the producer was Hudson Faussett; and the directors were Grey Lockwood and Kirk Browning. In the August 7, 1953 edition of *TV Guide*, the program was reviewed this way: "The situation comedy idea, of course, is not new to TV. In fact, it's been a staple of the medium almost from the start, and since *I Love Lucy* first hit pay dirt, they've become almost as numerous as panel quiz shows. But the good ones are still fun to watch, and *My Son, Jeep* is a good one."

My World and Welcome to It Sheldon Leonard Productions/Paramount Studios/Cinema General Studios. NBC. Monday nights 7:30. September 15, 1969–September 7, 1970. 26 color episodes were filmed with a laugh track.

It took a long time for this concept to become a series. It originated as a pilot made in 1959 titled *The Secret Life of John Monroe* with Arthur O'Connell in the title role. More than a decade later, it became *My World and Welcome To It* and was based upon the late James Thurber's work. The opening credits, which disrupted the sleep of an animated dog said, "based on stories, inspirational pieces, cartoons, and things that go bump in the night." John Monroe was brilliantly played by William Windom. John had a good job at *Manhattanite Magazine*, a nice family, and yet was rather disappointed with his lot in life. John loved the women in his life—his domineering wife, Ellen (Joan Hotchkis), his super-intelligent brace-faced 10-year-old daughter, Lydia (Lisa Gerritsen), and his mother, Mrs. Monroe (Betty Kean). And yet he was absolutely terrified of these women (in fact, one episode of the show revolved around John's misogynistic tendencies). John's escape from his problems was his home office in the attic—and he would, in fact, frequently immerse himself in his own whimsical drawings, much in the fashion of *The Secret Life of Walter Mitty*. John's two most frequent flights of fantasy involved his Westport, Connecticut house taking the form of his battle-axe wife, and the frequent personification of animals. Not only did poor John have troubles at home, he also had problems at work. John's boss, publisher Hamilton Greeley (Harold J. Stone), didn't always "get" John's sense of humor (the two men had very different ideas about what was funny). Luckily, John had a friend and confidant in fellow writer, Phillip Jensen (*I've Got a Secret* panelist, Henry Morgan), with whom he would often commiserate at Billy Cochrane's Bar. Monroe directly addressed the viewers numerous times in each episode.

Among the best episodes (and there were many) were "Christabel," in which Lydia's asparagus and raspberry loving poodle passed on and her sadness about the loss of the dog was exacerbated by her notion that her dad just didn't care. Dad proved her wrong by writing a touching tribute to the canine and by bringing home a cute little puppy to take its place. Two great episodes ("The Ghost and Mr. Monroe" and "Seal in the Bedroom") revolved around John's inability to handle criticism of his work. In "The Disenchanted," Lydia decided to run away from home because her parents refused to intervene to get her seat in class changed away from Johnny Basco, who enjoyed pulling her hair and copying her schoolwork without permission. John decided to join her—he was running away from a problem with a noisy, shaky, disruptive freight elevator near his desk at work.

The program was produced by Danny Arnold; the executive producer was Sheldon Leonard; writers included Ruth Brooks Flippen, Rick Mittleman, Melville Shavelson, Phil Sharp, Paul Wayne, Harvey Bullock, R. S. Allen, and Marion Hargrove; and directors included Arnold, Lee Philips, Leonard, Melville Shavelson and Hal Cooper. The theme song was by Warren Barker and Arnold. Despite cancellation, *My World and Welcome To It* garnered two Emmy Awards ("Best Comedy" and "Best Actor In A Comedy"—William Windom). There was quite an outcry from devoted fans of this very literate sitcom upon its cancellation, and NBC considered bringing it back. However, this was quite an expensive little show to produce (mostly because of the animation, provided by David H. DePatie and Friz Freleng), and NBC decided to just let the sleeping dog (in the opening and closing credits) lie. To this day, the program has quite a devoted cult following. Reruns were seen on CBS as a summer replacement in 1972 and were again briefly shown on cable channel WWOR-TV. Susan Gordon, who portrayed Lydia in the pilot passed away on December 11, 2011. William Windom died on August 16, 2012, at the age of 89.

Nancy Sidney Sheldon Productions/Screen Gems. NBC. Thursday nights 9:30. September 17, 1970–January 7, 1971. 17 color episodes were filmed without a laugh track.

Even though this romantic comedy was about the daughter of the President of the United States, the intention was to first make it a show about making a marriage work in the modern world, and then to bring in the complications brought about by Nancy's extraordinary political ties. In fact, we never got to see the President, nor did any of the episodes focus upon Washington, D.C., politics. Nancy Smith (Renne Jarrett) had fallen head over heels in love with a veterinarian named Adam Hudson (Broadway actor John Fink) from Center City, Iowa. Their romance was like any other romance—except for the Secret Service agents who followed them everywhere (William Bassett as Agent Turner and Ernesto Macias as Agent Rodriguez). Nancy had a pixie-like quality and yet she was the impulsive one, while Adam was very homespun and down to Earth. They were both extremely insecure about meeting one another's family and friends, fearing they wouldn't fit in. Jarrett told me, "There were many comparisons to Tricia Nixon. There was a resemblance between Tricia and me." Nancy also had a chaperone, Abby Townsend (Celeste Holm). Renne said, "Celeste taught me a lot. She gave me lots of hints about acting for the camera. She was very nice." Being the daughter of a career politician, Nancy certainly did not have the average childhood. Adam didn't have the most normal adolescent years either—he was raised by his Uncle Everett Hudson (Robert F. Simon), who remained by his side. Others in the cast included Frank Aletter as Tom Daily, the President's assistant; and Eddie Applegate as Willie Maxwell: local reporter. Among guest stars, Renne remembered one in particular: "Farrah Fawcett—she wasn't a star yet, but when she came on the set every single head turned. She had that certain something—you could see it even then."

Each episode of *Nancy* followed the young couple's progress. The title of the debut says it all—"It's A Good Day for Meeting the President's Daughter." Already in the second episode, "Guess Who's Coming to the White House," Adam missed his own engagement party to care for a sick cow. Less than two months after the program's debut, Adam and Nancy were pronounced "man and wife" (on November 5, 1970) in episode number eight titled "Here Comes the Groom." Logically, the next episode was "Honeymoon for Twelve," in which Adam and Nancy devised a plan to get some real "alone time" away from Abby, Uncle Everett, and the Secret Service men. Renne said, "The outdoor scenes, especially the ones on horseback, were done at the Disney Golden Oak Ranch in Newhall, California." We never did get to find out if President Smith became a grandfather, or won a second term in office, as *Nancy* lasted only a few more weeks. Competition from *The CBS Thursday Night Movie* and *The Odd Couple* on ABC proved insurmountable.

It seems really innocent by today's standards, but Renne told me, "We got a lot of mail from mothers of teenage daughters who were incensed by an open-mouthed kiss between Adam and me. They thought that our innocent kiss was way too sexual. It was a different place and time."

The show's creator and executive producer was Sidney Sheldon; the producer was Jerome Courtland; writers included Mark Rowane, Christopher Golato, Allan Devon, Sheldon, Jean Holloway, and William Canning; and directors included Courtland, Alan Rafkin, Claudio Guzman, E. W. Swackhamer, Allen Baron, Lou Antonio, and Herb Wallerstein. Renne remembered, "Most of the early episodes were directed by E. W. Swackhamer, whom I liked a lot. Everyone called him 'Swack.' It's amazing how much things change, however, when the director changes. We were somewhat ill-at-ease with some of them. Claudio Guzman was great—we laughed a lot." The theme song's lyrics were written by Sheldon, and the music was provided by Sid Ramin. In Renne's opinion, "We were on too late. Many teenage girls were fans of the show, but couldn't stay up until 10 on a school night." There was another possible reason for the show's abrupt cancellation, as Renne opined, "We were on before *The Dean Martin Show*. It's a fact that

***Nancy*—Renne Jarrett and John Fink (photograph courtesy of Renne Jarrett).**

Dean was not a fan of our show as a lead-in, and at that time his opinion carried a lot of weight."

The Nancy Walker Show T. A. T. Communications. ABC. Thursday nights 9:30. September 30, 1976–December 23, 1976. 13 episodes were videotaped at Metromedia Studios, only 12 aired.

Nancy Walker had done movies and Broadway, but by the 1970s had focused on television. She was Rosie in a series of Bounty Paper Towel commercials and also had recurring roles on *Family Affair* and *McMillan and Wife*, but it was her role as Ida Morgenstern on *The Mary Tyler Moore Show* and *Rhoda* which solidified her as a household name. On the final day of September in 1976, right after *The Tony Randall Show* on ABC, we caught our first glimpse of *The Nancy Walker Show*. She portrayed Nancy Kitteridge, who ran a highly successful talent agency from her luxurious apartment ten months of the year. The other two months were always spent with her husband (William Daniels as Kenneth Kitteridge) when he returned from active duty as a Lieutenant Commander in the navy. Nancy had been savoring this routine through 29 years of marriage, but then suddenly her whole world was turned topsy-turvy when Kenneth announced his retirement from the service. He was now home to stay and wanted her to dissolve the business she loved. He was also unhappy about her gay roommate (among the first recurring gay characters on TV), Terry Folson, who got his room and board covered by being Nancy's male secretary. The surname Folson was merely a scrambling of the actor's surname, (Ken) Olfson. As if that weren't enough, visiting on a regular basis was the Kitteridge's sad sack, hypochondriacal daughter, Lorraine (Beverly Archer), whose first words were invariably a very exasperated, "Hello, mother." Also in the cast were Glen (James Cromwell), Nancy's son-in-law; Teddy Futterman (William Schallert), a TV executive whom some say resembled Fred Silverman; and Michael Futterman (Sparky Marcus), Teddy's obnoxious six-year-old son.

Episodes include "TV and War," in which Kenneth's memoirs were drastically altered by Nancy in an attempt to make the story more TV-worthy. In "Rival Agents," both Nancy and her biggest competitor (Michelle Laurita) overheard producers discussing a new, up-and-coming talent in need of an agent, and these competitors one-upped each other in an effort to sign that talent. In a two-parter called "The Anniversary," Nancy and Kenneth celebrated their 30th anniversary by smoking what they thought was a marijuana cigarette. It wasn't, but they still got an imaginary high from it.

The program was created and produced by Norman Lear and Rod Parker; writers included Parker, Mark Evanier, and Dennis Palumbo. I asked Palumbo if Lear was very "hands on" for this program and he said, "No, he pretty much stayed away from this one. I think he had his hands full with Carroll O'Connor and Bea Arthur at the time." Alan Rafkin was the director. The theme song, "Nancy's Blues," was written by Marilyn Bergman, Alan Bergman, and Marvin Hamlisch (and performed by Nancy). Only a few weeks after the demise of *The Nancy Walker Show*, Nancy had a new sitcom on ABC called *Blansky's Beauties*, which also failed to catch on. Kay Gardella of *The New York Daily News* wrote of *The Nancy Walker Show*, "Nancy is more attractive in her own series, which is well-paced, well-written and well cast. Some of the dialogue is hilarious. The series is just good fun."

The Nanette Fabray Show (see *Westinghouse Playhouse*)

Needles and Pins Screen Gems/David Gerber Productions. NBC. Friday nights 9:00. September 21, 1973–December 28, 1973. 14 color episodes were filmed with a laugh track, only ten aired.

Set in the vicinity of 7th Avenue (Fashion Avenue) and West 36th Street in Manhattan, *Needles and Pins* brought the rat race of the garment district to Hollywood. Nathan Davidson (Norman Fell), usually called simply "Mr. D.," was the owner of Lorelei Fashion House (in a building with the number 463 emblazoned on it). The daughter of a friend of his, Wendy Nelson (acting newcomer Deirdre Lenihan), came all the way from Nebraska to "get a feel" for the garment business. She was instantly surrounded by a cast of characters including Charlie Miller (Bernie Kopell), the firm's main salesman; Max Popkin (Larry Gelman), the fabric cutter; Myron Russo (Alex Henteloff), the pattern maker; Sonia Baker (Sandra Deel), the bookkeeper and secretary; Mr. Singer (Milton Selzer), Lorelei's main fashion competitor; and the flamboyant Harry Karp (Louis Nye), Lorelei's newest designer and brother-in-law to Nathan, who, when things were going his way would invariably say, "oh, perf."

In the debut titled "The Girl from Seventh Avenue," young Wendy came to Lorelei to observe the goings-on. She was instantly mistaken for a model and unwittingly managed to sell 600 copies of a dress just by trying it on. She was hired on the spot and didn't return to her native Nebraska. In "Union Trouble," everyone at Lorelei went on strike—that is, except for the only non-union employee, Wendy.

The program was created by Adele and Burt Styler; the producer was Hy Averback; the executive producer was David Gerber; writers included the Stylers, Bess Boyle, Norman Paul, Jack Elinson, Karyl Geld, Charlotte Brown, Ed Jurist, Everett Greenbaum, Jim Fritzell, and Sid Dorfman; and directors included Averback, George Tyne, Peter Baldwin, and Ernest Losso. The catchy theme song was provided by Marvin Hamlisch. The funny debut episode is available for viewing at the Paley Center for Media in Beverly Hills.

The New Andy Griffith Show ADA Productions/Warner Brothers Studios. CBS. Friday nights 8:30. January 8, 1971–May 21, 1971. Ten color episodes were filmed with a laugh track. Sponsors included Pillsbury, Lifebuoy Soap, Pepsodent Toothpaste, and Excedrin PM.

The New Andy Griffith Show replaced another Andy Griffith show called *The Headmaster*, which lasted only 13 weeks. This replacement lasted even less time. Instead of being a sheriff, as on the original *Andy Griffith Show*, here Andy was the "mayor pro tem," filling in for the mayor of Greenwood (population 12,785, elevation 475 feet) who had abruptly decided to retire. Andy and the rest of the Sawyer family packed up their big blue station wagon, and left Raleigh, North Carolina, so that Andy could take this job (he had previously been working for the government at the state capital). Andy had a wife named Lee (Lee Meriwether) and two young children—a boy named T. J. (Marty McCall) and a girl named Lori (Lori Rutherford). Lee remembered, "Those kids were so polite and well-behaved. They were always on time, always knew their lines, and were never a problem. One could see that they had wonderful upbringing." Lee's older sister, a gloomy, gossipy hypochondriac named Nora (Ann Morgan Guilbert), lived with the Sawyers. Nora was also the receptionist for a local doctor in Greenwood, and she freely discussed very personal patient ailments at the dinner table. Also in the cast were Glen Ash as Buff MacKnight, the rotund town councilman; Susan Davis was his girlfriend Verline; and Ruth McDevitt played Violet Gossage, Greenwood's eldest member of the town council.

Episodes include the surreal debut titled "My Friend, the Mayor," in which Goober (George Lindsay), Emmett (Paul Hartman) and Barney Fife (Don Knotts) all came to visit their old friend Andy Sawyer as the same characters they played on the old *Andy Griffith Show*. It didn't make much sense since Andy had a different last name, a different wife, different children, a different job, and a different show. Lee Meriwether said, "They were looking for something more familiar for Andy. He'd been so out of his element on *Headmaster*. That show dealt with a lot of very serious subjects. Here, with Barney, Emmett and Goober, at least in the debut episode, it was as if Andy were back home." In "Get Me Glen Campbell," Buff MacKnight promised that he could get Glen Campbell to perform at the upcoming Greenwood Centennial celebration, but because of a mix-up, what he got was a much older string and bucket player named Glenn Campbell (Glenn with two "n's"). The situation, however, was corrected and the real Glen Campbell made it just in time for the event. Meriwether told me, "I loved that my character, Lee, was so nervous about meeting Campbell—so worried that she'd been sweating. It was a lot of fun." In "Town Square," Violet Gossage offered Andy inheritance money willed to the town by the late Henry H. Gossage. With that money, it was decided that a fountain would be built in his honor in the town square, but the townspeople mistakenly thought Andy had spent the money on a new fur coat for his wife, Lee.

The program was created and produced by Aaron Ruben; the executive producer was Richard O. Linke; directors included Lee Philips and Elliott Lewis; and writers included Ruben, Jim Fritzell, and Everett Greenbaum. Greenbaum made a cameo appearance as a "man on the street" in the "Get Me Glen Campbell" episode. Music was provided by Earle Hagen. After the cancellation of *The New Andy Griffith Show*, it was replaced with summer reruns of the show it had replaced, *The Headmaster*. Kay Gardella of *The New York Daily News* reviewed the debut episode this way: "It was an amusing 30-minute episode. It certainly is superior to *The Headmaster*." Meriwether recalled, "I auditioned for the role of the wife on *Headmaster*, but didn't get it. How interesting that I got to play Andy's wife anyway on this other show." Andy Griffith died on July 3, 2012, at the age of 86.

The New Bob Cummings Show Revue Studios/Universal. CBS. Thursday nights 8:30. October 5, 1961–March 1, 1962. 22 black-and-white episodes were filmed with a laugh track. Sponsored by Kelloggs.

This was the third of four sitcoms starring Bob Cummings. This one began with the title *The Bob Cummings Show*, a title which had previously been used for Bob's most successful show (but called *Love That Bob* in syndication). This new program was being annihilated on Thursday nights by *Dr. Kildare* on NBC and by *The Real McCoys* on ABC, so to draw more attention to it, the title was changed to *The New Bob Cummings Show*, beginning with the December 28, 1961, episode titled "La Dolce Roma." However, nothing was "new" about it. It was the same show which had debuted on October 5, 1961. In fact, Bob's character wasn't all that different from the first *Bob Cummings Show* (1955–1959), on which Bob (then a photographer) was always surrounded by beautiful women. In this "new" program, Bob was a pilot with an aerocar (a car which, when wings were added, would take off) and once again he was surrounded by beautiful women. Instead of being Bob Collins, here he was Bob Carson, and he had a bodyguard/manservant named Lionel played by the deadpan Murvyn Vye (he always called Bob "Boss"). Bob took up residence in a nice bachelor pad in Palm Desert, California, next to Desert Air. The airstrip owner's daughter, easily excitable teen tomboy Henrietta "Hank" Gogerty, was played by Roberta Shore. To add excitement and intrigue to the plots, Bob and Lionel were amateur sleuths—a wrinkle which took them to exotic locales, and put them in peril in almost every episode.

Episodes include "Very Warm for Mayan," in which Bob and Lionel assisted an American archaeologist and his wife in bringing an ancient cuneiform tablet across the border from Mexico, and danger followed them back to California. In "North by Southeast," Bob's half of a winning lottery ticket in Hong Kong was almost his undoing. In "National Satin," Bob uncovered illegal fixing activity at the horse racing track, and almost met his own photo finish in the process. Some of the outdoor airport scenes for this sitcom are thought to have been filmed at the small southern California Flabob Airport.

The program was created by Roland Kibbee; the producer was Bob Finkel; writers included Roscoe J. Armbruster, Jr., Steve Fisher, Sheldon Stark, Ron Bishop, Lee Karson, Mel Diamond, Howard Leeds, Bob Fisher, Jerry Adelman, Alan Lipscott, Sheldon Keller, Lee Erwin, Austin Kalish, Glenn Wheaton, Elroy Schwartz, and Milt Rosen; and directors included Don Weis, John English, Earl Bellamy, and David McDearmon. Music was provided by Esquivel. Bob took one more stab at a sitcom with *My Living Doll* in 1964, but met with similar results.

A New Kind of Family Gordon–Eisner Productions/Paramount. ABC. Sunday nights 7:30 (September 16, 1979–October 21, 1979), and Saturday nights 8:30 (December 15, 1979–January 5, 1980). 13 episodes were produced before a live audience, only ten aired.

ABC had extremely high hopes for this sitcom. In fact, ABC dangled this show under Eileen Brennan's nose while she was still doing *13 Queens Boulevard*. Instead, *A New Kind of Family* became one of the first casualties of the 1979–1980 season, even after a major cast overhaul. This was the story of Kit Flanagan (Brennan), a recent widow who decided to start a new life 3,000 miles away, moving from New York to Los Angeles with her three kids in tow—13-year-old Hillary (Laurie Hendler), nine-year-old Andy (David Hollander), 15-year-old Tony (a very young Rob Lowe), and the family dog named Heinz (O. J.) They leased an apartment without having seen it. Here's the rub—another family, the immensely conservative Stones (Gwynne Gilford as divorcee Abby Stone and Connie Ann Hearn as her 13-year-old daughter Jill) had just leased the same apartment on Loma Linda Drive. Realizing that a pooling of the two family's finances would make for an easier life, the Flanagans and Stones all moved in together. Their neighbor and landlord, Harold Zimmerman, was played by Chuck McCann.

Up against *60 Minutes* on CBS and *Disney's Wonderful World* on NBC, *A New Kind Of Family* was an instant flop. After only six episodes had aired, the show was pulled from the lineup and retooled. Gone was the Stone family, replaced by an African American family led by divorcee Jess Ashton (Telma Hopkins). Jess also had a daughter, Jojo (Janet Jackson [she previously played Penny on *Good Times*]). The show returned, now on Saturday nights, up against the second half of the very popular *CHiPs* and again failed to find an audience, lasting only a few more weeks. In one of the episodes from the second format, Kit bowed out of a camping trip with the kids at the last minute so that she could be reunited with a visiting former beau named Michael Jansen (Robert Hogan). However, Kit's alone time with Michael was interrupted when Jojo came home sick.

The program was created by Margie Gordon and Jane Eisner, who also served as executive producers; writers included Nick Arnold; and directors included Herbert Kenwith. One episode of *A New Kind of Family* is available for viewing in the UCLA TV Archives. Kay Gardella of *The New York Daily News* reviewed the show this way: "The way Eileen Brennan delivers a line, she could make any series look good. She's one of the most adept comediennes around today."

The New Phil Silvers Show Gladasya Productions/United Artists Television. CBS. Saturday nights 8:30 (September 28, 1963–November 8), and 9:30 (November 15–June 27, 1964). 30 black-and-white episodes were filmed at 20th Century–Fox Studios. Sponsors included Gravy Train, Tang, SOS Soap Pads, and Maxwell House Coffee.

Traditionally, shows with the word "new" in their moniker haven't fared well (*The New Bob Cummings Show*, *The New Loretta Young Show*, *The New Odd Couple*, *The New Temperature's Rising*, *The New Andy Griffith Show*). This "new" show was no exception. The main problem was that *The New Phil Silvers Show* wasn't very different from the old *Phil Silvers Show*. Here, instead of being Ernie Bilko in the army, he was Harry Grafton (he even had graft in his name)—the foreman and maintenance supervisor of Osborne Enterprises. Even Herbie Faye (Fender on the old show) came along for the ride as Waluska. Like Bilko, Harry Grafton was always conjuring up get-rich-quick schemes which invariably backfired.

Also in the new cast was the very tall and very gullible Jim Shane as Lester; Steve Mitchell as Fred Starkey; Bob Williams as Bob; Buddy Lester as Nick; Norm Grabowski conveniently played Grabowski; and Pat Renella (sometimes Bert Convy) portrayed Roxy. Grafton also had a boss named Fred H. Brink, played by Stafford Repp. If Grafton pinched the nose on the portrait of his boss on the wall of his own office, the walls would separate, revealing a secret living room with an easy chair, an ottoman, a lamp and an end table. Since Grafton didn't actually get very much work done, this room was utilized often (at least whenever Brink wasn't in the vicinity).

The New Phil Silvers Show—**Phil Silvers and Elena Verdugo (CBS).**

Episodes include "The Birthday Boy," in which Grafton overheard that the boys were raising money, so he assumed it was for his own birthday and a surprise party. He was greatly disappointed when he later found out that the guys were all chipping in for Ollie's (Bobs Watson's) new baby. In "75 1/2 Trombones," Fred Starkey won Grafton's latest pool, but when Fred discovered that the prize (an army tank) was still overseas, he threatened to blow the whistle on Harry to Mr. Brink. Harry then tried to raise the funds necessary to get the tank into the United States by teaching youngsters how to play musical instruments. Phil's real-life wife, Evelyn Patrick, made a rare guest appearance as Della in the episode called "The Tortoise and the Harry"—an episode about turtle racing. Actor Leo De Lyon guest starred in an episode called "Stop the Factory, I Want to Get Off," and he told me, "Phil caught me playing a piano on the set in between scenes and broke out his clarinet. It was the first time we had ever worked together and we started playing duets on the set. The director started getting nervous because we were using valuable studio time.

We became great friends, and soon after the show was canceled, Phil took me on tour with him. We toured together for four consecutive years, and remained friends until his passing. He was a great guy."

Well, *The New Phil Silvers Show* became even newer in episode number 18, called "Leave It to Harry," in which three new regulars (and Harry's home life) were added. The new additions were Elena Verdugo as Harry's sister, Audrey, and her two children—Susan and Andy (Sandy Descher and Ronnie Dapo respectively). The changes didn't help the ratings very much and *The New Phil Silvers Show* disappeared early in the summer of 1964.

The program was created by R. S. Allen and Harvey Bullock; the producer was Rod Amateau; directors included Amateau, David Davis, Guy Scarpitta, Thomas Montgomery, and Al Lewis; and writers included Ben Starr, Phil Sharp, Danny Simon, Ed Jurist, and David Davis. A few episodes can be viewed in the UCLA TV Archives.

Phil Silvers' production company was called Gladasya, because one of his most frequently used phrases was "Glad to see ya." His company also gave us *Gilligan's Island* and *It's About Time.*

Ninety Bristol Court (see *Harris against the World*, *Karen* and *Tom, Dick and Mary*).

No Time for Sergeants Warner Brothers Studios. ABC. Monday nights 8:30. September 14, 1964–September 6, 1965. 34 black-and-white episodes were filmed with a laugh track. Sponsors included Schick Stainless Steel Blades, and L and M Cigarettes.

Exactly eleven days later, another hillbilly named Gomer joined the military and went on to a five-year run in prime time. However, this show about hayseed Will Stockdale only lasted a single season. The official way it was described in the series' closing credits was: "from the play by Ira Levin, as presented by Maurice Evans, based on the novel by Mac Hyman." The Mac Hyman novel was made into a play and a movie, both of which starred a young Andy Griffith. When the series came to TV, Andy was too busy being the sheriff of Mayberry. Coincidentally, this program aired opposite *The Andy Griffith Show* on Monday nights. The role of Will Stockdale went to Sammy Jackson. A native of Georgia, Private Stockdale wasn't well-schooled, but he was very clever and resourceful. He immediately rubbed a lot of people the wrong way at Andrews Air Force Base because he continually found better ways of doing things, and did them with a very sunny disposition. In the debut episode, Stockdale actually saw his being placed on PKP (permanent kitchen police) as a promotion. In fact, he improved the food so significantly, even the officers began eating meals he'd prepared right along with the enlisted men. Will had a girlfriend named Millie Anderson (Laurie Sibbald) who worked as a waitress. Her grandfather, Jim Anderson (Andy Clyde), appeared in several episodes, including "The Spirit of Seventy-Five," in which he was approaching his 75th birthday and, despite his transparent protests to the contrary, really did want a fuss to be made about the landmark he was about to hit. Grandpa Jim had great disdain for the Air Force's proximity to his farm, as their planes invariably shook up his cattle. Also in the cast was Blue, Stockdale's sad sack of a bloodhound, who was the focus of the episode titled "Bloodhounds Are Thicker than Water," in which Stockdale, in order to keep the dog by his side, joined the air police and attempted to turn the docile Blue into a fierce sentry dog. Stockdale had another close friend on the base named Airman Ben Whitledge (Kevin O'Neal). Ben was the subject of an episode titled "Bully for Ben," in which Stockdale erroneously spread the word that Ben held a black belt in karate.

As far as the "Sergeants" on *No Time for Sergeants*, Stockdale answered to his NCO Sergeant King (Harry Hickox, who had been a real sergeant in World War II), and got under the skin of others in command—including Paul Smith as Captain Martin, Hayden Rorke as Colonel Farnsworth, and George Murdock as Captain Krupnick. In a play on the Officer Krupke character from *West Side Story*, one episode was titled "O Krupnick, My Krupnick," in which Captain Martin, seeking a promotion, attempted to get Stockdale transferred to Krupnick's outfit.

The program was produced by William P. D'Angelo; the executive producer was William T. Orr; writers included Elon Packard, Norman Paul, William Burns, John L. Greene, Ed James, and Seaman Jacobs; and directors included Richard Crenna, Leslie Martinson, Jeffrey Hayden, Hollingsworth Morse, Sidney Lanfield, and Charles R. Rondeau. The theme song was by George Duning, and music was provided by Frank Perkins. The entire production was supervised by George Burns. A series of three *No Time*

No Time for Sergeants—Left to right, Sammy Jackson and Harry Hickox (ABC).

for Sergeants comic books based upon the TV series were released by Dell and each initially sold for twelve cents.

Norby Norby Productions. NBC. Wednesday nights 7:00. January 5, 1955–April 6, 1955. Filmed at 20th Century Movietone Studios in New York City without a laugh track. Sponsored by Kodak film.

Most likely, the thing that hurt this show the most was its timeslot. Only a handful of NBC affiliates aired the program at its scheduled time on Wednesday nights at 7:00. However, it also had a few things in its favor—it was created by David Swift of *Mr. Peepers* fame (in fact, this show has the same slow, gentle, repetitive, methodical pacing of *Mr. Peepers*). Most importantly, it was the first sitcom filmed in color (on Eastman color film). To emphasize its historic significance, the program was sponsored by Kodak. It starred the very likable David Wayne as Pearson Norby (his wife called him "Pierce," most others called him simply "Norby"). Pearson Norby's very supportive wife was named Helen (Joan Lorring). The Norbys had two children, Diane and Hank (Susan Hallaran and Evan Elliot respectively). Together they lived in the small New York town of Pearl River (population 12,000). Many of the outdoor scenes used on the show were actually filmed in Pearl River.

Norby had worked at the Pearl River First National Bank for six years, and had been the head teller for two years. Also at the bank were the "watchdog of office waste," the very frugal Mr. Rudge (Ralph Dunn) who had the employees bring in their own fountain pens and ink to allay costs; and the bank president—the rather stuffy-yet-kindly Maude Endles (Carol Veazie). There was evidence of nepotism at the bank because the biggest slacker there was Oliver Wendell Prue (Lamont Johnson)—the Vice-President of the bank, and nephew of Mrs. Endles. The switchboard operator, Wahleen Johnson, was portrayed by Janice Mars. In one of the show's best episodes, "Wahleen's Romance," Wahleen made her co-workers believe that her own wedding day was not far off after everyone in the office created a fuss over a passing car with the words "just married" written on the back.

In the debut, to his surprise, Norby was named the successor to the elderly Thurmon Newell, the director of small loans, who just retired. Norby was so overwhelmed by the news, he ran all the way home to tell his wife, Helen, instead of taking the car.

Besides creating the show, David Swift also served as producer; directors included Richard Whorf, Rogers Brackett, and Swift; and writers included Harvey Orkin, James Lee, David Rayfiel, Paul West, Poot Pray, and George Kirgo. David Wayne later attempted sitcom stardom again in *The Good Life* and *House Calls*. For a long time, it was thought that all episodes of *Norby* had been lost in a fire, but, luckily, copies have surfaced.

O.K. Crackerby Beresford Productions, Ltd./United Artists. ABC. Thursday nights 8:30. September 16, 1965–January 6, 1966. 17 black-and-white episodes were filmed with a laugh track. Sponsors included Bristol-Myers and Quaker Oats.

O.K. Crackerby (*Okay Crackerby* in the pilot) was a self-made Stillwater, Oklahoma, millionaire many times over (in fact, he was the richest man in the world). After leaving Oklahoma, Crackerby (Burl Ives) settled in Palm Beach, Florida in the Hotel Havenhurst. When he was unable to secure the entire top floor penthouse there for the Crackerby family, he simply made one phone call, and within five minutes owned the hotel (which then instantly became the Havenhurst Crackerby Hotel). There were a few things Crackerby wouldn't tolerate—not getting his way, being told he couldn't accomplish something, and (especially) lacking the grace to climb socially (he had so many rough edges, he just didn't fit in). One could take this boy out of Oklahoma, but one couldn't take the Oklahoma out of this boy. He was a widower with three children and he wanted those children to get a proper education so that they wouldn't experience these same societal obstacles. After much searching, he found the right person to hire as a tutor for his children in an unemployed, almost penniless Harvard graduate named St. John Quincy (pronounced SIHN- Jihn KWIHN- zee). St. John (Hal Buckley), however, wanted none of it. He and Crackerby didn't hit it off very well, but getting back to my earlier point that Crackerby was averse to not getting his way, St. John eventually accepted the position. It was obvious that he was enamored with the Crackerby children (and they liked him). There was the eldest daughter, 16-year-old Cynthia Crackerby (Brooke Adams), who made it very plain that she had a crush on St. John. Then there was the youngest son, nine-year-old Hobart (Joel Davidson), who didn't like anything (but he liked St. John). Finally, there was the middle child, the husky 13-year-old O.K., Jr. (Brian Corcoran). Also in the cast, Dick Foran played Slim (O.K.'s business partner); Laraine Stephens played Susan Wentworth (St. John's girlfriend, who thought he should take the job); and John Indrisano played the chauffeur. There was also an occasional appearance made by Gertrude, Crackerby's basset hound.

Episodes include "The St. John Raid," in which O.K.'s extroverted old Oklahoma friend Aggie Cranepool (Kathleen Freeman) attempted to steal St. John away from the Crackerby family. Crackerby fell for a woman (Phyllis Avery) whom he saw at the airport (in "Who Was that Lady You Saw Me With?"). When she instantly vanished almost into thin air, he had his entire staff track her down.

The program was created by playwright Abe Burrows and *TV Guide* critic Cleveland Amory (it's unclear whether he ever reviewed his own show). The program was produced by Rod Amateau, Norman Henry, Charles Stewart, and Burrows (briefly); writers included Burrows (early episodes only), George Balzer, Rich Eustis, Al Rogers, Terry Ryan, Robert C. Dennis, Earl Barret, Richard Baer, Tony Webster, James Menzies, Arnold Margolin, James Allardice, Tom Adair, Bill O'Halleren, and Jim Parker; and directors included Rod Amateau, Leonard Horn, Jack Shea, Claudio Guzman, James Sheldon, Ezra Stone, Thomas Montgomery, Seymour Robbie, Gary Nelson, and David Nelson. Music was provided by Ralph Carmichael, and the theme song was written by Robert Emmett Dolan and Burrows. Burl Ives was probably best known to television audiences as the snowman on the perennial holiday special, *Rudolph, the Red-nosed Reindeer*. He also had numerous top-twenty hit singles such as *A Little Bitty Tear*, *Funny Way of Laughing*, and *Call Me Mr. In-Between*.

Occasional Wife Screen Gems. NBC. Tuesday nights 8:30. September 13, 1966–August 29, 1967. 30 color episodes were filmed with a laugh track. Sponsors included Lever Brothers and Brown and Williamson.

The show began with the words, "This is a modern fable about two young people who made a bargain." The bargain they made accounted for the laughs in the show. Peter Christopher (Michael Callan) worked for the New York branch of the Brahms Baby Food Company (their slogan was "Every meal a lullaby"), a company in which families and a corporate image were of utmost importance. Thus, the single status of Christopher was hampering his chances at a promotion. He got an idea from a hat-check girl named Greta Patterson (Patricia Harty, years later known as Trisha Hart). Initially, her surname on the program was to be Veblen, but was changed to Patterson. She wore a phony wedding ring when checking hats on the job to help fend off the advances of single men. This idea of a "staged wedding" led Peter to utter these words to Greta: "I want you to be my wife ... occasionally." He agreed to pay for her rent (she moved in two floors above him on the ninth floor of his 58th Street apartment building), her art school classes, and her contact lenses (she was quite adept at negotiations). She even got him to buy her a ring (albeit a cheap one for $15.00). In return, she'd be at his beck and call and pretend to be his wife. This arrangement finally got Peter's boss, Max Brahms (Jack Collins), off of his back. They continued the charade for family, as well, to get Peter's mother (Sara Seeger) off of

Occasional Wife—**Michael Callan and Patricia Harty (NBC).**

his back. She wanted nothing more than to see her son finally settling down with a nice girl. In fact, he took great umbrage at her queries as to whether he were "eccentric," as she so gently put it. Comedy ensued when guests dropped in unexpectedly. They'd see Peter with a girl he was dating or Greta with a guy she was seeing; getting out of those situations unscathed seemed to get harder each week. The most confused person was the tenant on the eighth floor (between Peter and Greta's apartment), played by Bryan O'Byrne, who saw all sorts of bizarre behavior on the fire escape between the "couple's" apartments. Guest stars included E. J. Peaker as Ginger Snap in "The Promotion," Paul Sand as Harvey in "No Cookie for Dessert," Herb Edelman as Uncle Harry in the episode titled "Marriage Counselor," Sally Field as Nancy in "No Talent Scouts," Richard Dreyfuss and Rose Marie in "Fair Play for Gypsies," and Vic Tayback as the prisoner in "Kangaroo Kandidates."

The program was produced by Harry Ackerman and Bob Claver; it was created by Fred Freeman and Lawrence J. Cohen; writers included Cohen, Robert Riley Crutcher, Martin Donovan, Richard Baer, Peggy Chantler Dick, Lila Garrett, Bernie Kahn, Gene Thompson, and Martin Ragaway; and directors included Richard Kinon, Ernest Pintoff, Claver, Jerry Bernstein, Paul Junger Witt, John Erman, Gary Nelson, and Russell Mayberry. The theme song was written by Ernest Pintoff and Howard Greenfield. The narrator was legendary Dodger's baseball announcer, Vin Scully. During the show's run, Michael Callan and Patricia Harty fell in love and got married in real life (that is, until 1983). A review by Bob Hull of *The Los Angeles Herald-Examiner* read, "A light-hearted, potentially sophisticated comedy." Reruns were briefly shown on the HA! cable network.

Off the Record Independent Television Producers Association/Wanamaker Studios. DuMont. Tuesday nights 7:00. October 19, 1948–October 26, 1948. Two episodes were broadcast live.

This early live sitcom starred Zero Mostel and Joey Faye. The setting was a radio station. Mostel, who was accustomed to performing on stage, demanded the availability of a live studio audience for the show. However, the Wanamaker Studios were quite small and couldn't accommodate a live audience. Disappointed, and claiming breach of contract, Mostel walked away from the project after only two episodes had aired, and very quickly *Off the Record* was off the DuMont TV schedule. The program was produced by Martin Gosch. To my knowledge, no episodes exist. However, a local 1948 WPIX-TV Channel 11, New York program with Mostel and Faye titled *Channel Zero* has survived and can be viewed at the Paley Center for Media.

Oh! Those Bells Davana, Inc./MGM Studios. CBS. March 8, 1962–May 31, 1962. 13 episodes were filmed with a laugh track.

The German-born Wiere brothers (Herbert, Harry and Sylvester) began in vaudeville. They then made the successful transition to motion pictures such as *The Road to Rio* and *Hands Across the Border*. They performed their slapstick routines frequently on *The Ed Sullivan Show*. In 1962, CBS finally green-lighted their madcap comedy series, originally to be titled *The Wiere Brothers*, but later changed to *Oh! Those Bells*. Herbert, Harry and Sylvester Wiere became Herbert, Harry and Sylvester Bell, who worked for the Cinema Rents Hollywood prop shop. Their boss at the shop was the easily flustered Mr. Henry Slocum (Henry Norell). Also at the shop was the lovely Kitty Mathews (on whom Sylvester had a crush), played by Carol Byron. The Bell boys had a home life, too (they all lived together in a bungalow), and their landlady was Mrs. Stanfield (Reta Shaw).

Episodes include "Money Mix-up," in which a box of phony money, intended as a movie prop, got confused with $10,000 in real money stolen from a charity. A couple of thieves attempted to steal the real money, but kept getting the prop money instead. In "Too Many Spooks," Mr. Slocum set the Bell boys up in a house he bought at an estate sale after the Bells were evicted by their landlady, Mrs. Stanfield. However, Slocum had neglected to tell the boys that the house was allegedly haunted, and came complete with secret rooms, moving walls, moving beds, flying bats, flying knives, eerie voices, and a portrait on the wall with eyes that followed you wherever you went. Actor Johnny Eimen, who guest starred in the episode titled "The Camping Trip" recalled, "There was a lot of energy there on the set. The camping scene was done on a soundstage, with dirt, tents, and phony trees."

The program had a couple of gimmicks it used and re-used. Whenever something went wrong, Sylvester uttered the word, "Oops." Also, whenever any one of the Bell brothers had a brainstorm, a bell would ring. The Wiere brothers got to perform their vaudeville act, especially their musical shenanigans, in almost every episode.

The program was created by Jules and Sam White, who had previously directed Buster Keaton and The Three Stooges. Some of the more inspired slapstick moments on this short-lived sitcom actually resembled some of the Stooges' best work. Jules and Sam White also produced the show; the executive producer was Ben Brady; writers included Arthur Phillips, Si Rose, and Seaman Jacobs; and the directors were Charles Barton, Norman Abbott, Abby Berlin, Danny Dare, and Jack Arnold.

A few years after the demise of this series, the Wiere brothers again did their schtick in the Elvis Presley movie *Double Trouble*. After the death of Sylvester in July of 1970, the two remaining brothers greatly curtailed their performances. It's interesting to note that *Oh! Those Bells* was originally intended to begin airing on November 13, 1960, but a sponsor could not be found. Almost 16 months later, it was finally on the CBS prime time schedule, albeit briefly. A couple of episodes can be viewed in the UCLA TV Archives.

On Our Own Time-Life TV Productions. CBS. Sunday nights 8:30. October 9, 1977–August 27, 1978. 22 episodes were videotaped before a live audience in New York City.

Along with *Calucci's Department*, *Ball Four*, *Ivan the Terrible*, and *Kate and Allie*, this sitcom was recorded at CBS in New York City. This was a rarity in the 1970s, as most shows (except for a few game shows and soap operas) were done in Hollywood. This was the story of two ambitious young ladies who had just taken their first step up the corporate ladder at the Bedford Advertising Agency on Madison Avenue in New York City. Julia Peters (Bess Armstrong) was Protestant, cute, petite, naïve, and recently promoted to copywriter. Her best friend, Maria Teresa Bonino (Lynnie Greene), was Catholic and extremely adherent to what she was taught by nuns. She was 23 years old, stood six-feet-one inches tall, weighed 127 pounds, was nicknamed "Stretch," and was unusually uncomfortable around attractive men. Also working at the agency was the sexy, sultry, worldly April Baxter (she only had to buy her own lunch once in her life), played by Dixie Carter. Comedian Jimmy Brogan told me, "I was the warm-up for their live audience. A few years later I got to work with the wonderful Dixie Carter again on *Out of the Blue* on ABC." Among April's throngs of male admirers was co-worker Eddie Barnes (John Christopher Jones), who was the creative producer of TV commercials. Also in the cast was salesman Craig Boatwright (Dan Resin), who was always telling lengthy dirty jokes to anyone within earshot; Toni McBain (Gretchen Wyler) was the very sophisticated head of the agency and carried her little dog, Flotsam, with her everywhere; and Toni's boss was the dimwitted board chairman J. M. Bedford (Bob Randall) always heard (never seen) barking out orders over the intercom. Julia's landlord, Mr. Fibelman (Larry Best), who recited old sayings for every situation that cropped up, appeared in several episodes as well.

Episodes include the debut, "Never Trust an Actor with His Clothes Off," in which Julia and Maria were in charge of hiring a man for a deodorant commercial they had written. However, Toni wanted the actor in the commercial to be wearing only his boxers, and the shy girls had to audition all of the men dressed that way. When one of those men (John Getz as Tom Ericson) asked both girls out on dates, it almost ruined their friendship. In "Honesty Is Not the Best Policy," Julia and Maria were asked to entertain a new client (Scott McKay as Leyland Bartlett, a wood magnate) for dinner. Mr. Bartlett fell for Julia, and after quite a few drinks, passed out on her bed, leading to many raised eyebrows at the office the next day. In "Julia in the Dark," a blackout in the office building trapped Julia (who was working late) with a stranger from another floor named Barry Spalding (James Naughton). The two of them quickly fell in love, albeit briefly, as he was only in town for a short while completing a project.

The program was produced by Sam Denoff; the executive producer was David Susskind; the creator was Bob Randall (the voice of J. M.); writers included Randall, Andrew Smith, and Bruce Kane; and directors included James Burrows, Mel Shapiro, Lee Bernhardi, and Doug Rogers. Music was provided by Bob Israel and Walt Levinsky. I had the opportunity to see one of the episodes of this show recorded in New York and Bess Armstrong graciously came out to greet the studio audience and sign autographs after the show. She also appeared in a few other single season sitcoms, *All Is Forgiven* in 1986 and *Married People* in 1990; Dixie Carter enjoyed a long run in *Designing Women*; and Dan Resin became "The Ty-D-Bol Man" in a series of popular commercials.

On the Rocks John Rich Productions. ABC. Thursday nights 8:30 (September 11, 1975–January 8, 1976), and Monday nights 8:00 (January 12, 1976–May 17, 1976). 23 color episodes were videotaped before a live audience at Golden West Studios.

ABC used to promote their Thursday night sitcoms (*Barney Miller* backed with *On the Rocks*) as "funny cops, funny robbers." The robbers were in a "minimum security prison" known as Alamesa. The new inmates were hardly new at all—most had been in Alamesa before. There was the clever, wise-cracking Latino named Hector Fuentes (Jose Perez); his old inmate friend from "the class of 1968" DeMott (Hal Williams); and Cleaver who had a sunny disposition (Rick Hurst). All three blamed their incarceration on a "gross miscarriage of justice." There was one newbie—Nicky Palik (Bobby Sandler), who stole six cars—all at once (he claimed he did it for his fiancée). In the debut, while the new inmates were getting acquainted, Fuentes was attempting to use his streetwise cunning to land a prison job in the kitchen or in the library. Those jobs, however, went to DeMott and Palik (respectively), and Fuentes went instead to the farming area outside, and had to tend the pigs. Mel Stewart portrayed the tough "by the rules" guard named Mr. Gibson; the more inmate-friendly and lenient guard, Mr. Sullivan, was portrayed by Tom Poston. Warden Wilbur Poindexter was played by Logan Ramsey.

Episodes include "To Catch a Thief," in which there were thieves among the thieves—someone had stolen Fuentes' canned pineapple chunks. In "Hector Convinces Nicky to Lose a Fight," newcomer Palik had his first behind-bars brawl. In "Dear John," Palik's fiancée broke off their engagement and also broke his heart. The show's final first-run program was an hour-long episode called "Retrospective."

The program was produced and directed by John Rich; the creators and writers were Dick Clement and Ian La Frenais (also of *Billy*). Music was provided by Jerry Fielding. The National Association for Justice attempted to get *On the Rocks* canceled because of the unrealistic and comical way in which prison life was portrayed. It was all for naught, as the show only lasted a single season anyway. *On the Rocks* was based upon the long-running British show called *Porridge*. A few episodes can be viewed in the UCLA TV Archives.

One Happy Family A Mark Goodson/Bill Todman Production/Desilu Studios. NBC. Friday nights at 8:00. January 13, 1961–March 10, 1961, and May 12, 1961–September 8, 1961. 15 black-and-white episodes were filmed before a live audience. Sponsors included the Block Drug Company.

Mark Goodson and Bill Todman were best known for a long list of amazingly successful game shows. However, they did dabble in other types of programming. There were drama shows such as *The Web* and *The Richard Boone Show*; there were Westerns—*Jefferson Drum*, *The Rebel* and *Branded*; there was even a variety show, *The Don Rickles Show*. Oh, and there was this one sitcom, a funny-yet-unsuccessful series called *One Happy Family*.

It was about three generations of the same family all living under the same roof, trying to be *One Happy Family*.

Recently married, Dick and Penny Cooper were played by Dick Sargent and Jody Warner, respectively. Dick had aspirations of becoming a TV meteorologist; scatterbrained Penny was just happy to be Mrs. Cooper. These newlyweds originally planned to crash at her parents' place for one night, but they stayed. Penny's parents were Barney and Mildred Hogan, played by Chick Chandler and Elisabeth Fraser, respectively. As if that weren't enough, Penny's grandparents lived there, too—Grandpa Charley Hackett (Jack Kirkwood) was always eating and his wife, Lovey (Cheerio Meredith), was very fond of harness racing. Barney and Charley worked together at Hogan Plumbing Company—Barney was the boss, and Charley worked in the shipping department. Willard Waterman appeared in a few episodes as Mr. Douglas.

Episodes include "Charley: Executive at Large," in which Charley left the plumbing company after being admonished by Barney for a shipping error which cost the company an account. Charley then went to work for Barney's biggest competitor, S. B. Crowley (Alexander Lockwood). In the episode titled "Barney Gives Dick the Business," Barney tried to get Dick to work for the plumbing company so that he could buy Penny all the things she desired. Dick hadn't been making a lot of money in meteorology, but didn't wish to give up his dream. Instead of hurting Barney's feelings, Dick and Charley cooked up a scheme to make Barney renege on the job offer. Before going on hiatus, this show aired nine original episodes. Two months later, upon its return to the prime time schedule, six more original episodes aired.

Writers included Seaman Jacobs, Si Rose, Sid Dorfman, and Al Lewis—the latter also served as creator and director. A few episodes can be viewed in the UCLA TV Archives.

Our Man Higgins First Company of Writers Productions/Screen Gems—ABC. Wednesday nights 9:30. October 3, 1962–September 11, 1963. 34 black-and-white episodes were filmed with a laugh track. Sponsors included Pontiac and The American Tobacco Company.

The Dick Van Dyke Show really caught on in its second season and this was bad news for the new sitcom up against it on ABC called *Our Man Higgins*. Based upon the radio program called *It's Higgins, Sir*, that title was also used as the title of the debut episode. He didn't like being called "Mr. Higgins," but rather simply "Higgins" (Stanley Holloway). He was a butler inherited by the MacRoberts family who lived at 617 Dunwoody. Actually, he was inherited along with a small fortune ($50,000) in a 250-year-old 127-piece silver service. These were a matching set—the MacRoberts family couldn't have the silver without taking the butler. They were willed to the MacRoberts family by the late Sir Doogal (Lord Roberts of Scotland), and the silver was brought into the United States duty-free as an art collection. The MacRoberts family consisted of the patriarch, Duncan R. MacRoberts, an executive, played by Frank Maxwell, and his wife Alice (Audrey Totter). They had three children—the infrequently-seen Joanie (Regina Groves), the middle child; 13-year-old Tommy (Rickey Kelman); and the youngest, nine-year-old Dinghy (K. C. Butts).

Episodes include the debut, "It's Higgins, Sir," in which the newly arrived Higgins quickly wore out his welcome when he swatted young Tommy on the backside with a mop and was asked to leave. What the MacRoberts parents didn't know until later was that Tommy and his dog had tracked in mud onto a freshly washed kitchen floor. When reprimanded by Higgins, the youngster mouthed off, kicked the butler in the shins, purposely knocked over a bucket of water, and thus he deserved what he got. Amends were made and Higgins got to stay. In the episode "Half-A-Higgins," Duncan's long-lost relative, Ernie MacRoberts (Alan Carney) surfaced after being presumed dead (MIA) in the armed services, and wanted half of the inheritance—including half of Higgins.

The program was created and produced by Paul Harrison; the executive producer was Harry Ackerman; writers included Richard Murphy, Mort Lewis, Al Schwartz, Alvin Sapinsley, Joanna Lee, Bernie Gould, Fred F. Finklehoffe, Ray Singer, Dick Chevillat, Walter Black, Nate Monaster, Norman Katkov, and John McGreevey; and directors included Murphy, Earl Bellamy, Gene Nelson, Sidney Lanfield, Andrew McCullough, Leslie Goodwins, Fred DeCordova, William D. Russell, Paul Harrison, and Oscar Rudolph. Music was provided by Frank DeVol. Going into commercial breaks, Higgins would say, "And now a word from our benefactor." A couple of episodes can be viewed in the UCLA TV Archives.

Out of the Blue Paramount Studios. ABC. Sunday nights 7:00 (September 9, 1979–October 21, 1979), and Sunday nights 7:30 (Dec 16, 1979). 13 color episodes were filmed (most employed a laugh track, but a couple were recorded before a live audience)—only nine aired.

Much as in *The Smothers Brothers Show*, a probationary angel was summoned to Earth to lend a helping hand. However, in this show, the angel's name was Random (comic Jimmy Brogan) and the location was Chicago (the *Chicago Sun-Times* building and Wrigley Field were seen in the opening credits), instead of Los Angeles. Brogan told me, "The opening credits were shot in Hancock Park, California with inserts of Chicago added in later. The cast never actually did any filming in Chicago, but for a time I'd lived in River Forest, near the windy city, in my youth. I pointed out that some of the cactus and other plant life in the outdoor scenes around the Richards' home would not be indigenous to Chicago, so they covered all of those up." The pilot for the show never aired. As Brogan remembered, "It was more of a presentation episode and ran only about 18 minutes. The Boss Angel in that episode was male, but they made it a female role for the series and the brilliant Eileen Heckart was their choice. We used to run our lines in her dressing room, and she was just a natural."

Random's mission on earth was to assist a family of five orphaned Richards children who lived with their aunt Marion (Dixie Carter) after the death of their biological parents in a plane crash. As Brogan recalled, "Dixie Carter didn't appear in the presentation episode, but was added for the series after that presentation episode at ABC's direction. I was very happy about that. I'd worked with her when I was the warm-up for the live audience on her earlier series called *On Our Own*."

The kids and their ages were as follows: Chris (Clark Brandon), 16; Laura (Olivia Barasch), 13; Stacey (Tammy Lauren), ten; and the twin boys Jason and Shane (Jason and Shane Keller), eight. Brogan shared, "I was recently reunited with the Keller twins. We went to lunch, and they told me they used to get beaten up in school by classmates because they were on TV. I would have thought otherwise." Hannah Dean played the saucy-but-loving housekeeper Gladys. Her role, in fact, was much like that of Carter's. As Brogan told me, "There were now two characters fulfilling the same function on the show—being the adult in the household, and there just wasn't much for Dixie to do. Because of that, after about seven episodes, Dixie decided to leave the show." Olivia Barash told me, "Our show was on back-to-back with *A New Kind of Family* on Sunday nights on ABC. At the time, I was dating Rob Lowe, who played Tony Flanagan on that show."

There are some who would call *Out of the Blue* a spinoff of *Happy Days* and *Mork and Mindy*, but in reality its connection to those two shows was merely promotional. Random appeared on an episode of *Happy Days* titled "Chachi Sells His Soul." Mork (Robin Williams) appeared on the debut episode of *Out of the Blue* titled "Random's Arrival." Brogan recalled, "Robin was amazing. We did his scenes on a Saturday because of his *Mork and Mindy* schedule. He only had to look at the script once or twice. He just absorbed his lines." Barash concurred, saying, "I adored Robin Williams. I loved having the chance to work with him. I was also in a lunchtime yoga class with him and Cindy Williams." Brogan also recalled a future celebrity appearing on the show: "Corey Feldman, who was about seven at the time, appeared in a scene which took place in a doctor's office."

Episodes include "The Hustle," in which the family took up a collection to buy Aunt Marion a nice gift for her birthday. However, Chris tried to amass even more money for an even nicer gift, and gambled away all the money shooting pool with a guy who turned out to be a pool hustler. Random then stepped in to win the money back.

The program was created by Thomas L. Miller and Robert L. Boyett; it was developed by Barry Kemp; the producers were Austin and Irma Kalish; and the executive producers were William Bickley and Michael Warren. Writers included Laurie Gelman, Alan Moskowitz, and Kemp; directors included John Tracy, Peter Baldwin, Scott McGibbon, and Jeff Chambers. Music was provided by Charles Fox. This *Out of the Blue* is not to be confused with several subsequent shows with that same title. Competition from *60 Minutes* on CBS and *Disney's Wonderful World* on NBC seemed insurmountable. Brogan, with tongue in cheek, told me, "Even I wasn't watching." He also shared, "We knew the end was coming. The ratings weren't good. On one of the last episodes, we filmed before a live audience—the producers were attempting to retool the show, adding Peter Scolari as a 'bad angel.' The show was going to be retitled *Heaven Help Us*, but ABC didn't pick up this new version of the show." Jimmy found out about the demise of the show "from the *New York Times*. Believe it or not, I read about it before I was told about it. It was a wonderful experience, however—working on the Paramount lot at that time, surrounded by all of the *Happy Days*, *Laverne and Shirley* and *Taxi* talent. It was unforgettable."

Ozzie's Girls Filmways (Distributed by Viacom). First-run syndication. 1973–1974. 24 color episodes were videotaped with a laugh track. Sponsors included Procter and Gamble.

After a seven-year absence following the cancellation of *The Adventures of Ozzie and Harriet*, the Nelsons were back. This time, the boys had both moved out and to help "keep up with the times," Ozzie and Harriet decided to take in a boarder in the boys' old room in that same old house on Sycamore. Mike Wagner, who portrayed Mike (Susan's boyfriend) on the show, recalled, "The program was done in very familiar surroundings—Stage Five at General Service Studios on Las Palmas. That's where the old show was done." Well, the Nelsons initially wanted only one boarder, but because of a mix-up there were two. Jennifer (Brenda Sykes, who had been discovered on *The Dating Game*) was actually promised the room first, but her arrival at the Nelson's home was delayed because her bus was late. Ozzie thought a hippie girl named Susan (Susan Sennett) who came to the door inquiring about the room was Jennifer and gave the room to her. Here's the rub—Susan was white, and Jennifer was black. To keep Jennifer from

AUG.26 SEPT.1

LOS ANGELES TIMES

TV TIMES

OZZIE AND HARRIET COMING BACK WITH A NEW SERIES

Ozzie's Girls—**Clockwise from top, Ozzie Nelson, Susan Sennett, Harriet Nelson, and Brenda Sykes (photograph courtesy of Mike Wagner).**

getting the wrong impression about the Nelson's intentions, she was invited to stay, too (since the room was very large and it had two beds). For some reason, Jennifer became known as Brenda after the first episode. Brenda and Susan liked including Ozzie and Harriet in a lot of their plans, making the elder Nelsons feel very youthful. We also found out everyone's astrological sign in the debut episode—Ozzie and Susan were Pisces, Harriet was a Cancer/Moon Child, and Jennifer/Brenda was an Aquarius.

Unlike the original Ozzie and Harriet show, this sequel was recorded on videotape. Mike Wagner told me, "That made it easier for Ozzie.

He was quite the perfectionist and was famous for a lot of retakes. Using videotape made it easier for Ozzie to instantly see and keep the best take."

Episodes include the pilot, in which David and Ricky were seen in flashbacks. In "Murder Mystery Mystery," Ozzie made repeated attempts to find the missing page from his mystery novel—the page which named the killer. In "The Candidate," Susan ran for class president, and stirred up a political furor. A young Mark Harmon made his acting debut as Mark Johnson in that episode. Wagner remembered, "Mark Harmon and I both attended Harvard Military School together, and later we both went to UCLA—he was a football star, and I was a communication major. Coincidentally, we met again on that memorable episode."

Although he didn't appear in any episodes, David Nelson was still involved in *Ozzie's Girls* as producer; Al Simon was executive producer; Ozzie Nelson was the director; and writers included Ozzie Nelson, Don Nelson, Arthur Alsberg, John L. Greene, Arthur Phillips, Dick Bensfield, and Perry Grant. Music was provided by Frank McKelvey. Wagner said, "We were all set to begin a second season of the show, but Ozzie became seriously ill shortly after season one and everything suddenly came to a screeching halt."

The end credits of each episode were unique curtain calls, specifically made for that episode, often with the actors carrying their own names on low budget cardboard signs. Episodes of the program were completed and edited so close to their intended airdate, many stations were unable to get promos for that week's show on in time. Susan Sennett later became Susan Sennett Nash in 1977 when she married rock star Graham Nash (of the Hollies, and Crosby, Stills and Nash). They had three children together.

Papa Cellini ABC. Sundays 4:30PM. September 28, 1952–November 16, 1952. Broadcast live.

This program focused upon situations in the home of the Cellinis, an Italian-American family who resided in New York. Tiro Virolo portrayed the family patriarch, Papa Cellini; Ada Ruggieri was Mama; Carol Sinclair was their daughter Nita; and Aristide Sigismundi was their son, Antonio. To my knowledge, no episodes exist.

Paper Moon The Culzean Corporation/Paramount Studios. ABC. Thursday nights 8:30. September 12, 1974–January 2, 1975. 13 color episodes were filmed without a laugh track. Sponsors included American Home Products, Ralston Purina, and Lehn and Fink.

Attempts have been made countless times to bring hit movies successfully to television. The hit Peter Bogdanovich movie, which starred Ryan O'Neal and daughter Tatum, was based upon a novel titled *Addie Pray* by Joe David Brown. Television quickly jumped on the *Paper Moon* bandwagon and turned this Depression-era period piece into a weekly TV sitcom. In the title roles on TV were Christopher Connelly as Moses "Moze" Pray of the Dixie Bible Company and future two-time Academy Award Winner, Jodie Foster was his daughter, Addie. Eleven-year-old Jodie already had plenty of sitcom experience, with semi-regular roles on *My Three Sons*, *Bob & Carol & Ted & Alice* and *The Courtship of Eddie's Father*. The Prays worked very well in tandem as slick con artists (getting money out of people through a myriad of get-rich-quick schemes). In one episode, Moses charmed and distracted a store clerk enough to get him to exchange two

Paper Moon—**Christopher Connelly, Jodie Foster (photograph courtesy of Jean Cummings).**

ten dollar bills for his five dollar bill multiple times. Somehow, the Prays managed to stay just ahead of the long arm of the law. They traveled along the Kansas countryside in a rather moody 1931 convertible roadster.

Episodes include "Imposter," in which Moses attempted to pass Addie off as the long-lost daughter of a very wealthy recluse. In "Long Division," Moses swindled a college graduate into teaching Addie how to do long division. In "Settling," the debut, the slick Prays were themselves conned when Moses gave in to Addie's pleas to settle down, give up the con game, and buy a house. The seemingly honest old man from whom they purchased the house then skipped town with the money, and when the real owner returned from a trip, the Prays were quickly evicted, and once again living a nomadic life.

The program was produced by Robert Stambler; the executive producer was Anthony Wilson; writers included Alvin Sargent; and directors included James Frawley. Music was provided by Artie Butler. The theme song, "It's Only a Paper Moon," was written by Harold Arlen, Yip Harburg, and Billy Rose. This expensive little show was filmed on location in Kansas. The program was reviewed by Cecil Smith of the *Los Angeles Times* this way: "*Paper Moon* is a reasonable facsimile of the hit movie. The opening script strikes the right note." One episode was rerun on TV Land.

The Partners Don Lee Productions/Universal City Studios. NBC. Saturday nights 8:00 (September 18, 1971–January 8, 1972), and Friday nights 8:00 (July 28, 1972–September 8, 1972). 20 color episodes were filmed with a laugh track.

Not unlike his classic Maxwell Smart character on the long-running *Get Smart*, here, instead of a bumbling spy, Don Adams was a bumbling police officer named Detective Lennie Crooke. His original "partner" on *The Partners* was to have been Godfrey Cambridge, but the two actors didn't hit it off too well, and instead Rupert Crosse got the role of Detective George Robinson, an African American police officer who was every bit as much a bumbler as Lennie Crooke. Crosse had been an Oscar nominee for his role in *The Reivers*. Adams wanted the program to deal with more social issues, but NBC wanted it to be more in the slapstick mold, and NBC won. While chasing the bad guys, Lennie and George broke almost every rule in the code book along the way (including forgetting to read the perpetrator his or her Miranda rights). Whatever rules were broken along the way were certain to be reported to their impatient Captain Andrews (John Doucette) by the precinct snitch, Sergeant Higgenbottom (Dick Van Patten). There was always added confusion to each case as a character named Freddie Butler (Don's cousin, Robert Karvelas) would invariably confess to every imaginable crime, although he was actually guilty of none. There were indeed some classic slapstick moments in this short-lived sitcom, including a hurried Lennie forgetting his pants on his way to work leading to a pants exchange in the small front seat of the squad car; Lennie and George rolling down a steep mountain after misjudging the backyard of a criminal's hideout; a trigger-happy Lennie shooting up a noisy cuckoo clock which startled him; losing a dead body over and over again (in the episode cleverly titled "Abra Cadaver"); and Lennie jumping over a hedge in pursuit of a criminal and landing in a kiddie pool full of water. All of the well-timed slapstick was for naught, however, as *The Partners* on NBC was up against *All in the Family* on CBS on Saturday nights, and was pummeled in the ratings. After being canceled in January of 1972, a few previously unaired episodes were shown during the summer of 1972, this time on Friday nights.

The program was created by Don Adams; the producers were Arne Sultan, Earl Barret, and Lee Wolfberg; writers included Adams, Barret, Sultan, Burt Styler, Bruce Howard, Ed Simmons, Lawrence Marks, Milt Rosen, Ben Starr, and Jerry Mayer; and directors included Adams, Gary Nelson, Richard Benedict, Joseph Pevney, Christian Nyby, Charles Rondeau, Earl Bellamy, and Barret. The theme song was provided by Lalo Schifrin (*Mission: Impossible*) and other music was provided by Richard Hazard. Several episodes of the show were later edited together as a TV movie called *Confessions of a Top Crimebuster*. Cecil Smith of the *Los Angeles Times* wrote, "It brings laughter back to the tube in great howling masses." A couple of episodes can be viewed in the UCLA TV Archives.

The Paul Lynde Show An Ashmont Production/Screen Gems. ABC. Wednesday nights 8:00 (September 13, 1972–May 30, 1972), and Saturday nights 8:30 (June 9, 1972–September 8, 1973). 26 color episodes were filmed before a live audience.

This sitcom had a very unique history. It

***The Paul Lynde Show*—Left to right, Jane Actman, Elizabeth Allen, John Calvin, Paul Lynde, Milt Kamen, Anne Meara, Jerry Stiller. From the episode "Howie's Inheritance" (photograph courtesy of Jean Cummings).**

began in 1962 as a pilot called *Howie*, which was based upon a stage play of the same name by Phoebe Ephron. A full decade later, this pilot was reworked as the debut episode of *The Paul Lynde Show*. First and foremost, both starred Lynde (as Walter Simms in the pilot, and as Paul Simms in the series). Both have Simms married (to Edith portrayed by in the pilot by Peggy Knudsen, and to Martha portrayed by Elizabeth Allen in the series). In each, the couple had two daughters, Barbara (portrayed by Mary Mitchel in the pilot, and by Jane Actman in the series) and Sally (Sherry Alberoni in the pilot, and Pamelyn Ferdin in the series). Sherry Alberoni Van Meter (as she's known today) recalls, "Paul Lynde was really, really silly fun." She added, "I remember having a crush on Will Hutchins." Speaking of Will Hutchins, he portrayed Howie Dickerson in the pilot, but ten years later Howie was portrayed by John Calvin in the series. Howie was a tall, blonde, handsome genius who knew the stock market inside and out. However, his biggest drawback was his inability to keep a job. Both the pilot and the debut episode of the series featured a fertility statue, much to Paul's dismay. Both the pilot and the series were produced by William Asher. The pilot was written by Sidney Sheldon. Sherry Alberoni Van Meter also told me, "I recall it being the first live audience TV show I did, and I really enjoyed the audience—their reactions and feedback."

The 1972–1973 ABC series had the Simms family living in Ocean Grove, California. Howie's parents appeared in several episodes. They were portrayed by the real-life couple of Jerry Stiller and Anne Meara (as Barney and Grace Dickerson, respectively). Every episode featured a put-upon Paul over-reacting to and wise-cracking about the latest dilemma to arise in the Simms home. Paul's wife greeted him after work each day with a double martini—his means of coping with the bizarre goings-on around him. He would often have more than one.

At the law office, Herb Voland played Paul's boss, J. J. McNish; James Gregory appeared in several episodes as T. R. Scott; and Allison McKay was Paul's receptionist, Alice.

A memorable line from the debut episode

called "Howie Comes Home to Roost," came when Martha asked her husband, Paul, "How goes the rat race?" Paul's response was, "The rats are winning." In the episode titled "No Nudes Is Good Nudes," in which Howie got a job in an all-nude musical production of *Oh, Bombay* (a take-off on *Oh, Calcutta*), Paul referred to all of those involved in the production as "nudie loonies," but he, too, became one of them by the end of the episode.

Many episodes featured great guest stars, such as Anson Williams as Jimmy in "Whiz Kid Sizzles as Quiz Fizzles"; Ray Walston and Charlotte Rae guested in "Meet Aunt Charlotte"; and Tom Bosley and Gordon Jump guest starred in "The Congressman's Son."

Writers included Ben Starr, Bernie Kahn, Lawrence Marks, Leo Rifkin, Phil Sharp, Barry Blitzer, and the teams of Ron Clark and Sam Bobrick, Ed Jurist and Stan Dreben, Bob Fisher and Arthur Marx, William Raynor and Myles Wilder, and Bob Carroll and Madelyn Davis (nee Pugh); and directors included William Asher, Bruce Bilson, Jack Donohue, Ernest Losso, George Tyne, Jerry London, Oscar Rudolph, and Coby Ruskin. Apparently, stiff competition on the other networks (*Adam-12* on NBC, and *The Carol Burnett Show* on CBS) was the undoing of this sitcom. Paul's other sitcom credits include *Stanley*, *Bewitched*, *The Munsters*, *The Pruitts of Southampton*, and *The New Temperature's Rising*. *The Paul Lynde Show* was briefly rerun on the short-lived Screen Gems Network.

Paul Sand in Friends and Lovers MTM Enterprises. CBS. Saturday nights 8:30. September 14, 1974–January 4, 1975. 15 color episodes were filmed before a live audience.

Paul Sand was an up-and-coming star. He won a Tony Award for *Paul Sills' Story Theater* on Broadway. He made numerous guest appearances on *The Carol Burnett Show*. He portrayed a lovestruck tax auditor named Robert on *The Mary Tyler Moore Show*. That got the attention of the powers-that-be at MTM and before long he had his own sitcom. Here he was Robert again—Robert Dreyfuss, the bass player for the prestigious Boston Symphony Orchestra. Robert, who had been living in Denver for the last three years, returned to Boston and auditioned for and immediately joined the symphony in the debut (he also reunited with his old girlfriend, Maggie Joplin, played by Lynn Lipton). Also in the orchestra was a young Steve Landesberg as Austrian violin player Fred Meyerbach; the orchestra's manager was Jack Riordan (Dick Wesson); and the sarcastic, overweight Mason Woodruff (Craig Richard Nelson).

Dour-faced Robert had trouble with the ladies, but fell head over heels in love very quickly. Robert's girl problems were fodder for lots of jokes from his sister-in-law, Janice Dreyfuss (Penny Marshall). Affection-starved Janice was married to Robert's older brother, the aggressive and very fit Charlie Dreyfuss (Michael Pataki). The two brothers were nothing alike. In the debut, Janice and Charlie's 3-year-old son, Brendan is alluded to, but not mentioned again in later episodes.

Several episodes had musical titles. For example, the debut episode (with guest star Henry Winkler as egotistical cellist Ronald De Laura) was titled "Getting to First Bass." Episode four was called "Fiddler in the House." One of the funniest episodes of this short-lived show (one of MTM's first ever canceled shows, along with *The Texas Wheelers*) was called "Maid in the Snow," which took place over the Thanksgiving holiday. Fred and his health nut girlfriend, Trudy (Karen Morrow), rented a cabin to go skiing. Morrow told me, "I ran into Steve Landesberg years later, and he called me 'Twudy,' with the same German accent of his character on the show. He was wonderful." In the episode, Janice tagged along with husband Charlie, hoping for some romantic "alone time" with him (but this never came to fruition). Also in tow was Robert, who became quite a burden because he had a bad cold and a bad back (from changing a tire). Since he was bedridden for the entire weekend, he required someone to babysit for him. That someone was Janice. While the others were out skiing, Janice and Robert were stuck indoors and just plain miserable. Morrow recalled that during some of the rehearsal downtime "Paul Sand and Penny Marshall played what they called 'theater games.' These were extremely creative improv games, and they got the guest stars involved, too. It was a lot of fun, and hard to keep up."

The program was produced by Steve Pritzker; the executive producers were Allan Burns and Jim Brooks; directors included Peter Bonerz, Bob Claver, Alan Rafkin, and Jay Sandrich; and writers included Linda Bloodworth-Thomason, Mary Kay Place, Mark Rothman, Lowell Ganz, Phil Mishkin, James L. Brooks, Burns, Bud Wiser, Elias Davis, and David Pollock. Pollock, who was also one of the story editors for this series, recalls, "Paul Sand used to insert the word 'really' into a lot of his dialogue, and it drove the script writers crazy." Pollock and his writing partner Elias Davis wrote the episode titled "From Russia with Lust." The show's classical-tinged theme song was provided by Pat Williams. Seiji Ozawa of the Boston Symphony Orchestra was a consultant for the show. A couple of episodes can be viewed at the Paley Center for Media.

Peck's Bad Girl Talent Associates. CBS. Tuesday nights 9:00. May 5, 1959–August 4, 1959. 13 black-and-white episodes were filmed with a laugh track. Sponsors included Pharmaceuticals, Incorporated (Geritol, Devarex, Serutan and Sominex).

Twelve-year-old Patty McCormack was already a star, having done *The Bad Seed* both on Broadway and on film (the latter of which garnered her a Best Supporting Actress Oscar and Golden Globe nominations) as the evil Rhoda Penmark. She made the leap to television in another "bad" role in *Peck's Bad Girl* during the spring and summer of 1959. However, in this role, she wasn't all that "bad"—Torey Peck was just a young lady teetering on the fence between being a tomboy and a young lady. Very loosely based upon the old George W. Peck stories and *Peck's Bad Boy* movies, which starred Jackie Cooper, Torey Peck opened and closed each episode (serving as narrator) with a "set-up" and a "wrap-up." The head of the middle-class Peck household was Steve Peck (Wendell Corey), a research physicist. His wife, Jennifer, was played by Marsha Hunt; Torey's seven-year-old brother, Roger, was played by Ray Ferrell; her girlfriends/schoolmates included Reba Waters as Francesca, Bernadette Withers as Trudy, and Trudy Ziskind as Lois.

Most episodes focused upon Torey and her girlfriends' adjustments to "that awkward age," and their discovery of and uncertainty about the opposite sex. One episode of this short-lived series is available for viewing at the UCLA TV Archives (called "Slumber Party"), in which Torey envisioned her dad, Steve Peck, on the cover of an upcoming *Life* magazine because of his work in physics. At a slumber party at the Peck house, Torey's girlfriends swooned over him and found him every bit as dreamy as their favorite movie actors—that is, until they saw him attempt to dance, at which time they discovered what a total square he really was.

The program was produced by Stanley Rubin; the executive producer was Norman Felton; writers included Shirl Gordon, William Danch, and Bill Manhoff; and directors included Don Taylor, Sherman Marks, John Rich, Arthur Hiller, and David Greene. Music was provided by Wilbur Hatch; the theme song was written by Jerry Goldsmith. Patty (sometimes called Patricia McCormack) would later go on to recurring roles in *The Ropers*, *Dallas*, and *The Sopranos*. She also made a few 45rpm records, including a song called "Bubble Gum" on the Dot Record label (Dot 15762) in 1956. Reruns of *Peck's Bad Girl* were aired during the summer of 1960 as a replacement for the canceled *Dennis O'Keefe Show*.

Peter Loves Mary Four Star/Mirisch/Mount Tom Productions. NBC. Wednesday nights 10:00. October 12, 1960–May 31, 1961. 32 black-and-white episodes were filmed with a laugh track. Sponsored by Procter and Gamble.

Entertainers and real-life husband and wife Peter Lind Hayes and Mary Healy took several stabs at TV fame and fortune, but they never quite clicked. There was a lot of singing and dancing and some comedy on *The Peter and Mary Show*, which morphed into *The Peter Lind Hayes Show* in TV's infancy. There was also a daytime variety show called *The Peter Lind Hayes Show* and another prime time show called *Star of the Family*. Years later, they tried again with this sitcom (1960), titled *Peter Loves Mary* at Four Star Studios. Here, they portrayed Peter and Mary Lindsey, married entertainers who decided to move to the country for a more sedate life. Actually, this was what Mary wanted—Peter loved the hubbub of the big city, but as the title suggests, *Peter Loves Mary*, so he went along with it. They settled in the Connecticut suburb of Oakdell at 927 Linwood Drive, along with their two children—towheaded Leslie (Merry Martin) and young Steve (Gil Smith). They had a housekeeper who moved with them named Wilma Cervanko, who was played by Bea Benederet. Coincidentally, while Bea was playing this character named Wilma, she was also supplying the voice of Betty Rubble who lived next door to a different Wilma on *The Flintstones*.

Episodes include "Wilma," in which the Lindseys were convinced that their friends, Bill and Claire Rogers (David Lewis and Joan Tompkins), were planning to steal away their extremely efficient housekeeper and terrific cook, but they were merely attempting to assist Wilma in replacing a treasured broken vase. In "A Star Is Born," Peter and Mary found out the hard way that talent wasn't necessarily passed down from generation to generation when their daughter, Leslie, was exposed as having none. In "The Classic Car," money which was supposed to have been used for a boat was instead invested into a rundown 1928 Dusenberg by Peter and neighbor Barry Watkins (Ronny Graham), much to the dismay of their wives.

The program was produced by Billy Friedberg; writers included Terry Ryan, David Schwartz, Friedberg, Norman Barasch, Carrol Moore, Mel Diamond, Mel Tolkin, Sam Locke, and Joel Rapp; and directors included Sidney Miller and Robert Butler. The program was briefly syndicated in recent years (along with numerous other Four Star Studios sitcoms) on the Performance Channel in the UK. Bea Benederet benefited greatly by the single season status of this program because she had *Petticoat Junction* awaiting her in the near future.

The Phyllis Diller Show (see *The Pruitts of Southampton*)

Pistols and Petticoats A Kayro-UTV Production/Universal City Studios. CBS. Saturday nights 8:30 (September 17, 1966–January 1967), and Saturday nights 9:30 (January 1967–August 19, 1967). 26 color episodes were filmed with a laugh track. Sponsors included Procter and Gamble and The American Tobacco Company.

Not to be confused with *Petticoat Junction*, also on CBS, this was the story of the Hanks family of Wretched, Colorado, in the 1870s. They were quite adept with weaponry, that is, with the exception of Henrietta's city-bred daughter, Lucy (played by Carole Wells in the series, but Chris Noel in the unaired pilot). The widow, Henrietta Hanks, was played by the actress nicknamed "the oomph girl" in the movies, Ann Sheridan (from such films as *Angels with Dirty Faces*). Her pistol-packing mom, Grandma Hanks, was played by Ruth McDevitt, and she was married to Andrew (Grandpa Hanks), played by Douglas V. Fowley (who couldn't see a thing without his glasses, let alone shoot straight). The Hanks family was so tough they even had a wolf named Bowser as a pet. Wretched had an inept, bumbling Sheriff named Harold Sikes, (Gary Vinson). He and Lucy Hanks were an item. Recurring roles included Pat Buttram as Jake Turner—the patriarch of an entire family of outlaws; Jay Silverheels was Great Bear; Alex Henteloff was Little Bear; Lon Chaney, Jr., was Chief Eagle Shadow; Robert Lowery was land owner Buss Courtney; and Marc Cavell was Gray Hawk.

The unaired pilot was later reworked and used as episode number eleven, titled "Quit Shootin' Folks, Grandma," in which the Hanks family attempted to put down an Indian uprising. In "The Golden Fleece," lifelong outlaw Jake Turner attempted to go straight, but his lawless family led him back into a life of crime and a scam involving phony gold mines. Sadly, the same night the episode titled "Beware the Hangman" aired, the show's star, Ann Sheridan died of cancer at the age of 51 on January 21, 1967. Despite her chronic illness, Sheridan appeared in almost all of the episodes, although she was often very weak and ill. Episodes were filmed very far in advance.

The program was created by George Tibbles; Joe Connelly was the producer; writers included Lois Hire, Tibbles, Marty Roth, Bill Kelsay, John Bradford, Suzanne Summers, Brad Thomas, Bud Freeman, George F. Slavin, Stanley Adams, and Paul West; and directors included Sidney Lanfield, Alan Rafkin, Connelly, Larry Dobkin, Leslie Goodwins, David Alexander, Joseph Pevney, Harry Harris, Earl Bellamy, Douglas Tibbles, and Ezra Stone. The theme song was written by Tibbles (lyrics) and Jack Elliott (music). Several episodes were edited together to make the 1967 TV movie called *The Far Out West*. A new color DVD set of 17 select episodes from the series are available from Euro Video/Mammut Home Entertainment in Germany as *Pistoles Und Petticoats* (however, they are overdubbed in German with no English subtitles).

Please Stand By Bob Banner Productions/Viacom. First-run Syndication. 1978. 27 episodes were videotaped at KTTV Studios.

The theme song began with the lyrics, "Please Stand By, while we change our direction. Say goodbye to the life that we've known. Leaving the city, taking a chance to do what we want to do, Please Stand By for something really new." This was the story of an oil executive in Los Angeles named Frank Lambert (Richard Schaal), who quit his job to chase the dream of running a TV station. The small, decrepit station was KRDA, Channel Four in De Queen, New Mexico, run out of a garage. Frank also had a wife named Carol (Elinor Donahue) and three children—daughter Susan (Darian Mathias); son Rocky (Bryan Scott); and son David (Stephen Michael Schwartz). Donahue told me, "Stephen Michael Schwartz is Richard Schaal's real-life son-in-law." The station was off the air more than it was on the air, thanks to its staff of misfits—Dennis "Crash" Lopez (Danny Mora); Vicky James (Marcie Barkin); and Sam (Gary Oakes).

Donahue recalled, "It was a time when I really needed a job, and it was a guaranteed 27 weeks of work. We did a pretty extensive promotional tour for the show, and while in New York, we were staying at the United Nations Plaza Hotel. That night, there was a rather severe storm with a lot of lightning and thunder, and my hotel room had these floor to ceiling windows through which I could see every lightning bolt. I was so scared, I went over to the hotel room that Richard Schaal was sharing with his girlfriend and asked if I could sleep there with them. Very generously, they both welcomed me in." Elinor had another amusing story about that tour: "While promoting the show, I did a fundraiser with Henry Winkler for KCET-TV. There was a cue card for Henry to read to introduce me. On the card, in big print was the title of our show, *Please Stand By*. Poor Henry thought that they were telling him to stop and thought the station was off the air, misunderstanding the cue card. There was a long, confused pause before I was introduced."

Episodes of note include one in which both Frank and Rocky needed to have their tonsils removed, but it was Frank who acted more like a child; in another episode, Frank and David attempted to install a second bathroom in the house.

Executive producers were Bob Banner and Ed Warren.

Popi ITP Allied Artists. CBS. Tuesday nights 8:30 (January 20, 1976–February 1976), and Tuesday nights 8:00 (July–August 24, 1976). Eleven episodes were filmed with a laugh track.

This sitcom about a widower with two sons replaced another sitcom about a widower with two sons (*Joe and Sons*). Neither was successful. Based upon the 1969 movie of the same name starring Alan Arkin and Rita Moreno, *Popi* was about a Puerto Rican immigrant (Hector Elizondo as Abraham Rodriguez) who took on three part-time jobs to make ends meet. He was a kindly, hard-working man who wanted nothing more than a better life for his two motherless boys—nine-year-old Junior (Anthony Perez) and younger brother Luis (Dennis Vasquez). In the pilot episode which aired May 2, 1975, Abraham's romantic interest (with marriage first and foremost in her thoughts) was neighbor Lupe played by Liz Torres (Edith Diaz in the series). Others in the cast included Angelo Maggio (Lou Criscuolo) and Mr. Diaz (Frank Lugo). Despite the opening theme song, "It's Gonna Be Terrific," the program fared so poorly in the ratings, it was pulled from the CBS lineup after only five episodes had aired. The remaining unaired episodes, and a couple of reruns aired during the summer of 1976 in a different time slot, but the ratings were still unimpressive.

Episodes include one in which Abraham attempted to keep his mischievous boys out of trouble by signing them up for the boy scouts; in another untitled episode, nine-year-old Junior came down with a bad case of puppy love and began making plans to marry his young sweetheart (Dominique Pinassi); and in yet another the boys found a stray Great Dane and brought him home to their tiny apartment where the dog wreaked havoc.

The program was created by Lester and Tina Pine; the executive producer was Herbert B. Leonard; writers included the Pines, Earl Barret, Arne Sultan, and Bill Taub; and directors included Bruce Bilson, Alfred Viola and Hy Averback.

Pride of the Family Sam Perrin Productions/Revue Studios/MCA, Hollywood. ABC. Friday nights 9:00. October 2, 1953–September 24, 1954. 39 black-and-white episodes were filmed with a laugh track. Sponsored by Bristol-Myers (Ipana Toothpaste, Bufferin, Dial Soap, and Dial Shampoo) and Armour.

Paul Hartman had previously starred in a seminal short-lived live TV sitcom called *The Hartmans* in 1949. He later portrayed Emmett Clark, the handyman on both *The Andy Griffith Show* and *Mayberry R.F.D.* In between, he starred as Albie Morrison, the head of advertising and classified ads on a small newspaper called *The Chronicle* in *Pride of the Family* (sometimes called *The Paul Hartman Show*)—more famous for its stars than for its success. Albie's wife Catherine was played by Fay Wray (of *King Kong* fame). They had two children—a teenage boy named Junior (Bobby Hyatt) and a teenage girl named Ann (Natalie Wood). Barbara Billingsley made one of her first TV appearances as Albie's childhood sweetheart in the episode titled "Albie's Old Flame."

Albie was the typical bumbling, fumbling TV dad (not unlike Chester A. Riley or Stu Erwin). He invariably had good intentions, but those intentions always seemed to go awry. In the debut, Ann needed $600 so that she could join her class on their graduation trip. Through a long series of misunderstandings and miscues, Ann and Catherine were led to believe that Albie had designs upon committing suicide for the insurance money so that Ann could go on that trip. In "Honest Albie," our star was put on the horns of a dilemma when he was called upon to judge a flower contest. Trouble ensued when the winning mums belonged to Catherine. In "Albie Helps the Lovelorn," a newlywed bride named Mrs. Martha Gilbert (Connie Marshall) placed an ad in *The Chronicle*'s classifieds in an attempt to get her husband (who walked out after their first spat) to come back home. Albie got himself in big trouble when the ad accidently ended up as the big story on the front page.

The characters on the program were created by Sam Perrin; writers included Fred Howard, Irving Phillips, Paul Schneider, Al Gordon, Jack Fleischmann, and Hal Goldman; and directors included Robert S. Finkel and Herschel Daugherty. Select episodes of this show were rerun on CBS in prime time during the summer of 1955. One episode exists in the Peabody Awards Collection, Athens, Georgia.

Professional Father McCadden Productions. CBS. Saturday nights 10:00. January 8, 1955–July 2, 1955. 18 black-and-white episodes were filmed before a live audience at General Service Studios. Sponsors included Helene Curtis Cosmetics, and Spray Net.

The most notable thing about this short-lived sitcom was its stars—almost everyone in the cast went on to bigger and better things. Pediatrician/child psychologist Dr. Thomas Wilson was played by Steve Dunne (who would also star in *The Brothers Brannagan*, host two game shows, *Double Exposure* and *You're On Your Own*, and serve as announcer for *What's This Song?*). Dr. Wilson's wife, Helen, was played by Barbara Billingsley (later Beaver's mom), who admitted years after this program was canceled that she was terrified of the live audience. Their neighbor was Fred Davis (Joseph Kearns, of *Dennis the Menace*); his wife, Nurse Madge Davis, was played by Phyllis Coates (*The Adventures of Superman*). The Wilsons' daughter was the clumsy Kathryn "Kit" Wilson (Beverly Washburn, later of *Old Yeller*). She also had a minor hit record called "Everybody Loves Saturday Night" on the Smash Record Label of Chicago (Smash number 1855). Also in the cast was Ted Marc as the Wilson's baseball-loving son, Thomas "Twig" Wilson. Jr. Washburn recalled, "Ted Marc and I became great friends, almost like a real brother and sister. We both had schooling for three hours each day on the first floor of CBS Television City. He really didn't enjoy acting, and after the show was canceled he did very little else on TV. He later became a very successful fencing instructor." Ann O'Neal was the Wilson's surly, wise-

Professional Father—**Top left to right Barbara Billingsley, Steve Dunne. Bottom row left to right Ted Marc, Beverly Washburn (photograph courtesy of Beverly Washburn).**

cracking housekeeper, Nana, and Arthur Q. Bryan was Mr. Boggs, the neighborhood handyman.

The premise for this show must have looked great on paper—a child psychologist who was very adept at the office, but very inept with his own children at home. However, the show failed to garner an audience, partly because of its time slot—10:00 on Saturday nights. It replaced another failed sitcom, *That's My Boy*. One of the few surviving episodes of *Professional Father* focused upon Dr. Wilson's futile attempts to go fishing with his neighbor, Fred Davis. A series of interruptions, including son Twig's on-again/off-again baseball game, put the kibosh on those plans. It should be noted that *Professional Father* and *Leave It to Beaver* have more than just Barbara Billingsley in common—Twig's baseball team was called "The Beavers," and both the Wilsons and the Cleavers had an Aunt Martha ("Aunt Martha Comes to Visit" aired April 9, 1955). Also, both sitcoms were on CBS.

The program was created by Harry Kronman and the executive producer was Ben Feiner. Directors included John Claar, James Sheldon, and Sherman Marks; and writers included Kronman and Jerry Adelman. Music was provided by Lud Gluskin and Paul Baron. The opening credits are, cleverly, shown on a doctor's prescription pad. Washburn fondly recalled two of the behind-the-scenes guys, "Director James Sheldon had his own clothing line, which we wore on the show. We got to keep the clothes, too. And the creator of the show, Harry Kronman, gave me a beautiful bracelet after the program was canceled. I still have it today." Beverly also remembered, "The program aired at 10 p.m. on Saturday nights—too late for a family show." In the February 26, 1955, edition of *TV Guide*, the program was reviewed this way: "*Professional Father*, starring Steve Dunne as a child psychologist who can't cope with his own children, is built on a promising program idea."

The Pruitts of Southampton/The Phyllis Diller Show A Phildil Production, Ltd./Filmways. ABC. Tuesday nights 9:00 (September 6, 1966–January 3, 1967, under the *Pruitts* title), and Friday nights 9:30 (January 13, 1967–September 1, 1967, as *The Phyllis Diller Show*). 30 color episodes were filmed with a laugh track (17 *Pruitts*, 13 *Diller*). Sponsors included L & M and Lark Cigarettes, Colgate Toothpaste, and Listerine.

Self-deprecating stand-up comedienne Phyllis Diller attempted sitcom stardom in this show which went through a few changes over its single season run. It was first known as *The Pruitts of Southampton*, and had a wonderful Vic Mizzy theme song which pretty well summed up the premise of the show: "The Pruitts of Southampton live like the richest folk, but what the folks don't know is that the Pruitts are flat broke." Phyllis Pruitt was a once-wealthy widow, but after an audit it was found that she owed the IRS ten million dollars. The IRS thought that if the word got out about the Pruitts, it would cause a stock market collapse, so the news was kept under wraps until the Pruitts could pay the money. However, there were some conditions—Phyllis had to close up 52 of the 60 rooms in the mansion and live in only eight, fire all of the staff (except for Sturgis, the butler, played by Grady Sutton), store her priceless art collection, get by on one automobile, and do all of her own cooking. It was a Horatio Alger story in reverse. Phyllis also had a pretty 22-year-old blonde daughter named Stephanie (Pam Freeman) and an elderly Uncle Ned (Reginald Gardiner) who had been in charge of Phyllis' finances until the audit—a responsibility then bestowed upon Mr. Fred Baldwin (Richard Deacon) of the IRS, who became a live-in financial accountant. Paul Lynde had a recurring role as Phyllis's talent scout brother, Harvey. After 17 weeks of that, the show moved to Friday nights retitled *The Phyllis Diller Show* (and gone was that wonderful Vic Mizzy theme song). There were even more changes—the mansion was turned into a boarding house to raise money to pay the IRS—and a couple of new characters were added: John Astin as Phyllis's inventor brother-in-law Rudolph Angus Pruitt and Marty Ingels as Norman Krump, the neighborhood handyman. Astin and Ingels had formerly been paired on *I'm Dickens, He's Fenster*.

Episodes include the debut called "Phyllis Goes Broke" which included a bevy of expository information, and "Phyllis, Queen of the Road," in which Phyllis used cunning to get an advance from the IRS by befriending a group of local hobos. Fearing media coverage and its impact on the stock market, Mr. Baldwin and his boss, Mr. Maxwell (Charles Lane), acquiesced. Under the new title, *The Phyllis Diller Show*, episodes include "My Sister-In-Law, Phyllis," in which Rudy Pruitt attempted to make a deal with the IRS to put up money to finance his amazing "pizza-making machine."

The program was created by David Levy.

***The Pruitts of Southampton*—Phyllis Diller makes a mess of things in the kitchen (photograph courtesy of Fred Wostbrock).**

Levy also served as executive producer; writers included Lawrence J. Cohen, Fred Freeman, Ray Kammerman, Sid Mandel, Lou Derman, Elon Packard, and Joseph and Carol Cavella; and directors included Nat Perrin, Hollingsworth Morse, Gene Nelson, Oscar Rudolph, and Ralph Levy. The *Pruitt's* theme song was performed by Phyllis Diller. The show was loosely based upon the novel *House Party* by Patrick Dennis. Diller would again attempt TV success and fail in the short-lived variety series called *The Beautiful Phyllis Diller Show*. Numerous episodes of *The Pruitts of Southampton* can be viewed in the UCLA TV Archives. Phyllis Diller died on August 20, 2012, at the age of 95.

Quark David Gerber Productions/Columbia Pictures Television. NBC. Friday nights 8:00. February 24, 1978–April 14, 1978. Eight episodes were filmed with a laugh track at The Burbank Studios. Sponsors included General Foods.

Not many sitcoms of this era begin with the letter "Q"—*The Queen and I* and *Quark*. The latter was created by David Gerber and Buck Henry as a parody of space adventure epics (*Star Wars*). In physics, a quark is a specific kind of charged particle, but in this sitcom set in the year 2222, *Quark* was Adam Quark (Dick Benjamin), commander of Perma One, a gigantic space station which collected space garbage—quote, "garbage, the final frontier." The UGSP (United Galaxy Sanitation Patrol) also became involved in many intergalactic adventures, as well as battles with the evil Gorgons. All orders came from "The Head" (Alan Caillou) who governed the entire universe and was only seen on a TV screen (sans body). He was usually thinking because, being just a head, "he wasn't very good at athletics." Next in the chain of command was Palindrome (Conrad Janis), the fastidious chief architect of Perma One (Quark's boss). The first officer was one of the more colorful characters, a transmute named Gene/Jean (Tim Thomerson)

Quark—Denny Miller as "Zoltar" (photograph courtesy of Denny Miller).

who had both male and female traits. He would be threatening to throw punches one moment, and then showing off his latest needlepoint in the next. The science officer was the deadpan, emotionless Ficus (Richard Kelton) who was a vegeton—a humanoid vegetable who required the proper amount of moisture or his middle would turn brown. The co-pilots and second in command were Betty 1 and Betty 2 (buxom identical blonde twins Tricia and Cyb Barnstable), one of whom was the clone of the other, but no one was certain which. Douglas V. Fowley portrayed the eyepatch-wearing chemist O. B. Mudd who lost sight in one eye after a microscope incident. Mudd was the creator of the "Cervo Mechanical Android" better known as Andy, the cowardly robot (Bobby Porter), who was little more than a walking junk pile. Mudd was gone after the pilot episode, but Andy remained a regular member of the dysfunctional crew. Also gone after the pilot, was Quark's pet pile of sometimes vicious and always hungry ectoplasm named Ergo.

Episodes include "The Good, the Bad and the Ficus," in which, after traveling through a black hole, a ship with the entire crew's identical but evil opposites was created. The "Good Quark" was then drawn into a fight to the death with the "Evil Quark." In "Goodbye Polumbus," Denny Miller guest starred as Zoltar. Denny told me, "I don't remember very much about it except that I was a superhero and wore a huge Z on my chest." There was also a two-part episode titled "All the Emperor's Quasi-Norms." The director of that two-part episode, Bruce Bilson, told me, "Right before we started filming the episodes I noticed that one of the Barnstable twins had put on a few pounds. They were supposed to be identical, so I told her about it. She cried and cried, but in very quick order, she dropped those extra pounds." The executive producer was David Gerber; writers included Stuart Gillard, Buck Henry, Steve Zacharias, Bruce Kane, Jonathan Kaufer, and Robert Keats; and directors included Bruce Bilson, Hy Averback, and Peter H. Hunt. Music was provided by Perry Botkin, Jr. Reruns were briefly shown on the HA! cable channel. Only months after cancellation, Conrad Janis surfaced in yet another sci-fi sitcom, *Mork and Mindy*.

The Queen and I Bing Crosby Productions/Paramount Studios. CBS. Thursday nights 7:30. January 16, 1969–May 1, 1969. 13 color episodes were filmed with a laugh track.

The Queen and I was a midseason replacement for *Blondie* on CBS on Thursday nights, and after 13 weeks, it too needed a replacement. This was the story of a decrepit, aging ocean liner known as the *Amsterdam Queen*. Its owners were considering retirement and pondered putting the ship permanently "out to sea" (they had even considered selling it for scrap). This news was immensely upsetting to the ship's purser, the opportunistic Charles Duffy (Larry Storch), who very badly wanted to keep his job. Duffy proved very resourceful in his attempts to keep the business and the ship afloat by holding private parties, weddings, and bar mitzvahs when in port. He also wasn't above encouraging the passengers to leave bigger tips. The crew was definitely on Duffy's side and supported his efforts, with one exception—First Officer Oliver W. Nelson (the flamboyant Billy DeWolfe), who made very conscious attempts to get Duffy fired. Director Bruce Bilson told me, "Billy DeWolfe was great, but he was never called Billy—it was always Mr. DeWolfe." Also in the cast were Carl Ballantine as the steward named Seaman Becker; Pat Morita was Barney the cook; Dave Willock was radioman Ozzie; Barbara Stuart was Wilma the nurse; Liam Dunn was Captain Washburn; Dave Morick was Max Kowalski; and Reginald Owen was the ship's owner, Commodore "Doodles" Dodds.

In the debut titled "Duffy's Cruise," Duffy and the crew got some much needed business

***The Queen and I*—Larry Storch as Purser Charles Duffy (CBS).**

when a distress call from a marooned ship near Bermuda meant lots of new passengers for the *Amsterdam Queen*. In "The Promotion," Duffy tried to secure a promotion for his nemesis, First Officer Nelson, so that he would leave the ship and get off his back once and for all—but his concerted efforts fell short. In "My Karate Lies over the Ocean," Duffy attempted to boost Barney the cook's confidence in a martial arts competition in which his black belt opponent was to take a dive. Barney's victory, however, went right to his head.

The program was created by Howard Leeds; the producer was Edward Feldman; writers included Laurence Marks, and Arthur Julian; directors included Feldman and Bruce Bilson. Music was provided by Jerry Fielding. The debut episode of *The Queen and I* can be viewed at the UCLA TV Archives. Coincidentally, *The Queen and I* left the prime time schedule on May 1, 1969 (May Day).

Rango Spelling/Thomas Productions/Desilu. ABC. Friday nights 9:00. January 13, 1967–September 1, 1967. 17 color episodes were filmed with a laugh track. Sponsors included Crest Toothpaste and Alka-Seltzer.

This sitcom replaced the second half of the canceled *Hondo* on Friday nights on ABC and was sold to the network without a pilot. Tim Conway previously had a four-year run in *McHale's Navy*, but finding success in a starring role proved elusive. This was the story of a clumsy, bumbling, inept Texas Ranger who somehow still managed to come out on top at the end of each episode. Even though it was rarely mentioned, his full name was Rango Starr—an obvious parody of the Beatles' legendary drummer, Ringo Starr. Rango's father was head of the Texas Rangers and thus he placed his son at the Deep Wells Ranger Station (Company "B") because it was a quiet post, and it was thought Rango wouldn't cause much trouble there. Rango's father guessed wrong. Rango's harried immediate commanding officer, Captain Horton (Norman Alden), kept trying to keep Rango out of the crime-solving loop, but somehow he always got wind of the goings-on, and invariably fouled things up (at least initially), until some lucky turn of events near the end went his way. Rango's partner in crime-solving was a Native American named Pink Cloud (Guy Marks). Pink Cloud was an Indian scout, but actually much preferred the white man's world to his own.

Episodes include "The Spy Who Was Out Cold," in which Rango mistook a Secret Service man for a gun-runner, and sided with the actual criminals, only to stumble upon a secret room which housed the real criminals' guns. In "Diamonds Look Better around Your Neck than a Rope," Rango thought the real jewel thief was the loan officer, but upon accusing him of the crime got his guilty daughter to confess. One episode ventured across the border; in "In a Little Spanish Town" Rango and Pink Cloud were seeking El Diablo in El Rita. Through a bizarre chain of events, the heavy-drinking El Diablo ended up in the back of Rango's truck, and no one was more surprised than Rango himself.

The program was created by Harvey Bullock and R.S. Allen; the producer was Aaron Spelling; the executive producer was Danny Thomas; writers included Frank Gill, Jr., G. Carleton Brown, Scott Anderson, Herbert Finn, Ray Singer, Alan Dinehart, Allen, and Bullock; and directors included Murray Golden and Sidney Lanfield. Music was provided by Carl Brandt, and the theme song was written by Earle Hagen and Ben Raleigh (and performed by Frankie Laine, who also did the theme for *Rawhide*). Tim Conway wouldn't fare much better in his other starring roles in *The Tim Conway Comedy Hour*, *Turn On*, or *The Tim Conway Show*, but his later work as a regular on *The Carol Burnett Show* made him famous. Episodes of *Rango* can be viewed in the UCLA TV Archives.

The Red Hand Gang A D'Angelo/Bullock/Allen Production. NBC. Saturday mornings. September 10, 1977–January 21, 1978. 12 episodes were filmed without a laugh track.

This was a live action Saturday morning sitcom/adventure series which focused upon five "kid detectives." Frankie (Matthew Laborteaux) was the leader as well as the eldest; J. R. (J. R. Miller) was the athlete of the group; Joanne (Jolie Newman) was a dedicated tomboy; Doc (James Bond III) was African American and the scholar of the bunch; and Li'l Bill (Johnny Brogna) was Frankie's little brother. The gang also had a dog named Boomer, who would later have his own NBC series called, appropriately, *Here's Boomer*. Each episode of *The Red Hand Gang* employed a real throwback to an earlier era—a cliffhanger.

Episode titles include "The Mystery Boat," "The Face at the Window," "Doc's Big Idea," "Monkey Business," and "Devil's Canyon." Guest stars included Van Williams (as NFL star O.K.

Okens). As kidnappers in five consecutive episodes, Maureen Arthur was Lola, Anthony Zerbe was Marco, and James Hampton was Tasker (usually called "Meathead"). Hampton told me, "Director Charles Rondeau, with whom I worked on *F Troop*, recommended me for the show. If I remember correctly, a lot of the people involved with *Love, American Style* were involved in *The Red Hand Gang*." William P. D'Angelo had indeed produced the first two seasons of *Love, American Style*. Hampton also said, "What a great bunch of kids, but I think Boomer enjoyed doing the show the most, because all he had to do was play, get petted by the cast and crew, and gobble dog treats all day. What a life!"

The executive producers were William P. D'Angelo, Harvey Bullock and Ray Allen; writers included Bullock, R. S. Allen, and Ray Irvings; and the director was Charles Rondeau. Music was provided by Score Productions, Incorporated (including the catchy "La La" theme song). It was never explained, but for some reason Frankie played an odd musical instrument called an ocarina in every episode (resembling "The Pied Piper of Hamlin"). The series is available on DVD from Fabulous Films in the UK.

Roll Out 20th Century–Fox. CBS. Friday nights 8:30. June 5, 1973 (pilot), October 5, 1973–January 4, 1974 (series). 13 color episodes (counting the pilot) were filmed with a laugh track.

The same guys who gave us *M*A*S*H*, gave us this period piece set in France during World War II. Based upon stories of an actual World War II transport unit, this show's focus was the exploits and hijinks of the 5050th Quartermaster Trucking Company of the U.S. Army's Red Ball Express—a mostly African American company which delivered supplies to the front lines. Military discipline and ethics were not always an option. Each truck had a name emblazoned on its side—Ella, Lady Day, Brown Bomber, A-Train, and Hard Way. The latter belonged to World War II's equivalent of Hawkeye and Trapper John, Corporal Carter "Sweet" Williams (Stu Gilliam) and the much more timid and sensible Private Jed Brooks (Hilly Hicks), who were the unit's best drivers. Their sergeant was B.J. Bryant (Richard Ward in the pilot, and Mel Stewart in the series, who called people "double clutchers" when angry), their lieutenant was Robert Chapman (a young Ed Begley, Jr.), who wanted to be a novelist, and their captain was Rocco Calvelli (Val Bisoglio), who loved opera music . When the boys needed an escape, they would visit a seedy place owned by Madame Delacort (Fifi D'Orsay in the pilot, Penny Santon in the series). Each of the remaining members of the unit had great nicknames, such as "Phone Booth," "Sgt. Grease," "High Strung," "Jersey," and "Wheels." The latter was portrayed by Garrett Morris, who would later go on to *Saturday Night Live* and *Two Broke Girls*.

Episodes include "Sweet Millions," in which Sweet and Jed found a sack in a tree filled with hundred dollar bills. Sweet and Jed's vastly different lifestyles mushroomed into a big fight in the episode titled "No Wages—All Fear." They were also able to sneak in a Christmas episode titled "Christmas Time '44" just a couple of weeks before cancellation.

The program was created by Gene Reynolds and Larry Gelbart; Reynolds was also producer; and directors included Reynolds, Robert Butler, and Bruce Bilson. Bilson told me, "I really thought this was a winner. I was rather surprised when the show didn't catch on." Writers included Gelbart and Rick Mittleman.

Roller Girls The Komack Company. NBC. Monday nights 8:00 (April 24, 1978–May 1, 1978), and Wednesday nights 8:00 (May 3, 1978–May 10, 1978). 4 episodes were videotaped before a live audience.

James Komack was a very successful TV producer, but this was not his biggest success story. It was, however, a lot of fun. *Roller Girls* revolved around the cutthroat world of women's Roller Derby, and a fledgling expansion team known as the Pittsburgh Pitts. The owner of the team, Don Mitchell (Terry Kiser), did almost anything to succeed, get on a winning streak, and get out of paying his bills. The episode titled "Roller Girls," flashed back to the team's first day together. On the team, there was a very tall country girl named Mongo Sue Lampbert (Rhonda Bates); an erudition named Selma "Books" Cassidy (Joanna Cassidy) who was the arch enemy of teammate Lampbert (they were always getting into scrapes in the locker room); a feisty, no-nonsense African American player named J.B. Johnson (Candy Ann Brown); a newcomer to roller derby, a dizzy blonde (to whom manager Don was attracted) named Honey Bee Novak (Marcy Hanson); and a wise-cracking Japanese-/Eskimo-American named Shana "Pipeline" Akira (Marilyn Tokuda). Tokuda recalled, "I got word of the audition at the last possible minute. Physically, I was bursting with energy having just

Roller Girls—Left to right rear—Marcy Hanson, James Murtaugh, Terry Kiser, Rhonda Bates, Joanna Cassidy. Left to right front—Marilyn Tokuda and Candy Ann Brown (photograph courtesy of Marilyn Tokuda).

worked out at the gym; I showed up in workout clothes, which was great because I looked athletic—like someone who could potentially be a member of a roller derby team. Jimmy Komack instantly took a liking to me—something about a mischievous, puckish quality. In his lingo, I 'was always peering around corners.' I went back for several more auditions, about five callbacks, a screen test, and got the part. It was a very exciting new challenge. I had previously worked as a back-up singer and dancer in Las Vegas with Mac Davis and Connie Stevens. When I won the role of Pipeline, I gave my notice that I was leaving Mac, not because I hated my work; Mac was great to work for ... I just had to make a decision that I wanted to break out of being back-up for someone else and establish myself as an actor, I had to move on. It would have been crazy for me not to take the opportunity to become a regular in a series. Komack was a great guy—a wonderful, creative, robust ball of energy. I was grateful to him for creating an Asian-American character; I had played my share of stereotypical roles, and here was this energetic, fun character who didn't have an accent. It was refreshing and wonderful." The snobby, out-of-place announcer (he had formerly been an FM radio opera commentator) Howie Devine was played by James Murtaugh. Marilyn Tokuda told me, "James Murtaugh was extremely funny and witty. He had a very dry sense of humor." Marilyn also remembers Candy Ann Brown, with whom she has remained friends to this day: "Candy was amazing. I remember being so impressed when I found out that she had worked with Michael Bennett. In fact, one of the characters (Richie) in the long-running Broadway musical, *A Chorus Line*, was based on Candy's story." Marilyn also revealed that "we girls trained with the Los Angeles Thunderbirds. I did my own skating, and the teams we played against on the show were real roller derby participants." In reality, Marilyn is Asian-American and not part Eskimo, but on the show she was often seen donning a Save the Whales t-shirt, and, as she remembered, "I had a hook. I would often quote humorous, somewhat corny sayings from my old Alaskan grandfather."

Manager Don had promised the girls that they'd all be living in a beautiful condominium with a pool and a tennis court. When this didn't come to fruition, his excuse was that the condo wasn't yet ready because the construction crew had run out of wood. The girls had to "temporarily" take up residence in the back of their locker room. Don also didn't have the money to cover their first paychecks, so he cooked up a scheme involving the adoption of orphans so that the girls wouldn't think he was a total creep, walk out, and turn their backs on the team.

The program was created by James Komack (who also served as executive producer); the producers were Stan Cutler, George Tricker, and Neil Rosen; writers included Tricker, Neil Rosen, Gary Belkin, and Cutler; and directors included Komack, Burt Brinckerhoff, and Gary Shimokawa.

Room for One More Warner Brothers Studios. ABC. Saturday nights 8:00. January 27, 1962–September 22, 1962. 26 black-and-white episodes were filmed with a laugh track. Sponsors included Armour and Company and Block Drug Company.

Room for One More was a mid-season replacement for *The Roaring Twenties*, but it instantly faced tough competition from *Perry Mason* on CBS and from *Tales of Wells Fargo* on NBC. This was the story of the Rose family of Los Angeles. The patriarch of the bunch was engineer George Rose (Andrew Duggan); his wife was Anna (Peggy McCay); their two natural children were nine-year-old Flip (Ronnie Dapo) and ten-year-old Laurie (Carol Nicholson); and their two adopted children were 14-year-old Jeff (Timmy Rooney, Mickey's real-life son) and 16-year-old Mary (Anna Carri). However, as the show's title suggested, there was always "room for one more," and a vast array of young waifs had temporary stays in the warm and loving Rose residence. They also had a mutt named Tramp who is not to be confused with the Tramp who lived with the Douglas family on *My Three Sons*, also on ABC. The program was loosely based upon the autobiography of Anna Perrott Rose, and the 1952 Cary Grant movie, originally titled *Room for One More*, but later renamed *The Easy Way*.

Episodes include "A New Twist," in which George twisted an ankle tripping over one of the kids' toys. The incident, however, came at a very opportune time, as George was attempting to get out of taking Anna to a Saturday night dance, and he milked the injury for all it was worth. In "Bonjour, Rose Family," a visiting French boy named Marcel (Michel Petit) rubbed the other Rose children the wrong way because of his good manners and constant offers to help with household chores. In "A Trip to the Beach," it never failed; every time George attempted a vacation away from the children, something went wrong, and this time was no exception, as Aunt Harriet backed out of her babysitting offer at the last minute because of a washed out bridge.

The program was produced by Ed Jurist; the executive producer was William T. Orr; writers included Bob O'Brien, Phil Sharp, Henry Sharp, Lawrence Marks, Sam Locke, Michael Fessier, Mel Tolkin, Leo Rifkin, Michael Morris, Arnold Horwitt, Milt Rosen, Jerry Davis, Iz Elinson, Larry Rhine, Milton Pascal, and Leo Solomon; and directors included Leslie Martinson, Andrew McCullough, Gene Reynolds, Marc Lawrence, Charles R. Rondeau, Norman Tokar, and Seymour Robbie. The theme song was written by Mack David and Jerry Livingston. Andrew Duggan went on to co-star in *Twelve O'Clock High*, *Lancer* and *Rich Man, Poor Man* and Peggy McCay had a long run in *Days of Our Lives*. A few episodes can be viewed in the UCLA TV Archives.

The Rounders MGM Studios. ABC. Tuesday nights 8:30. September 6, 1966–January 3, 1967. 17 color episodes were filmed without a laugh track. Sponsors included R. J. Reynolds Tobacco.

The Rounders was originally a novel by Max Evans. Then, in 1965, it was a comedy Western motion picture starring Chill Wills, Glenn Ford, Henry Fonda, and Sue Ane Langdon. *The Rounders* was then adapted for TV by Marion Hargrove in the fall of 1966. This was the story of two wild, crazy, skirt-chasing cowboys—Ben Jones (Ron Hayes) and Howdy Lewis (Patrick Wayne, John's son) who were deep in debt to their boss, the crafty Jim Ed Love (Chill Wills reprising his role), the owner of a vast expanse of ranch land (The J. L. Ranch) in Texas. Jim Ed also owned an oil well he affectionately called "Hazel." Jim Ed, the second richest man in Texas, was always dressed in white suits and drove a pimped station wagon. Meanwhile, his two ranch hands got around the range on a moody old roan horse named "Old Fooler." After a hard day on the job, Ben and Howdy would usually head over to the nearby town of Hi-Lo and spend all of their pay on wine, women and song at the Longhorn Café. The boys had girlfriends (Ben had Ada played by Bobbi Jordan, and Howdy had Sally played by Janis Hansen), but neither cowpoke was ready to settle down anytime soon. Also in the cast on a recurring basis were Jay Silverheels as *Wall Street Journal* subscriber/Native American John Tallgrass; Andy Devine as the richest man in Texas, Honest John Denton; and J. Pat O'Malley as Vince, Jim Ed's right hand man.

Episodes include "Don't Buffalo Me," in which John Tallgrass agreed to give an important connecting piece of land to Jim Ed Love if a buffalo hunt could be arranged for him. Opportunists Ben and Howdy located a buffalo, purchased it, and were poised to make a tidy profit on the resale to Jim Ed—that is, until the buffalo ran away. In "Man of the Year," Jim Ed Love attempted to drastically change his image in order to win the Texas Man of the Year award. The personality overhaul soon became a larger task than that of Eliza Doolittle in *My Fair Lady*. In "Efficiency Is for the Experts," Jim Ed hired a no nonsense efficiency expert named Laura Jean Layton (Melodie Johnson) to get the two lazy cowpokes to complete their chores on time.

The program was produced by Ed Adamson and Burt Kennedy; writers included Adamson, Teddi Sherman, Judith Plowden, Milton Gelman, Marion Hargrove, and Norman Lessing; and directors included Kennedy, Hollingsworth Morse, Alexander Singer, Allen Reisner, and Tom Gries. Music was provided by Lyn Murray, and the theme song was by Jeff Alexander. Up against the still-popular *Red Skelton Show* on CBS on Tuesday nights, *The Rounders* disappeared from the ABC prime time schedule very early in 1967. The program was rerun briefly on Ted Turner's TNT cable channel several years ago when Turner acquired the MGM TV library.

Run, Buddy, Run Talent Associates. CBS. Monday nights 8:00. September 12, 1966–January 2, 1967. 16 color episodes were filmed with a laugh track. Sponsors included Procter and Gamble, Menley and James, and Ralston Purina.

In between his other two single season sitcoms (*The Cara Williams Show* and *The Girl with Something Extra*), Jack Sheldon starred in *Run, Buddy, Run* and one can plainly see in the opening credits that Buddy did indeed do a lot of running. Twenty-eight-year-old Buddy Overstreet, a bookkeeper, was in a steam bath and overheard the syndicate's plan to kill some guy named "Renty," and another named "MacGregor." Buddy was also privy to their nefarious project known as "Chicken Little." Buddy was unable to escape the steam bath without being seen, and from that point on, Buddy was on the run. Buddy contacted his brother, Albert (who lived at 122

Mapleton Road on Long Island with his wife, Ruth), played by Bernie Kopell, but that proved to be a poor decision because Albert unwittingly led the hoods directly to Buddy. He was running from the men of Devere Enterprises, headed by its chieftain, Mr. D., played by Bruce Gordon. Mr. D. frequently took advantage of his closed circuit TV system (a camera built into the wall of his office which sent his reports to members of the organization in all 50 states, and beyond). Through this system, he was kept apprised of the whereabouts of one Buddy Overstreet. The mantra uttered by Mr. D. on that camera in each episode was "Get him." He'd also frequently mention that Buddy Overstreet was "wanted dead or dead." Mr. D. had a nerdy son named Junior (Jim Connell), who was always trying to impress his dad but continually fell short. Mr. D. also had a couple of henchmen who were huge disappointments—Wendell Krimm (Nick Georgiade) and Harry (Gregg Palmer).

Buddy described himself as an "unemployed jack-of-all-trades"—a most apt description, as he managed to elude the underworld while taking on jobs as Texaco gas station attendant Horace Powers (in the debut, "Steam Bath and Chicken Little"); horse groomer and jockey Buster Watts (in "Win, Place and Die"); a soda jerk (in "Buddy, the Lifesaver"); a worker in a health spa (in "Killer Cassidy"); a hotel worker (in "Grand Mexican Hotel"); a nightclub waiter (in "My Son, the Killer"); and a professional boxer (in "I Want a Piece of That Boy"). The powers-that-be at *Run, Buddy, Run* were aware of the upcoming cancellation and brought some closure in the episode titled "Buddy Overstreet, Please Forgive Me," in which Mr. D. developed a terminal illness and a change of heart—he welcomed Buddy to join the syndicate. In the episode titled "Buddy Overstreet, Please Come Home," Jackie Joseph portrayed Mr. D.'s receptionist Miss Ogelthorpe. She described Jack Sheldon as "sweet and dear." Jackie also told me, "Jack's mom taught my baby girl to swim—she was a professional teacher."

The program was produced by Jack Elinson, Dan Melnick, and Leonard Stern; the creator was Stern; the executive producer was David Susskind; writers included Mel Tolkin, Ernie Chambers, William Raynor, Myles Wilder, Budd Grossman, Bill Freedman, and Ben Gershman; and directors included Stern, Bruce Bilson, Gene Reynolds, Jack Arnold, Gary Nelson, and Joshua Shelley. Music was provided by Jerry Fielding, and the theme song was written by Frank Wedlaw. There was one *Run, Buddy, Run* comic book released by Dell in the fall of 1966—it sold for twelve cents. Jack Sheldon also had a successful career in music—he played trumpet on *The Merv Griffin Show* and also sang several of the memorable *Schoolhouse Rock* episodes. Jack also got to sing and play in the *Run, Buddy, Run* episodes titled "Grand Mexican Hotel," and "My Son, the Killer." TV Land reran a couple of episodes.

Sally A Caulross Production/Paramount Television. NBC. Sunday nights 7:30. September 15, 1957–March 30, 1958. Approximately 26 episodes were filmed with a laugh track. Sponsors included The Chemstrand Corporation and Royal McBee Typewriters.

The program's two stars had previously starred in live sitcoms—Joan Caulfield (as Sally Truesdale) had been Liz Cooper on *My Favorite Husband*, and Marion Lorne (as Myrtle Banford) had been Mrs. Gurney on *Mr. Peepers*. This series called *Sally* was filmed, however, and in fact was the first filmed TV series for Paramount Television. *Sally* had two formats. Initially, eligible bachelorette Sally Truesdale had left her job as a department store clerk to accompany the daft wealthy widow, Myrtle Banford, on a trip around the world. After that premise ran dry, Sally and Myrtle were suddenly back home, working at the Banford and Bleacher Department Store. Several new cast members were added for format two: Gale Gordon as Bascomb Bleacher, Sr. (part owner of the store); a young Arte Johnson as his incompetent son Bascomb, Jr.; and singer Johnny Desmond as Jim Kendall from the advertising department who became Sally's boyfriend.

Several episodes can be viewed at the UCLA TV Archives. From the first format, an episode of note is "To Myrtle, with Love," in which Sally got Myrtle a most unusual birthday gift—a gigolo named Msr. Coucheau (Frances Lederer) from an escort service. Myrtle and Coucheau became quite an item (Myrtle called him her little "poopshin"), but Sally found out later that Coucheau really had designs on her. From the second format, in an episode titled "The Cosmetician," Sally and Myrtle created a special facial crème made out of plums (called Plum De Vie, meaning Plum of Life). The product sold like hotcakes, but there was one problem—the product didn't work and a long line of ladies demanded their money back. In "Sally, the

Love Doctor," Bascomb, Jr., fell in love with Sally. The love, however, was unrequited and Sally then devised a plan have him meet the pretty new girl at the glove counter (Carol Nugent).

The program was produced by Frank Ross (the Ross in Caulross Productions); writers included Bob O'Brien, Irving Elinson, Alan Lipscott, Robert Fisher, and Philip Shuken; and the director was William Asher. It's interesting to note that at the end of each episode, Sally gave us a preview of the next week's show. The music played during that preview was identical to the opening theme for *The Donna Reed Show*'s first season, which wouldn't debut until the fall of 1958, long after *Sally* had been canceled.

The Sandy Duncan Show Jefferson-Sultan Productions/Paramount Studios. CBS. Sunday nights 8:30. September 17, 1972–December 31, 1972. 13 color episodes were filmed before a live audience. Sponsors included Lever Brothers and Pepsodent Toothpaste.

Nine months after her emergency eye surgery, Sandy Duncan was back as Sandy Stockton in a brand new eponymous Paramount sitcom. So much had changed from the successful but short-lived *Funny Face* (except the theme song). The new program was filmed before a live audience, and Sandy was now a student teacher at UCLA (no longer a student studying to be a school teacher). She was also a part-time secretary at the Quinn and Cohen Advertising Agency (she would occasionally get work in TV commercials through the agency, too). Her boss, Bert Quinn, was played by Tom Bosley. Hilary, the scatter-brained receptionist, was played by Pamela Zarit. Sandy now had a new apartment (2A) in a different apartment building. She also had a new set of friends, including Kay Fox played by Marian Mercer, and motorcycle cop/aspiring author Alex Lembeck (M. Emmet Walsh).

In the episode titled "Write On," Alex finished a novel about motorcycle cops on which he'd been working for a year. Even though Sandy and Kay secretly thought it was one of the worst things they'd ever read, a Hollywood producer wanted to make it into a movie—a comedy. The problem was that Alex had written it as a drama. In "Richer the Third," Sandy had a very wealthy secret admirer (Richard Hardington III, played by Keith Charles) who kept sending her lavish gifts after seeing her in a waterbed commercial and instantly falling in love. A whirlwind romance developed, followed by a very quick marriage proposal, which Sandy reluctantly declined.

This new Sandy Duncan program was developed by Arne Sultan and Earl Barret; the producer was Barret; writers included Lawrence Marks, Albert E. Lewin, Sultan, and Barret; and directors included Jack Donohue and Dan Dailey. Without the cushion of being sandwiched between *All In The Family* and *The New Dick Van Dyke Show* (which *Funny Face* had), this show failed to garner an audience and disappeared after 13 episodes. Duncan later took the reins of *The Hogan Family*, after Valerie Harper was let go (then known as *Valerie*) and would become a regular fixture in a series of commercials for Wheat Thins crackers. Episodes can be viewed in the UCLA TV Archives.

The Sanford Arms Tandem Productions/Toy Productions. NBC. Friday nights 8:00. September 16, 1977–October 14, 1977. Seven episodes were videotaped before a live audience at KTLA Studios, only four aired.

In season five of *Sanford and Son* there was an episode titled "The Sanford Arms," (October 3, 1975) in which Fred and Lamont Sanford became landlords of an apartment complex. Two years later, that became the title of a series (after Redd Foxx left for an ABC variety series, and Demond Wilson left because of a salary dispute). In the new series, *The Sanford Arms*, we were told that Fred and Lamont had moved to Arizona (because of Fred's arthritis). The new owner, a widower named Phil Wheeler (Theodore Wilson), was an old army buddy of Fred's, and he tried to make the Sanford place into a successful hotel. Wheeler had an arrest record for punching a policeman who used a racial slur. He did have some hungry mouths to feed—his 19-year-old daughter Angie (Tina Andrews) who worked as a cocktail waitress at a seedy bar called The Foxey Fox; and a bright 12-year-old wisecracking son named Nat (John Earl). Phil had a lovely girlfriend named Jeannie (Bebe Drake-Hooks), who was none too pleased that she got less attention than the hotel. Some of the *Sanford and Son* regulars were on board, too—Bubba Hoover (Don Bexley) was now the bellboy and maintenance man, and Aunt Esther Anderson (La Wanda Page) was in charge of collecting the mortgage money (Phil owed the Sanfords $20,000 and Esther was unyielding in her pursuit of that money). In the debut episode, "Goodbye Fred, Hello Phil," Grady Wilson (Whitman Mayo) was unaware that Fred and Lamont had moved. Grady was back because his daughter, his son-in-law and two grandchildren (all from his *Grady* spinoff series) had moved from Santa Monica to Chicago, and he opted to stay in California. *The Sanford Arms* failed to catch on and was gone after four episodes (even though seven had been videotaped). When Redd Foxx returned a few years later with his new series simply titled *Sanford*, it was as if *The Sanford Arms* had never occurred. In *Sanford*, Fred was back in the junk business in the same old Sanford house, but Lamont had gone to Alaska to work on the pipeline.

The program was produced by Woody Kling; the executive producers were Saul Turteltaub, Bernie Orenstein, and Bud Yorkin; writers included Turteltaub and Orenstein; and directors included Russ Petranto. The theme song was by Henry Mancini. The program was reviewed by John J. O'Connor of *The New York Times* this way: "It's an entirely new show, and perhaps surprisingly, it shows some promise."

The San Pedro Beach Bums 20th Century–Fox/ABC. Monday nights 8:00. September 19, 1977–December 19, 1977. Ten hour-long episodes were filmed with a laugh track.

The pilot episode was a TV movie called *The San Pedro Bums*, which aired on May 13, 1977 (and can be viewed at the UCLA TV Archives). When the pilot became a series that fall, the word "beach" was added to the title. That beach was Cabrillo Beach in San Pedro and the five fun-loving bums lived on a houseboat called *Our Boat* (not unlike the premise of *It's a Man's World*). It should be noted that the houseboat in the pilot was called the *Challenger*. The bums were Buddy Binder (Christopher Murney), the self-confident leader; introvert Ed "Dancer" McClory (John Mark Robinson), called "Dancer" because he could not sit still; "Moose" Maslosky (Darryl McCullough), the gentle giant; Boychick (Chris DeRose), the suave ladies' man (in the pilot, he was played by the diminutive Jeffry Druce); and Anthony "Stuf" Danelli (Stuart Pankin), the insatiable eater. Pankin told me, "They really had the Bowery Boys in mind here. This was all brand new to me and very exciting. It was my first job on TV—I had done mostly theater work, previously. My character's father ran a fish store on the show, and the cast often got to take home some delicious fresh fish after we'd wrapped up the filming." Representing the fairer sex on the show were Susan Mullen as Suzi Camelli; Louise Hoven as Louise; Lisa Reeves as Marge; and Nancy Morgan as Julie.

Episodes include the debut, "The Angels and the Bums," in which *Charlie's Angels* guest starred to help out with the Miss Harbor Beauty Contest. Pankin recalled, "Farrah Fawcett wasn't there, but Jaclyn Smith, Kate Jackson and Cheryl Ladd were. It was a great way to cross-promote another Aaron Spelling program. We also did an episode aboard *The Love Boat* (titled "The Bums Take a Cruise"), one of the final episodes of the show. The wonderful Jack Arnold directed that episode (he'd directed *It Came from Outer Space*, a favorite of mine). I'll never forget—we got word of our cancellation the week we did that show, and to console everybody, Jack Arnold had a nice food spread for us after we wrapped up filming for that week."

The program was created by E. Duke Vincent; the executive producers were Aaron Spelling and Douglas S. Cramer. Pankin remembered, "Aaron Spelling was very hands-on—he had to approve our costumes, scripts, and reshoots. He was very good to me, too—my agent had negotiated my contract for much less than the other actors, and Aaron raised my salary to be comparable. It was great for me, and a very astute move for him." Writers included E. Duke Vincent, William Raynor, Myles Wilder, Earl Barret, Ben Starr, Simon Muntner, and Ron Friedman; directors included Barry Shear, Earl Bellamy, George Tyne, Jack Arnold, Allen Baron, Don Weis, and Gene Nelson. Music was provided by Pete Rugolo. This was yet another example of a failed attempt at an hour-long sitcom. The program's stiffest competition was *Little House on the Prairie*.

The Second Hundred Years Screen Gems. ABC. Wednesday nights 8:30 (September 6, 1967–February 28, 1968), and Thursday nights 7:30 (March 7, 1968–September 19, 1968). 26 color episodes were filmed with a laugh track.

This program was reminiscent of *The Patty Duke Show* in that Monte Markham played dual roles—Ken Carpenter, a modern-day conservative, and Lucius Carpenter, a joyful, rugged free spirit (Ken's grandfather). This was the far-fetched plot: in 1900, Lucius "Luke" Carpenter, while prospecting for gold in Fairbanks, Alaska, was lost in a glacier slide at the age of 33. Sixty-seven years later, a huge avalanche caused him to thaw out, surprisingly unscathed. Even though, technically he would have been 100 years old, he hadn't aged a day (the analogy given in the pilot was that Luke was very much like a package of succotash in one's freezer—as fresh as the day it was frozen). Luke's son, Edwin Carpenter, a real estate salesman (Arthur O'Connell) was 67 years old, lived in Woodland Oaks, California, had been too young to have memories of his dad, and was physically much older-looking. Edwin's son, Ken, was 33 years old and an exact double for Luke, and this wrinkle (or granddad's lack of any wrinkles) led to plotlines involving mistaken identity. Luke still thought William McKinley was President, so there was a lot of comedy mined from his adjustments to 1967 (television, exploration of space, automobiles, rock music), and by the generation gap created by three generations of Carpenters all living under one roof. Because Luke's defrosting was such a freak occurrence, the military wanted to keep it a secret, and that onus belonged to army doctor Colonel Garroway (Frank Maxwell). The colonel tried to keep Luke out of the public eye as much as possible, but Luke was extremely curious about this new world of which he'd suddenly become part. The colonel had a hippie daughter named Marcia (Karen Black) and an army nurse named Lucille Anderson (Bridget Hanley).

The program was produced by Hugh Benson, Bob Claver, and Richard Bluel; the executive producer was Harry Ackerman; writers included Ed Simmons, James Henerson, Martin A. Ragaway, Stan Cutler, Martin Donovan, Ron Friedman, Lila Garrett, Bernie Kahn, Skip Webster, Gene Thompson, Peggy Chantler Dick, Douglas M. Dick, J.E. Selby, Stanley H. Silverman, John O'Dea, and Jay Simms; and directors included Jud Taylor, Richard Kinon, Gene Reynolds, Claver, John Erman, Claudio Guzman, Paul Junger Witt, Robert Rosenbaum, and Russell Mayberry. Music was provided by George Duning. Reruns were briefly shown on the USA Network. Monte Markham later starred in yet another single season sitcom, *Mr. Deeds Goes to Town*.

Shirley's World ITC/Pinewood Studios, London. ABC. Wednesday nights 9:30. September 15, 1971–January 5, 1972. 17 color episodes were filmed without a laugh track. Sponsors included Eastman Kodak, Warner Lambert, and Lehn and Fink.

This program was a very expensive flop and it was Shirley MacLaine's one and only foray into episodic television. *Shirley's World* really encompassed the entire world. Shirley played Shirley Logan, a photographer (with a Nikon camera) for *World Illustrated* magazine (in a very posh building which also housed The Cotton Inc. Textile Company and The Braithwaite and Sons Accounting Firm) and each episode was filmed in exciting locales such as London, Hong Kong, Paris, and Tokyo. Shirley was persistent, bubbly, cunning, and impulsive. She was quite the women's liberation advocate, too. She was a great reporter with one shortcoming—she always managed to get too involved with her subjects and often found herself in great peril. Her editor was the gruff, tough, demanding yet kindly Dennis Croft (John Gregson).

Episodes include the debut, "The Berkeley Club Caper," in which Shirley's very first assignment was to interview the elusive Sir Harold (Charles Lloyd Pack). However, Sir Harold's favorite hangout was The Berkeley Club, a long-standing club "for men only." In "Thou Shalt Not Be Found Out," Shirley got the interview no one else could get. She pretended to be a maid in a hotel to speak with movie star Richard Burley (Nigel Davenport). Burley had recently separated from his equally famous wife. After interviewing Burley, Shirley's new goal became getting the couple back together, much to her editor's chagrin.

The executive producer was Sheldon Leonard; the creators were Frank Tarloff and Melville Shavelson; writers included Peter Miller, Frank Tarloff, Lew Schwartz, Philip Mishkin, Rob Reiner, Anthony Skene, Richard DeRoy, John Muir, Brian Degas, Jeremy Burnham, David Pursall, Jack Seddon, Tom Brennand, Roy Bottomley, T.E.B. Clark, and Patrick Alexander; and directors included Ralph Levy, Ray Austin, Charles Crichton, Frank Cvitanovich, Leslie Norman, Peter H. Hunt, Peter Sasdy, and Sidney Hayers. All 17 episodes of this comedy/drama/adventure are available on DVD from Network Video, UK.

Sirota's Court Peter Engel Productions/MCA-Universal Studios. NBC. Wednesday nights 9:00 (December 1, 1976–January 1977), and Wednesday nights 9:30 (April 1977). 13 episodes were videotaped before a live audience, a few were unaired.

A precursor to *Night Court*, this short-lived sitcom debuted on the same night as the ill-fated *McLean Stevenson Show* on NBC. This was the story of the Honorable Matthew J. Sirota, portrayed by Michael Constantine, in an undetermined big city. Sirota had been downgraded to night court because of his maverick attitudes and actions. In the opening credits, Sirota was called "tough but fair, a nice guy." The judge was called simply "Matt" by the court clerk, Maureen O'-Connor (Cynthia Harris); they had an on-again/off-again relationship for many years. Kathleen Miller played the very liberal public defender, Gail Goodman; Fred Williard portrayed the extremely conservative and very vain Assistant District Attorney, Bud Nugent; Ted Ross played private attorney Sawyer Dabney, the African American attorney who would take any case that came down the pike; and Owen Bush portrayed the bailiff John Bellson who had much reverence and respect for Judge Sirota.

In one of the best episodes, there were three problems plaguing night court—a gay couple with a marriage license wanted the ceremony to be performed by Judge Sirota; a filmmaker was arrested for allegedly creating pornography (the judge had to view the film in question to make the determination); and a gangster named "Blackie" Wilson, whom the judge sent "up the river" ten years prior, had been released early from prison and everyone in the courtroom was fearful that Blackie would seek revenge. Blackie was a changed man, and instead of a gun in his pocket, he had real estate brochures which he wanted to share with the judge.

The program was created by Coslough Johnson and Harvey Miller; the producers were Miller and Peter Engel; writers included Jack Winter, Jim Parker, Kenny Solms, Marc Sotkin, Judy Pioli, Miller, Chris Thompson, Gary Markowitz, Dennis Klein, Mike Kagan, Carole Ita White, and Jordan Tabat; and directors included Mel Ferber, Miller and Tom Trbovich. A couple of episodes of *Sirota's Court* are available for viewing at the Paley Center for Media.

The Smothers Brothers Show A Four Star/Knave Production. CBS. Friday nights 9:30. September 17, 1965–September 9, 1966. 32 black-and-white episodes were filmed with a laugh track. Sponsors included Alberto-Culver, and Tareyton Cigarettes.

Not to be confused with their popular and controversial variety show, this one came first and it came in sitcom form. This early Aaron Spelling show almost didn't happen, as the Brothers were unhappy with the early scripts from Phil Sharp. However, CBS brought in Fred DeCordova to salvage the project, and that combination worked. This was the far-fetched story of Dick Smothers, who had just gotten a job as a publishing executive at prestigious Pandora Publications. His life was falling into place nicely. And then "all heaven broke loose," as Dick's brother Tommy, who had been lost at sea two years earlier, suddenly showed up at Dick's "bachelor pad" at 452 Vista Del Mar in Los Angeles. Tommy was now an angel (Agent 009) trying to earn his wings by doing good deeds on earth. It took him a while to convince his brother, but through some "angel magic," and a phone call from the Assistant Section Chief for Temporarily-Assigned Angels (a.k.a. Ralph), Dick became a believer. However, Tommy was such a bumbler, it appeared as though he would be on earth and living in his brother Dick's apartment for a long time. Most episodes focused upon the good deeds Tommy was attempting, but always managed to screw-up. Others in the cast included Roland Winters as Dick's boss, Leonard J. Costello; Harriet MacGibbon played Mrs. Costello, the boss's wife; Marilyn Scott was their daughter Diane Costello; and Ann Elder played Dick's girlfriend, Janet.

Some of the episodes had very clever titles—"A Boarding House Is Not a Home," "Harried Italian Style," "The Girl from Ralph," "Immaterial Witness," "How to Succeed in Business and Be Really Trying," and "Is Your Wig Wam?" One episode even reflected the slogan of one of the show's sponsors, Tarreyton Cigarettes, titled "We'd Rather Fight than Switch."

The program was produced by Fred DeCordova; the creators were Aaron Spelling and Richard Newton; writers included Alex Gottlieb, Chris Hayward, Allan Burns, Arnold Margolin, Jim Parker, Lila Garrett, Bernie Kahn, Arnold and Lois Peyser, Arthur Weingarten, Gerald Gardner, Jinx Kragen, David Zeitlin, Dee Caruso, Jack Raymond, Randall Anthony, Peter Gregory, Ray Allen, Ralph Goodman, Gene Thompson, and Joseph Hoffman; and directors included DeCordova, Charles Barton, Sidney Miller, Bruce Humberstone, Norman Foster, Murray Golden, Andrew McCullough, and Richard Kinon.

The Smothers Brothers were said to be very uncomfortable doing a scripted show and both were secretly very relieved when the show was cancelled after one season. Nick at Nite aired reruns in the 1980s.

So This Is Hollywood Arrowhead Productions. NBC. Saturday nights 8:30 (January 1, 1955–June 25, 1955), and Friday nights 10:30

(July 1, 1955–August 19, 1955). 24 black-and-white episodes were filmed with a laugh track. Sponsors included Toni Hair Care Products and Pamper Shampoo (with announcer Jack Narz).

The opening credits began with searchlights and then the faces of the four regulars appeared inside the four letter O's in *So This Is Hollywood.* Those four regulars were Queenie Dugan (Mitzi Green)—a seasoned movie stunt woman and on-screen double (Cass Daley was the original choice to play the role but she was replaced at the last moment). Her roommate in the La Paloma Courts on Sweetzer Street in Hollywood was fellow actress/starlet Kim Tracy, played by Virginia Gibson. Kim showed lots of promise, but as of yet hadn't found the right vehicle to jettison her to super-stardom. The girls worked for Imperial Artist Studios, whose net worth was over $100 million dollars. Imperial owned 82 theaters, and operated in 17 countries. Kim's agent/boyfriend, Andy Boone (Jimmy Lydon), was determined to make her dreams of stardom and great wealth come true. Queenie also had a boyfriend, a dim-witted fellow stunt actor named Hubie Dodd (Gordon Jones). Appearing occasionally was the temperamental movie diva, April Adams (for whom Queenie was a stand-in) played by Peggy Knudsen.

Episodes include the touching "Friend in Need," in which the girls discovered that their elderly neighbor, Oliver Hampton (Victor Moore), used to be a very famous and wealthy movie star, but had since fallen upon hard times. Their attempts to help the kindly old man bore fruit when they found him steady acting work, and thus, the ability to pay his bills and again realize a sense of purpose. In "Twinkle, Twinkle," a seemingly sweet little girl from the neighborhood named Cindy McGuire (Mimi Gibson—the real-life daughter of Virginia Gibson) morphed into a demonic Shirley Temple after Queenie and Kim recommended her to the studio to fill the void left by a child actress who had come down with a bad case of mumps. They had previously been warned by the girl's father, but paid no heed and then paid the consequences.

The program was created and produced by Edmund Beloin; writers included D. D. Beauchamp, Charles Stewart, Lowell Barrington, William Cowley, George O'Hanlon, and Dean Riesner; and the director was Richard Bare. A couple of episodes can be viewed in the UCLA TV Archives.

The Soldiers James Saphier Productions. NBC. Saturday nights 8:00. June 25, 1955–September 3, 1955. Broadcast live with a live audience. Approximately 11 episodes aired.

Tom D'Andrea and Hal March had been doing a comedy skit about soldiers on variety shows for years with great acclaim, most frequently on *The Colgate Comedy Hour.* In the summer of 1955, NBC gave them the opportunity to parlay that skit into a series. Tom and Hal played Tom and Hal. *The Soldiers* were two malcontent GIs who found fault with everything in the military—the food, the accommodations, the leadership, and the rules and red tape associated with it. They seemed to cause trouble wherever they went and with whatever they did. However, they had hearts of gold, and would do almost anything to help a friend in need.

Episode titles, as well as airdates are very sketchy. In one surviving episode, Tom and Hal were just hours away from a three-day pass. A fellow soldier, Freddy, was also eligible for the same three-day pass, but opted to stay in because he had no money—he had spent his salary on round-trip bus fare for his wife for their anniversary, but had no money left to wine and dine her. Tom and Hal raised the money needed by promising their bodies to scientific research, and the young couple got to have a happy anniversary dinner after all. In that episode, John Dehner played the very fastidious Lt. Zetterquist.

The program was often produced and directed by Bob Henry; Bud Yorkin produced a few of the episodes as well (among his first TV credits); and writers included Jack Douglas, Marve Fisher, Tom D'Andrea, and Hal March. Music was provided by Norman Luboff. The show was staged by Jackie Coogan, who later became involved in another military sitcom, *McKeever and the Colonel.* D'Andrea also played Gillis for many seasons on the William Bendix version of *The Life of Riley.* March had recurring roles in *The George Burns and Gracie Allen Show* and *My Friend Irma.* He was also the host of a few game shows—*The $64,000 Question*, *It's Your Bet* and *What's It For?*

Stanley Max Liebman Productions. NBC. Monday nights 8:30. September 24, 1956–March 11, 1957. 25 live episodes were produced with a live audience from New York. Sponsors included Pall Mall Cigarettes, Pamper Home Permanents, and Deep Magic Lotion.

This half hour sitcom was broadcast live

from New York City and featured Buddy Hackett as Stanley Peck who ran the newsstand inside New York's Sussex-Fenton Hotel. Stanley was quite the extrovert and thus became privy to a lot of goings-on around Manhattan. He would always have tickets to all the hottest shows in town. However, while trying to "do the right thing," Stanley somehow managed to get into some awful predicaments. His co-star was Carol Burnett playing his girlfriend, Celia Howard (she lived in apartment 5F and her phone number was 324–3098). Burnett told me, "I was unemployed and unemployment paid only $36.00 back then. Luckily, I had been seen in some summer stock in 1955 by the right people, and I was called in to read for a new live sitcom that Max Liebman was doing. He was looking for a girlfriend for Buddy Hackett on the show, and I got a call the next day that I got the job." Frederick Tozere played Mr. Phillips, the manager of the Sussex-Fenton Hotel, and although never seen on-camera, Paul Lynde (voice only) played Horace Fenton who served not only as narrator, but also Stanley's conscience. Up-and-coming sitcom star Dick Gautier appeared on-camera in several episodes in non-speaking roles. Gautier remembered, "I was contracted to appear on the show with appropriate billing. Well, the powers-that-be reneged at the 11th hour and my appearances received no mention in the credits. I was going to sue, but my agent told me that it wasn't really worth all the effort." Dick also said, "The most pleasant part of performing on *Stanley* was getting to meet Carol Burnett." Jane Connell portrayed both Mary Barbara and Jane. Don Pardo, the staff announcer for *Saturday Night Live*, as well as *Jeopardy*, *Judge for Yourself*, *Three on a Match*, and dozens of other game shows, was also the announcer for *Stanley*. Several episodes can be viewed at the Paley Center for Media.

A couple of episodes dealt with Stanley's overall lack of trust in Celia around other guys. In "Stanley Gets Jealous," Celia fell for a rock and roll singer (who sang a version of Elvis Presley's "*Don't Be Cruel*"). Stanley's insecurities surfaced yet again in "Celia and the Frenchman," when Celia's French pen pal (a young Efrem Zimbalist, Jr.) visited the United States, and made a point of meeting Celia. Burnett remembered, "The episode with Efrem Zimbalist, Jr., was one of the first ones I did. I remember it vividly." Stanley also had a reputation for being tardy and in "The Late Stanley Peck," Celia refused to believe Stanley's seemingly outlandish excuse that he was held up by robbers in the hotel basement. However, that time Stanley's story was true. Then, in "The New Year's Eve Episode," Stanley's lateness after getting separated from Celia on the subway almost caused him to miss a midnight kiss from Celia to welcome in 1957. Stanley also had a penchant for appearing to be someone he wasn't. In an untitled episode, Stanley attempted to impress Celia and her friends by pretending to be on friendly terms with numerous celebrities who visited his newsstand. Burnett had a unique memory about that episode, which aired on January 14, 1957: "It aired on the day that Humphrey Bogart died. I remember Buddy Hackett saying how wonderful it was that we could make people laugh to forget all of the sadness of that day." In "The Old-Fashioned Christmas," episode, Stanley had misgivings about the old-fashioned music box he had bought as a present for Celia. He had no confidence in the old adage, "it's the thought that counts."

All episodes were directed by David Brown; the most notable writers were two gentlemen who would go on to much bigger and better things—Woody Allen and Neil Simon. Burnett said, "We always called Neil Simon 'Doc.' I think the nickname came about because he wore glasses and kind of looked like a doctor. We worked together again later on *The Garry Moore Show*." About the live audience, Burnett told me, "A lot of the lines in the show weren't all that funny, but some 'plants' were placed in the live audience to enhance the laughter."

The lyrics to the opening theme song, written by Clay Warnick and Mel Pahl, are as follows: "Stanley, how is it coming? Stanley, are bluebirds humming? Stanley, Stanley, where do you go from here?"

Stockard Channing in Just Friends Little Bear Productions. CBS. Sunday nights 9:30 (March 4, 1979–June, 1979), and Saturday nights 8:30 (June, 1979–August 11, 1979). 10 episodes were videotaped before a live audience at KTLA Studios.

Mirroring Sandy Duncan, who had two different sitcoms in two different seasons with the same theme song, Stockard Channing starred in *The Stockard Channing Show* in 1980 and almost exactly a year earlier, *Stockard Channing in Just Friends*. Stockard was a hot commodity at the time because of the success of *Grease*, and a transition to TV seemed like a natural. As co-star Mimi Kennedy recalled, "The show was a Little

Bear Production, named after Stockard's dog. Her husband David ran the company with her—it was a family affair." Here in this earlier of the two sitcoms, Stockard portrayed Susan Hughes who had always gotten A's in physical education (which explained the sneakers used as candle holders on the mantle), was on the varsity field hockey team in high school, and held a BA in Slavic languages. She was newly separated from her husband, Frank (Lawrence Pressman), who lived in Boston, and had just taken an American Airlines flight to Los Angeles to start anew. Very quickly she got a used Volkswagen, an apartment, and a job as an assistant manager and trainer at the posh Fountain of Youth Health Spa in Beverly Hills. Her gruff, buff, and frugal boss was Milt D'Angelo (Lou Criscuolo). His motto was "Fat is my enemy." Milt's dimwitted son, Angelo D'Angelo (Albert Insinnia), was employed at the spa as well; behind the juice bar counter was naïve, baby-voiced Coral (Sydney Goldsmith); and Susan's snooty, staunchly conservative, wealthy older sister, Victoria was Mimi Kennedy. In real life, Mimi is a progressive, and when I asked her about "playing against type," she said, "It's fun to play the shadow side. I had Long Island lockjaw—holding your jaw tight as if all your money was in there and you couldn't let it fall out. I loved it—getting to play that sort of snobby person." Victoria was constantly fixing Susan up with successful but boring men, much to Susan's chagrin. Susan's new apartment was never locked, and so family, co-workers, friends and neighbors just walked right in without knocking. Her new neighbor, the deadpan Leonard Scribner (Gerrit Graham), did just that all the time. Leonard attempted numerous get-rich-quick schemes, but none of them panned out.

Episodes include "Last of the Red Hot Tubbers," in which Susan found it very difficult as a recently separated woman to get a line of credit, so she bought a hot tub from Leonard next door, and installed it in her living room. In "A Little Fright Music," a man from Victoria's past (Hamilton Camp), a percussionist for the touring Joplin Ballet, was back in town wanting to rekindle the old flame. Kennedy remembered this as her favorite episode: "I liked that one where Hamilton Camp came back into my life as my old flame, Heavy Evie. We had a great scene at the table. He sang 'Indian Love Song' to me. He was very funny. I loved it." Tom Selleck guest starred in an episode titled "A Fine Romance," and Mimi recalled, "I gasped when I first saw him. As I walked onto the set, his massive, gorgeous back was to me, and he turned to face me. I gasped again. Dimples, eyes, and he was so nice."

The program was produced by Al Rogers; the executive producer was David Debin; the creators were Nick Arnold and Eric Cohen; writers included Arnold, Cohen, George Bloom, and Earl Barret; and directors included Robert Drivas, Rick Bennewitz, Bob La Hendro, Jay Sandrich, J. D. Lobue, Joan Darling, and Will Mackenzie. Kennedy most liked working with the last two directors mentioned; she "loved Will Mackenzie—sensitive, funny, a good guy. Joan Darling was really nice, too." The theme song for both Stockard Channing sitcoms was written and sung by Delaney Bramlett of the famous duet Delaney and Bonnie. Stockard's character in *The Stockard Channing Show* was also Susan, but the last name was changed to Goodenow, and she was a consumer advocate. Only Sydney Goldsmith was carried over to the new show, but her character was then renamed Earline Cunningham. Mimi Kennedy was supposed to be part of the new show, but "I asked for $500 more (even then, that was chump change). That apparently constituted breach of contract, so one of the producers said that they should let me go. Gerrit Graham and Lou Criscuolo had already been let go, so now they would get to change the show completely—and they sure did." A DVD box set is available from VEI.

Struck by Lightning An Arthur Fellows—Terry Keegan Production/Paramount Studios. CBS. Wednesday nights 8:30. September 19, 1979–October 3, 1979. Six color episodes were filmed before a live audience, only three aired. Sponsored by Folgers Coffee.

This show followed *The Last Resort* on Wednesday nights on CBS, but only for three weeks. *The Last Resort* went on hiatus until December after abysmal early ratings, but *Struck by Lightning* never got that second chance. This was the story of an old Victorian lodge in Maine called the Brightwater Inn, which had previously been owned by Emil Stein, who passed away suddenly. The Inn was then willed to his grandson, an avid Boston Celtics fan and high school science teacher named Ted Stein (Jeffrey Kramer), who came to the Inn to have a look around before selling the place, with the help of a local realtor named Walt Cravin (Richard Stahl, whom director Joel Zwick called "a wonderful old pro—a great character actor"). Ted had two obstacles standing in his way—a longtime employee at the Inn named Nora (Millie Slavin) who thought she was more deserving of the inheritance, as well as the 230-year-old handyman named Frank Stein (Jack Elam). In a clandestine meeting, Frank Stein admitted that Ted's great-great-grandfather created him in his lab. Thus, he was Frankenstein's monster. It took a lot of convincing, but Ted finally believed Frank. Frank did his best to urge Ted to stay on at the Inn, because he was in desperate need of someone with a scientific background to re-create a necessary serum (needed every 50 years) to keep him alive. Frank was also in need of female companionship (he hadn't had a date in 187 years). All of that expository information came from the debut episode. In the episode titled "The Movie," Frank was upset about a Hollywood film about Frankenstein's monster being produced at the Inn. Director Zwick told me, "Jack Elam relished playing the monster on this show. He had a great sense of humor about himself, and used to tell me not to worry about directing him because even if one eye was looking the wrong way, the other eye would be looking the right way."

Struck by Lightning—**Jack Elam as Frankenstein's monster (photograph courtesy of Joel Zwick).**

The program was produced by John Thomas Lenox; writers included Fred Freeman and Lawrence J. Cohen; and the director was Zwick, who told me, "Unlike most sitcoms which take place on a sofa without much atmosphere, this show let me be really stylistic between the laboratory and that huge old house. I could really get creative—it was fun to shoot." Music was provided by Thomas Talbert. The opening theme song was "You Are So Beautiful," by Joe Cocker, and the closing theme song was "Keep Me Alive," composed by Alan Brackett and Joey W. Stec. Frank Torrez of *The Los Angeles Herald-Examiner* reviewed the show this way: "Elam does marvelous things with a script that, intentionally or not, supplies him with the best lines. The rest of the show leaves a lot to be desired." A few episodes can be viewed in the UCLA TV Archives.

Sunshine Universal Studios. NBC. Thursday nights 8:00. March 6, 1975–June 19, 1975. 13 color episodes were filmed without a laugh track.

The subject matter doesn't sound like fodder for a sitcom, but it was. *Sunshine* was originally a CBS-TV movie about a woman named Kate with bone cancer. Kate had a young daughter named Jill (Elizabeth Cheshire in the series). Her full name was Jill Patricia Hayden—Jill for Kate's maternal grandmother, Patricia for her sister, and Hayden for her new love, Sam Hayden (Chris DeYoung). Sam was not the baby's father—that was a man named Dave to whom Kate was once married, but he vanished before the baby was born (and he eventually sent divorce papers). Sam was in a musical trio along with a guy named Weaver (Bill Mumy) and another named Givits (Corey Fischer), earning barely enough to survive. To supplement his income, Sam often took temporary jobs as a dishwasher, cabdriver, or dog-walker. It was Sam's singing of the John Denver song "Sunshine on My Shoulders" at a party which brought Kate to his side, and thus the name *Sunshine* was chosen for the title of the movie and the series. Kate passed on in the movie, but excerpts from her journals were the basis for episodes of the series, as Sam became a widower living in Vancouver, British Columbia, trying to make ends meet to support his now five-year-old daughter. Jill was constantly seeking a mate for her dad, as well as a new mommy for herself. A positive maternal influence in her life was a neighbor named Nora (Meg Foster) who worked in a local psychedelic shop. The cast of the movie was almost identical to that of the series.

Episodes include "Leave It to Weaver," in which Weaver quit the trio and joined a "pop music" group called Eric (Kim Milford) and the Rangers. Sam tried replacing Weaver with an old musical acquaintance named Eddie Flint (Burke Byrnes), but it just didn't work out. However, all was well by the end of the episode, and Weaver returned to the trio. By the way, in this episode, when asked his first name, the response was, "It's Weaver, just Weaver." In "Why Sam's Paid," Sam got a job as a private investigator and had the unpleasant task of following a woman whose husband suspected her of infidelity. In "White Bread and Margarine," Sam had difficulty convincing a social worker (Mariclare Costello) that he could be a fit parent. The latter was a sticky wicket for some viewers and critics who shared the social worker's concerns.

The program was developed by Carol Sobieski; the producer was George Eckstein; writers included M. Charles Cohen, Corey Fischer, Sobieski, and Bill Mumy; and directors included George Eckstein, Daniel Haller, Joseph Sargent, and Bernard L. Kowalski. A couple of episodes can be viewed at the UCLA TV Archives. One final brand new chapter in this "dramedy" aired on December 12, 1977 in an NBC TV movie titled *Sunshine Christmas.*

The Super Metromedia Productions Corporation. ABC. Wednesday nights 8:00. June 21, 1972–August 23, 1972. 10 episodes were videotaped before a live audience.

Richard S. Castellano (the "S" stood for Salvatore) was a hot commodity in the early seventies—he'd just appeared in a couple of very successful films (*Lovers and Other Strangers* and *The Godfather*), so he thought he might parlay his luck into success on television. His attempts were in vain. In *The Super*, his first of two sitcoms (the other being the short-lived *Joe and Sons* in 1975, on which he was also named Joe), the 260-pound actor portrayed Joe Girelli, the superintendent of an old, nearly condemned apartment building in a lower middle-class neighborhood in New York City. The tenants encompassed every possible ethnic group imaginable and they were very impatient when work wasn't completed on time and efficiently. Among the most visible tenants were Officer Clark (Ed Peck); his wife, Dottie (Virginia Vincent); Mrs. Stein (Janet Brandt); and Louie (Louie Basile). In the Girelli household were Joe's wife, Francesca (Ardell Sheridan); his disobedient, wise-cracking son, Anthony (pronounced "Antny"), played by Bruno Kirby, Jr. (who for some reason was known as simply B. Kirby, Jr. in the credits); and Richard's real-life daughter (named Joanne on the show), Margaret E. Castellano. There were also recurring visits from Joe's arrogant, hot-shot lawyer brother, Frankie (Phil Mishkin, who also co-created and co-wrote the show).

The debut of this summer replacement sitcom was titled "The Super's Apprentice," in which Joe took his son on as an apprentice after being suspended from school. It was also a way to appease his wife who thought he should spend more time with the children. When Anthony proved to be all thumbs on the job, he came to the realization that being a super was not for him, and he returned to school. In "The Plague," Anthony came down with a case of German measles, and got the entire building put under quarantine. In "Joe's Extra Ticket," Joe suddenly had a long list of best friends upon obtaining extra tickets to a sold-out football game.

The program was produced and directed by

The Super—**Richard S. Castellano as Joe Girelli (ABC).**

Alan Rafkin; the executive producer was Gerald Isenberg; the creators were Rob Reiner, Phil Mishkin, and Isenberg; and writers included Reiner and Mishkin. A couple of episodes can be viewed at the Paley Center for Media.

The Tab Hunter Show Shunto Productions/MGM Studios, Culver City. NBC. Sunday nights 8:30. September 18, 1960–September 10, 1961. 32 black-and-white episodes were filmed with a laugh track. Sponsors included Westclox, Newport Filter Cigarettes, and Chrysler.

Fresh off his success in the movie version of *Damn Yankees* and a couple of big hit records on the Dot label (*Young Love* and *Ninety-Nine Ways*), Tab Hunter tried his luck at sitcom stardom. Tab portrayed Paul Morgan, a playboy with a Malibu Beach house, a long parade of beautiful women following his every move, and a successful comic strip called *Bachelor-At-Large* (based upon his sitcom character's real-life experiences). The original working title for the show was *Bachelor-at-Large.* Hunter said, "The beach house was constructed on a soundstage at MGM. We did shoot a few scenes on the beach in the Malibu Colony for certain shows." On this eponymous sitcom, he worked for a company called Comics, Incorporated, where his boss was John Larsen (Jerome Cowan); his friend, millionaire playboy Peter Fairfield III was played by Richard Erdman; his housekeeper, Thelma, was played by Reta Shaw. Thelma was constantly expressing her disapproval of Paul's womanizing ways. Even though he portrayed a cartoon artist, Hunter told me, "I am not an artist, but I have dabbled in painting over the years. I used to paint at silent film star Harold Lloyd's home years ago—at least once a week."

Every episode revolved around some beautiful woman—many of whom became quite famous. Mary Tyler Moore appeared in a minor role as a brunette in "One Blonde Too Many." Tab told me, "Mary Tyler Moore was indeed on our show, and she was excellent. We had some marvelous guests every week." Elizabeth Montgomery guested in "For Money or Love" as Peter's cousin; Patricia Crowley played a cold-hearted editor in "Operation: Iceberg"; Tuesday Weld played a starlet who tried to drown herself in "The Doll in the Bathing Suit"; Ruta Lee guested in "Turnabout"; and Suzanne Pleshette was a guest at a winter resort in "Weekend on Ice." Joanna Barnes appeared in two different episodes as two different characters—as Isabelle in "Dream Boy" and as Attorney Michael Carruthers in "Portia, Go Home." A couple of seasoned actresses guest starred—Spring Byington won a contest and got to spend a week with Paul in "The Matchmaker" and Nancy Walker was a military nurse in "I Love a Marine."

Directors included Richard Kinon, William J. Hole, Philip

***The Tab Hunter Show*—Tab Hunter as comic strip artist Paul Morgan at the drawing board (photograph courtesy of Tab Hunter).**

Rapp, and Norman Tokar; and writers included Richard Morgan, John Elliotte, and the team of Dick Conway and Roland MacLane.

Each episode featured a unique Zeke Zekley comic strip image during the opening credits which reflected the subject matter in that particular episode. Music was provided by Leon Klatzkin; and the catchy theme song was from Pete Rugolo. The program was a Shunto Production. Tab told me, "Shunto Productions was a contraction of the names Stanley Shapiro (who wrote the pilot), Tab Hunter, and Norman Tokar (director). Also, it sounded very Japanese and I love Japanese art and culture." Speaking of Japanese culture, Tab said, "The show was a huge hit in Japan, the UK and other parts of the world." The show didn't catch on in America however. Tab said, "Our time slot was Sunday nights opposite *The Ed Sullivan Show*—that should tell you something." After 32 episodes were produced, Tab recalled, "I was pleased to move on after we were canceled, but hated returning the Chrysler Imperial they loaned me. It was a great car."

Tabitha Ashmont Productions/Columbia Pictures. ABC. Saturday nights 8:00 (September 10, 1977–January 1978), and Friday nights 8:00 (January–August 25, 1978). 12 episodes were filmed with a laugh track.

There's a really good reason this show never caught on: it had an erratic schedule on ABC. It never seemed to air on consecutive weeks. The program was a combination of spinoff and update of the Stephens children (now grown-ups) of *Bewitched*. In fact, in the opening credits, there were a few scenes of Tabitha as a baby on *Bewitched*. Like her mother, Tabitha (now played by Lisa Hartman) had powers and a mere twitch of her nose would make the seemingly impossible possible. Her brother Adam (David Ankrum) did not inherit those powers (he took after his dad, Darrin Stephens, and inherited his dad's chocolate allergy). We didn't ever get to see the parents or grandparents on this show, but there were a few familiar faces—Bernard Fox reprised his role as Dr. Bombay in the episode titled "Tabitha's Party," and Gladys and Abner Kravitz (Sandra Gould and George Tobias) appeared on the episode titled "The Arrival of Nancy." Tabitha and Adam had a meddlesome Aunt Minerva (Karen Morrow), whom Tabitha called in emergencies. Minerva was always encouraging Tabitha to use her special powers, while her mortal brother Adam was invariably discouraging these powers. Karen Morrow told me, "The show really must've had an impact in foreign countries. I would have waiters at Indian restaurants recognize me as Aunt Minerva for many years after the show went off the air."

Tabitha and her brother Adam were both employed in the TV industry at KXLA. Some of Tabitha's co-workers simply called her "Tab." Tab and Adam worked for producer Marvin Decker (Mel Stewart) on The Paul Thurston Show. Paul was the handsome on-camera newscaster, a dim-witted egomaniac played by the ubiquitous Robert Urich (not unlike Ted Baxter of *The Mary Tyler Moore Show*, only less lovable and less funny).

In the original unaired pilot for the show, for some reason Tabitha was spelled *Tabatha*, and the entire cast was different (Liberty Williams played Tabitha with brown hair and Bruce Kimmel played Adam, who was a warlock, not a mortal as he was in the series). Another difference in the pilot was that Tabatha was working in San Francisco for *Trend Magazine*.

Episodes include "Tabitha's Weighty Problem," in which our young witch came down with a cold which caused her powers to go haywire every time she sneezed. The cold was ill-timed and wreaked havoc upon athletes while she covered a weight-lifting competition for KXLA. In "Mister Nice Guy," Tabitha cast a spell which humbled the vain Paul Thurston and turned him into a really nice guy. However, his changed behavior caused his TV show's ratings to plummet. In "Tabitha's Party," a love potion intended for Tabitha was accidentally ingested by the other party-goers.

The program was produced by George Yanok; the executive producer was Jerry Mayer; writers included Mayer, Roland Wolpert, Bernie Kahn, Martin Donovan, Yanok, and Robert Stambler; and directors included Charles S. Dubin, Bruce Bilson, William Asher, Murray Golden, Herb Wallerstein, George Tyne, and Charles Rondeau. Music was provided by Dick DeBenedictis and Shorty Rogers. The theme song, "It Could Be Magic," was written by Jeff Barry, and performed by Hartman. Karen Morrow recalled, "Early on, *Tabitha* had really good ratings, but the erratic scheduling of the show was likely its downfall." A DVD box set is available from Sony Entertainment. Ashmont Productions was a contraction of the names William Asher and (his wife) Elizabeth Montgomery.

Take It from Me ABC. Wednesday nights 9:00. November 4, 1953–January 20, 1954. 11 episodes were produced.

Sometimes called *The Jean Carroll Show*, *Take It from Me* starred this trailblazing comedienne named Jean Carroll (born Celine Zeigman), who was to greatly impact and influence Phyllis Diller, Joan Rivers, and Lily Tomlin. Carroll was attractive and was usually dressed in mink and expensive jewelry while doing her stand-up. She was a monologist who actually began her showbiz career in a dance act with her husband, Buddy Howe. When Buddy was drafted during World War II, Jean was forced to go solo, and gained such wild acclaim for her monologues, the act remained a solo when Buddy returned—he stepped aside and became her agent. Her monologues were not self-deprecating, but rather centered around family life and being driven crazy by her husband and children (something only male comedians were doing at the time). ABC thought she would be an ideal candidate for a sitcom, and her only venture into episodic TV began in the fall of 1953. Much like the early *Seinfeld* episodes, she began each episode of *Take It from Me* with a monologue, and there were also numerous asides spoken directly to the audience during the goings-on. An example of her wit and humor is: "The thing that attracted me to my husband was his pride. I'll never forget the first time I saw him, standing up on a hill, his hair blowing in the breeze—and he was too proud to run and get it." She was cast as an average New York housewife—complete with a klutzy husband named Herbie (Alan Carney) and an awkward, somewhat dopey daughter (Lynn Loring). There was also a nosey neighbor played by the epitome of nosey neighbors, Alice Pearce (later Gladys Kravitz on *Bewitched*). Jean, however, quickly became disenchanted with the series, and after only eleven episodes, she announced to ABC that she no longer wished to continue. Jean felt that Alan Carney was dreadfully miscast as her husband, and *Take It from Me* quickly disappeared from the Wednesday night lineup. Jean enjoyed stand-up much more than doing the series, and she appeared countless times on variety shows, most notably *The Ed Sullivan Show*, on which she allegedly received close to $10,000 per appearance. To my knowledge, no episodes of this sitcom exist.

The program was produced and directed by Alan Dinehart; writers included Cleman Jacoby and Arnie Rosen; and directors included Dick Linkroum. Music was provided by Bernard Green. Jean Carroll, long out of the limelight, died on January 1, 2010, in Hartsdale, New York, at the age of 98. The most readily available example of her work can be found on the Columbia Records album titled *Girl in a Hot Steam Bath* from 1960 (Columbia CS 8311). Her style of comedy involved long, repetitive stories which, with today's attention span, sadly just wouldn't fly. One of her stories on that album focused upon purchasing a mink coat, and took up about four-fifths of one side of the album. She also laughed along with us at many of her own jokes.

Tammy Uni-Bet Productions/Universal City. ABC. Friday nights 8:00. September 17, 1965–July 15, 1966. 26 color episodes were filmed with a laugh track.

Tammy was many things. She was three hit movies (*Tammy and the Bachelor*, with Debbie Reynolds, *Tammy Tell Me True* and *Tammy and the Doctor*, with Sandra Dee). *Tammy* was a number one song (by Debbie Reynolds on the Coral Record label—Coral 61851). In 1965, *Tammy* was also a TV sitcom. This *Tammy* was portrayed by yet another Debbie, Debbie Watson. In movies, Tammy's last name was Tyree, but on TV it was Tarleton. Eighteen-year-old Tammy lived on a houseboat on the Louisiana bayou with her grandfather Mordecai Tarleton (Denver Pyle) and Uncle Lucius (Frank McGrath)—and both claimed to be one-thirty-second Cherokee Indian. The Tarletons did a lot of fishing and also raised farm animals (among them Nan the goat, seen in the opening credits, and Enoch the mule). Later in the series' run, cousin Cletus (Dennis Robertson) and his guitar came to live with them on the houseboat. Our Tammy actually had two distinctly different lives—she was also a secretary (she could type 200 words a minute from training she got at Seminola Secretary School) for the mega-wealthy Brent family who lived on a plantation known as "The Bowers." The Brents were very kind to Tammy and very tolerant of her very southern ways and patterns of speech. However, Mr. Brent (Donald Woods) had a right-hand man, Dwayne Whitt (George Furth), who was a lot less accepting, and would rather have had the very prim and proper Gloria Tate (Linda Marshall) from next door get the secretarial job. The Tates were snobs without an ounce of humility—especially the matriarch of the family, Lavinia Tate (Dorothy Green), who disliked Tammy immensely, and especially hated her "swampisms." Lavinia was especially upset when her son Peter (David Macklin) took an interest in pretty Tammy.

In the debut titled "Tammy Leaves Home," Tammy passed all the tests and got the secretarial job at the Brent's plantation. She was then invited to a formal party at the Bowers and accepted. To make Tammy look bad, Lavinia Tate recommended that Tammy bring her "kinfolk" along. Tammy did, and fell right into Lavinia's trap, and Tammy's unsophisticated relatives were quite an embarrassment. Luck was on Tammy's side, however, as Mr. Brent admitted to having more fun at that party than he'd had in many years.

The program was produced by Paul Mason; the executive producer was Paul Wesson; writers included Elroy Schwartz, Peter Barry, Sandra Gould, Andre Stojka, Sam Locke, Joel Rapp, William Raynor, Miles Wilder, Paul David, John L. Greene, Dorothy Cooper Foote, Robert V. Barron, Jack Marlowe, Gail Ingram Clement, David Braverman, Robert Marcus, Ben Starr, George Tibbles, Frank J. Gill, Jr., G. Carleton Brown, Michael Fessier, Safford Lynne, Martin Grupsmith, and Gene Thompson; and directors included Charles Rondeau, David Butler, Earl Bellamy, Sidney Miller, Jerry Paris, Gene Nelson, Sherman Marks, Thomas Montgomery, Ezra Stone, Leslie Goodwins, Claudio Guzman, and Paul Harrison. Music was provided by Herbert Spencer, Jay Livingston, and Ray Evans. Four episodes of the TV series were edited together to make a 1967 movie titled *Tammy and the Millionaire*. The complete DVD set of *Tammy* is available in color in the PAL format from Alive Vertrieb Und Marketing in Germany.

The Tammy Grimes Show A Greenway/Tamworth Production—Twentieth Century-Fox. ABC. Thursday nights 8:30. September 8, 1966–September 29, 1966. Ten color episodes were filmed with laugh track, only four aired (and there were four more unproduced scripts). Sponsors included Behold Furniture Polish, and Bristol Myers' new Resolve Seltzer.

Tammy Grimes had won a Tony Award on Broadway for *The Unsinkable Molly Brown*. She then wanted to conquer TV, but met with disastrous results. This was the story of an heiress named Tamantha "Tammy" Ward who would one day be rich, but was placed on a very tight budget. Her money was "managed" by her frugal Uncle Simon Grimsley (Hiram Sherman), the president of the Perpetual Bank of America. Tammy had very expensive tastes and total disregard for "putting some away for a rainy day," and so Uncle Simon played a huge role in keeping her in the black. She was always scheming to get advances on her trust fund (usually to no avail), which she wouldn't officially inherit until she turned 30. Tammy arrived at work on a scooter and was in charge of "customer relations" at the bank. Maudie Prickett portrayed busybody housekeeper, Mrs. Ratchett. Tammy also had a fraternal twin brother named Terence Ward (Dick Sargent, who, on this show was credited as Richard Sargent). Terence was nothing like his sister—he was very straight-laced and downright square. Terence was one of eleven vice-presidents at the bank. He was also in the naval reserves and got called for duty in the debut titled "Officer's Mess." In that episode, Tammy got herself trapped on her brother's ship while sneaking on-board to say "bon voyage." In the second episode, "How to Steal a Girl Even if it's Only Me," Tammy was kidnapped by a bumbling group of newbie thugs who made a bevy of rookie mistakes. The problem: how to get ransom money from her tightwad Uncle Simon.

The program was created by George Axelrod; producers included Richard Whorf and Alex Gottlieb; and the executive producer was William Dozier. The few episodes of the show that made it to the airwaves were directed by Don Taylor; and writers included Ralph Goodman, Axelrod, Jack Raymond, Sid Morse, Gordon "Whitey" Mitchell, and Roland Wolpert. Music was provided by John Williams. Episodes can be viewed in the UCLA TV Archives.

The Ted Knight Show Hayoudo Productions/Paramount Television. CBS. Saturday nights 8:30. April 8, 1978–May 13, 1978. Six color episodes were filmed before a live audience.

In between *The Mary Tyler Moore Show* and *Too Close for Comfort* came this short-lived Ted Knight sitcom. The show opened with a ringing telephone. The phone was answered by a cheerful yet gravelly voiced receptionist who said, "Mr. Dennis Escorts. Wherever you want to go, we want to go with you." That receptionist, the irascible Dottie (Iris Adrian), was the sister-in-law of one Roger Dennis (Ted Knight). Roger was divorced. Dottie's husband, Burt Dennis (Normann Burton), was Roger's brother. The Dennis brothers were in business together in this high-class escort service venture with offices in a posh New York apartment building. Burt Dennis financed the business, and was a no-nonsense tyrant. Also employed at the escort service was Roger's easily distracted playboy son, Winston (Thomas Leopold), who was always hitting on the girls. Said girls consisted of Fawne Harriman, the "take charge" Honey; Cissy Colpitts was air-headed Graziella; Tanya Boyd was the company's only African American escort Phil Brown; Janice Kent was Cheryl, "the floozy"; Ellen Regan was the timid Irma; and Deborah Harmon was Joy. Claude Stroud played Hobart Nalven, the mail-man with a crush on Dottie.

Ted Knight readily admitted that doing this show was a mistake because it was too soon after *The Mary Tyler Moore Show*. Here's a quick synopsis of the six episodes: in "The Strike," the girls went out on strike for better pay; in "My Hero," when Graziella didn't get the raise she expected, she went to work for the competition; in "Hop To It," the comedy surrounded an inebriated Easter Bunny, and son Winston's new job in a clothing store; in "The Wedding," Honey posed as Roger's hot new girlfriend at his ex-wife's wedding; in "Sweet Sixteen," Roger was hired to escort a beautiful young lady to a birthday party. Problems arose when Roger discovered that this mature-looking woman was only 16. In "The Honeymoon Game," a woman hired Roger to pretend to be her husband on a TV game show.

This show was a spin-off of another relatively short-lived sitcom called *Busting Loose* with Adam Arkin (in the episode titled "Mr. Dennis Steps Out," which aired on October 25, 1977). Director Joel Zwick told me, "I heard that Mark Rothman and Lowell Ganz, with whom I'd worked on *Busting Loose*, were doing this new show. I contacted them, and they brought me over to direct an episode. In fact, I also got to play a character named Jim in that episode titled "The Honeymoon Game." *The Ted Knight Show* was produced by Martin Cohan and David W. Duclon; writers included Mark Rothman, Lowell Ganz, Susan Sisko, and Richard Rosenstock; and directors included James Burrows, Jerry Paris, and Zwick. Music was provided by Michael Leonard. This *Ted Knight Show* is not to be confused with the title for the later syndicated episodes of *Too Close for Comfort*. Zwick recalled, "This show about an escort service was really a bizarre concept. I think CBS was relying upon Ted Knight's star power at the time, but it just didn't catch on."

The Texas Wheelers MTM Enterprises, Inc. ABC. Friday nights 9:30 (September 13, 1974–October 4, 1974), and Thursday nights 8:30 (June 26, 1975–July 31, 1975). Nine color episodes were filmed without a laugh track. Sponsors included Bristol Myers.

The first two MTM shows ever canceled were *Paul Sand in Friends and Lovers* and *The Texas Wheelers*. The latter took place in the small Texas town of Lamont (population 5,367). This was the story of the four motherless Wheeler children and their lazy, crotchety, irresponsible, deadbeat, opportunistic yet somehow likable dad, Zack, played by Jack Elam. In the debut called "Wailin' Wheeler Is Dead," Zack returned to his immensely independent children after an eight month drinking binge, and was immediately confronted with his 16-year-old son's desire to quit high school. The four Wheeler kids were ten-year-old T.J. (Tony Becker); 12-year-old Boo, the only girl and a real tomboy (Karen Oberdiear); 16-year-old Doob (Mark Hamill); and the eldest, 24-year-old Truckie played by Gary Busey. Seeing Hamill and Busey in their early days is probably the most interesting element of this short-lived series.

In the episode titled "The Call," Zack was caught attempting to sneak away from the family again in the middle of the night. He was leaving to fulfill his dream of panning for gold at Superstition Mountain in Arizona. Truckie talked him out of going alone, so young Boo tagged along—and it's a good thing, because Boo was able to find help after Zack suffered a bad ankle sprain and couldn't hike back home. In "The Rebel," Truckie became weary of doing all of the chores around the house and decided to fashion a picket sign and go out on strike. There was even a bit of romance for the eldest Wheeler child in the episode titled "The Bookmobile," in which Truckie fell for Lamont's new devil-may-care bookmobile librarian (Christina Hart).

The program was created by Dale McRaven, who also served as executive producer; the producer was Chris Hayward; writers included McRaven; and directors included Jackie Cooper, Stuart Margolin, and James Frawley. The theme song, "Illegal Smile," was performed by John Prine. After an initial ill-fated four-week-run, the show went on a rather lengthy hiatus in October 1974, returning in June of 1975 as a summer replacement to burn off the five remaining unaired episodes. John J. O'Connor of the *New York Times* reviewed the show this way: "Refreshing—the perfect antidote for the dull hangovers trailing much of what is called warm family drama. The Wheelers are delightful." Episodes can be viewed in the UCLA TV Archives.

That Wonderful Guy Charles Irving Productions/ABC. Wednesday nights 9:00 (December 28, 1949–March 1, 1950), and Friday nights 8:30 (March 10, 1950–April 28, 1950). 17 live episodes were broadcast.

He would later go on to win two Academy Awards, but that very same Jack Lemmon had humble beginnings in early television. A native of Massachusetts, Jack Lemmon was a Harvard University graduate, Class of 1947. Not long afterwards, in 1949 at age 24 he was making guest appearances in the new medium of television on programs such as *The Philco-Goodyear Television Playhouse* and *Suspense*. Near the end of 1949, he landed a role in a brand new musical sitcom for ABC called *That Wonderful Guy*. Jack portrayed an enthusiastic, bumbling young valet named Harold for a pompous, demanding, acerbic theatrical critic named Franklin Westbrook (Neil Hamilton). Harold had aspirations of becoming a big time Broadway star. Mirroring his own real-life situation, his character had just graduated from drama school and was awaiting his big break. Until then, he tolerated the demanding Westbrook. Harold also had a girlfriend, played by Cynthia Stone, who would later become Mrs. Jack Lemmon in real-life.

The program failed to garner a sponsor and disappeared from the ABC prime time schedule after 17 weeks. Jack and Cynthia appeared on a short-lived summer replacement show in 1951 (for *Mama*) called *The Ad-Libbers*, hosted by Peter Donald. It was, basically, a live precursor to *Whose Line Is It, Anyway?* Jack and Cynthia continued to appear in episodic TV and it was a series of sketches they performed on *The Frances Langford—Don Ameche Show*, which led to their next series, *Heaven For Betsy* on CBS in 1952 (see that entry for more information). After many more guest starring roles on TV, including an episode of *Campbell's Summer Soundstage* similarly titled "One Swell Guy," Lemmon embarked upon a storied motion picture career which really got into gear with an Oscar-winning performance as Ensign Pulver in the 1955 smash *Mister Roberts*. Jack Lemmon and Cynthia Stone had one son together, Chris, in 1954, and they divorced in 1956. Chris starred in his own short-lived sitcom in 1979 called *Brothers and Sisters* on NBC.

The program was produced by Charles Irving; directors included Babette Henry and Hal Gerson; and writers included Charles Gussman and Russell Beggs. Music was provided by the Bernard Green Orchestra. This show was originally slated to debut in the fall of 1949, but was postponed. To my knowledge, no episodes exist.

Thicker Than Water Bob Banner Associates, Inc. ABC. Wednesday nights 8:00. June 13, 1973–August 8, 1973. Nine episodes were filmed in color before a live audience.

This dark sitcom was based upon the British show *Nearest and Dearest*, by Vince Powell and Harry Driver for Granada Productions. The British version had a five-year run; the American version lasted only nine weeks. This was the story of the Paine family (the Pledge family in the British version), purveyors of pickles. The family's proudest moment came when they won a gold medal for their gherkins. The patriarch of the Paine family, Jonas Paine (Malcolm Atterbury), was nearing his 80th birthday, but was in poor health and was bedridden. Waiting on him hand and foot for the past ten years was his loving and very responsible daughter, Nellie Paine (Julie Harris). However, it became obvious that Jonas' favorite child was his ne'er-do-well, womanizing, devil-may-care, alcoholic son, Ernie (Richard Long). Ernie had been estranged from the family for eight years, but upon hearing that his dad had taken a "turn for the worse," he feigned interest in the old man's health to insure he'd get part of the inheritance. This greatly antagonized Nellie, who thought she was more deserving. However, they discovered a stipulation in the will which stated that each of them would receive $75,000 if, and only if, they lived in the same house and ran Paine's Pure Pickle Company for five years. Others in the cast included a friend of the Paine family named Lily (Jessica Myerson); her silent husband, Walter (Lou Fant); and the factory's longest tenured employee, Bert Taylor (Pat Crenshaw).

The debut did have some humorous lines. Nellie, upon discussing her brother Ernie with her ailing dad said, "Blood is indeed thicker than water, but not when the blood is 90 proof." Ernie delivered a funny line when discussing a possible inscription for his dad's headstone, saying, "How about a Paine in the grass?"

The producer of the show was Tom Egan; writers included Rick Mittleman (who also developed the program); and directors included

Jerry Paris. The music was provided by Michael Melvoin. Episodes can be viewed in the UCLA TV Archives.

13 Queens Boulevard Toy Productions. ABC. Tuesday nights 10:30 (March 20, 1979–April 17, 1979), and Tuesday nights 10:00 (July 10, 1979–July 24, 1979). Nine episodes were videotaped before a live audience, only eight aired.

Toy Productions, which also gave us *What's Happening* and *Carter Country*, produced this short-lived adult comedy set in a diverse garden complex in the New York borough of Queens. The show had two brief runs in 1976—one in spring and one with a slightly different, all-female cast in summer. The theme song, "Everybody Needs Friends," remained the same for both incarnations.

The spring line-up consisted of Jerry Van Dyke as Steven Winters who worked for a sporting goods company; Eileen Brennan was his stay-at-home wife of 15 years, Felicia Winters (maiden name Sherman); Helen Page Camp portrayed widowed neighbor Millie Capestro; Louise Williams was her attractive young daughter Jill; and Marcia Rodd portrayed divorced neighbor and longtime friend of the Winters, Elaine Dowling, who worked for a company called Marcus of America. Rodd told me, "This character was more like my own self than any other in my long acting career." She also said, "The cast thought the show was going to be a runaway hit, but later we found out that ABC had designs on Eileen Brennan for another show for the fall called *A New Kind of Family*. Thus, *13 Queens Boulevard* was never really given a chance to prove itself."

Gone during the brief summer run were Jerry Van Dyke and Marcia Rodd. Felicia (Eileen Brennan) was now single. Added were Francis Lee McCain as Lois, Felicia's sister-in-law, and Karen Rushmore as neighbor and friend, Camille. This version of the show only lasted three weeks.

Episodes include the debut "For Better or Worse" which took place on the 15th wedding anniversary of Felicia and Steven. At the same time, Steven was getting a promotion, forcing a move to Akron, much to Felicia's chagrin. In the second episode called "The Reunion," Elaine opted not to accompany Felicia to their high school reunion. That is, until she discovered that her ex-husband of 17 years, Brad (Allan Miller), would be in attendance. Brad was now a publishing agent for a shipping company, financially well-off, and seemingly interested in rekindling the old flame. In "The Younger Man," eyebrows were raised when Elaine had a fling with Steven's 23-year-old nephew. In an episode with cast number two titled "Italian Holiday," Felicia rekindled an affair with an old boyfriend, Sergio Fontana played by Cesare Danova, but was crushed to find out he didn't wish to settle down. Almost every episode had a musical number ("I Married An Angel," "Al Di La," and "All of Me" were among the selections).

The program was created by Richard Baer and developed by Bud Yorkin, Saul Turteltaub and Bernie Orenstein for Toy Productions; directors included Will Mackenzie, Kim Friedman, and Nancy Walker. Music was supplied by Barry De-Vorzon. Toy productions combines the first letters of the names Turteltaub, Orenstein and Yorkin.

This Is Alice Filmed at Desilu for NTA (National Telefilm Associates). First-run syndication. Thursday nights 8:00. October 1958–August 1959. 39 black-and-white episodes were filmed a laugh track.

In this syndicated Desilu sitcom set at 857 Elm Street in River Glen, New Jersey, Alice was the female equivalent and the precursor to *Dennis the Menace*. She meant well, but her good intentions always seemed to backfire. Nine-year-old Patty Ann Gerrity got the lead role of Alice Holliday, but Kathy Garver told me, "I was part of the final three auditioning for the starring role of Alice. It was I, Patty Ann Gerrity, and Sherry Alberoni. I had passed the initial interviews and then, we were to prepare a scene and a song. The song I prepared was 'A Sweet Old-Fashioned Girl,' by Teresa Brewer. I must say, I was quite surprised that Patty got the role instead of me or Sherry. I think they were looking for a more realistic girl. Sherry and I were pretty slick for ten-year-olds. Although the part went to Patty, they liked me a lot and installed me as her best friend, Sally."

Tommy Farrell played Alice's father, newspaperman Chester Holliday; Phyllis Coates portrayed her mother, Clarissa Mae Holliday; freckle-faced Stephen Wootton played Alice's accomplice, Clarence "Soapy" Weaver; and Lucien Littlefield played the Colonel (Alice's grandfather, who had been a Georgia peanut farmer).

This was really a one-man-show with Sidney Salkow serving as creator, producer and director (and occasionally writer) of each of the 39 episodes. Episode highlights include "Quiz Show," on which Alice went head-to-head with her father's boss on a nationally-televised game show. In "Rock And Roll," Alice intervened when a rock and roll singer failed to answer her girlfriend's letter of adoration. In "Man's Best Friend," Alice got the butcher (Herman Strohm played by George Tobias) to muster up the courage to ask a socialite, for whom he'd been pining for years, out on a date. In an episode called "The Princess," Garver recalls, "I was supposed to cry. To get me to cry, the director (very cruelly, as I look at this in retrospect) kept saying, 'You can't cry because you're not a good actress—you're a horrible actress.' Well, certainly, he got me to cry. He then yelled 'cut' and said, 'That was brilliant.' Afterward he came up and said he was just kidding—that was just for the scene. I can now cry at the drop of a hat."

Each of the 39 episodes had a distinctly different opening credit: Alice as a queen on a throne; as an organ grinder with a monkey; as flower girl at a wedding; at a printing press; as Santa Claus; and dozens more.

Those Endearing Young Charms NBC. Sunday nights 6:30—30-minutes in length (March 30, 1952–April 27, 1952), and Tuesday and Thursday nights 7:15—15-minutes in length (May 6, 1952–June 17, 1952). Broadcast live from Chicago.

Those Endearing Young Charms had been the title of a movie starring Robert Young, Laraine Day, and Anne Jeffreys. There is also a traditional Irish folk song called "Believe Me if All Those Endearing Young Charms" (from a Thomas Moore poem). In the spring of 1952, this was also the title of a TV sitcom. NBC put the show together in a mere six days—the first script was written on a Monday, okayed on Tuesday, casting was done on Wednesday, and the show debuted that Sunday, March 30, 1952. This quick turnover may be one of the main reasons for its short-lived status—it all happened just too quickly. The program was broadcast live from Chicago, but was set in a small New England town where the Charm family resided. The head of the household, Ralph Charm, was played by Maurice Copeland; his loving wife Abbe by Fern Persons; daughter Connie by Charon Follett; son Clem by Gerald Garvey; and colorful, eccentric, savant-like (he could memorize entire catalogs of items) Uncle Duff was played by Clarence Hartzell. Uncle Duff's photographic memory came in handy because the Charm family ran a mail order business. They sold a wide variety of household gadgets to earn their keep.

After just a few episodes had aired, the show was pulled from the Sunday night lineup and shortened from a 30-minute show to a 15-minute show which now aired twice a week (Tuesday and Thursday nights at 7:15, replacing *The Bob and Ray Show* beginning on Tuesday, May 6, 1952). The program struggled in its new time slot as well, and disappeared from the NBC lineup for good on June 17, 1952.

The program was produced and directed by Ben Park and writers included Bill Barrett. To my knowledge, no episodes exist.

The Tim Conway Show Timkel Andromeda Productions. CBS. Friday nights 8:00. January 30, 1970–June 19, 1970. 12 episodes were filmed at CBS Studio Center with a laugh track.

This show had one major obstacle: it was scheduled on CBS very irregularly. After debuting in late January, it was off for the entire month of March, had only one airing in April, and then skipped a couple of weeks again in May and June of 1970. Tim Conway was having trouble finding a successful new show after the demise of *McHale's Navy* in 1966. In this one, Tim was again paired with Joe Flynn, who had portrayed Binghamton on *McHale's Navy*. Replacing *The Good Guys* in midseason, Tim portrayed Timothy "Spud" Barrett, the chief pilot for Triple-A (Anytime, Anywhere Airlines). Joe Flynn was Herbert T. Kenworth, the president of Triple-A, and Spud's co-pilot on the Lucky Linda (a decrepit, pea green 99 Beechcraft plane with the numbers N646CF). Director Bruce Bilson recalled, "Joe Flynn would drive up very proper in his chauffeured Rolls Royce, but was soon ready for whatever the script entailed, including falling down face first in mud." A slogan on the wall of the pilots' shabby offices read "We're cheaper than a bus." Spud and Herbert were quite the bumblers, but all in all were good pilots (although Herbert never totally got over his fear of flying). Others in the cast included Ann Seymour as K. J. Crawford, the owner of Triple-A's biggest competitor, Crawford Airlines; her son Ronnie was played by Johnnie Collins III; Fabian Dean played Harry at the never-crowded airport burger stand; and Becky, who worked at the airport (and on whom Spud had a crush), was played by Emily Banks.

Episodes include "All of Our Aircraft Is

Missing," in which, to duck from creditors, Spud and Herbert fabricated a story about the Lucky Linda being stolen. In another episode, Triple-A managed to wrest a lucrative mail-delivery contract away from Crawford Airlines when Spud demonstrated his amazing abilities as a pilot while caring for a baby in the cockpit. Still other episodes have clever titles such as "The Boys in the Bandwagon" and "The High and the Blighty."

The program was produced by Burt Nodella; the creators were Kenny Solms and Gail Parent; writers included Frank Gill, Jr., William Raynor, and Myles Wilder; and directors included Alan Rafkin, Harry Falk, and Bruce Bilson, who told me, "It was quite coincidental that Burt Nodella and I, who both went to UCLA at the same time, worked on the same show." The theme song was written by Dan and Lois Dalton. Music was performed by Jerry Fielding.

Tom, Dick and Mary—**Left to right, Don Galloway, Steve Franken and Joyce Bulifant (photograph courtesy of Joyce Bulifant).**

Tom, Dick and Mary Kayro-Vue/Universal City Studios. NBC. Monday nights 8:30. October 5, 1964–January 4, 1965. 13 episodes were filmed with a laugh track.

Up against *The Andy Griffith Show*, this show, *Tom, Dick and Mary*, didn't have a chance. It was the last of the trio of shows in the *Ninety Bristol Court* cluster on Monday nights and is most noteworthy because of its cast. It was originally announced that Burt Metcalfe would be Tom, but Don Galloway, later Detective Sergeant Ed Brown on *Ironside*, got the "Tom" role (Dr. Tom Gentry, currently an intern). Steve Franken, formerly Chatsworth Osborne, Jr., on *The Many Loves of Dobie Gillis* was "Dick" (Dr. Dick Moran, also an intern). Joyce Bulifant, later Mrs. Murray Slaughter on *The Mary Tyler Moore Show*, was "Mary" (Mrs. Mary Gentry, recently married to Tom). Bulifant told me, "I felt so bad for Bert Metcalfe at the time, but he certainly went on to bigger things as a producer on *M*A*S*H*." Tom, Dick and Mary were all sharing an apartment to defray costs (interns didn't make much money). The newlywed Gentrys weren't thrilled to have a roommate (they wanted more "alone time"), but the extra money certainly came in handy. Tom and Dick's boss, the chief of staff at the hospital, was Dr. Krevoy (John Hoyt), and as on *Harris Against the World* and *Karen*, Cliff Murdock (Guy Raymond) was also their handyman. The name "Cliff Murdock" reappeared on *The Bob Newhart Show* in a recurring Tom Poston role as Bob's old friend, Cliff "The Peeper" Murdock.

Episodes include "Mary Gentry, Girl Cupid," in which Mary attempted to find a nice girl for Dick, who had quite a playboy reputation. In "And Baby Makes Four," Dick made great strides in his medical career by delivering his first baby—but the baby's father had serious misgivings about becoming a father. In "Hail! Dick the King," Dick saved the life of a visitor from a small foreign country, and, as was customary in that country, the grateful patient became Dick's servant. Bulifant told me, "I was actually quite relieved when the show was canceled, because I was free to go to London with my husband at the time, and my son, Charlie." *Tom, Dick and Mary* and *Harris Against the World* disappeared after 13 weeks, but *Karen* was given a full-season commitment from NBC.

The program was produced by Les Colodny and Joel Kane; writers included Terry Ryan, Lee Erwin, Arnold and Lois Peyser, Tom and Frank Waldman, Lou Shaw, and Richard Baer; and directors included Lawrence Dobkin, E. W. Swackhamer, Jeffrey Hayden, Sidney Miller, and Dick Wesson. Steve Franken died on August 24, 2012, at the age of 80.

The Tom Ewell Show A Four Star Ewell-Carroll-Martin Production/Four Star Studios. CBS. Tuesday nights 9:00. September 27, 1960–July 18, 1961. 32 black-and-white episodes were filmed with a laugh track. Sponsors included Quaker Oats and Procter and Gamble.

Tom Ewell had previously starred in motion pictures with two of Hollywood's most beautiful and iconic women—Marilyn Monroe in *The Seven Year Itch* and Jayne Mansfield in *The Girl Can't Help It*. In this eponymous sitcom, Tom portrayed real estate salesman Tom Potter and he was once again surrounded by women. He truly was the only rooster in this hen house. Tom was a huge sports fan, so he was always seeking male companionship and male bonding to balance out his life, but usually to no avail. There were, however, a few recurring male characters on the show—Norman Fell was Tom's co-worker Howie Fletcher; Barry Kelley was Tom's friend, Jim Rafferty; and Vance Meadows was neighbor boy, Stanley.

Tom played a bumbling husband who had a beautiful wife, Fran (Marilyn Erskine, who was, for a time, married in real life to movie director Stanley Kramer); a live-in mother-in-law whom he called "Mother Brady" (Mabel Albertson); and three blond daughters—Carol (Cindy Robbins), who was 15, Debbie (Sherry Alberoni), who was eleven, and Sissie (Eileen Chesis), who was seven. The two youngest daughters were not natural blonds—their hair was bleached blond for most, but not all 32 episodes. Even the dog, Mitzi, was female.

Sherry Alberoni Van Meter (as she is known today), who played middle daughter Debbie, told me, "At that time they were also filming Steve McQueen's *Wanted: Dead or Alive* on the same lot, and Steve would sometimes take me for a ride around the lot on his motorcycle." She also recalled encounters with another cast on the Four Star lot: "I remember playing with the kids on *Peter Loves Mary*." She recalls *The Tom Ewell Show* as a "very family-oriented set. Tom Ewell was very nice, very approachable. He smiled a lot."

In one particular episode, "Debbie Takes up the Tuba," Sherry recalls, "I played trumpet since I was seven or eight, so they figured I could play tuba, too. That took a lot of lung power."

Guest stars included Billy Mumy, who

***The Tom Ewell Show*—Top left to right, Sherry Alberoni, Marilyn Erskine, Eileen Chesis, Cindy Robbins and Mabel Albertson. In the doghouse, Tom Ewell with Mitzi the Dog (photograph courtesy of Sherry Alberoni Van Meter).**

played Jeffrey in an episode titled, "Tom Puts the Girls to Work"; Groucho Marx's second banana, George Fenneman, played Randy Rambo in "The Prying Eye," an episode in which Tom was accused of being a "peeping Tom"; and Alice Ghostley appeared as two totally different eccentric characters in two different episodes—as spinster Lavinia Barrington in "I Don't See It," and later as Tom's idiosyncratic sister, Polly, in "The Chutney Caper." One of the most unique guest appearances involved one of the "stars" in Four Star Productions, Dick Powell, who appeared as himself in the episode titled "Site Unseen." A great deal of the historic Four Star Studios complex could be seen in that particular episode.

Most of the early episodes were written by teams who had long associations with Lucille Ball, including Bob Carroll, Jr., and Madelyn (nee Pugh) Martin. They are the "Carroll" and "Martin" in "Ewell-Carroll-Martin Productions." Madelyn affixed the "Martin" to her name after marrying producer Quinn Martin. Also from the Lucy camp were Fred S. Fox and Iz Elinson. Later episodes were written by the teams of Michael Morris and Max Wilk, and Milton Pascal and Larry Rhine. Most episodes were directed by Hy Averback, whom Sherry Alberoni Van Meter says, "worked great with kids, and made it so much fun."

In the October 10, 1960, issue of *Time* magazine, the show was reviewed this way: "*The Tom Ewell Show* (CBS) leads a relentless parade of situation comedies, all designed to show that American family life is as cute as a freckle on a five-year-old. The show, which might also be titled 'Father Knows Nothing,' presents the comic with the excavated face as a bumbler named Potter who is trapped in the customary format: Harassed Man Beaten Down by Wife, Three Daughters, Mother-in-Law."

This show was also called *The Trouble with Tom*. Tom Ewell took another shot at sitcom stardom in 1981 as Dr. Jerome Kullens in the very funny but short-lived *Best of the West*.

Too Young to Go Steady A David Susskind Production/Talent Associates in association with Screen Gems. NBC. Thursday nights 8:30. May 14, 1959–June 25, 1959. Seven black-and-white episodes were broadcast live from New York. Sponsors included Oldsmobile (Florence Henderson and Bill Hayes starred in the commercials) and General Foods.

Too Young to Go Steady may have had a very short life in prime time, but there's a lot to say about it. The original pilot had a cast full of big names. Don Ameche portrayed the dad, attorney Tom Blake, and Polly Rowles played Mary, his wife. They had two kids—14-year-old tomboy Pamela (who just discovered boys), played by Tuesday Weld, and her doting 17-year-old brother, Johnny played by Doug Lambert. Pamela had a best friend named Timmy Barnes, played by a very young Joyce Bulifant. In this pilot, Pamela and Timmy were caught passing notes in their history class, and to their complete embarrassment, they were intercepted and read aloud by the teacher. The notes were about a boy named Bob Shaw (Ronnie Welsh) and Pamela's yearning to have Bob ask her to the prom. Bob eventually did ask Pamela out, but to her disappointment, he asked her to a movie and not to the prom. This pilot can be viewed in the UCLA TV Archives. Bulifant told me, "I had only done theater prior to *Too Young to Go Steady*. It was the first thing I ever did on television. Having been trained in the theater, I tried to project my voice as if I were performing in a theater. The director then told me that I didn't have to yell—there were microphones to pick up my voice. I wasn't even aware at the time that it became a series. It was a long time ago, but I guess the cast of the pilot was busy with other roles when the series aired because it was totally recast."

Indeed, it was recast. Donald Cook now played the father, Tom Blake; Joan Bennett was the mother, Mary; Brigid Bazlen was 14-year-old Pamela; Martin Huston was her big brother Johnny; and Lorna Gillam played Pamela's best friend Timmy Barnes. There was one other big change—the series was broadcast live from New York. One surviving kinescope can be viewed in the New York branch of the Paley Center for Media (titled "Father Takes up Golf"). Pamela gave her dad some tips about golf and completely forgot about a school project due the next day, so she copied the work of a schoolmate named Peter Brant (Clay Hall), but it's he who got in trouble. Pamela then had to come clean when the accusatory finger pointed at Peter got him kicked off the basketball team. A very blatant network promotional tool was visible in the Blake household—an NBC peacock screen in the living room fireplace simply cannot be missed. *Too Young to Go Steady* has the distinction of being the last completely live prime time sitcom. However, the program couldn't find an audience and disappeared after only seven episodes. The opening credits featured a scrolling drawing of a telephone cord which connected the cast. The principal of Pamela's school was named Mr. Woodman (Victor Thorley), the same name as the principal on the 1970s hit *Welcome Back, Kotter*.

The producers were Michael Abbott (pilot) and Ronald Alexander (series). The executive producer was David Susskind; the creator was Alexander; writers included Alexander; and directors included Paul Bogart (pilot), Frank Pacelli and Alexander (series).

A Touch of Grace Grace Productions/Herman Rush Associates. ABC. Saturday nights 8:30. January 20, 1973–June 16, 1973. 13 color episodes were filmed before a live audience.

She had already won a Tony Award for the stage production of *Come Back, Little Sheba*, as well as an Oscar and Golden Globe for the movie version. Then came two Emmys for her role in the TV sitcom, *Hazel*. Before retiring and calling it a career in 1974, Shirley Booth took one more stab at TV success in 1973 with *A Touch of Grace*, a show with the unenviable task of competing against the CBS lineup on Saturday nights. It was based upon the hit British show, *For the Love of Ada*, and it cast Shirley as Grace Simpson, a recently widowed, yet very spry 65-year-old woman who moved in with her extremely conservative and very square daughter, Myra Bradley (Marian Mercer), and her son-in-law, supermarket worker Walter (Warren Berlinger). Grace, ever the meddler, continually asked the stuffy couple why, after years of marriage, they were still childless and hadn't yet made her a grandmother.

In the debut, Grace suddenly increased her visits to the cemetery. Myra and Walter thought it was because she missed her deceased husband so much, but then came to find out that Grace was actually visiting a new boyfriend—gravedigger Herbert Morrison (J. Pat O'Malley). Grace brought Herbert home on one particular night because the kids were supposed to be out. However, they came home earlier than expected and were taken aback when they discovered that Grace wasn't home alone. In "The Weekend," Grace and Herbert made plans to spend a weekend together at the "Bayside Lodge," raising the disapproving eyebrows of Myra and Walter. Writer David Pollock who, along with Elias Davis, wrote three episodes of the show told me, "While briefly living in London, working on *The Des O'Connor Show*, I got to see *For the Love of Ada*—the show upon which *A Touch of Grace* was based, so I had a feel for the show. However, our three scripts ('The Working Girl,' 'The Reunion,' and 'Saturday Night at the Movies') were freelance, so Elias and I were never obliged to go to the tapings."

The program was produced by Saul Turteltaub and Bernie Orenstein; the executive producers were Herman Rush and Ted Bergmann; writers included Turteltaub, Orenstein, Elias Davis, and David Pollock; and directors included Carl Reiner. Reiner remembered, "Shirley Booth was an absolute pleasure to work with. She was a brilliant comedienne. I'd been a fan since her days as the original Miss Duffy on the radio version of *Duffy's Tavern*." Music was provided by Pete Rugolo. In the thirteenth and final episode of this charming yet dark little show, Herbert the gravedigger proposed to Grace, and she accepted. The debut episode is available for viewing at the UCLA TV Archives.

The Trouble with Tracy National General Television Productions, Inc./CFTO Studios. 1970. First-run syndication, every weekday. 130 episodes were recorded with a laugh track.

The Trouble with Tracy was shot in Toronto, but the program was set in New York City. The program was loosely based on the radio and TV sitcom called *Easy Aces* (and was written by one of the stars of that program, Goodman Ace). Because of time restraints, a small budget, and five new episodes per week, some of the old *Easy Aces* scripts were adapted and updated for *The Trouble with Tracy*. For those same reasons, there were very few retakes, and many dialogue flubs were left in. The original intent was to call the show "The Married Youngs," since Young was the couple's last name. The show's pilot bears that name, but for the series the title became *The Trouble with Tracy*. The very dizzy and naïve Tracy Young, who wore a lot of miniskirts, was played by Diane Nyland. Her husband, Doug (Steve Weston), headed an advertising agency and, despite all the "troubles with Tracy," he loved her very much and usually just rolled his eyes, but rarely lost his cool. Doug had a secretary named Sally Anderson (Bonnie Brooks) and a "flower-child" brother named Paul (Franz Russell) who was always short on cash. Tracy's meddling mom, Mrs. Sherwood (Sylvia Lennick), appeared occasionally.

A typical episode had Tracy watching a cheesy TV mystery series, for which her husband's ad agency had gotten sponsors. Doug disliked the show very much and thought of it as an insult to his intelligence, but Tracy loved it and watched it religiously. *The Trouble with Tracy* came into play when all of the events leading up to the murder on that TV show started playing out in real-life (beginning with a new neighbor who needed help carrying a trunk to his car). Comedy ensued after several more eerie coincidences played out. We would discover at the end of the episode that the new neighbor was one of the writers of that mystery series.

The program was produced by Seymour Berns, who named the series after his own daughter, Tracy. The executive producer was Murray Chercover; directors included Paul Kimberley. Music was provided by Al Kasha and Joel Hirshhorn. In Canada, reruns of *The Trouble with Tracy* ran until the mid 1980s.

Tugboat Annie (see *The Adventures of Tugboat Annie*)

Turnabout—**A confused Sharon Gless and John Schuck (photograph courtesy of Mel Carter).**

Turnabout Sam Denoff Productions/Universal City Studios. NBC. Friday nights 9:00 (January 26, 1979–February 14, 1979), and Friday nights 9:30 (March 7, 1979–March 23, 1979). Six color episodes were filmed with a laugh track.

The entire absurd premise of this show was summed up in the opening credits (narrated by Sterling Holloway). In short, it was the story of a couple of very successful people (Sam Alston, played by John Schuck, and Penelope "Penny" Alston, played by Sharon Gless) who loved each other very much and yet each envied each other's job. One day, while driving together in their convertible, Penny saw an item of interest for sale by a roadside gypsy (Dena Dietrich), and against Sam's wishes, purchased this allegedly magical statue for $40. That night, while discussing their jobs (he was a sportswriter, and she was the vice president of the Geoffrey St. James Cosmetics Company), each again reiterated their wish to have the other one's job and the other one's life. Well, the magic statue granted that wish—his personality was now in her body, and hers in his. She smoked cigars, he broke down in tears a lot, and each now had to go to the other's place of work and attempt to carry on as if nothing had happened (inciting confusion for his boss, the gruff Al Brennan, played by Bruce Kirby, and her boss, Geoffrey St. James, played by James B. Sikking). The Alston's neighbors and friends, the Overmeyers (Jack, played by Richard Stahl, and Judy, played by Bobbi Jordan) were equally confused by the noticeable changes—suddenly Penny knew a lot about sports and poker, and Sam knew a lot about fashion, make-up, and cooking. Comedy ensued when Penny had to shave in the morning (and was covered in tissue paper afterwards) and Sam put on way too much lipstick, couldn't walk around well in high-heel shoes, and feared he was pregnant. Actor/singer Mel Carter guest starred in the episode titled "Statutory Theft," and told me, "That was the episode in which the magic statue was stolen. I played Officer Johnson, and I recall having a moustache and wearing a brown and tan uniform. Performing on that show was a very pleasant experience." Carter also added, "Once directors discovered that I'd had big hit records such as *Hold Me, Thrill Me, Kiss Me* and *All of a Sudden My Heart Sings*, they would usually give me a few more lines in the program—a bigger role."

The program was developed by Steven

Bochco and Michael Rhodes; the producers were Arnold Kane and Rhodes; the executive producer was Sam Denoff; writers included Jim Rogers, Sylvia Necht, Barbara Avedon, Barbara Corday, Ken Hecht, and Richard Baer; and directors included Richard Crenna, Alex March, Arnold Laven, William P. D'Angelo, and Tony Mordente. Music was provided by Jack Elliott and Allyn Ferguson. The program was loosely based upon the 1931 novel *Turnabout*, by Thorne Smith (who also gave us *Topper*), and the 1940 *Turnabout* movie, which starred Adolphe Menjou. The show's developer, Steven Bochco, went on to bigger and better things such as *Hill Street Blues*, *NYPD Blue* and *L.A. Law*. Episodes can be viewed in the UCLA TV Archives.

Two Girls Named Smith ABC. Saturdays at noon. January 20, 1951–October 13, 1951. Broadcast live from New York City. Sponsors included Glim Dishwashing Detergent and Bab-o Soap (B. T. Babbitt).

This was the story of two actresses named Peggy who portrayed two up-and-comers named Smith. There was Peggy Ann Garner (Oscar-winner for her role in *A Tree Grows in Brooklyn*, as Barbara "Babs" Smith) and Peggy French (as Francis "Fran" Smith). Both women, cousins who shared the same last name, moved from Omaha to New York City to pursue their dreams: Babs as a singer; Fran as a fashion designer. Babs and Fran acquired an apartment at 514 East 51st Street where their landlord, Mr. Basmany (Joseph Buloff), was also their friend and advisor.

Kermit Kegley appeared as Fran's boyfriend, attorney Jeffrey Carter. Richard Hayes, Peggy Ann Garner's real life husband at the time, apparently played Babs' boyfriend (although this cannot be confirmed by actual episodes). Garner missed a few weeks of the show in July and August, and was replaced by Nina Foch. Then, after a very brief return, Garner left the series for good in September of 1951 (possibly because of illness), and her replacement, Marcia Henderson (portraying the same character), had no boyfriend. It was rumored that Garner left the series to spend more time with her husband, making it highly unlikely that Hayes was a regular. *TV Guide* and other printed sources mention Babs as having a boyfriend, but neither a performer nor character name is given. While at least one episode of the Marcia Henderson version of the series exists—from which information was taken—there appear to be no extant copies of the Peggy Ann Garner version. This could be attributed to the fact that the series was broadcast live. In addition to the problems with live television (in one episode, for example, an air raid siren was heard sounding in the background—but the cast simply ignored it and continued the story), there were problems behind-the-scenes as a piracy lawsuit was brought about by the creators of the book and movie *My Sister, Eileen*. Ruth McKenney, Jerome Chodorov and Joseph A. Fields felt the premise for this show and its characters were much too similar to their own creation.

The program aired at noon on Saturdays. *A Date with Judy* preceded it and its principal competition was *The Big Top* on CBS (NBC and DuMont apparently did not supply network programming at this hour of the day and in areas where local NBC and DuMont stations existed, the time slots were filled with local kid shows and western movies). On October 20, 1951, *Two Girls Named Smith* was replaced by *The Betty Crocker Star Matinee*. Peggy Ann Garner was also a panelist, albeit briefly, on an NBC Sunday night discussion series called *Leave It to the Girls*. Garner's last television appearance occurred in 1980 (in an uncredited role) in the TV movie *This Year's Blonde* (as the stepmother).

The program was produced by Richard Lewis; directors included Cort Steen, Charles Durbin and Mervyn Nelson; and writers included Peter Barry. Music was provided by Jacques Press. It is unclear how many episodes were broadcast. The program was cancelled when it was dropped by its sponsor, B. T. Babbitt.

The Tycoon Danny Thomas Entertainment. ABC. Tuesday nights 9:00. September 15, 1964–September 7, 1965. 32 black-and-white episodes were produced with a laugh track. Sponsors included The American Tobacco Company, Prell Shampoo, and Gleem Toothpaste.

In between *The Real McCoys* and *The Guns of Will Sonnett*, Walter Brennan starred in this almost forgotten single season sitcom as Walter Andrews, an eccentric millionaire who did things his own way. Despite objections from everyone in his circle, those things always seemed to work out just fine. For a billboard ad campaign, it was recommended that Walter use a blonde bathing beauty, but he objected, stating, "The policy of the Thunder Corporation is to avoid controversial subjects—so, add a brunette and a redhead." Walter was the chairman of the board for the huge California conglomerate called The

Thunder Corporation. Walter's definition of "chairman of the board" was "too ornery to get along with, and too smart to fire" (although Walter actually did get the boot, albeit briefly, in episode number three titled "Walter Gets Fired"). His co-workers included company president Herbert Wilson (Jerome Cowan) and his personal secretary, Betty Franklin (Janet Lake). At work, Walter was totally in charge, but at home—well, that's another story. Widower Walter lived with his granddaughter, Martha Keane (Pat McNulty), and housekeeper Una Fields (Monty Margetts). Walter's personal assistant and private pilot, Pat Burns, was played by Van Williams. The number on Walter's private plane was QX62114. Walter also had a classic car. He'd climb into it when he needed "alone time" to think things through (much like Dobie Gillis did near Rodin's "The Thinker").

Episodes include "Shotgun Merger," in which a new Thunder Corporation assembly plant was to be built in Fontana, California, but there was one big obstacle—the owner of the land, Nick Santino (Vito Scotti), didn't want to sell. Santino grew grapes on his land, and eventually Walter made a deal with Santino to put a hothouse on the property and branch out into the fresh fruit business, thus putting the original idea on hold. In "Honest Man," Walter insisted he'd never told a lie in his life, but then failed a polygraph test (the company's newest toy) because of one old lie. Walter tried to atone for that lie by returning to his hometown, but it seemed the lie actually made the lives of all concerned better. In "Mr. Fixit," stubborn Walter opted to fix things around the office by himself. However, when he made a bad impression upon a prospective client because of dirty overalls and greasy hands, he changed his tune.

The program was produced by Charles Isaacs; the executive producer was Danny Thomas; writers included Isaacs, Paul David, Fred Fox, Iz Elinson, and John L. Greene; and directors included Sheldon Leonard, Alvin Ganzer, and Jean Yarbrough. Music was provided by Les Baxter. Given Walter Brennan's star power, and the fact that the program was sandwiched between two hit shows on Tuesday nights (*McHale's Navy* and *Peyton Place*), it's rather amazing that *The Tycoon* failed to catch on. Numerous episodes can be viewed in the UCLA TV Archives.

The Ugliest Girl in Town Screen Gems. ABC. Thursday nights 7:30. September 26, 1968–January 30, 1969. 20 color episodes were filmed with a laugh track, only 17 aired. Sponsors included Yardleys of London.

In between the movie *Some Like It Hot* and the TV sitcom *Bosom Buddies*, came this short-lived sitcom about a man who had to dress like a woman. The plot was rather involved. The theme song asks the question, "Who owns that fabulous face?" It was Timothy Blair (Peter Kastner), who was 23 years old, weighed 140 pounds, was 5-feet 7-inches tall and made $97 a week as a talent scout in Hollywood for the Harper Talent Agency. He fell for a visiting British actress named Julie Renfield (Patricia Brake), to whom he had to deliver a contract. Julie initially turned him down for a date, but his persistence endeared him to her. Before very long, they were very much in love with one another, but after the filming, she had to return to London, and he was heartsick. In the meantime, to take his mind off his broken heart, he posed for some hippie pictures to help out his brother Gene Blair (a photographer, played by Gary Marshal—not to be confused with writer/producer/director/ Garry

***The Ugliest Girl in Town*—Peter Kastner as "Timmie" (photograph courtesy of Jean Cummings).**

Marshall). Gene needed these pictures in a hurry after an earlier set of pictures was accidently destroyed. It was all rather farfetched, but said pictures wound up in the hands of David Courtney (Nicholas Parsons), head of the London Modeling Agency. Because Tim had long hair in the pictures, Mr. Courtney thought the pictures were of a girl. He liked her "earthy" quality, and Tim became Timmie (the hottest thing since Twiggy) as the charade kept snowballing. There was a big advantage to this happenstance—Tim got free airfare to visit Julie in London. Oh, there was one snag, however—while in London, Gene found himself deeply in debt after some big gambling losses (he wasn't allowed to leave the country), and so the Blair Brothers were stuck there until Gene could pay off his creditors.

Episodes include "The Paris Incident," in which Julie and Timmie were booked into the same hotel room (a real no-no in 1968) for a fashion show put on by the Lonsoir Company, so Tim slept in the bathtub. In "My Sister: The Genius," Julie tried to keep her visiting 16-year-old sister from finding out the true identity of Timmie. When sis made the inevitable discovery, she threatened to blow the whistle to Mr. Courtney. In "The Cover-Up Girl," Timmie was asked to pose for some nude photographs, but a clever scheme kept the naked truth well hidden. Every episode began with Tim addressing the audience, setting up the episode ahead. The show's fashion sense definitely had an *Austin Powers* texture to it.

The program was produced by Bob Kaufman, Jerry Bernstein and Jerry Davis; writers included Brad Ashton and Kaufman (who was also the show's creator); and directors included James Frawley, Ray Austin, and E.W. Swackhamer. The theme song was written by Helen Miller and Howard Greenfield, and performed by the Will-O-Bees. Almost every episode also had an original song written by Carole Bayer Sager.

This much-maligned sitcom would definitely rival *My Mother, the Car* as one of the most outlandish creations of the 1960s. A few episodes can be viewed in the UCLA TV Archives. The "man dressed as a woman" premise resurfaced briefly in the 2012 ABC sitcom *Work It*.

Valentine's Day 20th Century Studios. ABC. Friday nights 9:00. September 18, 1964–September 10, 1965. 34 black-and-white episodes were filmed with a laugh track. Sponsors included Excedrin, Goodyear, General Foods, and Breck Shampoo.

Hal Kanter was the creator and executive producer of this sitcom. It's always very easy to distinguish a Kanter show from others—he loved to play around with the credits. He did it on *The George Gobel Show* (with comments such as, "Starring, of all people, George Gobel"). He did it on *Julia* (with comments such as, "Brought to you with pride" and "Brought to you with a smile"). Well, *Valentine's Day* was no exception—here it was "Intentionally brought to you by," "Brought to you with love by," "Ardently brought to you by," "Happily brought to you by," and "Purposely brought to you by." The opening credits featured a black-and-white cartoon drawing of New York City and a roving cartoon taxicab weaving through traffic.

Much like Bob Cummings's role on *The Bob Cummings Show*, handsome playboy Valentine "Val" Farrow (Tony Franciosa) had a seemingly endless harem of beautiful women in his life. And what a bachelor pad he had (a brownstone on 23rd Street in Manhattan). Janet Waldo recalled, "Tony Franciosa really loved women, but there were occasional exceptions. When Tony was playing love scenes with a beautiful model or actress, very rarely the actress would be someone he didn't like so much. One time I recall him kissing his co-star passionately—and then, when the director said 'cut,' Tony practically dropped the girl on the floor, he let go so fast." He was also surrounded by lovely ladies at work—his receptionist, Molly (Mimi Dillard), and his secretary, Libby (Janet Waldo). Waldo told me, "Libby was just your run-of-the-mill secretary. Looking back, I wish I'd played her kookier." Valentine's occupation was non-fiction editor for Brackett and Dunstall Publishing (at 50 Park Avenue). His boss was O.D. Dunstall (Jerry Hausner). Janet remembered, "Jerry Hausner and I go way back. We worked together a lot and he was a dear friend." In the debut called "The Life You Save Is Yours," a mysterious black-veiled "lady" turned out to be Valentine's old long-lost army buddy, Rockwell "Rocky" Sin (Jack Soo) in disguise. Rocky (who called Val, "Boss") had saved Val's life in the Korean War. Val owed him a favor, which Rocky collected by becoming Val's live-in housekeeper and valet. Rocky had a gambling problem, and this job allowed him to pay off his bookie. Occasionally, we also got to see the handyman, Mr. Fipple (Eddie Quillan). Anne Francis was originally intended to be in the cast, but she had her own show, *Honey West*, around the corner. Both Val and Rocky relished being single—that is, until the episode called "Bride and Gloom," in which Val saw a play about a sad, lonely guy who simply refused to marry, and saw an eerie parallel to his own life. He then had a change of heart, albeit a brief one, and began proposing to every girl he met. Val's military career was the focus of an episode called "Two Weeks with Pay." Val was finally able to take a two-week-vacation, but it was cut short when he was recalled for two weeks of active military duty.

Guest stars included Marlo Thomas (pre-*That Girl*) in "Follow the Broken Pretzel"—a spy caper involving top secret papers which turned out to be merely recipes; Mamie Van Doren played herself in "Yen Ku Horowitz" in which a female stand-up comic tried to get a part in Ms. Van Doren's next picture; George Gobel played Delmore Link who had written a book about the game of poker in an episode called "The Hottest Game in Town;" and the Cleveland Browns' great Jim Brown made a cameo appearance and attempted to get an old friend's book published in "For Me and My Sal." Waldo said, "My favorite episode was 'Viva Valentine,' in which I got to speak French."

Directors included George Marshall, William Graham, Alan Rafkin, Seymour Robbie, Jerry Hopper, Barry Shear, Bruce Humberstone, Christian Nyby, Leslie Goodwins, Bernard Wiesen, Hal Kanter, and Howard Morris (whom Waldo called "my favorite director. He was a very controlled actor and a very uncontrolled director. He was so creative"); writers included Kanter, Michael Fessier, Ken Kolb, Al Lewis, Alan Scott, Max Hodge, Morris, David P. Harmon, and the teams of Ben Gershman and Bill Freedman, Bill Davenport and Charles Tannen, Bruce Howard and Bud Nye, Robert C. Dennis and Earl Barret, and Michael R. Stern and Jack Gross, Jr. Waldo told me, "Hal Kanter was an amazing, wonderful, and extremely funny man. The business will never be the same without him."

This would be Tony Franciosa's only sitcom. He would later surface in *The Name of The Game*, *Search*, and *Matt Helm*. Waldo said, "I loved doing this show. Tony Franciosa was such a talent. He didn't receive the kudos he should have as an actor. He was a bit insecure, however. He was never happy with his scenes and always wanted to reshoot them. The wonderful Hal Kanter had a great comeback—'Tony, you can't be Hamlet every week.' Tony was a very dedicated actor, a perfectionist. But he always worried that the changes he suggested to the director might be accepted without question because they were from him. Then he would see the show and he would say, 'why did they let me do that?'" Janet also remembered, "Tony was devastated when the series was cancelled. ABC then had second thoughts about the cancellation, but Tony was so hurt he then wanted nothing to do with a second season. It's too bad, because the rest of us would love to have continued the series." A few episodes can be viewed in the UCLA TV Archives.

Viva Valdez Rothman/Wohl Productions/ Stan Jacobson Productions/Columbia Pictures Television. ABC. Monday nights 8:00. May 31, 1976–September 6, 1976. 13 episodes were videotaped, only 12 aired.

Viva Valdez was the story of a Chicano family (long before the preferred term became Latino), living in a changing world, attempting to hold on to a few traditional Mexican values amidst all of that change. The Valdez family lived in East Los Angeles at 363 1/2 La Hambre Street (translated: "hungry street") and shopped at the Zamora Brothers Mexican Food Store. The patriarch of the family, Luis (Rodolfo Hoyos), had a plumbing business, and his eldest son, Victor (James Victor), worked with him. Luis was married to Sophia (Carmen Zapata). There were two other Valdez children—boy-crazy teen cheerleader Connie (Lisa Mordente) and artistic, slick ladies' man Ernesto (Nelson D. Cuevas). Two cousins also visited frequently—12-year-old Pepe (Claudio Martinez), who wanted nothing more than to play professional baseball, and Jerry (Jorge Cervera, Jr.), who had just arrived from Mexico speaking very little English. One of the early episodes, "My Fair Jerry," focused upon him. Other episodes include "Father and Son Day," "The Nurse's Pipes," "Nervous Breakup," and "The Apprentice" (the final episode).

The program was produced by Phil Mishkin and Alan Rafkin; the creators and executive producers were Bernard Rothman, Jack Wohl, and Stan Jacobson; writers included Earl Barret, Howard Albrecht, Steve Zacharias, Sol Weinstein, Mishkin, Julie Russo, and Bernie Kahn; and the lone director was Rafkin. The theme song was performed by Shorty Rogers, and written by Julius Wechter.

The Wackiest Ship in the Army John M. Schenck Enterprises, Inc./Screen Gems. NBC. Sunday nights 10:00. September 19, 1965–September 4, 1966. 29 hour-long color episodes were filmed without a laugh track. Sponsors included Alberto-Culver and Liggett and Myers Tobacco.

The Wackiest Ship in the Army was loosely based upon the real-life exploits of the *USS Echo*—a decrepit schooner from the 1870s which was a gift from New Zealand during World War II. The wooden ship was not detectable by radar or sonar, and because of its size it could sail in shallow water. It was used to plant spies behind enemy lines. The ship became the *USS Kiwi* when it became the subject of a popular story by Herbert Carlson, which then led to the 1960 motion picture which starred Jack Lemmon and Ricky Nelson. In 1965, *The Wackiest Ship in the Army* came to television on NBC as an hour-long mixture of comedy, drama and adventure set in the South Pacific. The program had stiff competition from the second half of *The ABC Sunday Night Movie*, and *Candid Camera* and *What's My Line?* on CBS. Friction was a huge part of each episode because when on land Major Simon Butcher (Jack Warden) was in charge, but when at sea Lieutenant Richard "Rip" Riddle (Gary Collins) called the shots—and their methodology differed greatly. Also in the cast were Mike Kellin as CPO Willie Miller; Rudy Solari as Gunner's Mate Sherman Nagurski; and Mark Slade as Radioman Patrick Hollis.

Episodes include the cleverly titled "I'm Dreaming of a Wide Isthmus," an episode aired right before Christmas of 1965 in which the crew's objective was to invade an enemy-held island and destroy its supplies. In "My Island," the *USS Kiwi* sought a place to land so that the fever-wracked crew could get medical attention. The island turned out to be a neutral haven which had never experienced war—that is, until the Japanese came ashore for a surprise visit. In "The Stowaway," an eager news correspondent named Lori Adams (Ruta Lee) became somewhat of a pest when she insisted upon finding out why that 19th century ship was being used in a 20th century war. Ruta Lee shared this great anecdote with me: "It was the last shot of the day, three cameras rolling ... we were losing light. They were to get a shot of us rowing out from the tropical beach to the ship in the small boat. We rowed 50 yards into the bay and our boat filled with water and sank. Water in the boat immediately filled further with pee, as we were laughing hysterically. I adored the cast, and how nice it is that Gary Collins and I have continued to be close, personal friends."

The program was produced by Herbert Hirschman, Joseph Dackow, and E. W. Swackhamer; the executive producer was Harry Ackerman; writers included Julian Barry, Danny Arnold, Sam Perrin, Carey Wilber, Art Wallace, Jack Sher, Marion Hargrove, John O'Dea, Mary Loos, Richard Sale, Lou Shaw, Bill Jacobson, Ed Adamson, Robert Buckner, Arthur Rowe, Herbert Margolis, Stephen Kandel, and Arnold Belgard; and directors included Claudio Guzman, E. W. Swackhamer, Larry Peerce, Arnold, Robert Totten, Herschel Daugherty, Ralph Black, Murray Golden, Leo Penn, Harmon Jones, Alex Nicol, Mark Rydell, Mel Ferber, Richard C. Sarafian, Oscar Rudolph, Joseph Sargent, and Robert Stevens. The theme song was written by Howard Greenfield, Helen Miller and Jack Keller. Music was conducted by Nelson Riddle, and the music consultant was Don Kirshner. The show was briefly syndicated on the long-defunct cable channel CBN in the late eighties. In the 1965–1966 television season, NBC had another color military sitcom based upon a Jack Lemmon movie (and also set in the South Pacific) called *Mister Roberts*. Neither show was invited back for a second season. Jack Gould of *The New York Times* called *The Wackiest Ship in the Army* "the most successful of this season's many endeavors to capitalize on humor in uniform." Gary Collins died October 13, 2012, at the age of 74.

The Waverly Wonders Lorimar Productions. Friday nights 8:00. September 8, 1978–October 6, 1978. Nine episodes were videotaped, only five aired.

Super Bowl champion quarterback Joe Namath played a washed-up quarterback-turned-basketball coach named Joe Casey in this extremely short-lived sitcom. Casey coached at Waverly High School in Eastfield, Wisconsin, where he also taught history. On his hapless team were "Italian Stallion" Tony Faguzzi (Joshua Grenrock); introverted John Tate (Charles Bloom); sly and cunning Hasty Parks (Tierre Turner); and tomboy Connie Rafkin (Kim Lankford)—coincidentally, the team's best player. Among the other faculty members were Linda Harris (Gwynne Gilford)—the pretty principal, and George Benton (Ben Piazza)—the former coach whom the kids called "old prune-face."

Episodes include "Joe Checks Out the Librarian," in which a romance intended to be totally clandestine went public, leading the kids to refer to Mr. Casey as "lover boy." In "Joe Goes to the Press," Joe used a ghostwriter to send a letter to the editor debating a local sportscaster's cruel criticism of his team.

The program was produced by Steve Zacharias and Bruce Kane; the executive producers were Lee Rich and Marc Merson; the creators were William Bickley and Michael Warren; writers included Thad Mumford, Dan Wilcox, Brook Smith, Jim Rogers, Marty Farrell, Deborah Zoe Dawson, Victoria Johns, Dennis Koenig, Stephen Neigher, John Rappaport, Alan Eisenstock, Larry Mintz, Roger Garrett, and Sally Wade; and directors included Dick Martin, Jeff Margolis, and Bill Persky. This show was annihilated in the ratings by *Wonder Woman* on CBS and *Donny and Marie* on ABC.

We'll Get By Helix Productions. CBS. Friday nights 8:30. March 14, 1975–May 30, 1975. 12 color episodes were videotaped before a live audience. The debut episode aired as a special on Thursday March 6, 1975, at 10:30 p.m.

This program had a cutesy theme song by Peter Matz, with lyrics about "learning to be a family." However, getting that TV family together was the first big hurdle. The three kids remained the same, but the parents changed from pilot to series. In the unaired pilot, Ned Beatty played the patriarch of the family, lawyer George Platt, and Elizabeth Wilson was his loving wife, Liz. In the series, set in New Jersey, it was Paul Sorvino in the title role and Mitzi Hoag played his wife. Their three teenage offspring were curly-haired Jerry Houser as Michael "Muff" Platt (the eldest); Devon Scott (George C. Scott's daughter) as Andrea; and Willie Aames as Kenny. Henry Jones made an occasional appearance as Liz's father. The generation gap, teenage angst, school, dating, family, and just "getting by" were fodder for the twelve episodes.

The funny debut called, "Family Portrait," involved daughter Andrea's excessive use of the telephone. In "Muff's Time Out," Muff's wanderlust led him to consider quitting school and hitchhiking to the west coast. In "A Woman's Place Is in the World," Liz had second thoughts about attending night school to better herself (and become a teacher) because she felt that no one in her family could hold down the fort without pandemonium. She went through with her studies, but her misgivings became reality—Dad burned the eggplant dinner, nobody did the dishes, nobody sewed Kenny's torn jacket, and Muff didn't put away his football gear.

The program was produced by Marc Merson; the creator and co-producer was Alan Alda; writers included Alda and Susan Silver; and directors included Jay Sandrich and Jack Shea. Just about everyone on the show went on to other successes—Paul Sorvino did *The Goodfellas* and *Law and Order;* Jerry Houser had a very successful voice-over announcing career; Devon Scott did *The Tony Randall Show;* Willie Aames joined the cast of *Eight Is Enough;* and Henry Jones went on to *Phyllis*. The theme song was written by Sheldon Harnick and Joe Raposo. The unaired pilot is available for viewing at the Paley Center for Media in Beverly Hills, and one regular season episode is available for viewing in the UCLA TV Archives.

Wendy and Me Natwill Productions/Warner Brothers Studios. ABC. Monday nights 9:00. September 14, 1964–September 6, 1965. 34 black-and-white episodes were filmed with a laugh track. Sponsors included El Producto.

George Burns had it proven to him on *The George Burns Show* that he just couldn't go it alone. He needed a co-star. He needed a Gracie. He found someone who could carry off the same kind of word-twisting "Gracie schtick" in Connie Stevens. Connie played the scatterbrained Wendy Conway. George Burns said of the Wendy character, "It's too bad they don't have conclusion jumping in the Olympics, because with Wendy in it the Russians wouldn't have a chance." Indeed, conclusion jumping and misunderstandings were the fodder for all 34 very funny episodes. To get Connie Stevens for the role, George had to agree to produce another Warner Brothers sitcom, *No Time for Sergeants*, which preceded *Wendy and Me* on Monday nights.

The action took place in the Sunset DeVille Apartment complex in Los Angeles at 4820 Highland. Burns played himself, owned the building, lived in apartment number nine (104 in some episodes), and, much like he did on *The George Burns and Gracie Allen Show*, served as the narrator (or interlocutor). He knew everything that was going on around him. He was always rehearsing in his apartment just in case vaudeville ever made a comeback. The Conways lived in apartment number 17 (217 in later episodes). Wendy's Trans-Globe Airlines pilot was husband, Jeff, portrayed by Ron Harper. Ron told me, "I think the change in the apartment numbers was to better convey the fact that George

Wendy and Me—**Left to right, Ron Harper, Connie Stevens, George Burns, and James Callahan (photograph courtesy of Ron Harper).**

lived on the ground floor and that we lived on the second floor." Jeff's co-pilot, Danny Adams (James Callahan), was a chronic womanizer and lived in apartment 19 (219 in later episodes). If he had to go even one evening without seeing a woman, he'd go through withdrawal. Also in the building was the kindly but befuddled Mr. Bundy (J. Pat O'Malley). Poor Mr. Bundy would be asked to assist Wendy in all of her hair-brained schemes. Whenever he'd confront his boss, George Burns, about Wendy's latest bizarre request, George's response was invariably, "Do it." George said the same two words in each episode going into commercial breaks. Harper recalled, "George Burns always lit a fresh cigar. He never reused any." Ron also said, "Gracie Allen passed away during the year we did the show. George was so distraught, he immersed himself in his work. Burying himself in his work got him through it."

Ron remembered the other members of the cast: "Connie and I have remained good friends until this day. James Callahan was a wonderful friend. In fact, at a Valentine's Party which we both attended, I hit it off better with James' blind date. That woman, Sally Stark, later became my wife (with James' blessing, of course). I miss him very much. And J. Pat O'Malley was wonderful. While on a promotional tour for the show, I brought James Callahan and J. Pat O'Malley to my hometown of Turtle Creek, Pennsylvania, to meet my family. J. Pat O'Malley and my family hit it off extremely well."

Episodes include "Mountains to Molehills," in which Wendy, in an attempt to guarantee that Danny Adams would pass his airline physical the next day, took charge of his little black book and attempted to keep Danny at home all evening. In "Danny's Double Life," Danny secured an apartment in another building for a friend, the friend's wife, and their baby. However, Wendy was under the impression that the other apartment was for Danny, and that the wife and baby were his. In "Wendy's Five-Thousand-Dollar Chair," a chair on which Wendy was seated in a restaurant broke. When the insurance men called her at home after the accident, she thought they were attempting to get her to pay for the broken chair, but they were actually offering her a settlement to keep her from suing them. A young Raquel Welch guest starred as Lila in the episode titled "Wendy Sails in the Sunset."

Directors included Richard Crenna and Gene Reynolds; writers included Norman Paul, Elon Packard, and William Burns. Music was provided by George Duning.

This program faced some stiff Monday night competition from *The Lucy Show* on CBS, and *The Andy Williams Show* on NBC. Episodes can be viewed in the UCLA TV Archives. Connie Stevens attempted sitcom success again years later in another short-lived show, *Starting from Scratch*.

Wesley CBS Television Productions. CBS. Sunday nights 7:30 (May 8, 1949–June 12, 1949), Tuesday nights 9:30 (July 19, 1949–August 23, 1949), and Tuesday nights 8:00 (August 30, 1949). 13 episodes were broadcast live.

Wesley Eggleston (played originally by Donald Devlin) was a precocious 12-year-old boy, almost a teenager, but not in much of a hurry to grow up. He enjoyed living in a rural area (unidentified), being a kid, and playing with his best buddy, Alvin (Billie Nevard) who was more like a brother. In fact, he would have traded his older sister, Elizabeth (Joy Reese), for a brother any day of the week—they fought a lot. Wesley had a good relationship with his parents, Mr. and Mrs. Eggleston (real-life married couple Frank and Mary Thomas), although there were some minor and very normal disagreements. Also in the cast were Joe Sweeney as Grandpa and Jack Ayers as Elizabeth's boyfriend. After the June 12 episode, the show went on hiatus for a month, and Donald Devlin was replaced for unknown reasons by Johnny Stewart in the role of Wesley Eggleston for the remaining seven episodes beginning on July 19.

The most interesting part of *Wesley* occurred behind-the-scenes. The show's writer, Samuel Taylor, went on to write screenplays including the Alfred Hitchcock classic *Vertigo*, which starred Jimmy Stewart. The director, Franklin Schaffner, went on to produce many of TV's best and longest running live anthology shows such as *Playhouse 90*, *Studio One*, and even *Person To Person*, with Edward R. Murrow. Schaffner, together with the producer of *Wesley*, Worthington Miner, formed the Unit Four production company in 1955. Miner was the producer and executive producer of many prestigious TV programs such as *Medic*, *Frontier*, *The Kaiser Aluminum Hour*, and *The Play of the Week*. To my knowledge, no episodes of *Wesley* exist.

Westinghouse Playhouse (Yes, Yes Nanette/ The Nanette Fabray Show) Beejay Productions/Revue Studios. NBC. Friday nights 8:30 (January 6, 1961–April 1961), and Friday nights 9:30 (April 1961–July 7, 1961). 26 black-and-white episodes were filmed with a laugh track. Sponsored by Westinghouse.

This vehicle for Nanette Fabray had an interesting premise. It was loosely based upon her real-life experiences. She portrayed a former Broadway star who fell madly in love with a screenwriter named Dan McGovern (Wendell Corey), who had been a widower for six years. After a whirlwind courtship, they were wed. Dan's nickname for his new bride was "Nanny Goat." There was one snag—Dan hadn't told Nancy (Jacklyn O'Donnell) and 15-year-old Buddy (Bobby Diamond), his two children from his previous marriage. This led to all sorts of problems in the debut episode, "Amateur Mother," including a palpable distance and rudeness from the kids toward their new stepmom (albeit briefly), and also from the housekeeper, Mrs. Harper (Doris Kemper). Mrs. Harper and the kids eventually adapted to, and favorably accepted Nan later in that, and all subsequent episodes. Nan took over many of the household chores at that point, thus Mrs. Harper was only seen on occasion. There was another interesting change—the program altered its title a couple of times. It was initially called *Westinghouse Playhouse*, but somewhere along the way it became *The Nanette Fabray Show* and *Yes, Yes Nanette* (a take-off on the Broadway hit *No, No Nanette*).

Episodes include "Planned Picnic," in which Nan made an attempt to get her disorganized family into a routine which accounted for every moment of every day. Needless to say, it just didn't work out, and all soon returned to their old haphazard ways. In "Moth Trap," both Dan and Nan encountered old flames from show business. Upon becoming reacquainted, Dan and Nan immediately realized just how very shallow their old lovers were and devised a scheme to make them leave. In the episode called "For Better or Worse," we found out that Nan was a Taurus, Dan was a Scorpio, and Mrs. Harper was a Sagittarius.

The program was produced by Larry Berns

and created by Nanette's real-life husband, Ranald McDougall; writers included Si Rose, Seaman Jacobs, Luther Davis, Alan Lipscott, Bob Fisher, Benedict Freedman, John Fenton Murray, Hugh Wedlock, and Howard Snyder; and directors included Herschel Daugherty and Jerry Hopper. Music was provided by Axel Stordahl. Several episodes can be viewed at the Paley Center for Media.

We've Got Each Other MTM/Company Four Productions. CBS. Saturday nights 8:30. October 1, 1977–January 14, 1978. 13 color episodes were recorded before a live audience at CBS Studio Center. Sponsored by Sure Deodorant.

Even sandwiched between *The Bob Newhart Show* and *The Jeffersons*, this MTM domestic sitcom failed to attract an audience, and had a very short prime time life. Well, they were hardly Angelina Jolie and Brad Pitt—the Hibbards were very plain-looking folks. The most interesting part of their story was the role reversal angle of the show. Pudgy Stuart Hibbard, played by Oliver Clark, worked at home. Not only was he the chief cook and bottle washer, he conducted his business out of the Hibbard household. Stuart was a copywriter for the unique and, frankly, useless gadgets in the Herman Gutman Mail Order Catalog. One constant distraction for Stuart was his very fit but extremely dimwitted next door neighbor, Ken Renford (Martin Kove), who was a swimming pool contractor, and often quite a nuisance. Meanwhile, Stuart's wife, long and lanky Judy Hibbard (Beverly Archer), worked as the office manager at a busy photography studio in Los Angeles. Her boss was the skittish, absent-minded Damon Jerome (Tom Poston). Mr. Jerome was a very good photographer, but he lacked business savvy and was quite forgetful. One of the studio's top models was the moody, self-involved, demanding and acerbic Dee Dee Baldwin (Joan Van Ark). Judy and Dee Dee frequently came close to fisticuffs. Keeping the peace was their African American secretary, Donna (Ren Woods). Donna apparently had no last name, and the actress who portrayed her is now known as Renn Woods with an extra "n." I asked her about that and she said, "That domain name was taken. There's an on-line store in the UK known as Renwoods. I added an 'n' to lessen the confusion."

Renn remembers her co-stars very fondly: "It was an enchanted set. This was one of the best experiences of my entire career. Grant Tinker was so kind, funny and charming—I'm a 'Tinker Girl.' Tom Poston was so sweet—he could make one feel as though they were the most important person on earth. He was also a notorious prankster and whoopee cushions were his specialty. Joan Van Ark was an absolute delight, Beverly Archer was one of the most straight ahead normal people in the business, and poor Oliver Clark was so nice but not in the best of

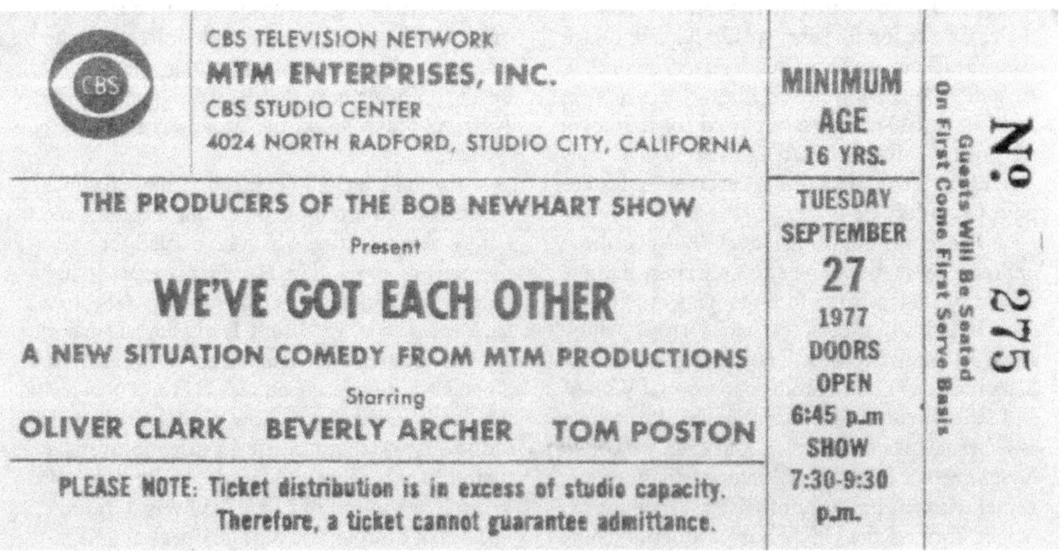

We've Got Each Other—unredeemed ticket to a taping.

health. I never got to know Martin Kove very well. All of his scenes were at the Hibbard's home—I don't think we did even one scene together."

In the debut, Judy had just quit her job at the photography studio as working with Dee Dee had simply become intolerable. Just as Judy was starting to settle in, enjoying being unemployed, Stuart devised a scheme to get her back to work because having her underfoot was driving him crazy. In "Pumping Iron," after ogling numerous body builders using the studio for a photo shoot, Judy inspired Stuart to become more physically fit with the help of fitness guru, Ken. In return, Stuart agreed to teach Ken some new polysyllabic words each day.

The program was created by Tom Patchett and Jay Tarses, who also served as executive producers; the producer was Jack Burns; writers included Mary-David Sheiner, Sheila Judis Weisberg, Sy Rosen, Jack Burns, Madeline DiMaggio, Kathy Donnell, Lloyd Garver, Tarses, and Patchett; and directors included James Burrows, Tony Mordente, Asaad Kelada, Lee Bernhardi, Michael Zinberg, George Tyne, Will Mackenzie, and Harvey Medlinsky. The theme song, "As Long as We've Got Each Other," was by Nino Candido; other music was provided by Clark Gassman. Two episodes can be viewed at the Paley Center for Media.

A *New York Times* review of the program by John J. O'Connor was positive: "As in most MTM efforts, the situations are simple and the comedy is inspired. The season's most promising entry."

When Things Were Rotten Crossbow Productions/Paramount Studios. ABC. Wednesday nights 8:00. September 10, 1975–December 24, 1975. 13 color episodes were filmed with a laugh track.

The Adventures of Robin Hood, starring Richard Greene, ran for three seasons on CBS in the mid–1950s. However, this particular 1975 interpretation of Robin Hood had Mel Brooks written all over it. This was a parody in which

When Things Were Rotten—**Left to right, David Sabin, Dick Van Patten, Dick Gautier, Richard Dimitri, Bernie Kopell (photograph courtesy of Jean Cummings).**

Robin was rather zany (as were his Merry Men). Set in 12th century England, Robin Hood was played by Dick Gautier, who told me, "I wish we got to wear the kind of tights they make today. The ones we had tended to droop and wrinkle a lot. It was hilarious—the entire cast was constantly pulling them up." Also in the cast were Friar Tuck as portrayed by Dick Van Patten; Alan-a-Dale by Bernie Kopell; Bertram and Renaldo (identical twin brothers) were both played by Richard Dimitri (Bertram was the Sheriff's right-hand man, while Renaldo was one of Robin's Merry Men); the Sheriff of Nottingham was played by Henry Polic II; peace-loving Maid Marion by Misty Rowe; Little John by David Sabin; Prince John by Ron Rifkin; and Princess Isabelle by Jane A. Johnston. Sight gags, one-liners, slapstick, and humorous asides directed to the viewer were plentiful. The most memorable moments were those involving anachronisms, such as a reference to *The Galloping Gourmet*; the proposed cutting down of Sherwood Forest to build a housing complex; the Merry Men doing the Bunny Hop; the inclusion of songs such as "My Melancholy Baby," "My Way," "Wedding Bell Blues" and "Stop in the Name of Love"; a working intercom system in the castle; a nurse asking a patient if he had medical insurance; and the destruction of the Rock Of Gibraltar (to which Prince John added, "I've always wanted 'a piece of the rock,' a line from those Prudential Insurance commercials). Gautier remembered his favorite line, "It was in the debut episode where the townspeople were told to hold their tongues, and they did—literally." The comedy came at you fast and furious. Critics loved it, but ratings weren't strong, and it quickly disappeared.

Gautier recalled, "We had rigorous training to be able to accomplish the necessary feats on horseback, and especially for the swordplay. We weren't using epees like they use in fencing, we had swords. Now, Errol Flynn in the movies had three weeks to complete his sword fights—we had to complete ours in one afternoon, leading to many hilarious outtakes with Henry Polic and me. I wish I could find those outtakes."

Episodes include the debut, "The Capture of Robin Hood," in which the narcissistic Robin was challenged to an archery contest. It was a trap, and he was thrown into the castle dungeon, only to be rescued by his Merry Men disguised as a conga band. In "Ding Dong, the Bell Is Dead," Prince John purloined the Abbey Bell. The onus was then on the Merry Men to steal it back. In "Quarantine," everyone (including Robin and his Merry Men) was quarantined in the castle for what was thought to be "the plague," but actually turned out to be bad ox meat prepared by the castle cook (Joe E. Ross). Gautier remembered, "It was such a funny, happy set—a blast. We laughed day and night almost non-stop."

The program was created by Mel Brooks, John Boni, and Norman Stiles; the producer was Norman Steinberg; writers included John Regier and Gary Markowitz; and directors included Norman Abbott, Bruce Bilson, Peter Bonerz, Jerry Paris, and Coby Ruskin. The clever theme song and its lyrics were from Charles Strouse and Lee Adams (of *Bye Bye Birdie* fame). In 1993, Brooks went to the Robin Hood well one more time (with more success) in *Robin Hood: Men in Tights*. Dick Van Patten appeared in both the TV series and the movie. Reruns were briefly shown on the HA! cable network.

Who's Watching the Kids? Henderson Productions/Paramount Studios. NBC. Friday nights 8:30. September 22, 1978–December 15, 1978. Ten color episodes were filmed before a live audience.

This show had an interesting history. First of all, it shared a lot of personnel (both on and off camera) with the equally short-lived *Blansky's Beauties* from 1977. *Who's Watching the Kids?* originated as an hour-long pilot called *Legs* on May 19, 1978 on ABC. It garnered enough "legs" in the ratings to be placed on the new NBC fall programming schedule. Yes, the pilot and the series aired on different networks. Caren Kaye remembered, "Indeed, a different network, but the producers liked the idea and gave it a shot." At first, the show was about two Las Vegas showgirls (Caren Kaye as Stacy Turner, and Lynda Goodfriend as Angie Vitola), who worked in a cheesy nightspot called "Club Sand Pile." They shared an apartment and each had a big responsibility—taking care of their younger siblings. Stacy was the caretaker for her younger sister Melissa Turner (Tammy Lauren), and Angie took care of her younger brother, the street-savvy Frankie Vitola (Scott Baio). Marcia Lewis played Mitzi Logan, the girls' landlady and emcee at the "Club Sand Pile." Mitzi always entered the apartment through an open window, never the front door.

There were many similarities between the pilot and the actual series, except that the show was now called *Who's Watching the Kids?*, and in the series the girls had an arrangement that while at work, the kids would be "watched" by a couple of guys who lived in the same apartment complex—TV cameraman Bert Gunkel—sometimes called "Gunk" to his dismay (Jim Belushi, then known as James Belushi), and local KVGS-TV newscaster Larry Parnell (Larry Breeding). Larry had aspirations of becoming a world famous newscaster, and for inspiration had a large photo of NBC's David Brinkley on the wall in his living room. In one of the better episodes, "Hit and Run," Bert and Larry had a falling out. Bert was so upset over the argument, he visited a local bar, had quite a few too many, and in a drunken stupor hired a hit man to kill Larry. Bert then had to find the hit man to call it off, but he remembered very little about the man, thus finding him proved almost impossible. As the series progressed, the focus on the guys grew, while the girls were being phased out (with Caren Kaye eventually disappearing completely). Caren told me, "The head of the studio changed, and apparently Fred Silverman was not a fan of the original format or me. I went to Garry Marshall and asked to be released from my contract, as I saw what was down the road. Garry is a wonderful man, and allowed me to leave and move on to other shows while still collecting my salary. That was not my intent, but I am forever grateful." Larry, Bert and the kids became the focus of the remaining episodes of *Who's Watching the Kids?* These changes didn't help a bit, and after ten episodes nobody was watching the kids.

The show was created by Garry Marshall, Bob Brunner, and Arthur Silver; the executive producers were Marshall, Tony Marshall, and Don Silverman; producers included Marty Wadler and Gary Menteer; writers included Roger Garrett; and directors included David Ketchum. The theme song was written and performed by Charles Bernstein. Kaye reminisced about a couple of her co-stars: "Jim Belushi was like a little brother to me, and Scott Baio—I worked in three shows with him, and kept urging him to go to college just in case." One episode was rerun on TV Land.

Willy Desilu Studios/Official Films. CBS. Saturday nights 10:30 (September 25, 1954–March 26, 1955), and Thursday nights 10:30 (April 7, 1955–July 7, 1955). 39 black-and-white episodes were filmed with a sweetened laugh track (28 episodes—format one, 11 episodes—format two). Sponsors included General Mills

Much like *The Lucy Show*, *The Doris Day Show*, *Sally*, *The Joey Bishop Show* and *It's About Time*, this early sitcom called *Willy* changed formats midstream. The original working title was *My Aunt Willy*, and in the beginning, Willa "Willy" Dodger (June Havoc, the younger sister of Gypsy Rose Lee), opened a law office six months prior to the debut episode. She found it difficult being a lady lawyer in 1954. Garnering the trust of the people of tiny Renfrew, New Hampshire, was a big challenge. Until now, she had no clients whatsoever and items in her office were being repossessed (including much needed law books). Willy lived in a rather large old house with her dad, Papa Dodger (Weaton Chamber), her older sister, Emily Dodger (Mary Treen); and Emily's son, Franklin Dodger (Danny Richards, Jr.). The family all thought that Willy should have remained at her old job as a store clerk, but they were supportive of her struggling law practice because Willy's grandfather, William Makepeace Dodger, had been a respected circuit judge in Renfrew. Willy's on-again/off-again romantic interest was the town veterinarian, Charley Bush (Whitfield Connor). Ranger the dog was portrayed by Rags. Ranger turned out to be Willy's very first client when he was accused of chasing a neighbor's cow. The cow was so traumatized by the event that it could no longer give milk. Speaking of dogs, the town dog catcher, Jim Baxter, was played by a very young Aaron Spelling, who would go on to create a TV empire. *Willy* replaced the Bert Parks game show *Two in Love*.

This small town proved to be too limiting for an up-and-coming lawyer, so in March of 1955, Willy moved to the big city where she now gave legal counsel to a vaudevillian organization run by Perry Bannister (Hal Peary). Now that Willy had moved out and was working for the Bannister Vaudeville Company, all of the old regulars were gone—even the dog. Added to the fray was Sterling Holloway as Harvey Evelyn, the repertory company's manager. A few weeks after the format change, the time slot changed from Saturday nights to Thursday nights. Neither helped the ratings very much and after 11 new format episodes, *Willy* was canceled by CBS.

The program was directed by William Asher and George M. Cahan; June Havoc's real-life husband, William Spier, was the producer. Spier also created the show and co-wrote many of the episodes along with Louis Pelletier, Robert Fisher, and Alan Lipscott.

Window on Main Street A Rodney-Young Production/Temopic Enterprises, Inc./Desilu Studios. CBS. Monday nights 8:30 (October 2, 1961–February 1962), and Wednesday nights 8:00 (February 1962–September 12, 1962). 34 black-and-white episodes were filmed with a laugh track. Sponsors included Scott Paper and Toni.

Much in the same way Andy Griffith left *The Andy Griffith Show* at the peak of its popularity, Robert Young left *Father Knows Best* after its most successful season. Young had grown tired of the role of Jim Anderson—he'd originated it on radio in 1949 and was looking for a new challenge. Utilizing the same creative team, the result was an intelligent, well-written, but low-rated single season sentimental sitcom called *Window on Main Street*. The original working title was *The Robert Young Show*. Young portrayed a mildly successful author named Cameron Garrett Brooks, who left his hometown of Millsburg 27 years earlier seeking fame and fortune. Now, after the death of his wife and child, he returned to Millsburg (which had changed dramatically) to write about the people who lived there. Brooks reconnected with a boyhood buddy named Lloyd Ramsey (Ford Rainey), who was now the editor of *The Courier News*. Lloyd's secretary, Chris Logan (Constance Moore), had a 13-year-old son named Arny (Brad Berwick), who instantly developed hero worship for the returning author. Brooks' new home was a suite (room 212) in the Majestic Hotel (a place he had dreamed of staying as a boy) with a balcony that had a wonderful view of Main Street. It was young Arny who coined the phrase "window on Main Street," which became the title of Brooks' book about Millsburg. Other recurring characters included desk clerk Harry McGil (Warner Jones) and elderly chambermaid Lavinia Webster (Mary Adams).

The pilot, "The Return," was especially well done, and utilized a wonderful surprise ending, in which the mysterious Tina Holtzman from Cameron's past turned out to be none other than Chris Logan (a widow) who worked at the newspaper. Her given name was Christina, but wished to be called Tina as a young girl (but Chris later in life). In "The Teacher," after Arny got an eyeful of his favorite teacher, Miss Wilma Henderson (Lisabeth Hush), necking with Harry, the desk clerk, in a parked car, he shunned her and his grades began to suffer. In "The Boy Who Got Too Many Laughs," Michael J. Pollard portrayed Ziggy Vance, the class clown, who hired Mr. Brooks to write him a moving speech so that people (namely his love interest, Sally, played by Dana Whittaker) would begin to take him seriously.

The program was added to the CBS prime time lineup without a pilot. The creator was Roswell Rogers; the producer was Eugene B. Rodney; writers included Rogers, Theodore and Mathilde Ferro, John McGreevey, Joel Malone and Tommy Tomlinson; and directors included

***Window on Main Street*—Left to right, Ford Rainey, Constance Moore, and Robert Young (photograph courtesy of Jeff Huybloom at *www.fatherknowsbest.com*).**

Richard Dunlap and Byron Paul. Numerous episodes are available as bonus features on each of the six season DVD box sets of *Father Knows Best* from Shout Factory, and the "Christmas Memory" episode is available on a set called *Merry Sitcom.*

Wonderful John Acton An Edward A. Byron Production. NBC. Sunday nights 10:00 (July 5, 1953–August 31, 1953), and Tuesday nights 8:30 (September 8, 1953–September 22, 1953). 13 black-and-white episodes were broadcast live without a laugh track, and a few had a live audience. Sponsors include Revlon.

Where *Mama* was a family's story told from a daughter's perspective, *Wonderful John Acton* was from a grandson's perspective. We never saw, but only heard the adult version of Kevin, who served as the narrator (the voice of Les Damon). We did get to see the 12-year-old version of Kevin on screen. More than *Mama*, this show was a precursor to *The Wonder Years* (and coincidentally the person reminiscing in both programs was named Kevin). Kevin Acton had a paper route, loved rabbits, and was played by Ronnie Walken (who later became Christopher Walken). The Acton family resided in the Ohio Valley town of Ludlow, Kentucky (just across the Ohio River from Cincinnati). Our story took place in 1919. John Acton (Harry Holcombe) was referred to as "Wonderful John Acton" by narrator Kevin—thus, the name of the show. John had come to America from Dublin in 1888. He was a widower and was the county clerk in Ludlow, where he also had a sweet shop (candy and ice cream). John's initials, "JNO Acton," appeared on the front window of the sweet shop (however, we never did find out what the "N" and the "O" stood for). The Acton family lived behind the store; John owned the entire building. Kevin's widowed mother (John's daughter), Julia (Virginia Dwyer), was a "red-haired saint with a sense of humor," according to narrator Kevin. She refused to let her only offspring be called "a poor fatherless child." A picture of Kevin's dad in a military uniform sat in a frame in the background. John's sister, Bessie Acton, was played by Jane Rose. Also living behind the store was Terrence Acton (Ian Martin). Kevin called him "great uncle" with a lot of emphasis on the word "great." "Great Uncle Terrence" could build the best kites and dream the best dreams, according to Kevin. Terrence never forgot a promise. Terrence also worked in the sweet shop, but was very bad at balancing the books. John could never tell if they were in the red or in the black. In maybe the only surviving episode, titled "Uncle Terrence Balances the Books," Terrence got a new-fangled cash register from Peter Bodkins, Jr. played by Roger Sullivan (the Bodkinses were friends of the Actons). However, once Terrence locked up the money and valuables in the "metal contraption" (as John called it), he couldn't get it open again.

The program was produced by Edward A. Byron; writers included Martha Wilkerson, Byron, Robert J. Shaw, and William Kendall Clarke; and directors included Grey Lockwood. Music was provided by John Gart.

Working Stiffs Frog Productions/Huk, Inc./Paramount Studios. CBS. Saturday nights 8:00. September 15, 1979–October 6, 1979. Seven episodes were filmed before a live audience at Paramount Studios Stage 19, only four aired.

This program was the first casualty of the 1979 fall TV season (because of fierce competition from NBC's *CHiPs*). *Working Stiffs* featured two very talented physical comedians, Michael Keaton, as Mike O'Rourke (the younger brother), and Jim Belushi, as Ernie O'Rourke. They had a tough time in the job market and decided to ask their Uncle Harry (Michael Conrad) for a job in the building he owned (the O'Rourke Building in Chicago). Uncle Harry was initially against the idea of hiring family, but when the boys recalled that he'd promised them a job at their communion, he acquiesced. The ambitious yet clumsy O'Rourke brothers were given a maintenance job, and were instantly at odds with their new boss, Al Steckler (Val Bisoglio), but tried to hold down the job anyway to make their Uncle Harry proud, and to put food on their table (the only things in their refrigerator were candy and spoiled milk). The O'Rourke brothers shared an apartment above the Playland Café and became good friends with the owner, Mitch Hannigan (Alan Arbus), and his pregnant waitress, Nikki Evashevsky (Lorna Patterson).

In the debut called "The Preview Presentation," Mike and Ernie were called upon to change a light bulb on the building's clock (which, of course, was on the building's edifice on the top floor). The brothers had quite a harrowing experience on the ledge just getting to the clock, unaware that a trap door behind the clock would have made it a much easier task. In "Looking for Mr. Goodwrench," a new do-it-all tool allowed Steckler to fire one of the O'Rourke brothers—but which one?

In "The Bank Robbery," an up-and-coming Pee Wee Herman made a guest appearance as Heimlich, the Playland Café's delivery boy.

The program was produced by Harry Colomby; the executive producers were Bob Brunner and Arthur Silver; writers included Marc Sotkin, E. Jack Kaplan, and Alan Aidekman; and directors included Penny Marshall (the debut episode), Norman Abbott, and Greg Antonacci. The theme song's music and lyrics were written by Jack Carone. Reruns were shown briefly on A&E and the HA! cable networks.

The Wren's Nest A Shirling Hollover Production. ABC. Thursday/Friday/Saturday nights (thrice weekly) at 7:15. January 13, 1949–April 30, 1949. Approximately 48 fifteen-minute episodes were broadcast live without a laugh track and without a live audience.

Sam Wren and Virginia Sale both had numerous movie credits on their respective resumes. He had appeared in *The Old Grey Mayor* and *Marked Woman* and she had appeared in light fare such as *Topper* and *The Thin Man Goes Home*. Very early in 1949, this "married in real-life couple" also portrayed a married couple living in New York in this short-lived fifteen-minute live sitcom called *The Wren's Nest*, which aired on Thursday, Friday and Saturday nights. Episodes dealt with raising twelve-year-old twins, Chris and Ginny, and the minor calamities of everyday life. The biggest problems on *The Wren's Nest* revolved around Virginia hiding an expensive new hat she'd just purchased, or what she served Sam's boss when he came over to dinner.

A kinescope of *The Wren's Nest* is available for viewing at the UCLA TV Archives. In this episode, Sam had a hankering for fudge and decided to take a stab at making some. He had to improvise along the way because he was missing a few of the ingredients listed in the cookbook. There was no chocolate in the house, so he used hot cocoa powder. There was no corn syrup in the house, so he again had to substitute. His creation ended up looking like anything but what was intended, and when he tried to use an oral thermometer to see if the temperature of the fudge was the temperature suggested in the cookbook, he accidentally broke it in the fudge. Because the thermometer contained mercury, he was unable to ingest the finished product.

The program was written by Virginia Sale; directors included Charles Howard and Tom DeHuff.

A Year at the Top T. A. T. Communications/ Norman Lear Productions. CBS. Friday nights 8:00 (August 5, 1977), and Sunday nights 8:30 (August 14, 1977–September 4, 1977). Five episodes were videotaped before a live audience.

A Year at the Top was over "a year in the making" before it finally aired, briefly, in the summer of 1977. It was originally an NBC project and the first pilot had a different cast (with Robert Alda and Vivian Blaine). For CBS, it was initially slated to be a mid-season entry (beginning in January 1977), but "production and conceptual problems" led to the show constantly being recast, reconfigured, and delayed. Producer Darryl Hickman clarified these conceptual problems: "Norman Lear liked our pilot but CBS didn't, so a friend of Norman Lear's named Al Burton and I reconceptualized the show and geared it to a younger audience. This pilot CBS liked." Singer/songwriter Ron Dante told me, "I auditioned for this pilot, but didn't get the part. They were looking for a foursome originally, and then a trio, and a duet when it finally became a series." It was the story of two wide-eyed songwriters chasing their dream of fame and fortune. They'd written some songs together, as well as a Broadway musical. Greg (Greg Evigan) and Paul (Paul Shaffer) left their hometown of Boise, Idaho, and headed to Hollywood "for their big break." In the hour-long pilot episode (available for viewing at the Paley Center for Media), they were accompanied by Greg's girlfriend, Linda (Priscilla Lopez, who was a singer who wanted to make it on Broadway); Grandma Belle Durbin (Nedra Volz); and her son, their Uncle Mickey Durbin (Mickey Rooney). As Hickman remembered, "Mickey was a creative genius, but irrepressible and difficult to handle. On one occasion, the director called my office and asked me, as the producer, to come down to the rehearsal hall and talk to him. Mickey and I had a long history together. I asked him to step out into the hallway. We had a discussion, and he promised not to cause any more problems, and indeed he didn't. It was smooth sailing from then on." It was Uncle Mickey who brought the boys to Paragon Records—he had some old connections there. Unfortunately, upon arrival at the Paragon offices, Mickey was told that his connection had passed on, and the business was under new management. Mickey was then scolded by the bossy receptionist, Miss Worley (Priscilla Morrill), that no one got in to see Frederick J. Hanover (Gabriel Dell). Hanover was a wicked, smarmy, extremely flamboyant "idol maker," who had created the sensation known to the world as Billy Worthy (Tim Thomerson). There was one other very important point about Hanover—he was the "son of satan," and for one's "year at the top," one had to sign a contract selling one's soul to the devil. He'd gotten Billy Worthy to sign, but Hanover's dad, the devil, called on the (appropriately) red "hotline" phone demanding two more souls immediately. Seizing the opportunity, Hanover decided to make the boys from Boise into superstars (Hanover pronounced Boise as "Bwa-ZAY"). However, Greg and Paul were merely songwriters and couldn't sing or play instruments—that is, until they met Hanover. Linda and Uncle Mickey were suspicious of the goings-on, but Greg and Paul suddenly had their every dream fulfilled and were having way too much fun to notice. Luckily, however, because of the show's extremely short run, Greg and Paul never did get around to signing that contract with the devil. Whenever they did try to discuss the terms of this contract with anyone, their words were instantly intercepted with bizarre non-sequiturs such as, "There's a squirrel in my shorts."

The program was created by Woody Kling, developed by Don Kirshner, and produced by Darryl Hickman. Norman Lear was the executive producer. Hickman said, "Norman was very loyal to actors. Nedra Volz and Priscilla Morrill were two of his favorites, and he used them in many of his projects." Darryl also told me, "I thought we had a good, unique show, but I don't think CBS was fully behind the project. That's the nature of the business." Writers included Sandy Veith, and directors included Alan Rafkin and Marlena Laird. The theme song was written by Paul Shaffer and Howard Greenfield.

Yes, Yes Nanette (see *Westinghouse Playhouse*)

Young and Gay (The Girls) CBS. Sunday nights 7:00. January 1, 1950–March 26, 1950. 13 episodes were broadcast live.

Author Emily Kimbrough wears the distinction of having two of her books from the 1940s turned into TV sitcoms in the 1950s. *It Gives Me Great Pleasure* inspired *The Eve Arden Show* in 1957, but long before that, a short-lived sitcom was based upon a book she co-wrote with Cornelia Otis Skinner, called *Our Hearts Were Young and Gay*, about their funny, real-life adventures on a post-graduate fling in Europe (they both graduated from Bryn Mawr College), and their eventual search for careers after settling down in New York's Greenwich Village in the roaring 20s. Skinner wanted to be an actress and Kimbrough wanted to make it as a writer. It was thought that those adventures would make great fodder for a TV sitcom. The program debuted on New Year's Day 1950, replacing *Tonight on Broadway*.

The title of the book was shortened for the TV sitcom to simply *Young and Gay*, and after only two episodes, on January 15, 1950, the title was again changed—this time to *The Girls* for the remainder of the show's short run. Mary Malone portrayed Emily Kimbrough and originally Bethel Leslie portrayed Cornelia Otis Skinner. However, Leslie received an offer she simply couldn't refuse and left to work opposite Helen Hayes in a play titled *The Wisteria Trees* (based upon Anton Chekhov's *The Cherry Orchard*) and was replaced for the few remaining episodes by Gloria Stroock (older sister of actress Geraldine Brooks). Also in the cast was Kenneth Forbes as Todhunter Smith II.

The program was produced by Carol Irwin and directed by David Rich and Frank Schaffner. To my knowledge, no episodes exist. Mary Malone went on to become the second of three actresses to portray Mary Aldrich on the TV adaptation of *The Aldrich Family*; Bethel Leslie had recurring roles on daytime soap operas such as *Another World* and *All My Children*; and Gloria Stroock went on to roles in such films as *The Day of the Locust* and *The Competition*.

Young Mr. Bobbin NBC. Sunday nights 7:30. August 26, 1951–May 18, 1952. Broadcast live from (what is now known as) NEP Metropolis Studios in Manhattan. Sponsors included General Foods, Jello.

Jackie Kelk had a long run as Jimmy Olsen on the radio version of *The Adventures of Superman*. He also played the first Homer Brown on *The Aldrich Family* on TV. This was his only starring role. The original working title was *Young Mr. Button*, but it became *Young Mr. Bobbin* and revolved around 18-year-old recent high school graduate Alexander Hawthorne Bobbin who had dozens of aspirations, but he was lacking in the ability department. The stories revolved around his attempts to mature and establish himself in the grown-up world. Bobbin was head-over-heels in love with the girl next door, Nancy (Pat Hosley). She liked Bobbin, too, but chose to play hard to get, lest he think he was the only man in her life. Nancy's younger sister, Susie (Laura

Young Mr. Bobbin—**Left to right, Jane Seymour, Jackie Kelk, and Nydia Westman (photograph courtesy of Brian J. Bohnett).**

Weber), continually tried to get the couple together. Resembling *Bringing Up Buddy*, which would come almost a decade later, Bobbin lived in a very old house with his two spinster aunts who had raised him—tall and tidy Clara (Jane Seymour) and short and daft Bertha (Nydia Westman).

In the untitled episode which aired March 16, 1952, Bobbin's boss recommended that he apply for membership in the town's best club as an aide to make more business contacts. However, he was blackballed by the club and when his friends attempted to help him become a clubman, the results were disastrous.

Up against *The Jack Benny Program* on CBS on Sunday nights, *Young Mr. Bobbin* had trouble finding an audience, and disappeared after only one season. To my knowledge, no episodes exist.

Sitcom Topical Index

Addresses

Apartment 3-C—Said apartment was at 46 Perry Street in New York City.
Blondie—Lived at 4224 Shady Lane Avenue.
The Debbie Reynolds Show—Lived at 804 Devon Lane, Los Angeles.
The Dennis O'Keefe Show—Lived in The Parkview Apartments, Apartment 12-A in New York City.
Duffy's Tavern—Located at Third Avenue, New York City.
Fibber McGee and Molly—Lived at 79 Wistful Vista.
Grady—Moved in with his daughter and son-in-law at 636 Carlisle Street, Santa Monica, California.
The Honeymooners—Lived at 328 Chauncey Street, Benson Hurst, Brooklyn, New York.
The Life of Riley—Lived at 1313 Blueview Terrace.
Life with Luigi—Ran an antique shop at 21 North Halstead in Chicago.
Love on a Rooftop—The newlyweds lived in a rooftop apartment at 1400 McDougal Street, San Francisco.
Many Happy Returns—Walter Burnley lived with his children at 609 North Elm Street, New York City.
Mulligan Stew—Lived at 1202 Circle Drive in the mythical town of Birchfield, California.
My Mother, The Car—Lived at 485 Maple.
Ninety Bristol Court—This was the address for *Harris Against the World*, *Tom, Dick and Mary*, and *Karen*.
O. K. Crackerby—Lived in the penthouse of the Hotel Havenhurst, Palm Beach, Florida.
Peter Loves Mary—Moved to 927 Linwood Drive in Oakdell, Connecticut.
The Smothers Brothers Show—Lived at 452 Vista Del Mar, Los Angeles.
This Is Alice—Lived at 857 Elm Street, River Glen, New Jersey.
Two Girls Named Smith—Lived at 514 East 51st Street in Manhattan.
Viva Valdez—Lived at 363½ La Hambre Street, Los Angeles.
Wendy and Me—Lived in the Sunset DeVille Apartments, Apartment 17 (later 217), 4820 Highland, in Los Angeles.
Window on Main Street—Resided in Room 212 of the Majestic Hotel in Millsburg.

Airline-related

Flying High—Three pretty, sensible stewardesses working for Sunwest Airlines.
From a Bird's Eye View—Mishap-prone British stewardess and her level-headed partner working for a London-based airline.
The New Bob Cummings Show—Wealthy playboy who is also a pilot.
The Tim Conway Show—Bumbling pilot (Tim Conway) for tiny Triple-A Airlines.
Wendy and Me—Married (to scatterbrained Wendy) pilot Jeff Conway and his friend and co-pilot Danny Adams.

Big Families

Anna and the King—American school teacher Anna Owens instructs the children of the King of Siam.
Bonino—Widowed opera singer Fortunato "Babbo" Bonino tackles a family of eight children.
Fair Exchange—Two families of four, united in an overseas swap of their teenage daughters for a year.
The Hathaways—Walter and Elinor Hathaway as the "parents" of three chimpanzees they refer to as their children.
Ivan the Terrible—Moscow waiter Ivan struggles to support nine people who live under his inadequate roof.
The Jimmy Stewart Show—In their twilight years, James and Martha Howard must welcome their son, Peter, and his family to live in their home after a fire destroyed theirs.
Joe's World—Detroit painter Joe Wabash, his wife Katie, and their five children try to make ends meet.

Make Room for Granddaddy—Nightclub entertainer Danny Williams and his wife Kathy contend with the six-year-old son of their eldest child, Terry.

The McLean Stevenson Show—Four generations living under one roof. Mac and Peggy Ferguson; their two kids; their daughters two sons; and Peggy's mother.

Mr. T. and Tina—A large Japanese family tries to adjust to American ways in Chicago.

The Montefuscos—A large family gathers every Sunday night for a big Italian dinner in their parents' Connecticut home.

A New Kind of Family—Two large families, the Flanagans and the Stones, share a Los Angeles home to save on expenses.

One Happy Family—Three generations living under one roof—grandparents of the bride (the Hacketts), parents of the bride (the Hogans), and the newly wedded Coopers.

The Paul Lynde Show—On the verge of a nervous breakdown, Paul Simms struggles to deal with his job and large family.

Room for One More—Fond of children, George and Anna Rose have four—two natural, two adopted—but there's always *Room for One More*.

The Texas Wheelers—Deadbeat dad mooches off his four offspring.

The Tom Ewell Show—A man (Tom Potter) attempting to cope with a house full of women.

Viva Valdez—Close-knit Latino family in east Los Angeles with four children and a live-in cousin who recently arrived from Mexico.

We'll Get By—The large Platt family trying to "get by" in suburban New Jersey.

Wonderful John Acton—Weekly reminiscences from Kevin Acton about his grandfather, John Acton, and the rest of his large family in rural Kentucky in 1919.

Blue Collar–related

The Cop and the Kid—Middle-aged policeman as the ward of a troubled young African American orphan.

Grindl—Jill-of-all-trades assigned a different temporary job each week.

The Honeymooners—Mishaps and shattered dreams of bus driver Ralph Kramden and sewer worker Ed Norton.

I'm Dickens, He's Fenster—Inept, accident-prone carpenters (Harry Dickens and Arch Fenster), attempt to cope with life.

Ivan the Terrible—Ivan, head waiter at the Hotel Metropole in Moscow, supports nine people who reside in his very small apartment.

Joe and Mabel—Cab driver Joe Spartan attempts to avoid girlfriend Mabel Spooner's efforts to marry him.

Joe and Sons—Widowed steel worker struggles to raise his two teenage boys.

Joe's World—Painter Joe Wabash and his wife, Katie, oversee a family of five smart-aleck children.

Kallikaks—Rural Kallikak family attempts to survive on the profits of a small inherited gas station in Nowhere, California.

The Life of Riley—Riveter Chester A. Riley attempts to support his wife Peg, daughter Babs, and son Junior on his meager salary.

Lotsa Luck—New York City bus company lost-and-found department supervisor supports his mother, sister and ne'er-do-well brother-in-law.

Mack and Myer for Hire—Misfits Mack and Myer struggle to perform various jobs.

The New Phil Silvers Show—Phil Silvers is Harry Grafton—the scheming maintenance supervisor for Osborne Industries.

Popi—A Puerto Rican widower works three part-time jobs to support his two young sons.

The Super—Superintendent of a decrepit New York City apartment building, struggling to cope with his family.

Viva Valdez—Plumber Luis Valdez struggling to support his large Latino family in East Los Angeles.

Working Stiffs—Janitors Jim Belushi and Michael Keaton wreak havoc in a Chicago office building.

Doctors

AES Hudson Street—Frenzied doctors at the emergency ward of a hospital in a rundown area of Hudson Street in New York City.

The Bob Crane Show—Insurance executive Bob Wilcox leaves his lucrative job to fulfill his dream of becoming a doctor.

Doc Corkle—Short-lived sitcom about a friendly, neighborhood dentist, and his financial woes.

Don't Call Me Charlie—A veterinarian from Iowa is assigned to U.S. Army veterinary duty in Paris.

Husbands, Wives and Lovers—Hour-long sitcom focused upon five very diverse couples (one of the husbands, Ron Willis, is a dentist).

Kentucky Jones—Newly widowed veterinarian adopts a nine-year-old Chinese boy.

McDuff, the Talking Dog—Veterinarian Calvin Campbell is the only one who can hear the voice of the ghost of an English sheepdog.

Me and the Chimp—Dentist Mike Reynolds attempts to cope with his children's pet monkey.

My Living Doll—Psychiatrist Bob McDonald cares for a gorgeous female robot named Rhoda.

My Son, Jeep—Widowed physician named Dr. Allison is left to raise his teenage daughter and mischievous ten-year-old son, nicknamed Jeep.

Nancy—Adam Hudson is a veterinarian who marries the daughter of the President of the United States.

Professional Father—Child psychologist Dr. Thomas Wilson has more success with kids at work than in his own home.

Tom, Dick and Mary—Up-and-coming Dr. Tom Gentry and his new bride, Mary, share an apartment with Tom's best friend and fellow doctor Dick Moran to help pay the bills.

Dwellings

Actor's Hotel—Rural boarding house run by Carlo Corelli and his Uncle Antonio.

Apartment 3—C—Newlyweds struggling to survive the first year of marriage in a small apartment.

Hey, Landlord—"Boy landlord" Woody Banner and his friend Chuck run a converted Manhattan brownstone.

Hot L Baltimore—A once grand, but now rundown hotel in Baltimore, inhabited by a diverse group of zany folks.

Love on a Rooftop—Newlywed San Francisco couple living in a rooftop apartment and struggling on a small salary.

Mickey—Mickey Grady and his family attempt to run an inherited hotel.

The Sanford Arms—Widower Phil Wheeler purchases Fred Sanford's "junk empire" and turns it into the Sanford Arms Hotel.

13 Queens Boulevard—Life with the residents of a garden apartment complex in Queens, New York.

Eponymously Titled

The Betty Hutton Show—Betty Hutton as Goldie, a manicurist caring for the rich children of a late friend.

The Betty White Show—Washed-up actress Joyce Whitman given a new start on a TV series called *Undercover Woman.*

The Bing Crosby Show—Retired singer Bing Collins becomes electrical engineer.

The Buster Keaton Show—Buster Keaton employs trademark slapstick antics as a clerk in a sporting goods store.

The Cara Williams Show—File clerk Cara Wilton struggles to keep secret her married status to fellow employee, Frank Bridges, in a company that forbids employee marriages.

The Charlie Farrell Show—Events culled from the real life of actor Charlie Farrell, who also owned the Racquet Club in Palm Springs, California.

The Debbie Reynolds Show—Housewife Debbie Thompson seeks to become more than just a housewife despite hubby's objections.

The Dennis O'Keefe Show—Newspaper columnist Hal Towne tries raising his young son after his wife's death.

The Don Rickles Show—Don Robinson is an executive struggling to cope with a high-tech world and on-going challenges at home with his wife and daughter.

The Ed Wynn Show—Ed Wynn as John Beamer, a retired businessman who takes in college boarders.

The Eve Arden Show—Liza Hammond, a widow with fraternal twin daughters, becomes a touring lecturer after writing a book.

The George Burns Show—George Burns (alone after wife Gracie retires) becomes a producer in this sequel to *The George Burns and Gracie Allen Show.*

The Gertrude Berg Show—Widow and mother Sarah Green (Mrs. G.) attempts to fulfill her lifelong dream of attending college. The title was changed midseason from *Mrs. G. Goes to College.*

The Hank McCune Show—Hank McCune and his slapstick antics in one of television's first filmed sitcoms.

The Harvey Korman Show—Unemployed actor Harvey Kavanaugh and his daughter living in a big old house.

The Jean Arthur Show—Mother-and-son law team not always seeing eye-to-eye on cases.

The Jean Carroll Show—Jean Carroll as an average housewife with a clumsy husband and a precocious child. Also known as *Take it from Me.*

The Jim Backus Show—Jim Backus as John Michael O'Toole, owner of the Headline Press Service. Also known as *Hot Off the Wire.*

The Jimmy Stewart Show—A professor of anthropology coping with his son, daughter-in-law, and grandchildren who move into his house after theirs burns down.

The John Forsythe Show—A retired military man as headmaster of an all-girls school.

The Marge and Gower Champion Show—Dancers Marge and Gower Champion as themselves in this sitcom wherein they performed at least one dance number per episode.

The McLean Stevenson Show—McLean Stevenson as Mac Ferguson, a man with a hardware store, and a house full of relatives.

The Mickey Rooney Show—Mickey Rooney as Mickey Mulligan, a page for the IBC TV network. Also known as *Hey, Mulligan.*

The Nancy Walker Show—Nancy Walker as Nancy Kitteridge, a talent agent, whose husband abruptly retires from the navy, and throws the house into turmoil.

The New Andy Griffith Show—Andy Griffith in a

rural sitcom wherein he portrayed the mayor protem of a small town.

The New Bob Cummings Show—Bob Cummings as Bob Carson, a wealthy playboy and adventurer who was also an airplane pilot.

The New Phil Silvers Show—Phil Silvers as Harry Grafton, in charge of maintenance at Osborne Industries.

The Paul Lynde Show—Paul Lynde as attorney Paul Simms, with a wife, two daughters, and a well-meaning son-in-law named Howie who rubs Paul the wrong way.

The Phyllis Diller Show—Phyllis Pruitt is a millionaire who has lost her fortune in a revamped mid-season version of *The Pruitts of Southampton*.

The Sandy Duncan Show—Sandy Stockton, from the show *Funny Face*, now working for an advertising agency.

The Tab Hunter Show—Tab Hunter as Paul Morgan, a cartoonist and swinging young bachelor with a pad on the beach.

The Tammy Grimes Show—Tammy Ward is an heiress seeking ways to get her inheritance before she reaches 30.

The Ted Knight Show—Ted Knight had two different shows with this title. In the first, he portrayed Roger Dennis who owned an escort company. The other is the syndicated version of *Too Close for Comfort*.

The Tim Conway Show—Tim Conway and Joe Flynn of *McHale's Navy* were reunited in this sitcom in which they portrayed the owners of an extremely small airline.

The Tom Ewell Show—Tom Ewell as real estate agent Tom Potter contends with a house full of females (his wife, three daughters, and mother-in-law).

Ethnic-oriented

Bridget Loves Bernie—Wealthy Irish Catholic girl marries the son of a Jewish delicatessen owner.

The Cop and the Kid—Troubled young African American male is placed in the custody of a middle-aged Caucasian police officer.

Free Country—Lithuanian immigrants at the turn of the century.

Grady—A *Sanford and Son* spin-off wherein Grady moves in with his daughter Ellie and her family.

Ivan the Terrible—A large Russian family tries to make ends meet in a very small dwelling which houses nine people.

Life with Luigi—Italian-Americans living and working in Chicago. Outrage over the portrayal of Italian-Americans leads to its cancellation, despite good ratings.

Mr. T. and Tina—A large Japanese family in Chicago tries to cope with the customs and morals of their new home.

The Montefuscos—Italian-American family meets every weekend for Sunday dinner.

Popi—Puerto Rican widower works three part-time jobs in an effort to support his two motherless sons.

Viva Valdez—Large Latino family living in East Los Angeles.

Firsts

Eddie Albert—Long before starring as Oliver Douglas on *Green Acres*, he was Larry Tucker in *Leave it to Larry*.

Ted Bessell—Several years before becoming Don Hollinger on *That Girl*, he co-starred on *It's a Man's World*.

Barbara Billingsley—Several years before becoming June Cleaver, she had co-starring roles on *Professional Father* and *The Brothers*.

Carol Burnett—In her first TV series, *Stanley*, she played Celia Howard alongside Buddy Hackett.

Ellen Burstyn—Using the name Ellen McRae, made her TV sitcom debut on *I'm Dickens, He's Fenster* as Joan.

Judy Carne—Made her sitcom debut on an hour-long sitcom called *Fair Exchange*.

filmed—The first three filmed single season sitcoms are *The Life of Riley*, *Easy Aces*, and *The Hank McCune Show*.

Jodie Foster—As a child, got her start in two different single season sitcoms—*Bob & Carol & Ted & Alice* and *Paper Moon*.

Beverly Garland—Before playing Bing Crosby or Fred MacMurray's TV wife, she was Nina on *Mama Rosa* as Beverly Campbell .

Kathy Garver—Long before she was Cissy Davis on *Family Affair*, she had a recurring role as Sally on *This Is Alice*.

Mark Harmon—Made his first TV appearance as a jock named Mark Johnson on *Ozzie's Girls*.

Michael Keaton—Got his TV start as Lanny Wolf on the political sitcom *All's Fair*.

laugh track—*The Hank McCune Show* was the first sitcom to use a laugh track and set a precedent.

Jack Lemmon—Yet unknown, had his first starring role in *That Wonderful Guy*.

MTM cancellations—The first two MTM sitcoms to be cancelled are *The Texas Wheelers* and *Paul Sand in Friends and Lovers*.

Michelle Pfeiffer—Got started in a minor role as "The Bombshell" on *Delta House*.

Marion Ross—Long before she was Mrs. C. on *Happy Days*, she was Susan Green on *Mrs. G. Goes to College* and Kathleen on *Life with Father*.

Jane Rose—Decades before she was the mother-in-law on *Phyllis*, she was Bessie on the live sitcom *Wonderful John Acton*.

Dick Sargent—Co-starred in three single season sitcoms before becoming the second Darrin on *Bewitched*—*One Happy Family*, *Broadside*, and *The Tammy Grimes Show*.

Paul Shaffer—A few years before he became David Letterman's bandleader and sidekick, he played Paul on the short-lived sitcom *A Year at the Top*.

Jack Soo—Long before becoming a cop on *Barney Miller*, he was Rocky Sin on *Valentine's Day*.

Aaron Spelling—Before he created a TV empire as a producer, he played Jim Baxter, the dog catcher on *Willy*.

Christopher Walken—Got his start as Ronnie Walken on *Wonderful John Acton*.

Natalie Wood—Got her start in two different single season sitcoms—*Pride of the Family* and *Mayor of the Town*.

Five or Fewer Aired Episodes

Another Day—Four aired episodes.
AES Hudson Street—Five aired episodes.
Apple Pie—Two aired episodes.
Ball Four—Five aired episodes.
Coed Fever—One aired episode.
Doc Corkle—Three aired episodes.
Dorothy—Four aired episodes.
Flatbush—Three aired episodes.
Free Country—Five aired episodes.
Friends—Five aired episodes.
Hanging In—Four aired episodes.
Highcliffe Manor—Four aired episodes.
In the Beginning—Five aired episodes.
Ivan the Terrible—Five aired episodes.
The Kallikaks—Five aired episodes.
Mr. T. and Tina—Five aired episodes.
Off the Record—Two aired episodes.
Roller Girls—Four aired episodes.
The Sanford Arms—Four aired episodes.
Struck by Lightning—Three aired episodes.
The Tammy Grimes Show—Four aired episodes.
Waverly Wonders—Five aired episodes.
Working Stiffs—Four aired episodes.
A Year at the Top—Five aired episodes.

Gimmicks

Captain Nice—Mild-mannered chemist Carter Nash becomes superhero Captain Nice when he drinks a special potion he's created.

The Double Life of Henry Phyfe—Henry Phyfe, the exact double of deceased foreign spy U-31, becomes a reluctant replacement.

The Girl with Something Extra—Sally Burton can read some people's minds none of the time, some people some of the time, and a few people most of the time. Her new husband John falls into the latter category.

Good Heavens—Carl Reiner plays Mr. Angel who seeks out people performing good deeds and rewards them with the granting of a wish.

The Hathaways—Walter and Elinor have an unusual family—three chimpanzees they raise as if they were real children.

Highcliffe Manor—Helen Blacke inherits Highcliffe Manor and the Blacke Foundation, and all of the crazies who work there.

Holmes and Yoyo—Accident prone police detective Alex Holmes has a new partner named Yoyo, a robot with a few defects.

It's About Time—Two astronauts enter a time warp on their flight and wind up in prehistoric times, dodging dinosaurs and befriending cavemen.

Mr. Terrific—Stanley Beamish is the only man who can tolerate a power pill which turns him into a superhero. He fights crime for the Bureau of Secret Projects.

My Living Doll—Beautiful female robot AF 709 is left in the custody of a psychiatrist Robert McDonald.

My Mother, The Car—Among the most bizarre gimmicks of all time. Dave Crabtree buys a decrepit old 1928 Porter after he hears his mother's voice emanating from the vehicle. She has returned to guide his life.

My World and Welcome to It—Based upon the works of James Thurber, cartoonist John Monroe's drawings frequently come to life on screen.

Occasional Wife—Peter Christopher makes an arrangement with a hat check girl, Greta, to become his wife, occasionally, to appease his boss who will grant promotions only to married men.

The Pruitts of Southampton—Wealthy society family from Long Island must learn to live like normal folk when they lose their riches.

The Second Hundred Years—Luke Carpenter, thought to be killed in an avalanche, is thawed out unscathed. He may be 100, but hasn't aged a day since he was flash frozen. He just happens to be identical to his 33-year-old grandson, Ken (both roles played by Monte Markham).

The Smothers Brothers Show—Tom Smothers, who lost his life at sea, returns to Earth as an apprentice angel, and greatly disrupts his brother, Dick's life.

Struck by Lightning—When Ted Stein inherits an old inn, he also inherits Frank—the creation of his great-grandfather, Dr. Frankenstein.

Tabitha—Picking up where *Bewitched* left off, Tabitha Stevens has inherited her mother's powers, but her brother Adam has not. Tabitha works for a California TV station, where her powers often save the day.

The Ugliest Girl in Town—Timothy Blair (Peter

Kastner) becomes an earthy female model by accident and carries on that charade in England to be with his beloved Julie.

A Year at the Top—A songwriting team is given a chance to become superstars by Satan's son, posing as promoter Frederick J. Hanover. The catch is, they'll have to sell their souls to the devil.

"The Help"

Barefoot in the Park—Corie Bratter's mother, Mabel Bates (Thelma Carpenter), was a domestic for a wealthy Park Avenue family.

Bonino—The harried housekeeper for the large Bonino family was Martha the maid, played by Mary Wickes.

The Charlie Farrell Show—The housekeeper at the Racquet Club was Mrs. Papernow (Kathryn Card).

The Dennis O'Keefe Show—Hope Emerson portrayed housekeeper Amelia Sargent.

Dick and the Duchess—Beatrice Varley portrayed housekeeper Mathilda.

Father of the Bride—The Banks' housekeeper was named Delilah and played by Ruby Dandridge.

The Good Life—Albert and Jane Miller give up their hectic old life to become the cook and butler for the wealthy Duttons.

The Great Gildersleeve—Housekeeper Birdie Lee Coggins was played by Lillian Randolph.

The Halls of Ivy—Mary Wickes portrayed Alice, the housekeeper for Toddy and Vicky Hall.

Hangin' In—Nedra Volz plays Mr. Harper's wise-cracking housekeeper, Pinky.

The Hathaways—Mary Grace Canfield portrayed the Hathaway's housekeeper, Amanda Allison.

His Honor, Homer Bell—Jane Moultrie played Homer Bell's housekeeper, Maude.

The Laytons—Amanda Randolph as the housekeeper called Aunt Martha.

Love and Marriage—Midseason, the Bakers hire a housekeeper named Han Cho-Yee (Judy Dan).

McDuff, the Talking Dog—Veterinarian Dr. Calvin Campbell has a housekeeper named Mrs. Osgood.

Mr. Deeds Goes to Town—Longfellow Deeds has a butler named George (Ivor Barry).

My Son, Jeep—The housekeeper for the Allison family was Mrs. Bixby, played by Leona Powers.

Our Man Higgins—The MacRoberts family inherits a valuable silver service and a British butler.

Out of the Blue—Hannah Dean plays Aunt Marion's housekeeper, Gladys.

Peter Loves Mary—The Lindsey family has a housekeeper named Wilma (Bea Benederet).

Professional Father—The Wilson family's housekeeper was the wise-cracking Nana (Ann O'Neal).

The Pruitts of Southampton—Phyllis Pruitt had a butler she could no longer pay named Sturgis (Grady Sutton).

The Tammy Grimes Show—Maudie Prickett portrayed housekeeper Mrs. Ratchett.

Inconsistencies

The Betty White Show—Carla Borelli portrays Lisa Vincent in the debut episode, but Caren Kaye's Tracy Garrett character replaces her in the remaining episodes.

Camp Runamuck—Frank DeVol portrays Doc in the debut episode, but it's Leonard Stone in the remaining episodes.

The Cara Williams Show—The theme song changed from a vocal ("Cara's Theme") to an instrumental.

The Debbie Reynolds Show—The theme song changed from a vocal ("With a Little Love") to an instrumental.

The Egg and I—The role of Betty Blake was played originally by Pat Kirkland and later by Betty Lynn.

Fair Exchange—The program began as an hour, later shortened to a half hour.

Father of the Bride—Early episode opening credits feature an animated angel, later episodes feature the cast on a staircase.

Ghost Busters—In the opening credits, Larry Storch's character is listed as "Spencer" with a "c," but on the door to his office, it's spelled "Spenser" with an "s."

Gidget—Anne, Gidget's older sister, has black hair in the pilot, then goes blonde, and finally strawberry blonde.

I'm Dickens, He's Fenster—The opening credits for early episodes feature Dickens and Fenster each affixing a knob to the same door, but later episodes featured the actor's names amidst a bevy of tools on a pegboard.

It's About Time—First half of the season is set in pre-historic times; the remaining episodes modern times. Also, Imogene Coca's character is "Shag" in the first few episodes, but rather "Shad" in the remaining ones.

The John Forsythe Show—For about two-thirds of the season, Air Force Major John Foster was a girl's school headmaster. In the remaining episodes, John and Ed Robbins became undercover government agents.

Love on a Rooftop—Unexplained reason Julie Willis (Judy Carne) has a British accent, but her parents do not.

Mrs. G. Goes to College—This was the title for the first half of the season. It was changed to *The Gertrude Berg Show* to try to boost ratings.

My Living Doll—Rhoda, the female robot is left in the care of Dr. Bob McDonald for a majority of the episodes. When Bob was "let go" near the end of the season, Rhoda was cared for by Dr. Peter Robinson. Also, in the opening credits, "the doll" is seen most often wearing an evening gown; she is wearing a nightgown in others.

My Mother, the Car—Neighbor Phil Durkin is portrayed in early episodes by Bill Daily and in later episodes by Dave Willock.

The New Phil Silvers Show—First, the factory, Osborne Industries, manufactured a different product each week to fit that particular episode. Secondly, the program changed formats midstream, with the addition of sister Audrey and her two children.

Ninety Bristol Court—In midseason, only one (*Karen*) of the three adjoining sitcoms remained on the schedule. Gone were *Tom, Dick and Mary* and *Harris Against the World.*

Ozzie's Girls—Brenda Sykes's character was inexplicably named Jennifer in the pilot but Brenda for the remaining episodes.

The Pruitts of Southampton—The program was retooled midseason as *The Phyllis Diller Show.*

Sally—Initially, Sally Truesdale was the traveling companion for a wealthy widow named Myrtle Banford. Later in the season, they would both work for the Banford Bleacher Department Store.

San Pedro Beach Bums—The name of the houseboat changed from the pilot (*The Challenger*) to the regular series (*Our Boat*).

The Smothers Brothers Show—In some episodes, the opening theme song is a vocal (by Dick and Tom Smothers), and in others it's an instrumental version.

Tabitha—The spelling changed. In the unaired pilot, it was spelled *Tabatha.*

13 Queens Blvd.—The cast during the program's brief spring run differed quite a bit from the even more brief summer run. Gone in the summer were Jerry Van Dyke and Marcia Rodd.

Wendy and Me—In some episodes, Wendy and Jeff live in apartment 17, in others it's 217.

Wesley—Donald Devlin portrayed young Wesley Eggleston for the first two months of the show's run, followed by Johnny Stewart for the final month.

Who's Watching the Kids?—Caren Kaye bowed out of the show near the end of its run, and Lynda Goodfriend's character was greatly diminished.

Kids in the Spotlight

Brothers and Sisters/Co-Ed Fever/Delta House—Three ill-fated sitcoms about the antics of college kids and fraternities, all based upon *National Lampoon's Animal House.*

Camp Runamuck—The kids in an all-boys camp (Runamuck) and an all-girls camp (Divine).

Cliffwood Avenue Kids—The story of the youngsters who are part of the Cliffwood Avenue Club.

The Cop and the Kid—A troubled young African American male becomes the responsibility of a middle-aged longtime police officer.

Family Genius—Jack Diamond portrays child prodigy Tommy Howard, "the family genius."

Flatbush—Italian-American recent high school graduates form a gang called "The Flatbush Fungoes."

Gidget—Lots of fun in the California sun, sand and surf, and the joys of being a teenager in the 1960s.

Hank—While other kids were dropping out, Hank Dearborn was dropping in—to college that is, getting an education via numerous disguises and aliases.

The Hathaways—Walter and Elinor Hathaway raise three chimpanzees and think of them as their children.

My Son, Jeep—Dr. Robert Allison, a widower, has his hands full with a teenage daughter and a mischievous young son nicknamed "Jeep."

Peck's Bad Girl—Torey Peck (Patty McCormack) isn't so "bad," she is just having growing pains.

This Is Alice—Alice Holliday (Patty Ann Gerrity) always means well, but her good intentions always lead to calamity.

Too Young to Go Steady—A 14-year-old girl named Pam Blake (Brigid Bazlen) makes the slow transition from tomboy to young lady.

Wesley—Twelve-year-old Wesley Eggleston, nearing his teen years, but in absolutely no hurry to grow up.

Lawyers

Adam's Rib—The story of a husband and wife who both practice law—sometimes against one another in the courtroom.

The Associates—Three recent law school graduates who work for a Wall Street-based law firm.

Barefoot in the Park—Paul and Corie Bratter are newlyweds. Paul also just landed a job at the Kendrick, Keene and Klein Law Firm.

Father of the Bride—Stanley Banks (Leon Ames) is the "Banks" in the Williston and Banks Law Firm.

Fay—After her divorce, Fay (Lee Grant) rejoins the work force and becomes a secretary for a team of lawyers.

Harrigan and Son—Father and son law firm (Harrigan and Harrigan)—each with very different methodology.

His Honor, Homer Bell—Homer Bell (Gene Lockhart) as the kindly Justice of the Peace in Spring City.

The Jean Arthur Show—Mother and son law firm wherein Mom always seems to get involved with her clients.

The Marriage—Successful lawyer Ben Marriott (Hume Cronyn) and his wife Liz (Jessica Tandy) and their two children.

The Paul Lynde Show—Attorney Paul Simms, his wife Martha and their two children have their world turned upside down by their elder daughter's new husband, Howie.

Sirota's Court—Precursor to *Night Court*. Michael Constantine portrays the "firm but fair" Judge Matthew J. Sirota.

Too Young to Go Steady—Fourteen-year-old Pamela Blake's dad, Tom, is a lawyer.

We'll Get By—George Platt (Paul Sorvino) works as a lawyer supporting a wife and three kids in New Jersey.

Willy—June Havoc as a female lawyer named Willa Dodger, whose practice takes a long time to become established and start turning a profit.

Military-oriented

Broadside—World War II U.S. Navy WAVES stationed in the South Pacific.

Don't Call Me Charlie—Backwoods veterinarian Judson McKay stationed at an Army veterinary facility in Paris.

Ensign O'Toole—Peacetime military sitcom set aboard the destroyer USS *Appleby*.

The John Forsythe Show—Air Force Major John Foster's new career as the headmaster of an all-girls' school.

McKeever and the Colonel—A group of mischievous young men at the Westfield Military Academy.

Mr. Roberts—Douglas Roberts seeks ways to become part of the action rather than trapped aboard the USS *Reluctant*, a cargo ship stationed in the South Pacific during World War II.

Mona McCluskey—Mona makes more money as an actress, but her husband, Mike, a sergeant in the Air Force, insists that they live on his salary.

The Nancy Walker Show—Talent agent named Nancy Kitteridge's world is turned upside down when her husband abruptly retires from the Navy and is constantly under her feet.

No Time for Sergeants—Country bumpkin Will Stockdale wreaks havoc upon the Air Force.

Roll Out—The story of the "Red Ball Express," a supply troop, set in France during World War II.

The Soldiers—Tom D'Andrea and Hal March as Tom and Hal, two soldiers who find trouble in the U.S. Army.

The Wackiest Ship in the Army—Yet another military sitcom set in the South Pacific during World War II—this one, aboard a schooner called The USS *Kiwi*.

Movie-based

Adam's Rib—Ken Howard and Blythe Danner assume the roles of Spencer Tracy and Katherine Hepburn in the TV version.

The Adventures of Tugboat Annie—The Marie Dressler and Wallace Beery roles from the movie version are taken up by Minerva Urecal and Walter Sande in the TV sitcom version.

Anna and the King—Yul Brynner reprises his role as the King of Siam in this very short-lived sitcom based upon the play and movie titled *The King and I*.

Barefoot in the Park—Scoey Mitchlll and Tracy Reed assume the roles of Robert Redford and Jane Fonda in this TV version of the Neil Simon comedy.

Blondie—Penny Singleton and Arthur Lake had played Blondie and Dagwood in a series of movies, based upon the comic strip. Two different short-lived versions flop on TV more than a decade apart.

Delta House—Based upon the highly successful *National Lampoon's Animal House*. Four members of the movie cast return for the short-lived TV version.

Father of the Bride—Leon Ames and Ruth Warrick assume the roles made famous by Spencer Tracy and Joan Bennett in the 1950 movie version.

Gidget—Sally Field assumes the role originally made famous by Sandra Dee in a series of *Gidget* movies.

Going My Way—Gene Kelly takes on the Bing Crosby role in this single-season TV adaptation of the 1944 movie.

Mr. Roberts—Roger Smith assumes the Henry Fonda role on this military sitcom set during World War II.

Room for One More—Loosely based upon the Cary Grant movie, originally called *Room for One More*, and later retitled *The Easy Way*.

Tammy—Debbie Watson assumes the role on TV, made famous by both Debbie Reynolds and Sandra Dee in the movie versions.

The Wackiest Ship in the Army—Based upon the Jack Lemmon and Ricky Nelson movie of the same name, with Jack Warden and Gary Collins in the starring roles.

Music-involved

The Bing Crosby Show—Bing Crosby as Bing Collins, a retired crooner with a wife and two kids.

Getting Together—Bobby Sherman and Wes Stern portray a couple of songwriters who are having trouble making it in the music business.

It's a Business?—The story of competing song pluggers at the turn of the century.

Love and Marriage—Struggling song publisher who refuses to acknowledge the success of rock and roll, while his daughter tries to bring him up-to-date.

A Year at the Top—Two struggling songwriters are suddenly thrust into the limelight by a promoter who is really the son of Satan.

Newspaper-focused

The Adventures of Hiram Holliday—Proofreader corrects major error, saves newspaper from lawsuit, is awarded trip around the world.

Dear Phoebe—A former college instructor, Bill Hastings, writes an advice-for-the-lovelorn column under an alias.

The Debbie Reynolds Show—Unpredictable Debbie Thompson makes life difficult for her sports columnist husband, Jim.

The Dennis O'Keefe Show—Widower Hal Towne writes a popular syndicated newspaper column called "All Around Towne."

Honestly, Celeste—Celeste Anders gives up her job as a journalism teacher to become a newspaper reporter.

Ichabod and Me—Robert Majors takes the reins of a small, rural New England newspaper.

The Jim Backus Show—Michael O'Toole struggles to keep his newspaper and headline service afloat.

Pride of the Family—Albie Morrison manages the advertising department of a small town newspaper.

Notable Theme Songs

Accidental Family—An instrumental version (by Earle Hagen) of the traditional song "Old MacDonald Had a Farm," first published in 1917.

The Associates—"Wall Street Blues," the theme song, was performed by B.B. King.

Adam's Rib—The theme, "Two People," was composed by Perry Botkin, Jr., and Gil Garfield.

Ball Four—The theme, "Ball Four," was sung by Harry Chapin.

Barefoot in the Park—Theme song sung by Rock and Roll Hall of Fame inductee Darlene Love and the Blossoms.

Big John, Little John—Theme song written by Sherwood Schwartz and John Thomas Fox.

The Bing Crosby Show—"That's Life," the opening theme, and the closing signature, "It All Adds Up to Love," are performed by Bing Crosby.

Blansky's Beauties—Cyndi Grecco performs the vocal "I Want It All."

Blondie (1968)—Will Hutchins and Patricia Harty perform the theme vocal "Blondieeee."

Calucci's Department—The "Calucci's Department" theme song was written by Marvin Hamlisch.

Captain Nice—The theme, "Captain Nice" was written by Vic Mizzy.

Coed Fever—The theme "Coed Fever" was written by Henry Mancini.

The Debbie Reynolds Show—Debbie Reynolds performs the vocal "With a Little Love."

Dorothy—Dorothy Loudon performs the "Dorothy Theme."

The Double Life of Henry Phyfe—The theme, "The Double Life of Henry Phyfe," was composed by Vic Mizzy.

Dusty's Trail—The theme song was sung by Mel Street.

Fay—Jaye P. Morgan performs the theme "Coming into My Own."

Flying High—Pat Williams composed the theme song.

Funny Face—Jack Jones performs the theme "The Kind of Girl She Is."

Getting Together—The theme, "Getting Together," is sung by Bobby Sherman.

Gidget—Johnny Tillotson performs the "Gidget" theme.

The Girl with Something Extra—Dave Grusin composed and performed the theme song.

The Good Life—Tony Orlando performs the theme "The Good Life."

Good Morning, World—Dave Grusin composed and performed the theme song.

Harrigan and Son—Pat O'Brien and Roger Perry perform the theme (closing credits) "Harrigan."

The Harvey Korman Show—Harvey Korman performs the theme song "Living Life Today."

Headmaster—Linda Ronstadt performs the theme song "Only a Man."

Here We Go Again—Carol Bayer Sager and Peter Allen composed the theme "Here We Go Again."

Hey, Landlord—Quincy Jones performs the instrumental theme "Hey, Landlord."

Hizzoner—Star David Huddleston performs the theme "Hometown Blues."

The Honeymooners—Jackie Gleason and Bill Templeton composed the theme "You Are My Greatest Love."

Hot L Baltimore—Theme song composed by Marvin Hamlisch.

I'm Dickens, He's Fenster—The theme, "The Dickens and Fenster March," was composed by Irving Szathmary (brother of Bill Dana), who also wrote "The Get Smart Theme."

It's Always Jan—Earle Hagen and Herbert Spencer composed the "It's Always Jan" theme.

The Jean Arthur Show—Johnny Keating, Richard Quine and Richard Kennedy composed the theme "Merry-Go-Round."
The Jim Backus Show—The theme, "Hot Off the Wire," was composed by David Rose.
The Kallikaks—The theme song was performed by Roy Clark.
Karen (with Debbie Watson)—The Beach Boys perform the theme "Karen."
The Last Resort—Theme song written by Pat Williams.
Life with Luigi—Theme song, "Way Marie," written by Eduardo DiCapua.
Lotsa Luck—Theme song, "Lotsa Luck," written by Bill Persky, Sam Denoff, Jack Elliott and Allyn Ferguson.
Love on a Rooftop—Howard Greenfield and Jack Keller composed the theme.
Love Thy Neighbor—Solomon Burke performs the theme "Love Thy Neighbor."
Makin' It—David Naughton provides the vocal for the theme "Makin' It."
Mama Rosa—Theme song, "O Sole Mio," composed by Eduardo DiCapua.
Many Happy Returns—The theme song was performed by David Rose.
The McLean Stevenson Show—The theme song was performed and written by Paul Williams.
Mr. T. and Tina—The theme song, an instrumental version of the classic "Chicago," originally written by Fred Fisher in 1922.
Mrs. G. Goes to College—Herschel Burke Gilbert and Alfred Perry composed the theme "Alma Mater."
Mona McCluskey—Sonny Burke provided the upbeat version of the classic song, "Yessir, That's My Baby."
My Mother, the Car—The theme, "My Mother, the Car," was sung by Paul Hampton.
Nancy—The theme song was written by Sidney Sheldon.
Needles and Pins—The catchy theme song was written by Marvin Hamlisch.
The New Bob Cummings Show—The theme song was written and performed by Esquievel.
O. K. Crackerby—The theme song was written by Abe Burrows and Ralph Carmichael.
Occasional Wife—The theme song composed by Howard Greenfield and Ernest Pintoff.
Paper Moon—The theme song, the old standard "It's Only a Paper Moon," was written by Harold Arlen, Yip Harburg and Billy Rose.
The Partners—The theme song was composed by Lalo Schifrin.
Paul Sand in Friends and Lovers—The classical influenced theme song was composed by Pat Williams.
Pistols and Petticoats—The "Pistols and Petticoats" theme song was composed by George Tibbles and Jack Elliott.
The Pruitts of Southampton—The theme, "The Pruitts of Southampton," was performed by Phyllis Diller and composed by Vic Mizzy.
Quark—The theme song was composed by Perry Botkin, Jr.
Rango—Frankie Laine performs the theme "Rango."
Room for One More—The theme song, "Room for One More," was composed by Mack David and Jerry Livingston.
The Smothers Brothers Show—Tom and Dick Smothers perform "The Theme from The Smothers Brothers Show."
Stockard Channing in Just Friends—Delaney Bramlett performs "Stockard's Theme."
Struck by Lightning—Joe Cocker performs "You Are So Beautiful" as the opening theme.
The Tab Hunter Show—The theme song was composed by Pete Rugolo.
Tabitha—Lisa Hartman performs the vocal "It Could Be Magic."
Tammy—Jay Livingston and Ray Evans composed the classic theme song "Tammy."
The Texas Wheelers—The theme song, "Illegal Smile," was composed and performed by John Prine.
Valentine's Day—Van Alexander composed "The Theme from Valentine's Day."

Period Pieces

Anna and the King—Siam in the 1860s.
Broadside—World War II in the South Pacific.
The Chicago Teddy Bears—Chicago in the 1920s during prohibition.
Dusty's Trail—The old west in the 1880s.
Free Country—New York City in the early 1900s.
It's About Time—Prehistoric times (for the first few months of its run).
It's a Business—Vaudeville and song pluggers in the early 1900s.
Margie—Teenagers' lives in the roaring 20s.
Mr. Roberts—The South Pacific during World War II.
Paper Moon—Kansas during the Depression era.
Pistols and Petticoats—The old West of 1871.
Quark—Set in the future, the year 2222.
Roll Out—France during World War II.
Wackiest Ship in the Army—The South Pacific during World War II aboard the USS *Kiwi*.
Wonderful John Acton—Reminiscences about the year 1919 through the eyes of Kevin Acton.

Pets

The Bickersons—Cat (Nature Boy).
Blondie—Dog (Daisy).

Dusty's Trail—Horses named Blarney (Callahan's) and Freckles (Dusty's).
The Hathaways—Three chimpanzees—Charlie, Enoch, and Candy.
Ivan the Terrible—A vicious, never-seen dog named Rasputin.
Marge and Jeff—Cocker spaniel (Paisley).
Me and the Chimp—Chimpanzee (Buttons).
My Mother, the Car—Dog (Moon).
My World and Welcome to It—Dogs (Christabel and Irving).
A New Kind of Family—Dog (Heinz).
No Time for Sergeants—Bloodhound (Blue).
O. K. Crackerby—Basset hound (Gertrude).
Pistols and Petticoats—A wolf named Bowser.
Quark—A sometimes vicious pile of hungry ectoplasm named Ergo.
Room for One More—Dog (Tramp).
The Rounders—An old roan horse (Old Fooler).
Tammy—A mule (Enoch); Tammy's goat (Nan).
The Tom Ewell Show—A female dog named Mitzi.
Willy—Dog (Ranger).

Photographers

The Brothers—Harvey and Gilly Box try to make ends meet with a partnership in a San Francisco photography studio.
Shirley's World—A young reporter-photographer gets to see the world while working for *World Illustrated.*
The Ugliest Girl in Town—A misunderstanding over some last-minute fashion photos leads Timothy Blair into a charade as a female model named "Timmie."
We've Got Each Other—It's role reversal as Judy Hibbard works at a photography studio and her husband works out of their home.

Politicians

Grandpa Goes to Washington—Jack Albertson as Senator Joe Kelley.
Hizzoner—David Huddleston as Mayor Cooper.
Mayor of the Town—Thomas Mitchell as Mayor Russell of Springdale.
Mr. Smith Goes to Washington—Fess Parker as Senator Eugene Smith.
Nancy—Renne Jarrett is Nancy Smith, the daughter of the never-seen president of the United States.
The New Andy Griffith Show—Andy Griffith as Andy Sawyer, the mayor of the small southern town of Greenwood.

Rural

Accidental Family—Jerry Van Dyke as Jerry Webster, who owns a farm in California's San Fernando Valley.
Dusty's Trail—Crossing the lone prairie in a wagon train full of bumblers.
The Egg and I—Ma and Pa Kettle run a chicken farm.
Guestward Ho—The Hooten family leaves the hustle and bustle of New York in favor of a dude ranch in New Mexico.
Kentucky Jones—Widowed veterinarian raises an adopted boy on a 40-acre California farm.
The New Andy Griffith Show—Andy Sawyer leaves his government job to replace the mayor of the small town of Greenwood.
Pistols and Petticoats—The Hanks family in Wretched, Colorado, in the 1870s.
Rango—Tim Conway as an inept Texas Ranger.
The Rounders—Set in the modern-day west, two cowpokes find themselves in arrears to the wealthy Jim Ed Love.
Tammy—The Tarltetons are treated like outcasts by the plantation-dwelling Tates.
The Texas Wheelers—Set in rural Texas, four motherless children try to make it on their own.

School-based

Anna and the King—Anna Owens is hired to teach the King of Siam's many children.
Big John, Little John—Science teacher takes a small drink from the "fountain of youth" and intermittently reverts to his 12-year-old self.
The Bob Crane Show—A frustrated insurance executive changes his life course and goes to medical school.
Brothers and Sisters—Inspired by the success of *Animal House*, this is the story of fraternity shenanigans at Larry Krandall College.
Co-ed Fever—Inspired by the meteoric success of *Animal House*, this was the least successful of three shows attempting to cash in.
Delta House—Based upon *Animal House*, this version utilized some of the stars of the original movie focused upon fraternity hijinks.
Dorothy—Dorothy Banks teaches music and drama at the Hannah Huntley School for Girls.
Fair Exchange—A family from London and a family from New York participate in a student exchange program (a daughter swap).
The Halls of Ivy—The story of the staff and students of Ivy College, somewhere in the Midwest.
Hanging In—Louis Harper (Bill Macy) is offered the presidency of Braddock University.
Headmaster—Andy Thompson (Andy Griffith) is

the headmaster of a private prep school known as Concord.

The Jimmy Stewart Show—Anthropology professor at Josiah Kessel College, and his newly expanded family.

The John Forsythe Show—Former Air Force Major John Foster becomes the headmaster for an all-girls school.

McKeever and the Colonel—Mischievous cadets wreak havoc on the Westfield Military Academy.

Mrs. G. Goes to College—Gertrude Berg as Sarah Green, an elderly widow who decides to finally get a college education.

The Waverly Wonders—Joe Namath as Joe Casey, a quarterback-turned-history-teacher/basketball coach in Wisconsin.

Ships and Boats

The Adventures of Tugboat Annie—Rival tugboat captains in the Pacific Northwest.

The Baileys of Balboa—Sam Bailey (Paul Ford) runs a charter fishing boat in Balboa, California.

Broadside—U.S. WAVES stationed on a South Pacific island during World War II.

Ensign O'Toole—Set during peacetime aboard the USS *Appleby*, a Navy destroyer.

It's a Man's World—College students in a Midwestern town live aboard a houseboat.

Mr. Roberts—Set in the South Pacific in World War II aboard a cargo ship called the USS *Reluctant*.

The Queen and I—An aging ocean cruise ship, the *Amsterdam Queen*, and the many attempts to save it from being retired.

The San Pedro Beach Bums—Five young guys live aboard a houseboat called *Our Boat* in sunny California.

The Wackiest Ship in the Army—Story of a twin-mast schooner called the USS *Kiwi*, stationed in the South Pacific during World War II.

Showbiz-oriented

Accidental Family—Jerry Van Dyke portrays a widower who earns a living as a nightclub comedian.

Actor's Hotel—Carlo Corelli and his Uncle Antonio run a boarding house for showbiz folks.

The Betty White Show—An out of work actress gets a big break with her own action series.

The Bing Crosby Show—A former crooner retires to become an electrical engineer.

Blansky's Beauties—Nancy Blansky manages a group of Las Vegas showgirls.

Bonino—An opera singer greatly curtails making appearances to spend more time with his large family.

The Charlie Farrell Show—Charlie portrays himself, an actor, who runs the Palm Springs Racquet Club.

Funny Face—Sandy Duncan portrays a college student who earns money in TV commercials.

The George Burns Show—After his wife Gracie Allen retired, George became a producer, surrounded by many familiar faces.

Good Morning, World—A pair of disk jockeys try to make it with a morning radio show in Los Angeles.

Harry's Girls—Entertainer Harry Burns and three girls tour Europe with a nightclub show deemed too old-fashioned for the U.S.

The Harvey Korman Show—Harvey portrays an unemployed hammy actor who lives with his daughter.

Hathaways—Walter and Elinor Hathaway have three talented chimpanzees with a show business act.

He and She—Dick Hollister created the *Jetman* comic strip, which has been turned into a successful TV show.

Heavens to Betsy—Two young ladies try to make it big in show business.

The Hero—Sam Garret is very sure-footed on his popular Western TV show, but a klutz in real life.

Hey, Mulligan—Mickey Mulligan works as a page for a TV network, but keeps trying to break into show business himself.

Holiday Lodge—Wayne and Shuster are the social directors and often the entertainment at a ritzy summer resort.

It's a Business?—Song pluggers compete with one another at the turn of the century.

It's Always Jan—Janis Paige as a talented nightclub performer who never quite made it big.

Love and Marriage—A struggling music publisher avoids rock and roll, despite pressure from his daughter.

Make Room for Granddaddy—A sequel to *Make Room for Daddy*, with Danny Thomas as a nightclub entertainer.

Mama Rosa—Much like *Actor's Hotel*, Mama runs a boarding house for out of work show business folks.

The Marge and Gower Champion Show—A sitcom about a choreographer and his dance partner.

Mona McCluskey—Juliet Prowse portrays an actress who is forced to live on her military husband's meager salary.

My Sister, Eileen—Pretty-but-naïve Eileen Sherwood tries to make it in the big city as an actress.

The Nancy Walker Show—Nancy Kitteridge portrays a sarcastic yet successful Hollywood talent agent.

Peter Loves Mary—A show business couple adjusts to life in the suburbs.

So This Is Hollywood—Two young women take almost any roles to make it in show business.
Tabitha—In this sequel to *Bewitched,* Tabitha takes a job at a Los Angeles TV station.
That Wonderful Guy—Jack Lemmon as the valet for a snooty theater critic.
Two Girls Named Smith—Cousins Babs and Fran Smith experience the ups and downs of trying to further their show biz careers.
Who's Watching the Kids?—Trusty neighbor Larry Parnell keeps an eye on the younger siblings of a couple of Las Vegas showgirls.
A Year at the Top—A couple of struggling songwriters will suddenly enjoy "a year at the top" if they sign a pact with the son of Satan.

Spies/Detectives/Sleuths

Captain Nice—A timid police chemist invents a potion which turns him into a superhero crime fighter.
Dick and the Duchess—Dick Starrett is an insurance investigator and adjuster. His wife, Jane, somehow becomes entangled in each case, as well.
The Double Life of Henry Phyfe—After a spy known only as U-31 is murdered, his exact double, Henry Phyfe is called upon to make the enemy think he's still alive.
Glynis—Glynis Granville writes murder mysteries, but also finds herself really wrapped up in her work, and frequently in peril.
The John Forsythe Show—In the program's second format, John Foster and Ed Robbins become secret agents.
Mr. Terrific—A pill created by a scientist was designed to transform a common man in to a superhero. However, it only worked on one man, mild-mannered Stanley Beamish.
The New Bob Cummings Show—Bob Carson and his bodyguard and assistant, Lionel, are amateur crime-solvers, and often placed in harm's way.
The Partners—Bumbling detectives Crooke and Robinson somehow manage to solve crimes.

Sports-oriented

Ball Four—Based on the Jim Bouton book of same name, the story of the hapless Washington Americans baseball team.
Big Eddie—A reformed gambler is now the owner of a successful sports arena.
The Buster Keaton Show—Buster Keaton is a bumbling employee in a sporting goods store.
The Duke—A championship boxer gives up the ring in pursuit of culture.
The Joe Palooka Story—The cartoon pugilist with high morals comes to life.
The Roller Girls—The Pittsburgh Pitts are the focus in this sitcom about the roller derby.
Waverly Wonders—A former professional football quarterback now coaches basketball in a Wisconsin school.

Store Owners or Workers

Bridget Loves Bernie—Bernie's parents own a delicatessen in New York City.
The Dumplings—Joe and Angela Dumpling run a luncheonette in Manhattan.
Heaven for Betsy—Pete Bell works in the toy section of a New York department store.
The Kallikaks—A family inherits, and runs a small California gas station.
Leave it to Larry—Larry Tucker works with his father-in-law in a shoe store.
Life with Luigi—Luigi Basco runs an antique store in Chicago, his friend Pasquale runs an Italian restaurant.
Love Thy Neighbor—Ferguson Bruce and Charlie Wilson both work at Turner Electronics.
Many Happy Returns—The focus is upon the complaint/return department of Krockmeyer's Department Store.
The McLean Stevenson Show—Mac Ferguson runs a hardware store to support all of the generations of Fergusons in his home.
Menasha, the Magnificent—Menasha is the manager of a restaurant owned by the fastidious Mrs. Davis.
One Happy Family—The Hogans and the Hacketts run a family plumbing business.
Sally—Sally Truesdale and Myrtle Banford help run the Banford-Bleacher Department Store.
Those Endearing Young Charms—The Charm family runs a mail order business for household items.
Wonderful John Acton—The Acton family lives in back of their family-run candy store.

25 Famous Lines

1. "A—C—T—I—O—N."—said by Barton J. Reed (John McGiver) on *Mr. Terrific.*
2. "Annie Brennan, I'll get even with you if it takes the rest of my natural life."—said by Horatio Bullwinkle (Walter Sande) on *The Adventures of Tugboat Annie.*
3. "Bang, zoom, to the moon."—said by Ralph Kramden (Jackie Gleason) to wife Alice on *The Honeymooners.*
4. "The Bunco Squad, the Bunco Squad, the Bunco Squad"—the phrase on which Yoyo (John Schuck) always gets stuck on *Holmes and Yoyo.*
5. "C'mon, kids."—said by Elinor Hathaway (Peggy

Cass) to the three chimpanzees in her care on *The Hathaways.*

6. "Cu-cu."—what Goldie (Betty Hutton) would utter when something strikes her fancy.
7. "Do I have a son?"—asked by Mrs. Belmont (Kathleen Freeman) on *Lotsa Luck* to get her way.
8. "Do it!"—said by George Burns to the sponsor, and also to Mr. Bundy (J. Pat O'Malley) on *Wendy and Me.*
9. "Get him, get him, get him."—said by Mr. D. (Bruce Gordon) when speaking about Buddy Overstreet (Jack Sheldon) on *Run, Buddy, Run.*
10. "Hello, mother."—said with a heavy sigh by Lorraine (Beverly Archer), daughter of Nancy Kitteridge (Nancy Walker), on every episode of *The Nancy Walker Show.*
11. "Holy haystack."—uttered often by young Twig when amazed on *Professional Father.*
12. "I'd better be shoveling off."—said by undertaker Digger O'Dell (John Brown) on the Jackie Gleason version of *The Life of Riley.*
13. "It's Higgins, sir."—said by gentleman butler Higgins (Stanley Holloway) on *Our Man Higgins.*
14. "Love that Jill."—said by Jack Gibson (Robert Sterling) at the end of every episode of *Love That Jill.*
15. "Maaaaaaa."—said by Stanley Belmont (Dom DeLuise) on *Lotsa Luck.*
16. "Menasha, Menasha."—yelled in the opening credits of *Menasha, the Magnificent.*
17. "Murder?"—said by Glynis Granville (Glynis Johns), a mystery writer and semi-sleuth on *Glynis.*
18. "Norton, you are a mental case."—uttered by a frenzied Ralph Kramden (Jackie Gleason) on *The Honeymooners.*
19. "Oh, Johnny."—said with much exasperation, and with a thick French accent, by Angel Smith (Annie Farge') on *Angel.*
20. "Oh, my goodness."—uttered by a harried Paul Simms (Paul Lynde) on *The Paul Lynde Show.*
21. "Oh, perf."—a shortened version of "oh, perfect," said by Harry Karp (Louis Nye) on *Needles and Pins.*
22. "Oops."—uttered wide-eyed by Sylvie Bell (Sylvester Wiere) on *Oh! Those Bells.*
23. "There's got to be a better way."—said by Albert Miller (Larry Hagman) weekly in the opening scene on *The Good Life.*
24. "Toodles."—uttered frequently by Frances "Gidget" Lawrence (Sally Field) on *Gidget.*
25. "You're gonna get yours, Alice."—said by Ralph Kramden (Jackie Gleason) to wife Alice on *The Honeymooners.*

Wealth

The Betty Hutton Show—Goldie, a manicurist, becomes an heiress who is made legal guardian of three teenage children.

Bridget Loves Bernie—Her parents are Irish-Catholic and wealthy; his parents are middle-class Jewish delicatessen owners.

The Good Life—The Millers give up their hectic life to become butler and cook for the extremely wealthy Dutton family.

Love on a Rooftop—Newlywed Julie Willis tries, unsuccessfully, to keep it a secret that her parents are very wealthy.

Mr. Deeds Goes to Town—Longfellow Deeds inherits a large corporation and is instantly wealthy.

The New Bob Cummings Show—A wealthy bachelor owns and pilots several planes, and does some amateur sleuthing.

O. K. Crackerby—The wealthiest man in the world makes continued attempts to become part of high society.

The Pruitts of Southampton—One of the wealthiest families in the world suddenly has a reversal of fortune.

Sally—Sally Truesdale becomes the traveling companion of a wealthy widow named Myrtle Banford.

Tammy—A class clash as Bayou girl Tammy Tarleton works for the wealthy John Brent.

The Tammy Grimes Show—Tammy Ward is an heiress with many safeguards placed upon her fortune to keep her from blowing it foolishly.

The Tycoon—Walter Brennan as Walter Andrews, the eccentric chairman of the multi-million-dollar company known as the Thunder Corporation.

Widows and Widowers

Accidental Family—Jerry Van Dyke as widower Jerry Webster, raising a young son, Sandy.

The Baileys of Balboa—Sam Bailey (Paul Ford) as the widowed skipper of *The Island Princess.*

Bonino—Ezio Pinza as Fortunato "Babbo" Bonino, widower with eight children.

The Dennis O'Keefe Show—Dennis O'Keefe as widower Hal Towne, a columnist raising a young son.

The Ed Wynn Show—Ed Wynn as widower John Beamer, who raises his grandchildren and takes in college boarders.

The Eve Arden Show—Eve Arden as widow Liza Hammond, an author and lecturer raising fraternal twin daughters.

Gidget—Don Porter as widower Russell Lawrence, father of Gidget and Anne.

Harrigan and Son—Pat O'Brien as widower James Harrington, Sr., in a law partnership with his son James, Jr.

The Harvey Korman Show—Harvey Korman as widower and out of work actor Harvey Kavanaugh, raising a daughter in a big old house.

Hizzoner—David Huddleston as widowed Mayor Cooper, father of a grown-up son and daughter.

Ichabod and Me—George Chandler as widower Ichabod Adams, former owner of a small newspaper in New England.

It's Always Jan—Janis Paige as Jan Stewart, a war widow, nightclub performer, and mother.

The Jean Arthur Show—Jean Arthur as widow and lawyer Patricia Marshall, who practices law with her son, Paul.

Joe and Sons—Richard S. Castellano as widower Joe Vitale, a blue-collar worker raising two sons.

Lotsa Luck—Kathleen Freeman as widowed Mrs. Belmont, who lives with her son, Stanley and her daughter, Olive.

Many Happy Returns—John McGiver as widower Walter Burnley, who manages the complaint department at Krockmeyer's Department Store.

Mr. T. and Tina—Pat Morita as Taro Takahashi, the widowed head of a large Japanese family in Chicago.

My Son, Jeep—Jeffrey Lynn as widower Robert Allison, a doctor raising two children.

Nancy—Renne Jarrett as Nancy Smith, the daughter of the widowed President of the United States.

A New Kind of Family—Eileen Brennan as a recent widow raising three children.

O.K. Crackerby—Burl Ives as the richest widower in the world raising three children.

Paper Moon—Christopher Connelly as a widower and con artist with an eleven-year-old daughter.

Sally—Marion Lorne as wealthy widow Myrtle Banford, who takes on Sally Truesdale (Joan Caulfield) as a traveling companion.

The Sanford Arms—The widowed, new owner of the Sanford place makes it into a hotel.

The Second Hundred Years—Arthur O'Connell as widower Edwin Carpenter, whose father reenters his life.

The Texas Wheelers—Jack Elam as deadbeat widower Zack Wheeler, whose four children make it on their own.

A Touch of Grace—Shirley Booth as widow Grace Simpson who begins a relationship with widower Herbert Morrison (J. Pat O'Malley).

Writers

The Eve Arden Show—A widowed mother of twins embarks on a new career as a novelist.

Glynis—Glynis Johns as Glynis Granville, a murder mystery novelist and amateur sleuth.

My World and Welcome to It—William Windom as John Monroe, a cartoonist and humor writer for *Manhattanite Magazine.*

Westinghouse Playhouse/Yes, Yes Nanette—Nan McGovern is married to screenwriter Dan McGovern.

Window on Main Street—Cameron Garrett Brooks (Robert Young) returns to his hometown to write a novel about its people.

Names and Titles Index

Numbers in ***bold italics*** indicate main entries.

www.ingramcontent.com/pod-product-compliance
Lightning Source LLC
Chambersburg PA
CBHW081332090726
47907CB00011B/2452

* 9 7 8 0 7 8 6 4 6 8 1 2 6 *